9 1100000046686

D1615513

Ruth Fir

THE SOUTH AFRICAN VICTORY over apartheid quickly became the stuff of legend: the power of good triumphing over the forces of evil, the mighty Nelson Mandela offering a beacon of hope to oppressed peoples the world around. True, true, and of course much more complicated in reality. Alan Wieder's great accomplishment here is to provide a clear window into that complex reality, and in the process to rescue the revolution from its myth-makers. Focusing on the lives of the colorful and contradictory revolutionaries Ruth First and Joe Slovo, Wieder provides detail and context, personality and character to one of the epic struggles of all time. This book is a gripping social history, a love song to the revolution, and a passionate and enlightening portrait of a partnership, a love-affair, and two extraordinary activists who cast their fates with the dreams of people everywhere for justice and freedom.
—BILL AYERS & BERNARDINE DOHRN

DEMONIZED BY APARTHEID, Joe and Ruth were revolutionary heroes for black South Africans. They were formidable opponents in word and deed. This absorbing account does them justice and illuminates the complexity and richness of their often stormy relationship and extraordinary times.
—RONNIE KASRILS, anti-apartheid leader and solidarity activist; former Minister of Intelligence in South Africa; author, *The Unlikely Secret Agent*

WIEDER'S BOOK ENLARGES AND ENRICHES our understanding of the lives of First and Slovo, their intense and turbulent relationship, their personalities and impact on others, and their various roles as lawyer, journalist, under-ground operative, researcher, teacher, author, political and military leader, negotiator and cabinet minister. The evocation of the Johannesburg left during the 1950s—Gillian Slovo called them her parents' Camelot years—is vivid and well-observed. Ruth, Joe, and their circle combined commitment and camaraderie with conspiracy and concealment—and also with careless-ness and complacency. The account of tensions between the ANC and SACP, and Joe's efforts to reconcile African nationalism and socialism, is nuanced and important. The discussion of Ruth as writer-researcher and researcher-teacher makes use of earlier evaluations, but goes beyond them in an impor-tant assessment of her work as an academic *engagé*.
—COLIN BUNDY, former Principal of Green Templeton College, University of Oxford

IT HAS BEEN A REAL PRIVILEGE for me to read Alan Wieder's book. It brought me back in touch with two remarkable and complex people and ac-tivists. Ruth First and Joe Slovo emerge from this book as flesh and blood human beings facing monumentally difficult decisions. Each of them, and those dearest to them, paid a high price for their respective life choices. Yet Ruth and Joe's integrity and full-throated commitment to a different kind of South Africa not only played an important role in doing away with the obscenity that was apartheid, they also represent a clear road not taken in post-apartheid South Africa. This book evokes a vital period which became a focus of myth-making rather than the kind of clear-eyed, honest history Ruth and Joe would each have ultimately have deemed essential.

—DAN O'MEARA, author, *Volkskapitalisme*, and coauthor, *The Struggle for South Africa*

TO THE MOVEMENTS HE LED, he was known by his initials, JS. His last name had become anthemic when the mostly black guerilla army belted out 'Joe Slovo' in song as they marched on parade or executed sabotage missions in the secret war against apartheid. You can't really appreciate South Africa's transition to democracy without knowing why Nelson Mandela relied on his sense of strategy and how his bravery inspired a revolution committed to non-racialism. He was a communist known for red socks and a willingness to make compromises with capitalists that sealed the path to freedom. And just like Nelson's relationship with Winnie made him stronger through his long years in confinement, Joe's often tumultuous relationship with his wife and comrade Ruth First, a brilliant journalist and analyst, until her assassination, helped define the discourse of the ANC's painful years in exile. Now Alan Wieder has plunged into their past of domestic and political struggle to share their story with the scope, context, and detail that it deserves. And we all will appreciate his commitment and style in critically respecting their contributions and bringing this dynamic duo alive as the complex, loving and caring people they were.

—DANNY SCHECHTER, Founder and Director of "South Africa Now," Director of six films on Nelson Mandela

Ruth First and Joe Slovo in the War against Apartheid

ALAN WIEDER

Foreword by NADINE GORDIMER

MONTHLY REVIEW PRESS

New York

Library of Congress Cataloging-in-Publication Data
available from the publisher —

ISBN 978-1-58367-356-0 pbk
ISBN 978-1-58367-357-7 cloth

Monthly Review Press
146 West 29th Street, Suite 6W
New York, New York 10001

www.monthlyreview.org

5 4 3 2 1

Contents

My wife and partner, Joanie Krug, has had the most impact on my writing this book. Besides her multiple readings of the manuscript and her willingness to let me talk at length on Ruth and Joe's lives since late 2009, she has enthusiastically and lovingly promoted and celebrated my commitment and passion for the project. This book is hers as well as mine.

Foreword
by Nadine Gordimer

JOE SLOVO AND RUTH FIRST. We are entering their paths.

Both grew up unbelievers in Jewish or any religious faith. They met when Ruth was at the University of the Witwatersrand, Joe just returned from the South African Army in the war against Nazi Germany. His motivation for volunteering, eighteen years old, unemployed, lying about being underage for military call-up—his early alliance with communism, and so to the Soviet Union under attack—was decisive in the act. But there remained the devastating racial dilemma in South Africa. He wrote: "How do you tell a black man to make his peace with General Smuts—butcher of Bulhoek and the Bondelswarts? 'Save civilisation and democracy'—must have sounded a cruel parody. And fight with what? No black man was allowed to bear arms . . . if you want to serve democracy, wield a knobkerrie [wooden club] as a uniformed servant of a white soldier."

Joe Slovo's appetite for the pleasures of life is brought face-to-face with his political humanitarian drive when at the end of the war he took a holiday. From Turin to Cairo he went, and with other decommissioned soldiers somehow got to Palestine although travel was restricted because of Zionist resistance to British occupation; on to a kibbutz where "looked at in isolation, the kibbutz seemed to be the very epitome of socialist lifestyle. . . . it was populated in the main by young people with the passion and belief that by the mere exercise of will and humanism you could build socialism as one factory or one

kibbutz and the power of example will sweep the imagination of all
. . . worker or capitalist." Social theory aside, the dominating doctrine "on this kibbutz, as well on others, was the biblical injunction
that the land of Palestine must be claimed and fought for by every
Jew, and this meant the uprooting and scattering of millions whose
people had occupied this land for over five thousand years (no mention of the collusion of the Balfour Declaration of 1917)." The spirit
of the book admits issue can be taken with this view, whereas Slovo's
probing of concepts invoked by socialism become consistent to follow
with his lifelong political journey.

During Joe's absence from South Africa, membership in the Communist Party (CP) had grown fourfold in the period 1941–43 with
correspondingly the greatest call for action of the African National
Congress (ANC), although there are years ahead which the book follows in vivid attention, enlighteningly frank about a Communist-ANC
alliance. Joe and Ruth were both prominent in protests of the CP and
ANC against racist laws; two events among others—squatters' rights
in townships outside Johannesburg and Defense of the Basotho Peasants Organization in Basutoland. Joe wrote that they became lovers in
Basutoland. But he dated his "life with Ruth" as having "started off
with political tension." It's not clear—nothing glibly assumed in this
book—whether he is recollecting Students' Representative Council
meetings, the other student organization, Federation of Progressive Students (FOPS), or the Ismail Meer flat where his initial response to Ruth
and her friends was "sort of a little feeling of insecurity . . . these Smart
Alecks could formulate speech and so on . . . were just too big for their
boots . . . so my life with Ruth started off with quite a degree of political tension based on this nonsense." We echo in our own minds their
friend describing the differing qualities of Joe and Ruth—"She didn't
have a rapport with ordinary working class blokes . . . needed the better-
educated or bigger-thinkers . . . couldn't bring herself to be one of them.
And yet she would have given her life to protect them and their rights."

And did.

Ruth and Joe had fierce arguments throughout their lives together,
political and ethical, unlike the accepted domestic conflicts; the book
speculates that culture, "upbringing," hangover from "nature of
respective childhoods contributed to their disagreements." Ruth came
from a middle-class Johannesburg family, went to a private school and
on to university. Joe came to South Africa aged ten an immigrant from
Lithuania, speaking only Yiddish. But for themselves disagreement

was always an essential in the process of learning, discussions jolting one another out of too righteous a certainty that *he* or *she* understood, analyzed most clearly an issue of human lives. Here is self-honesty against revolutionary complacency.

In the incredible many contradictions in South African history, the Witwatersrand University and the University of Cape Town were the only "open" universities—half-open as students who were not white were permitted to do their course work there but excluded from "social, cultural, political, athletic activities." Among such students at the Witwatersrand University was a young Indian rebel intellectual from Durban, Ismail Meer. A love affair bringing together race difference and the sharing of searching intellect and politics, First and Meer found each other. A parliamentarian (all-white parliament) announced he had been told of a love affair between a European girl and a non-European: "This state of affairs can no longer continue." (*Double entendre* no doubt unintended.) A student affiliation of the Afrikaner Ossewa-Brandwag held protests against "black students and their fellow travellers, communists and Jews." Ruth and Ismail Meer joined a leftist student organization, Federation of Progressive Students (FOPS), many of whose leaders were members of the Young Communist League. (The early convolutions of the maze to be solved toward freedom.) The Communist Party accepted FOPS as means of inroad to the University; although FOPS had claimed that safer stance, progression as Trotskyites, others shunned it as a Communist front. Between denials, affirmations, accusation and manipulation of ANC elections FOPS was unable to claim the ANC Youth League as an ally. But its first chosen executive is seen as indeed Ruth First, the perfect conduit to the University. A newspaper calling itself *Mamba* ran a sideline that represented Ruth as "Truth Last."

Meer's flat was the meeting place for young leftists at the Witwatersrand University, revealed bluntly for readers by an habitué as "dreamy, bloody depressing . . . but warm with activity . . . always a hive." Nelson Mandela, law student along with Meer and eventually Slovo, described it as "here we studied, talked, even danced cold early mornings." He remembered "sleeping over"—dossing down?—in the flat. One is reading not of self-perceived martyrs but individuals greedy for life even while giving up so much personal fulfillment for a way of intense *certain* risk. A level of involvement, the process in making a life, living, hardly to be imagined. In this sense, among much else to come, this book is a revelation to be reckoned with.

The attachment between Ruth First and Ismail Meer ended, it appears in circumstances that ring an odd note in lives emancipated from the edicts of religious taboo that then sounded from synagogue and mosque. Her family, leftist, yet objected conventionally to the idea of marriage with a Muslim. His family had the matching taboo on marriage of a Muslim to a Jewish girl. During this smoke rising from the bonfire being stacked against South Africa's European-empowered and financed, evidently invincible apartheid. A smoldering opposition repeatedly defeated in the mission for UBUNTU. *"I am because you are."* The question as the pages are turned: What should have made humans in South Africa believe they were going to live and die, to attain this in their country?

Go for it.

Colloquial as that. The answers and denials of answers are in this book, the existence-odyssey of South Africans who wouldn't settle to live for less.

Joe Slovo and Ruth First. They met at the University of the Witwatersrand on his return from the South African Army. When exactly their intimate relationship began is an element integral to totality of their development as answerable to and for the dehumanizing of others. They worked together on two events among many others—squatters' rights in townships outside Johannesburg and defense of the Basotho Peasants Organization. It was in Basutoland, Joe wrote, they became lovers.

TAKING ON THE REGIME of South African apartheid is shown not to be an easy ride on whatever path. Most of Ruth's time was spent on party politics as precursor for the battle for freedom. Ruth and Joe, who discussed everyone, everything, reflected on their personal perceptions of Nelson Mandela. We overhear Ruth remembering him as "good-looking, very proud, very prickly, rather sensitive, perhaps even arrogant. But of course he was exposed to all the humiliation." Joe: "A very proud, self-contained black man who was very conscious of his blackness."

Ruth worked with Meer on a socioeconomic survey of Fordsburg, an impoverished area of central Johannesburg. Very practical, they helped women develop cooperatives, while initiating actions against merchants they believed were "gouging" local residents. Meer duly arrested and acquitted in court by the defense of Bram Fischer. It is intriguing to see the beginnings of the Afrikaner aristocrat to become the famous lawyer in the Rivonia Trial of Mandela. In Fordsburg he carried food in his hands to the local people. Freedom fighter himself, close comrade of Ruth and Joe, he was to share with Ruth paying for his political activism with his life, dying in the span of a life sentence, but alive forever in the story of the struggle for freedom.

Back from war, Joe Slovo had joined the Springbok Legion, a non-racial body for South African Army veterans. A predominantly white group (remember, blacks were not given arms!), its manifesto pledged to oppose any entity that sought to undermine democracy and support any individual party or movement working for a society based on the principles of Liberty, Equality and Fraternity. Ironically again: the appearance of Springbok Legion numbers transferred leadership roles in FOPS from founders like Ruth to men such as Joe. Ruth and Joe were fellow revolutionaries together in the Defiance Campaign of 1952. Their activism becomes breathless, compulsive to follow. Ruth's gifts as a writer were harnessed to their beliefs as she began work as a journalist on *The Guardian* in 1946, the year of Joe's return, and soon she was reporting firsthand on squatter camp conditions in the Transvaal and the Orange Free State. These as a warning of the violence that was to emerge with even more ferocity when the Nationalist Party won the 1948 elections: the entrenched apartheid regime. The Communist Party dispatched Joe, Ruth, and another comrade in an attempt to convince black township people that their massacre was probable if they followed their plan of resistance against their ghetto existence—a decision for human survival against political action? Police arrived at a township protest and people were beaten. As Joe, Ruth, and Rusty Bernstein were leaving, the police stopped them. Joe: "One asked us what were we doing so late at night in the veld?—Suddenly it seemed to dawn on him . . . he leered at Ruth . . . gave Rusty and me a winking look and giggled 'Jesus, and with those natives too, next time you's better find a safer spot. *Weg is julle!*'" (Get out!) The reaction reminds us about the era: "Government employees, police could not believe their eyes, whites in a black township, hardly suspect that these individuals were fighting against oppression of fellow South Africans wretchedly living there."

The "relationship," love affair of Joe and Ruth, emerges as their own business. Not a show for public curiosity to relish, or for us in our serious intention to understand them fully as we read. In his quoted autobiography, unfinished by his death, Joe says they started living together in 1949 and eight months later "we took off half-an-hour from our respective offices to get married." It comes as a commitment met among many others that are shared personal fundament. They are prominent in the Anti-Pass Campaign against the "pass-book" every black man had to carry on his person and produce to any policeman anywhere; a white boss/madam could supply a letter of authorization for him to be in the streets after six p.m.

Was there ever a more thorough, complete control by a self-elected ruling class over a color-designated outcast class? Racial divisions had existed in the, mainly white, Party in 1950, the year it was banned under the South African Unlawful Organizations Act. But the answer to the ban was the steep rise of black membership, while Party policy decisions were being taken in concurrence with Cominterm dictates "causing schisms." The Central Committee, which included Joe and Ruth, voted to dissolve the Party without any discussion among Party members. It was suggested (a recognition of realities?) this signal of the Party's lack of strategy to go underground at that stage in the Struggle was because "the rank and file would not be prepared or able to face dangers and difficulties of underground work."

On the government side the Minister of Justice appointed a "liquidator," a term usually associated with business—indeed, to seize the Party's assets. And compile a list of South African Communists. Joe's account of the way the Communists met with total liquidation is typical of his, and Ruth's, challenging, zestful bravado (which he dryly remembered as "bordered on extreme folly"). "Since none of us was ashamed of having been a communist, we would write a joint reply . . . that we would not resist being 'named' . . . indeed the liquidator's list was a roll-call of honours." Reading goes pell-mell with the radicalized ANC emerging with a newly created Youth League including Nelson Mandela, Oliver Tambo, and Walter Sisulu, and underground meetings of the communists which would lead to the home-grown South African Communist Party, SACP. The ANC was beginning to rebuild itself with the American and British-trained doctor, Alfred Xuma. Meanwhile, because Smuts had eased Pass Laws there were increasing numbers of black people moving to Soweto and Alexander townships and with them issues of poverty and resistance between original inhabitants and the local immigrants. As I read this book, the same situation, now on a scale called xenophobia, exists between South African blacks and the influx of refugees from conflicts in other countries of Africa, neighbors near and far.

The SACP's position on the ANC was that a nationalist move-ment could not end oppression because it did not address the issues of world imperialism and a class-divided—instance here, by color—South African society. Joe and Ruth, independent free thinkers ready to disagree even with Party discipline, work hard along other named persons to build an alliance of the emerging SACP with the ANC. As from the ANC side, did Sisulu and eventually Mandela. There's the claim that the profound influence of the alliance of white com-munists and black leaders "led to a large extent to the refusal of so many South African leaders to turn racialist as a result of white oppression." A perception, idea (depends on the political beliefs of the reader) that there was a direct relationship between a national liberation struggle of black victims under white-master government, and the struggle for socialism against capitalism. The attraction of socialism for African nationalism: as we are seeing now, as then, the call for nationalization of our principal underground resources is motivated against what can be called investment imperialism—ownership by individuals and companies who are not South African. Prompted to ask oneself, an endless debt to pay for the discovery of these precious metals and the knowledge of how to mine them to the surface of development of the country?

THE TENURE OF THE FIRST-SLOVO marriage was punctured by peri-ods when either was imprisoned in detention without trial. At the 1955 People's Congress Joe is one of the creators of the basic docu-ment of the SACP-ANC working in unison, the Freedom Charter. This unity was met by the apartheid government with the ultimate in legislation classifying all opposition, finally, as treason. The Treason Trial. Familiar with The Fort, then Johannesburg's main jail, as legal counsel with access to interview his prisoner clients in a room for that purpose, as an accused Joe is escorted to a cell as prisoner among some of the anti-apartheid activists he had represented in court. This incarceration was short. Charges withdrawn, as they were eventu-ally, after four years for others, when the court upheld the defense argument that the indictment was defective. It is exhilarating to read, partying along with what Joe writes as "Ruth's snap decision that a celebration was called for. At the Slovo house, midnight, what an Afrikaans paper headlined as 'Many Colours at Party' was invaded by police 'grabbing any black person holding a glass.'"

RUTH AND JOE were at underground meetings after the Suppression of Communism Act, 1950, fell upon the SACP. Meetings also held abroad in the conviction and need that the Struggle had support due from the outside world, in the universal struggle for humanity. Ruth traveled to the Soviet Union and China, broad spectrum of political ideas and practice—significant of the critical mind she kept while enacting the basic revolutionary precepts at home against apartheid oppression. Through the 1950s she and Joe leading public lives as journalist and advocate were fully active underground, although as individually banned persons could not attend political meetings, gatherings—sometimes even from meeting anyone other than family. Although we have become aware of their astonishing powers of resistance it is a shock, measured against understandable reaction, that "they still did not appear overly fearful." Was this possible because as a member of it says, "The underground Party was like a family—ties of mutual belief and affection . . . were strong." "The Party was their home."

We follow Joe and Ruth in the Defiance Campaign led by Nelson Mandela. They also represented the SACP-ANC alliance in their professional lives, Joe defending black South Africans in the courts, Ruth as a journalist taking up the challenge for *The Guardian* to report on African voices, issues. "In her first four weeks of the paper the twenty-two-year-old reporter had reported on a tin-workers' strike . . . visited a Sophiatown squatter camp, interviewed liberation leaders." She crept illegally into municipal workers' compounds, took photographs at night while holding a flashlight in her free hand. A Guyanese socialist revolutionary says she "confirms her professionalism along with what reads like political adventurism. She was concerned first of all to get the facts and to get them right." Bold and fearless, but in her code of honesty. She was eventually brought in to manage the Johannesburg office of *The Guardian*. The scope of the exposures she wrote, personally experienced, not secondhand from other sources, seems unique. There was nowhere she was afraid to go!

Without any religious community of purpose, she was an atheist, she goes with the activist Anglican pastor Michael Scott to investigate and expose slave-like conditions on farms in Bethal where police supplied forced labor to farmers. Ruth and Scott saw the dirt and degradation where workers lived, paid twelve pounds (South Africa still with English currency then) for six months' labor. Ruth wrote: "It is not every day that the Johannesburg reporter from *The Guardian* meets an African worker who silently takes off his shirt to shows weals and scars on back, shoulders, arms." Scott and First continued their investigations despite the government counter-investigation ordered by prime minister Smuts—a whitewash in all senses of the term predicted by her. Joe, undercover, joined in the investigations.

Two plainclothes detectives arrived at her office. Ruth was out; they waited for her. When she returned she saw them—called to a clerk, "Has Miss First come in yet?," he said "No," and before turning and walking out the door Ruth replied, "That's all right, I'll catch up to her later." Fast thinking. Only the buzz—which wasn't in the vocabulary of the 1950s, seems adequate: *cool*!

In 1963 Ruth was arrested under the 90-Day Detention Law and imprisoned, due to its extension without time limit, for *117 days*. These are the subject of her book, I am prepared to say, the unsurpassed testimony of total subjection of a human being, solitary confinement. The only contact to evidence one's existence the police interrogators who have the authority to set you free. Simply on the answers to their questions. The betrayal of others and the organizations to which you belong wholly, raison d'être so long as fellow human beings suffer oppression. The time span of reading this book—what relation has this to the timeless mental and spiritual suffering? But there is our need to know in order to be fully fellow-human.

We don't learn of Joe's reactions, feelings about those 117 Days cut apart from their life. He had spent five months in detention three years earlier, apparently not in solitary confinement. The personal had to be disciplined at whatever cost to reach the stoic standards of the blacks in suffering without a calendar limit. A commitment he knew he and she shared. Ruth's mother, Tilly, was permitted to see her once or twice in the presence of police and guards, and to bring her the sight of their children on the birthday of one. What this subjected the three girls to must have been dangerous for the mother in the cell, to be fought against as an urge to trade an end of the 117 days for release by giving relentless interrogators the answers to their repetition of questions that would betray comrades at the price of prison cells clanging on them, as on her.

Joe continued the nature of work they did together and singly. Ruth was a revolutionary with a brilliant pen; he also wrote excellently, this book turns one to his unsparing essay, "No Middle Road." It was not modesty, a meaningless virtue of the personal, but plain reality when looking back critically he writes he had been ill-prepared for the courtroom when he finished his law degree. A colleague says: "He was a good lawyer. How tough he was in court." Another: "Joe was first of all a fine human being . . . people from all walks of life and all shapes and sizes—all colors made no difference to him. He even struck up a friendship with Gert Coetzee." An Afrikaner nationalist who became a judge—it comes also as an opportunity to know the mind, conviction why and how of the enemy? Joe takes his position as a lawyer as having assisted him in terms of his political mission. Practically: "If one was an advocate, as I was, whose practice became more and more dominated by cases with the political aspects, access to prisoners . . . still remained in what was a great opportunity." He also irresistibly describes a judge having a courtroom "like Chaplin's *Modern Times*' production line, where he continually lessened charges against blacks who had killed other blacks." Irresistible not to take up in Joe's spirit: "Let them bump off one another, save us the trouble."

Slovo and First left for London, Joe in 1963; behind him, his contribution as one of the conceivers of the Freedom Charter, precursor of the Constitution in which our freedom is democratically entrenched, with today's campaigns to make changes to it, some alarmingly retrogressive, claimed to be relevant to present social norms of what justice is. Both left South Africa not to escape the doors of prison cells awaiting them but in the need of the anti-apartheid struggle for international support, not alone public demonstrations but Material. To begin with, money to defend anti-apartheid activists on trial, feed the stalwart protesters destitute in the townships.

Their paths intertwined, as with Ruth's exceptional gifts as a writer her books were translated and read in and far beyond the leftist press. An exception: her article on Bram Fischer rejected by the *New York Times*. Meanwhile, she was studying at the London School of Economics, evidently never satisfied that she had learnt firsthand what there was in the forces of the control of human society. She helps Govan Mbeki complete his book *The Peasants' Revolt* and writes the preface to Nelson Mandela's *No Easy Walk to Freedom* reminding its readers that "some of his speeches are missing or unavailable because in police files."

Both Ruth and Joe were involved in demonstrations speaking in revelation of the Rivonia Trial. They were based with the ANC and SACP; Ruth nevertheless triggered disdain from some Party members "for not towing the Soviet line." It is strangely disturbing to read her looking back critically at her works "Self-Alert Africa '63" and

117 Days. She says, "in the future I shall stick to facts like landowner-ship and mission schools." First and Slovo were assigned to different SACP groups; it seems cognizant of significances within them. Ruth not Stalinist. Joe was? Whatever, argumentative tolerance of thought, conviction in each—this is the ethos to be read of this marriage.

Both traveled wherever, whenever there was the chance to further in the world the cause of the ANC and SACP in the Struggle. Based with the Left in London they went individually to the Soviet Union, GDR (German Democratic Republic); she appeared on Swedish tele-vision and corresponded worldwide on African not only South African issues, later traveled in Africa and wrote notably among others an exposé book on Libya. She even became a member of the American Committee on Africa—despite the principles of the *New York Times* not to publish writings of revolutionaries. Significant recognition of her qualities outside the Left, she was appointed a United Nations Observer on the continent of Africa.

Joe in exile comes more and more to realization that apartheid's defeat will not be brought about unless South African exiles are sent back with the will to take up armed resistance to the apartheid regime. Clandestine, somehow to be effected in a police state. With fellow exiled ANC-SACP cadres arms are obtained and Joe takes on the recruitment of compatriots in exile, in African countries and Europe and, soon, South Africans who will leave home to respond to the opportunity of military training in the Soviet Union, the German Democratic Republic, and other countries. Not the parade ground summon most have been called up for as adolescents in South Africa. Guerrilla warfare. Umkhonto we Sizwe—the Spear of the Nation—the alarm, fear its announcement and emergence brought to the whites of the home country, and the flexing muscles of hope brought to the vast majority of the South African population held down under—to adapt the title of one of Ruth's books—the barrel of the apartheid gun. Joe at the SACP Central Committee meeting held in the Soviet Union (such meetings outlawed in South Africa) instigated special-ized training there and in the GDR for ANC-SACP members. His visits to Africa, Dar es Salaam, Lusaka, to consult with ANC leaders scattered in exile; it would have been another of the great experiences in this unique book if the discussions of MK with Oliver Tambo and Nelson Mandela could be read in it. But so much is offered by the work: the history of what ended our day-nightmare of apartheid.

LIFE IN LONDON is a juggling act of time and place and circumstances with revolutionary tactics colliding with the claims of family. Daughters were in London for periods, pursuing their education, living or not living with parents. Gillian, later, with her biography of the family, father and mother dominated by concern for the masses; Shawn with her documentary *A World Apart*—the Slovo-Firsts lived. Their children had been desired and planned for and it is clear were loved and missed; hardly to be seen together in anything like the conventional idea of personal relations. Political responsibility overwhelmingly backpacked, for all people to be recognized as free. Reading, we follow the primacy of the struggle above all other—the personal. It is a political education, take what sides you may, to be privy to the debates between Ruth First and Joe Slovo. Every aspect of the Struggle is there, including the Africans' fear of black nationalism being usurped in it—echoing, as with so much brought to light in this book, black nationalism in the South African vision of democracy today, while the colonial theft of land is recognized, must be dealt with, the respect of African culture once dismissed as "tribalism" is accepted as part of the justice of our Constitution created by white and black. But the demand for independent Traditional Courts will bring as justice certain inhuman subjections which are outlawed by that hard-won Constitution for all South Africans no matter color or sex. Darts of division fly in these pages. Ruth with her New Left "tendencies": Joe stated that a comrade exile had wanted to "remove" her from the Struggle because these "tendencies" were magnified with Soviet invasion of Czechoslovakia; her harmonious relationship with Tambo and other ANC leaders was in part because she was uncritical of the Soviet Party line.

Tambo comes to London to meet members of the SACP. He appoints Joe to draft a plan that would strengthen the ANC-SACP alliance. Even create a war council for armed struggle in South Africa.

Ruth asks, directing the question to leaders, Joe and others, and unsparing of herself as one of the recruiters of Special Operations cadres, why are we not back in Africa with them? The reader sees herself and Joe in acute consciousness of the difference between those who expedite revolutionary actions and those who go out to pursue them where imprisonment or death are the price tag. Leaders should be in Africa, although too well-known, infamous to the regime, to get away with clandestine presence in South Africa itself. The possibilities of Umkhonto we Sizwe in Mozambique newly liberated from Portuguese rule, comes on the territorial map of liberation.

MAPUTO, MOZAMBIQUE—the last we readers travel with the separate paths that ran parallel, then forked apart over discord, yet in the knot of a faith impervious, impossible to breach. Ruth, who has gained academic distinction at Durham University in England, is at Eduardo Mondlane University, Center for African Studies, political educator, Struggle recruiter for special operations along with other comrades landed up in Mozambique as a launching pad in the progress of the revolution. Mozambique no safe haven. The South African government forces assassinated ANC activists there. Joe—somehow finishing his essay with its determinative title "No Middle Road"—is totally occupied at the peak of special operations planning to send more exiles as armed cadres of Umkhonto we Sizwe from Mozambique to infiltrate South Africa. All manner of bizarre practical routes thought up with local ANC-SACP exile groups and supporters, in African unity of purpose, including FRELIMO victors in the end of Portuguese rule of their country—a connection to remind of the shared nature of struggle for freedom from colonial "ownership" of the African continent. One venture was a truck with MK men lying hidden in a load of industrial or supermarket supplies. The route equally ingenious—from Mozambique through Swaziland, Zimbabwe, and off the roads into the backveld of South Africa. There are three successful attacks carried out pointedly on apartheid South Africa's Republic Day, exploding oil refineries, Sasol and Mobil in the early hours with the intention, at least, of avoiding loss of life of workers there.

RUTH FIRST, SURVIVOR of so many dangerous situations, meets death in Mozambique. We know the unspeakable ending from the blare of media reports. Then it would seem unlikely that it could have new meaning, new impact: but here in its detail it has this. One of the uncountable meetings Ruth attended, called, in her mission for the freedom, the very lives of those with whom she lived in common humanity. She delays the meeting a few minutes, she wants to collect her mail. The African Center's director of the meeting half-chaffing complains: from the volumes of her letters people might think that she was director, not him. Her quick friendly jibe with a prick in it—"Well, don't you know if you want to get mail from people you have to write to them." She's back with the privilege of her copious mail, she's opening a letter, it explodes a bomb in her face.

ONE OF THE PATHS leads back to South Africa. Joe died a "natural" death from bone marrow cancer, end of a lifetime. He had returned in the 1990s to a country struggled free of apartheid, with so much new to create. He worked in negotiations for our Constitution on inalienable rights. April 27, 1994: the African National Congress came to power with Nelson Mandela as first president. Joe dances at the ANC celebration at the Carlton Hotel. Two weeks later, the day following inauguration, President Mandela appoints his cabinet. We understand Joe Slovo's anticipation of an appointment in the Justice Ministry. When he is announced *Minister of Housing*: public surprise and (in the complex rivalries of political loyalties) there is some political analysis of Joe's appointment as a "devaluation of the Left by Mandela."

Joe's reception of the ministry comes off as acceptation of reality he and Ruth were so devastatingly capable of. Speaking at a Financial Week meeting he says it for us once and for all: "Housing is not a privilege, it is a fundamental right. To live in an environment in degeneration is to produce a degraded people. We have striven endlessly for freedom and liberation. Now it is time to deliver." Reading this last sentence, it comes to us now just as it does when he argued "the government's role was not to build houses for people (presage of RDP) but rather to facilitate the building of affordable houses." A statement at down-to-plot level. "The cornerstone of my approach will be to seek an end to the undeclared war between communities and the private sector."

Dying, he worked until a few days before his last in 1995.

The end of Ruth First and Joe Slovo is not the end of what there is to discover in this book. There have been many amazing combinations of courage in bonding with the defining final necessity of focus— free South Africa. As an inquiry and with many answers to the how and why in human evolution since our primeval ancestor used fins as propellants to stand up on earth, we have sought, tried out religious faiths, philosophies, political orders, organizations of human life by which no one of us will escape, deny the equal needs of the other; to give our common humanity *actuality*.

Yet with Ruth First and Joe Slovo, this couple, man-and-woman, is one single coupling, in fundament of the absolute, the need, drive in striving for that freedom of the human state. The state of embattled Being, in itself. It is—no less—to be read out between the pages of this book.

Preface

WRITING *RUTH FIRST AND JOE SLOVO in the War against Apartheid* has been a three-year journey. In late 2009 I began reading and rereading Joe and Ruth's writings, books and articles about both people, Gillian Slovo's memoir, *Every Secret Thing: My Family, My Country*, as well as the literature on the African National Congress, the South African Communist Party, and the struggle against the apartheid regime. My reading has continued throughout the last three years. I watched Shawn Slovo's film, *A World Apart*, that provides a fictional account of her family, as well as the film *Catch a Fire*, which was produced by Robyn Slovo and portrays one of the incursions that Joe directed against the South African government. And there was Jack Gold's documentary, *90 Days*, about Ruth's 1963 imprisonment where she plays herself.

I AM AN ORAL HISTORIAN, and although I make extensive uses of the traditional sources just described, I wanted the heart of this book to be Ruth and Joe's stories told through the voices of the people who knew them. So I started to contact people who knew Ruth and Joe, including family, friends, comrades, colleagues, and critics.

After contacting dozens of people, I made a trip to London where I met with Shawn, Gillian, and Robyn Slovo. I then spent days in the archives of the Ruth First Papers at the Institute of Commonwealth Studies sifting through the immense collection of Ruth's writings and letters as well as newspaper accounts of her life and past interviews with people who knew her. I reviewed her multiple daybooks, her phone books, and studied photographs. It was after this visit that I began to earnestly contact people to interview. Initially, I conducted interviews by phone or Skype, but the majority of the interviews took place during two visits to South Africa in 2011. In February and March, I interviewed people in Cape Town and Johannesburg. Those who spoke with me knew Ruth and Joe at various times of their lives and they spanned different phases of both people's work and activism. Almost magically, each person that I met with provided me with the names of other people who they believed were essential to Ruth and Joe's story. I interviewed some people multiple times and others only once. At a minimum, interviews lasted approximately an hour. Most were longer, and one person spoke with me for eleven hours, while I met with another interviewee for sixteen hours. There were many surprises, and each of them enriched my understanding of Ruth and Joe. During this period I also worked in the archives of both the Mayibuye Centre at the University of the Western Cape and the African Studies Library at the University of Cape Town. Both collections included photographs, interviews, and letters that related to Ruth and Joe

When I returned to the United States in March, I had hours of interviews to listen to and transcribe, copies of papers from the archives, and a large number of contacts for further interviews. I continued to read, did phone interviews with people in England, the Netherlands, Canada, and Brazil, and planned a July and August trip to South Africa and Mozambique. At this point people who knew Ruth and Joe were excited about the project. Very few people refused interviews, although ironically there was a couple that actually lived in my city, Portland, Oregon, and worked with Ruth in Tanzania, who declined to meet.

I returned to South Africa, with my wife, Joanie Krug, at the beginning of July. I revisited people I had interviewed earlier in the year, met with new people, and did research at Mayibuye and the University of the Witwatersrand in Johannesburg. This second trip was especially powerful because I was able to interview people who had worked with Joe in the underground but had not yet spoken publicly about their experiences in the struggle. I suspect that a number of those I met with in February and March opened previously locked doors. I again spoke with people who knew and worked with Ruth and Joe in Cape Town and Johannesburg, but this time there were also meetings with individuals who knew Ruth and Joe in

Mozambique, where I was able to visit the office where Ruth worked at Eduardo Mondlane University.

Scattered interviews and more listening, transcribing, reading, and writing transpired through the remainder of 2011 and 2012. Writing and rewriting followed all of this, until *Ruth First and Joe Slovo in the War against Apartheid* was completed. Hopefully, this final version is better than any of those that preceded it.

A preface cannot fully exhibit the human connections that have made it possible to tell the stories of Ruth First and Joe Slovo. I trust that the pages that follow will breathe life into the work process that has been portrayed.

Acknowledgments

FOUR PRIOR BOOKS helped to guide my writing this oral history—Joe Slovo's *Unfinished Autobiography*, constructed posthumously by Helena Dolny; Gillian Slovo's *Every Secret Thing*; and Donald Pinnock's books, *Writing Left* and *Voices of Liberation*. But this book is an oral history; thus, my greatest substantive debt is to the people who invited me into their homes and offices to tell me their parts in the stories of Ruth and Joe. Their names are listed in the bibliography; their number is too large to cite on this page. However, there were people who were generous beyond any author's expectations. Thus, special thanks to Ronnie Kasrils and Rashid (Aboobaker Ismail). The many hours that they gave me make the book richer and much more personal than it would have been otherwise. I trust that I have honestly and accurately represented their words, as well as those of everyone who spoke with me.

Along the way contacts were made through what researchers un-academically refer to as "snowballing." The people I interviewed provided me with the names of other people to speak with about Ruth and Joe. In this regard, Helena Dolny, Hillary Hamburger, Terry Bell, John Pampalis, Vladimir Shubin, Pamela Dos Santos, and, I suspect, Ronnie Kasrils, kindly gave me the legitimacy that convinced people to talk. There were two other people I interviewed—Myrtle Berman and Paul Joseph—who, simply by staying in touch and discussing the project as it progressed, have made the book better. Finally, four of the people I interviewed did extensive reading of the full manuscript and their criticisms were invaluable. Norman Levy kindly helped me further question what I had written, but it was Dan O'Meara, Helena Dolny, and Albie Sachs whose line-by-line reads not only brought insights to my analysis, but also made me probe deeper into both Ruth and Joe's thinking and actions. Each of their critiques contributed to saving me from myself in terms of an understanding of the contexts and South African history surrounding the lives of Ruth First and Joe Slovo.

There have been many other readers as the project transformed from notes to manuscript to book. In the United States, Bill Ayers, Phil Wikelund, Jeffrey Mirel, Craig Kridel, and William Cobbett all read parts of the manuscript. As already stated, Joanie Krug read the book many times. Finally, the editor at Monthly Review Books, Michael Yates, as well as the copy editor, Erin Clermont, have been thoughtful, direct, and creative in their reads. Various South Africans also read the book prior to publication. Colleagues Peter Kallaway and Crain Soudien at the University of Cape Town read parts of the manuscript, and Russell Martin, my editor at Jacana Media, provided very helpful feedback in his ongoing reading of chapters. In addition, through Jacana, Colin Bundy offered immeasurable feedback from both micro and macro historical perspectives.

There were also people at libraries and archives, and others that provided documents and photographs that must be acknowledged. First, I would like to thank David Clover, Tansy Barton, and other librarians at the Institute of Commonwealth Studies. They were all especially forthcoming as they tolerated my rather intense reading of the library's collection of the Ruth First Papers. In fact, David brought documents to my attention that I probably would have over-looked. Robyn, Gillian, and Shawn Slovo administer the collection of their mother's papers. I thank them for making them available for me to read and allowing me to use photographs of their family. I am also deeply indebted to Matt Mahon and Leo Zelig who, through their work on the Ruth First Papers, provided photographs of both Ruth and Joe.

There were three additional archives were essential to writing the book. Andre Landman and Isaac Ntabankulu were especially helpful at the Centre for African Studies Library at the University of Cape Town. Andre uncovered documents in a collection of which I was unaware that brought important information to the project, and Isaac saved me by sending documents that I had forgotten across the pond after I had returned to the United States. Also in Cape Town, at the University of the Western Cape's Mayibuye Centre, Andre Mohammed, Coordinator of Historical Archives, kindly provided photographs. Finally, Debora Matthews allowed me to view Joe Slovo's papers at the University of the Witwatersrand's South African History Archives that were especially helpful for the last chapters of the book.

Besides formal archives, I relied on the good will of some of the people that I interviewed for documents and photographs. In this regard, I appreciate the kindness of Ronald First, Audrey and Max Coleman, Helena Dolny, Myrtle Berman, Kevin Tait, Pamela dos Santos, Mosie Moola, AnnMarie Wolpe, Paul Joseph, Ann Scott, Glenn Frankel, and Mike Feldman. Also Jack Gold kindly provided me with a copy of his BBC production, *90 Days*, in which Ruth played herself.

There were also people and institutions whose hospitality and support need to be recognized. As is generally the case when I am in South Africa, Peter Kallaway provided me with a place to live in Cape Town. Aslam Fataar and Azeem Badroodien and the Faculty of Education at Stellenbosch University supported my research in the country through my appointment as an Extraordinary Professor. Finally, my friend and colleague, Barnett Berry, provided backing through my appointment as a Senior Research Consultant at the Center for Teaching Quality.

Before closing my acknowledgments, I would like to thank Monthly Review Press, especially Michael Yates, Martin Paddio, and Scott Borchert, and Jacana Media's Russell Martin and Neilwe Mashigo, for their thoughtfulness and care in bringing *Ruth First and Joe Slovo in the War against Apartheid* to fruition. And, of course, I am deeply indebted to Nadine Gordimer, who was so generous in writing the foreword, both in terms of her time and praise; the latter touches my mind and my heart. In closing, the late, great, Louis "Studs" Terkel must be recognized. Without his work as a foundation, I would never have written this book.

Introduction

DURING THE LONG FIGHT against apartheid in South Africa several remarkable couples devoted their lives to the struggle— Winnie and Nelson Mandela, Albertina and Walter Sisulu, Hilda and Lionel Bernstein, and the intrepid Ruth First and Joe Slovo. Ruth and Joe began their activism the decade before the apartheid regime came into power. They became members of the Communist Party in the early 1940s as they fought racism, class disparity, and oppression in South Africa. Beginning in 1947 and ending prior to her imprisonment in 1963, Ruth was the editor of the Johannesburg office of *The Guardian*, a radical opposition newspaper that exposed the atrocities of the South African state, and featured the voices of black opposition leaders as well as oppressed people on the ground. Forced into exile in 1964, Ruth continued to speak back to power in South Africa through her activism, writing, and teaching. In 1982, she paid the ultimate price for her commitment to a democratic South Africa when she was assassinated by the apartheid regime. A year earlier, South African commandos were elated because they believed they had killed Joe Slovo, whom they referred to as "Enemy Number One." The commandos had instead mistakenly and tragically shot the wrong man, a Portuguese engineer, but there were further attempts on Joe's life. At the government's infamous interrogation and torture prison, Daisy Farm, there was a basement cell referred to as the "Slovo Suite."

The South African government demonized both Ruth First and Joe Slovo throughout the struggle years. With Nelson Mandela,

Walter Sisulu, and Govan Mbeki imprisoned for almost three decades beginning in 1963, Joe Slovo was, along with Oliver Tambo and Chris Hani, one of the most important leaders in the struggle against apartheid. He was the main strategist of the armed struggle, and later a key player in the negotiations with the apartheid regime that led to the country's first democratic government in 1994. This book—written three decades after Ruth was assassinated, and seventeen years after Joe's death—portrays the battle against apartheid through the partnered lives and separate paths of Ruth First and Joe Slovo.

Partially a narrative history, partially the oral history of a partnership, the book aims to present First and Slovo's lives immersed in the context of their time, historical flow, cultural and social surroundings, community, family, friends, colleagues, and comrades. These were complex individuals: their partnership, early years and beyond, was tested by their individuality, irreverence, ideology, infidelity, and intensity. Ruth and Joe's daughters, Shawn, Gillian, and Robyn, are on record stating that they each paid a high price for their parents' political commitment. Family, friends, and Ruth and Joe themselves have spoken of their intense private and public political disagreements. Yet letters between Ruth and Joe imply that the personal and political boundaries muddled, and in spite of the contrasts, they each believed that they made the other better, more thoughtful, smarter, and more effective.

Numerous times throughout the interviews with the people who knew Ruth First and Joe Slovo, I've been asked what prompted me to write about their lives. When I was a college student in the United States during the civil rights movement and the antiwar movement, I recognized the names Joe Slovo and Ruth First. I knew that they were South African freedom fighters, but I knew little else about them. Then, many years later, after doing work on race and education in the United States, I began to research and write on teachers who fought apartheid in South Africa. As my knowledge about the struggle grew, I read and heard more and more about Ruth and Joe, incomparable characters, strong personalities, courageous fighters.

Some of the teachers I interviewed were members of the African National Congress (ANC) or the South African Communist Party (SACP); some were younger United Democratic Front (UDF) activists; there were Pan Africanist Congress (PAC) and Black Consciousness (BC) people; and others were Trotskyists. Few of these teachers were known public figures, yet their stories are important to the struggle against the apartheid regime. As I worked on teacher stories between 1999 and 2008, I felt a growing camaraderie with First and Slovo. Both Ruth and Joe's roots were Eastern European and Jewish, as are mine; both were, at best, non-practicing Jews, as am I; both were, like me, politically left. Mostly though, I chose to write about Ruth and Joe because they represent the complexity, the contradictions, and also the very best of what it means to be revolutionaries committed to the struggle, both in South Africa and throughout the world.

I also discovered at least one parallel to my prior work in South Africa. In 2008 my book on Unity Movement stalwart Richard Dudley was published as *Teacher and Comrade*. I learned in my research that Joe Slovo was forever critical of the Unity Movement and viewed it as a do-nothing theoretical organization. Although there is some truth to his evaluation, it is also rather narrow. That said, Richard Dudley was first and foremost a human being, as was Joe Slovo. Sometimes, worlds even coalesce. In early February 2011, I went to the University of Cape Town to interview Gonda Perez, who was an Associate Dean of Health Sciences and had been the dentist for the underground struggle in Lusaka during the 1980s. As we greeted each other, she informed me that we had met at the launch for the Dudley book and that she and I were the only people in the world who admired both Richard Dudley and Joe Slovo. For Perez, they both were examples of the Yiddish term "mensch."

Ruth First could be thoughtful, contentious, generous, academic, intellectual, revolutionary, and more. Joe Slovo was tough, humorous, soft, harsh, congenial, thoughtful, political, musical, and revolutionary. Ruth's colleague at Durham University, Gavin Williams, spoke with me about Ruth, and his words might also describe Joe:

> In many respects what you saw is what you got. With Ruth there was no bullshit. But, she lived a complicated life. Obviously the personal which comes out in Joe's book, but she had so many commitments doing a wide, complex range of things that you can't understand her by knowing her in one context rather than in all contexts. None of us could have known her in all contexts.[1]

Ruth was sometimes compared to Rosa Luxemburg. Her commitment to the struggle against apartheid is given as testimony throughout the interviews I had with the people who knew her. In fact, Constitutional Court justice Albie Sachs said, "I once described her as a product of Lenin and the LSE" (London School of Economics).[2] Headlines from a newspaper interview with Ruth during her London years read, "I am a Revolutionary." Finally, her friend at the London School of Economics and beyond, American Danny Schechter, told me, "She was not playing the revolution, she was making the revolution, or trying to."[3]

Everyone I interviewed spoke of Joe Slovo as a revolutionary. Probably the most poignant comment, however, came from Jaya Josie, who worked with Joe during the eighties in Lusaka:

> For him the focus must be on South Africa and that was his main goal. He put every effort into the struggle and he took his role as leading Umkhonto we Sizwe[4] very seriously. What drove Joe was his commitment, his compassion. It was almost as if he would be very distraught if someone was hurt. That sort of commitment was almost religious in a way.[5]

When I spoke with Helena Dolny, Joe's second wife, she said, "I don't own the truth on Joe."[6] Though I clearly do not own the truth on Ruth or Joe, this book represents my description and interpretation of their stories in the struggle against apartheid. Ruth First and Joe Slovo were both leaders among leaders. They had different styles. They had different roles in the struggle. Their complex and vital places in the fight for a democratic South Africa need to be portrayed for the people that knew them, and more important for those who have come after them, both in South Africa and throughout the world.

1—From the Shtetl to South Africa

RUTH FIRST IS BURIED in Llanguene Cemetery in a dusty Mozambican suburb. Her grave lies next to those of other members of the African National Congress who were killed by the apartheid government in a 1981 raid, referred to as the Matola Massacre, where South African soldiers in blackface committed cold-blooded murder. Ruth's killing was no less brutal: the South African regime sent a letter bomb that detonated in her hands and sent shrapnel into the bodies of her colleagues at Eduardo Mondlane University. Joe Slovo is one of two white South Africans that lie in rest at Avalon Cemetery in Soweto, one of Johannesburg's massive black townships. His funeral, a national event, took place before a crowd of over 40,000 people packed into Orlando Stadium, home of Soweto's premier soccer club, where he was eulogized by among others, the Chief Rabbi of South Africa, Cyril Harris. Though the stadium was quiet during Joe's funeral, on the streets of the township on the way to the cemetery Joe Slovo was remembered by the South African people as they danced, laughed, and sang "Hamba Kahle Umkhonto" (Go Well, Spear of the Nation) in a celebration of Joe's life. At Avalon Cemetery, Joe was lowered into his grave not by the South African military, but rather by Umkhonto we Sizwe cadres, Joe Slovo's comrades in the fight against the apartheid regime.

Both Ruth and Joe's funerals and resting places offer stark contrast to their Eastern European Jewish roots in Latvia and Lithuania. Joe Slovo was born May 23, 1926, in Obelei, a small village close to Vilna, the city that Napoleon referred to as the "Jerusalem of Lithuania."

He left when he was ten years old and his memories were of a small Yiddish-speaking world and an ear-pinching rabbi. Ruth First was a native South African, born May 4, 1925; her father, Julius First, had immigrated with his mother and older brother to South Africa from Latvia in 1907 when he was ten years old. Ruth's mother, Tilly, whose birth name was Matilda Leveton, emigrated from Lithuania three years earlier.

Eastern European Jews began to come to South Africa in the late nineteenth century, an exodus that parallels even greater numbers moving to North America. Forty thousand had arrived in South Africa by 1914. Although there had always been anti-Semitism in Eastern Europe, it escalated greatly in 1881 with the assassination of the modestly liberal Russian tsar, Alexander II, who had freed over 40 million serfs and had also eased military conscription, opened up universities, and liberalized business practices for Russian Jews. Upon his death, in places like Latvia and Lithuania, Jews were removed from certain areas and excluded from many occupations and employment opportunities, an ironic foreshadowing of what was to happen to blacks in South Africa. In effect, Jews were ghettoized and were unable to support themselves and their families. In *World of Our Fathers*, Irving Howe refers to them as the "poor and the hopelessly poor." In addition, violent oppression, the worst form taking shape in the pogroms, made life unlivable—dangerous and life-threatening.

Though life had never been easy for the ancestors of Ruth First and Joe Slovo in the Diaspora, the families were part of a rich history. Vilna was one of the centers of Jewish piety, scholarship, and intellect and was later a city that celebrated the Yiddish writing and humor of Shalom Aleichem. Irving Howe's description of Yiddish might unwittingly be a portrayal of Joe Slovo: "Yiddish was a language intimately reflecting the travail of wandering, exile, dispersion; it came, in the long history of the Jews, like a late and beloved, if not fully honored, son."[7] In addition to Yiddish culture, a semblance of socialism began to grow in the last decade of the nineteenth century, as more and more Jews were displaced.

There is no detailed record of Ruth's family's journey. The reasonable assumption is that they made the same migration into Western Europe that was made by the masses of Jews. It might be that it was the success stories of two Lithuanian Jews, Sammy Marks and Isaac Lewis, who had both prospered economically when they immigrated to South Africa in the nineteenth century, that led the Levetons and

Firsts to choose South Africa. Ruth's family was part of the wave of immigration that began in 1882, after Alexander II's assassination, and ended with the beginning of the First World War in 1914. The Levetons and Firsts might have traveled overland, but more likely they sailed from the Baltic port of Libau, which, though more expensive, was safer than land travel. Most of the people who journeyed to South Africa initially departed from the European mainland to London, where they were aided and supported by an organization called the Jewish Shelter.

We can assume that the Levetons and Firsts made the long train trip from Cape Town to Johannesburg once they landed on the shores of South Africa. It should be remembered that Johannesburg was then in its infancy. The city began as a mining camp when gold was discovered in 1886. Rapid growth followed as the camp grew from 300 to 3,000 people by the end of the year. In 1892, a railroad line was built between Johannesburg and Cape Town, a city that dates back to the seventeenth century. By 1895, Johannesburg was the largest African city south of the equator. By the time Tilly and Julius arrived in Johannesburg approximately 200,000 people lived in the city including over 25,000 Jews. Tilly and Julius both attended the Jewish Government School in Doornfontein, the same school that Ruth and Joe would briefly attend as children.

Although there are no descriptions of Ruth's parents' childhood, awareness of the geography and culture of early twentieth century Johannesburg Jews is helpful, as is the early history of the left in South Africa. Jews worked as clerks in small shops adjacent to gold mines where blacks shopped for food and supplies. They also worked as tailors, carpenters, jewelers, cobblers, barbers, butchers, bakers, clerks, grocers, peddlers, drivers, shopkeepers, and gangsters. When they arrived in the city, they moved to low-rent neighborhoods such as Ferreirastown, Fordsburg, Doornfontein, and Yeoville. Tilly's family initially lived in Fordsburg and according to Ronald First, his birth family inhabited these neighborhoods as well as the more upscale Kensington because of the family's changing economic status. Like the rest of the population of Johannesburg, class distinctions quickly developed in the Jewish community. As some Jews accrued wealth even before Ruth First and Joe Slovo were born, Johannesburg was sometimes disparagingly referred to as "Jewhannesburg." At the other end of the continuum, poor Jews were called "Peruvians," a negative, racist epithet.

Ruth at a very young age with her father and uncle.
(courtesy of Ronald First)

The first twenty years of the twentieth century witnessed com-
peting movements among South African Jews. The large Zionist
movement that originated in Johannesburg with the Transvaal Zionist
Organization quickly affiliated with the South African Zionist Federation. Neither organization appealed to Tilly Leveton or Julius First.
By the time they married in 1924, they were each involved in socialist politics. Julius viewed the International Socialist League (ISL)
leader and Communist Party of South Africa (CPSA) founding member David Ivon Jones as somewhat of a mentor. Jones was one of the
key spokesmen of the Party and was committed to non-racial politics.
During the 1920 strike by black mine workers, Jones publicly called
for whites not to cross strike lines. Tilly noted that her future husband
was upset when in 1918 at age twenty he was not initially accepted
as a member of the ISL, but shortly after this rejection, both he and
Tilly were accepted for membership in the organization. Neither Tilly
nor Julius were practicing Jews at the time. This fact is only relevant
because the ISL in Johannesburg had various branches, one being
the active and vocal Yiddish Speaking Branch (YSB) that existed
between 1918 and 1920. Its members were deeply involved in the
arguments and debates held at West's Academy, the Johannesburg

socialist venue, when the ISL became one of the organizational leaders in the forming of the CPSA. There is no listing of Julius or Tilly in the records of the YSB: however, Julius First did become the chairman of the CPSA in 1923.

Ruth First was born a year after Tilly and Julius were married, on May 4, 1925. Similar to the story of her parents' lives during the first quarter of the twentieth century, there is not a great deal of information about Ruth's childhood. For the first ten years of her life, while her future husband Joe Slovo still lived in Lithuania, Ruth was growing up in Kensington, a relatively wealthy Johannesburg community. Ruth appeared to be strong and vocal even as a child, and the family lived a privileged life as upper-middle-class white South Africans. Ruth began kindergarten when she was four years old. The initial years of Ruth's education are sketchy, but it is known that just before she moved to the Jewish Government School in Doornfontein in 1936, about the same time Joe came to Johannesburg, her mother traveled to the Soviet Union. Tilly First had been awarded a trip to Yalta because of the family's contributions to the CPSA. Ronald First remembers the trip as a crucial experience for his mother, ideologically: "For my mother where the dedication became a mission, a vocation, something to pursue awake or sleeping, was her visit to Russia in 1936."[8]

Adele Bernstein, one of Ruth's new classmates at the Jewish Government School, remembered that Ruth was a reader who was articulate in class. Bernstein recalled her being "a skinny girl in a navy gym and white shirt who wore her fuzzy hair short. She was always neat, impeccably dressed and a bit of a class above us."[9] It is ironic that Ruth First went to school in Doornfontein, because the area was one of the immigrant Jewish enclaves in Johannesburg, and very, very Jewish, unlike Ruth's family. The area was bustling with Jewish signs everywhere: kosher butchers, synagogues, bakeries, and delicatessens lining the streets. Finally, recent immigrant children attended the school.

Joe Slovo was born in the village of Obelei in Lithuania in 1926. Later in life he visited his birth village twice, first in 1981 with his Soviet friend Alexei Makarov, and then again in 1989 with Makarov and Joe's second wife, Helena Dolny. In the introduction of *Slovo: The Unfinished Autobiography*, Joe speaks of his early years. He describes himself as a "thin, scraggy youth," and has memories of a green and ochre run-down wood house, yellow and mauve flowers, the river, and "dark winter mornings and winter nights, through the snow with paraffin lamp in hand, trudging to and from the synagogue school."[10] He also recalls Friday baths at the mikvah, the Jewish ritual bath, sledding, a large house where a more affluent relative lived, and festivals with singing, eating, and drinking. At the conclusion of his 1981 visit, Joe reflected on anti-Semitism and Jewish tribalism in the village and that a hundred-year-old Catholic Church was the most dominant building in Obelei. "I remember the rhyming chant . . . Jesus Christ lies in the earth dead like a horse. . . . We the chosen (for persecution?) were taught that we were superior to the *goyim*, and for boys the greatest taboo was the *shiksha*—a non-Jewish girl."[11] There is immense irony in the fact that in his ANC and SACP responsibilities Joe Slovo often visited the Soviet Union, the place of his birth. It might be that his reflections on anti-Semitism and Judaism are not far afield from his internal and intellectual struggles with aspects of the Soviet Union during the final decade of his life.

Wolfus Slovo, Joe's father, was by varied accounts a fisherman and a woodcutter in Obelei. His mother was a homemaker. Wolfus left Lithuania in 1928; Joe was two years old and would not see his father again until he was ten. When he was a toddler his mother, Chaya, sang him the lullaby, "Rosinkes und Mandlen" (Raisins and Almonds), a tune that wished for more riches for shtetl children. Wolfus Slovo immigrated to Argentina with plans to bring his family when he became settled. Although there is no evidence of his motive for choosing Argentina, it is not imprudent to assume that he had made some type of contact with the Jewish Colonization Society (JCS), an organization founded in 1891 by Baron de Hirsch with the mission of raising the material and moral status of Russian Jews. JCS had offices throughout Russia and worked to facilitate Jewish emigration. One of their programs was agricultural colonization in Argentina. Wolfus Slovo sailed from England to Buenos Aires, but it is unclear whether he ever became a part of any of the three agricultural colonies supported by the JCS. He opted to leave Argentina. In his memoir, Joe wondered how different things might have been if Wolfus had been successful in South America.

In 1936, with help from her family, the Sachs, Chaya Slovo prepared to immigrate to South Africa with Joe and her daughter Sonia. Joe Slovo met his father as a ten-year-old Yiddish-speaking boy. Although Wolfus had lived in South Africa for many years, he maintained Yiddish as his primary language. The family flat was located in

Doornfontein, the site of the Jewish Government School. The family's first house had a tin roof, typical for the area, but it was soon demolished to enable the building of the Apollo Cinema and Crystal Bakery, where both Joe's father and his sister Sonia later worked. Shortly after his arrival, Joe was enrolled in the Jewish Government School, and like all immigrant children, his head was shaved to prevent lice. Although many of the other children were also Yiddish-speaking immigrants from Eastern Europe, they quickly took to calling him the "Bald Bolshie." Business prospered and the family moved to a better house in Bellevue with Joe completing his primary education at Observatory Junior School and Yeoville School for Boys.

The family house in Bellevue was a row house situated on the tram line just across the street from the family's fruit stand, a business that was successful due to Chaya's extensive work regimen from five in the morning to eight at night. Joe remembers being a part of a gang of kids that he referred to as his smoking "club." He supplied them cigarettes from his parents' fruit stand until they were caught smoking at school and his father became vigilant about his behavior. Joe writes of his first crush and also of him and Sonia burying their dog, Spotty, who was killed by a car as it ran to greet Joe. He also reflects on the death of his mother, after only two years in Johannesburg. This, undoubtedly, was the event that changed the lives of the Slovo family. Joe's reflections on his mother's death are both ethnographic and psychological:

> I was not told of her death. I suddenly woke up in the middle of the night to find the mirror covered with a white sheet. The walk around the coffin, the hysterical wailing of women and, above all, the yellow, yellow face haunted me for years. But the shaft of horror and shock, which struck me on our return from the funeral still evokes a shudder within me. As we entered the dining room, staring at me from the mantelpiece was a large doll (a present for my sister Reina) completely wrapped in bright yellow cellophane paper. It was particularly horrifying since my mother had died in childbirth and I expected to see the stillborn child in the coffin.[12]

Joe Slovo admits that he did not have a rich recollection of his mother, but he does recall her warmth, her hard work, and her being pregnant. He also remembers his older sister, in defiance of Jewish law, privately reciting the Kaddish, the Jewish prayer for the dead, in respect for their mother. Chaya's death totally disrupted the family. Joe, who attended daily services at the synagogue prior to his Bar Mitzvah, began to question the existence of God. Because his mother was the force supporting the success of the fruit shop, it collapsed after her death. Wolfus returned to a life of transient work, which prompted him to send Reina to an orphanage, while Sonia went to work and live at the Crystal Bakery. Joe moved with his father to various rooming houses in Doornfontein, where, unbeknownst to him at the time, one of his neighbors was the future ANC leader Walter Sisulu.

As Joe was forced to leave school and watch his family life disintegrate, Ruth was proceeding with her traditional schooling. What was not traditional in Ruth's life was her family's commitment and involvement in socialist politics. Ruth lived a comfortable middle-class life and attended three secondary schools: Barnato Park, Jeppe Girls High, and an Afrikaner school. She loved clothes and was interested in boys. She was also immersed in radical politics through her parents, mostly from her mother's influence. Tilly and Julius First introduced Ruth and Ronald to the world of politics as children through weekly left-wing meetings on the steps of the Johannesburg City Hall, where the topics included Western imperialism and South African racism. As Tilly recalled: "When we used to go to the Town Hall steps (to hear Communist speakers) we took the children with us. We made them conscious. We wanted them to have an understanding of what was going on."[13]

Ruth definitely accepted her parents' political education. She met Myrtle Berman at Barnato Park and they became close friends. In the early 1960s, Berman and her husband, Monty, along with John Lang, Jerry Mbuli, and Baruch Hirson, founded the National Committee for Liberation, an organization that became the African Resistance Movement, with a manifesto that argued for armed resistance against the apartheid regime. When Myrtle was interviewed, she spoke about her first history class with Ruth at Barnato Park, and recalled that she and Ruth were the only ones who knew anything about the Soviet Union. Myrtle began asking Ruth questions, but since Ruth did not have answers, she invited Myrtle home to meet her mother.

One day after school I went home with Ruth. Got there about three o'clock and emerged at six o'clock with my head reeling,

Ruth, second from the right, with friends (courtesy of Myrtle Berman)

having had a three-hour lecture from Tilly on the history of socialism, the Russian Revolution, the origins of religion . . . without me saying a word! And I remember wandering home and telling my mother, who nearly had a fit.[14]

Ruth First's friendship with Myrtle Berman blossomed in earnest after Ruth took her home to meet Tilly. Myrtle's mother was fearful of her being associated with the Firsts, but she did not limit the girl's companionship. Descriptions of Tilly and Julius First by some of Ruth's friends, as well as Ronald First, help to paint a picture of the family dynamics. Berman was clearly impressed by Tilly First but added, "Tilly was really hard to get to know. I can't remember Tilly ever sharing with me anything about her own life, not a thing."[15] Rica Hodgson, who was also one of Ruth's friends, explained that Julius "exuded warmth which Tilly didn't."[16] Finally, Harold Wolpe, who was a neighbor of the Firsts and became Joe Slovo's best friend at university, remembered Tilly as "abrasive, very impatient. As a kid if Ruth made a child-like statement it didn't get a very good reception."[17]

As a fourteen-year-old, Ruth joined the Junior Left Book Club with Myrtle Berman. They would discuss books, sing, and pull slips of paper out of a hat with topics to research and report back on at the next meeting. One can envision Ruth and Myrtle riding their bikes to Dr. Max Joffe's office where the weekly meetings were held. Ruth read and discussed politics in South Africa and the Soviet Union with her parents. In the First home, social lives revolved around politics. When they picnicked or vacationed, it was with people like the

Buntings, whose son Brian Bunting later became one of the leaders of the SACP. Brian Bunting also spoke about Tilly First, and noted similarities between her and Ruth. "Yes, she's got good intellect, a very good brain. Very formidable person. A very nice person, but also difficult, very critical; sometimes rasping. When you've seen Tilly, you'll appreciate something about Ruth too, because Ruth's inherited a lot of that."[18] As something of a counterpoint, Dan O'Meara recalled Wolfie Kodesh telling him, "Ruth is a puppy dog compared with her mother."[19]

Ruth graduated from Jeppe Girls High School in 1941. Rica Hodgson recollects that she was brilliant and powerful, but at the same time vulnerable. Myrtle Berman recalled her being "sharp-tongued but also shy."[20] Describing Ruth First as vulnerable is interesting because adult friends like Ronald Segal, Barney Simon, and Wolfie Kodesh used the same descriptor. During her last year in high school, 1941, she was honored as the Literary Prefect at the School. A plaque with her name is still on display in the school library. Her award-winning essay, "On Poetry," was published in *The Magazine of Jeppe High School for Girls*: "Poetry became one of the ways in which the most intense emotions of the most sensitive men were put on record. The true poet makes his subject universal and immortal by stirring in his reader the same emotions that inspired him to expression."[21]

After graduating from high school, with average grades in spite of her brilliance, Ruth enrolled in the University of the Witwatersrand. However, before beginning she gave her own commencement address, not at her high school graduation, but rather on the steps of Johannesburg City Hall where her parents had taken her to political meetings from the time of her childhood. Her brother described listening to her speech: "What made a great impression on me was the first time I ever heard her speak, on the steps of the city hall in Johannesburg. And she was young, she was a brilliant orator."[22] Vulnerable, maybe; political, definitely; at this point she was clearly the daughter of Tilly and Julius First. According to her close adult friend, Ros de Lanerolle, when Ruth told the story thirty-some years after the event, her memories were not of an extraordinary accomplishment, but rather of her mother's criticism.

While Ruth was living in a middle-class home with her brother, parents, and domestic help, Joe was moving through different rooming houses, first with his father but then on his own. At the time, Joe's father was in and out of jail as a result of mounting unpaid debts. At

the first boarding house, Mrs. Leiserowitz's, Joe had his initial experience with communism when he met Max Joffe, a medical doctor and
a member of the Communist Party of South Africa (CPSA). Joe Slovo's memories are of Joffe "shocking the boarders when he talked of
votes for blacks and his opposition to the 'imperialist' war."[23] Joe later
attended Junior Left Book Club meetings at Joffe's medical office. Joe
moved from Mrs. Leiserowitz's house to the well-known boarding
house operated by Mrs. Sher, which is portrayed in Milton Shain's
book, *Memories, Realities and Dreams: Aspects of the South African
Jewish Experience.* Joe shared a room with his father and received
spending money from an aunt from the Sachs side of the family. He
would venture to her house every Friday afternoon and pay homage,
thus receiving a half-crown for school bus fare and maybe movies,
food, and gum. In *Slovo: The Unfinished Autobiography*, he compares
his aunt to the Bette Davis role in *Whatever Happened to Baby Jane.*
Soon after Joe and his father moved to Mrs. Sher's, Wolfus announced
that Joe could have the room to himself because he was going to move
in with a woman called Sophie Silberman. Joe had minimal involvement with his father after Wolfus remarried, and never seemed to
know Sophie or his half sister from the marriage, Rachel.

Joe's political education grew at Mrs. Sher's home. He was still
attending school, but his formal education was short-lived because he
was forced to get a job and support himself. Fortuitously, one of his
teachers was John O'Meara, who was a member of the CPSA and also
the uncle of one of Joe's future ANC friends in Tanzania and Mozambique, the political scientist Dan O'Meara. In his book, Joe describes
many of the other inhabitants at the boarding house and lists their
activities: rummy, poker, klabberjas (a card game), horse and dog rac-
ing banter, and, of course, political discussions (some continuations of
Jewish Workers' Club debates).

Joe was recruited by the Zionist-Marxist organization Hashomer
Hatzair when he lived at Mrs. Sher's. He recalls a Troskyist who cared
more about Jewish workers in Palestine than he did about blacks in
South Africa. Joe's thoughts were directed toward class disparity and
racism:

The combined inheritance of Zionism and boarding house armchair socialism (in terms of which a "kaffir remains a kaffir")
and the absence of any relationship with blacks other than in
master-servant form, made my transition to real radical politics

a difficult one. I well remember the discomfort I felt when I found myself seated between black youths at that first meeting of the Junior Left Book Club to which my teacher O'Meara had taken me.[24]

Joe Slovo's reflections are not unique and are as much if not more analytical than personal. There was both theoretical and practical racial tension among South African socialists throughout the twentieth century. Allison Drew documents the historical reality in *Discordant Comrades*. Although many in the South African Communist Party and the African National Congress were highly critical of what they labeled "armchair socialist" Trotskyists, other tensions and schisms existed throughout the twentieth-century history of both groups.

Joe took a job as a dispatch clerk at a pharmaceutical company called Sive Brothers and Karnovsky. Simultaneously influenced by the political discussions at the boarding house and even more by John O'Meara, he threw himself into left-wing politics. Mike Feldman befriended Joe during their teen years and he recalls him as fun-loving, social, and political. He accompanied Joe to a meeting at the Johannesburg City Hall and they both applied for membership in the Communist Party. Union leader Issy Wolfson informed them that they were too young and needed to work in the Young Communist League. Joe admired Wolfson, who was born in South Africa in 1906 and joined the CPSA in 1934. Wolfson quickly rose in Party ranks, becoming one of two spokesmen for white workers as well as a member of the Politburo. Joe was accepted into the Party on probationary status in 1942. He passionately committed to Party work and believed that the revolution was imminent, a belief he carried throughout his life working for a socialist revolution in South Africa. One of his other teachers in the Party was Solomon Buirski, who earlier as a leader in the International Socialist League had helped forge alliances with organizations like the non-racial Industrial and Commercial Workers' Union to recruit and politicize black workers. Joe was diligent as he sold Party publications including *The Guardian* and *Inkululeko* (Freedom) in Johannesburg's black townships. He and his comrades would often sit with the paper's readers talking and debating articles and politics. His initial political action, however, was organizing workers, mostly blacks, at Sive Brothers and Karnovsky where he worked:

We put up a literature stall in the black lavatory structure where we regularly sold Party publications, more especially the vernacular bi-monthly newspaper *Inkululeko*. We also operated an illicit wall newspaper in the same structure. Since we knew that no conventional white man would ever have the stomach to enter a black lavatory, it became quite a useful base for aspects of our work.[25]

In affiliation with the Black Chemical Workers, Joe helped facilitate the unionization of workers at Sive Brothers and Karnovsky. At the same time, he was a member of the National Union of Distributive Workers, a whites-only union that struck successfully for better wages in October 1942. As a result, the salaries of Joe and other white workers were raised, yet the strike had no effect on black workers, the same people Joe had organized. He goes to great lengths in his book to describe and analyze union and political racism within the South African left. As often as not, white workers fought to repress black workers because they were viewed as an economic threat. Thus racism, whether it was in workers or capitalists, connected to economics.

Joe Slovo continued to contest the racism that existed within the left; the owners of Sive Brothers and Karnovsky struggled with him as an employee. He was elected shop steward shortly after the strike, but more important, he continued his political work with his black coworkers. In March 1944, he was called in by one of the company's owners, Sammy Sive, and informed that he should curtail his political activities and be grateful that he had a job at "such a nice Jewish firm."[26] Sive explained, "At heart we are all communists."[27] He told Joe that the firm donated money to Medical Aid for Russia. Joe, by his own account, recalled that his response to Sive was somewhat "cheeky. . . . My torrent left him speechless. He just pointed a shaking finger toward the door and, as I moved towards it, I heard a deep sigh accompanied by that most expressive all-purpose Jewish lament, 'Oy vey.'"[28]

2 — War, Wits, Politics, and Ruth Meets Joe

JOE'S FIRST IMPRESSION of Ruth was that she and her intellectual friends at the University of the Witwatersrand were "just too big for their boots." [29] It was 1946; Joe was just returning from the army and the Second World War, and Ruth was in the midst of her social science studies at the university. They were both engaged in political protests and actions through the Communist Party of South Africa, already committed militants and engaged intellectuals, each looking toward a life of struggle for justice and equality. Joe brought the grit and experience of the streets and the war; Ruth evoked the style and sensibility of the brilliant researcher and writer she would become. "So my life with Ruth," Joe said later, "started off with quite a degree of political tension based on this nonsense." [30]

When Ruth First enrolled at the University of the Witwatersrand, Joe Slovo was sent to Italy by the South African Army to fight against Nazi Germany and fascist Italy. In June of 1941, Germany attacked the Soviet Union and the CPSA changed its policy of opposition to the Second World War, announcing that it would now support South African involvement in fighting against the Nazis. In addition, white members were encouraged to volunteer for military service. Because of the importance of South Africa's corporate and imperialist connections to the Allies, the country officially supported the war effort. Some Afrikaners felt a much greater sympathy for Germany and viewed Great Britain as the enemy. Some future leaders of the apartheid regime, most notably John Vorster, who went on to be prime minister (1966–78) and then president (1978–79), were imprisoned as enemy sympathizers during the war as a result of their overt support of Nazi Germany. In spite of the schism, over half of the South Africans who served in the Second World War were rural Afrikaners.

Joe Slovo's motivation for enlisting in the South African Army is not entirely clear. He was underage at eighteen, unemployed, and concerned about serving in a segregated army representing a segregated and racist country. However, he opted to join the cause. Quite possibly his strong allegiance to the Communist Party, and thus the Soviet Union, was the key factor. As part of the CPSA he had participated in Party recruiting efforts for white communists to fight the Nazis, but his analysis of harsh racism cuts to the core of the South African dilemma.

> To the average member of the voteless majority, the regime's exhortation to "save civilization and democracy" must have sounded like a cruel parody. And fight with what? At no stage was a black man allowed to bear arms; if he wanted to serve democracy he could do so wielding only a knobkierie (fighting stick, club), as a uniformed manservant of a white solder.[31]

Since he was only eighteen, and legal adult age was twenty-one in South Africa, Joe had to ask his father to give him permission to join the service. When Wolfus refused, Joe took it upon himself to declare himself twenty-two and scribble his name on the form. He was accepted without question, which he was sure was a common practice in South African recruiting offices. Assigned to the Signal Corps, he spent the next couple of months training. He was schooled in communications before traveling by train with other troops, all white men, to Durban. From Durban, Slovo departed by boat to Egypt before he was deployed to the front lines near Florence, Italy.

The exploits of the South African Army in the Second World War raised the country's standing in the world. The army was a prominent force in freeing Ethiopia from Italian rule, beating the Vichy French forces in Madagascar, and fighting bravely in both North Africa and Italy. In addition, the war provided a tremendous boost for the South African economy. Joe Slovo's tour of duty, however, saw none of this fighting. As a communications soldier, he was part of what has come to be known as the "chair corps." He was assigned to the Signal Corps with his young activist friends Mike Feldman and Barney Fehler, the

latter from the family of the well-known Johannesburg Jewish delica-
tessen, Fehler and Flax. When the war ended in 1945, Joe celebrated
on the streets, or more accurately, in the bars of Turin. His return
to South Africa took a rather circuitous path as he spent six months
vacationing by the sea in Italy before departing for Egypt. While in
Italy, he was able to obtain Trotsky's writings at a Catholic mission
library. From Cairo, Joe and some other returning soldiers decided to
take a detour and visit Palestine, not an easy journey at the time, as
travel was restricted because of Zionist resistance to British occupation. Slovo and his companions were able to hitch rides with military
vehicles and hop buses, landing in Tel Aviv after a two-day trip. Joe
briefly described the Palestine experience, but there is no mention of
the return to Cairo or the final trek back to Johannesburg. From Tel
Aviv, they landed on a kibbutz, and Joe later reflected on both Zionism and definitions of socialism:

> Looked at in isolation, the kibbutz seemed to be the very epit-
> ome of socialist lifestyle. . . . Social theory aside, the dominating
> doctrine on this kibbutz, as well as on the others, was the bibli-
> cal injunction that the land of Palestine must be claimed and
> fought for by every Jew. And this meant (as it did eventually
> mean) the uprooting and scattering of millions whose people
> had occupied this land for over 5,000 years, more's the pity.[32]

Issue can be taken with Joe's assertion that all people in kibbutzim
are Zionists, but his theoretical probing of socialism is consistent with
his lifelong political journey.

When Joe returned to South Africa, Ruth was in her final year as
a student at the University of the Witwatersrand. In her prison diary,
117 Days, she refers to her college years:

> My university years were cluttered with student societies,
> debates, mock trials, general meetings, and the hundred and
> one issues of wartime and postwar Johannesburg that return-
> ing ex-service students made so alive. On a South African
> campus, the student issues that matter are national issues.[33]

Majoring in Social Studies, Ruth received a Bachelor of Arts
degree in 1946. The bulk of her classes were in the social sciences—
Sociology, Social Economics, Social Anthropology, Social Legislation,

Mike Feldman, Barney Fehler, and Joe—Second World War
(courtesy of Mike Feldman)

Democracy and Society, Theory and Practice of Social Work, Native Law, Native Administration. She spent five years at Wits, possibly as an outgrowth of her formal education being a secondary priority to both her political and social awakening. Before sharing a flat with Patsy Gilbert and Winnie Kramer, Ruth lived at home, totally involved in leftist political work—both at the university and in the community. She attended political meetings, the Left Book Club, and the weekly orations at Johannesburg City Hall. Norman Levy recalls the City Hall meetings where conflicts arose. "They were a spirited group of Party protagonists. . . . Mike Feldman, Monty Berman and Joe Slovo, to name only the most prominent of the frontline defenders. . . . ready to move into action as soon as the heckling from the 'street fighters' became too disruptive."[34]

Like Joe and other political activists, Ruth spent time at Salmon's Bookshop, People's Bookshop, and Vanguard Bookshop where she could access Left Book Club publications as well as communist sources. Ruth and Joe visited and debated with their friends at Florian's Cafe, a Johannesburg coffee shop that was opened during their Wits years by German Jewish immigrants. In 1943, she formally became a member of the Young Communist League and edited the organization's paper, *Youth for a New South Africa*. Norman Levy cites a particular debate in which Ruth proposed, "All South African politics are native affairs."[35] Levy described Ruth in his memoir, *The Final Prize*: "I still see her image as she was at that first meeting: eighteen, curly-haired, short and ill at ease, pursuing her points at breakneck speed. She was earnest, self-conscious, and miserable with caring, but it was her energy and directness that marked her out from others."[36] As a precursor to the many letters she would pen two decades later as she was writing articles, books, and United Nation reports on Southern Africa, and in her position as the secretary of the Young Communist League, Ruth wrote to the director of the Institute of Race Relations, John Rheinallt-Jones, concerning government proposals on black farm labor. "The proposals are fascist in character and reminiscent of Nazi forced labour. Should they be adopted they will virtually reduce Africans to conditions of serfdom by restricting their freedom to seek more remunerative employment."[37] Although the Institute's research challenged the government, Rheinallt-Jones warned against anti-government protests.

Spurred by the war, membership in the Communist Party had grown exponentially; from 1941 to 1943 the growth was fourfold. Correspondingly, there was a greater call to action in the African National Congress. Although there were still years of debate ahead regarding a CPSA-ANC alliance, some of the black leaders of the CPSA—Moses Kotane, J. B. Marks, and Edwin Mofutsanyana for example—were making their mark in the ANC. In addition, the youth movement of the African National Congress, including Nelson Mandela whom Ruth knew at the University of the Witwatersrand, was calling for political action despite the fact that they were distrustful of the CPSA. Ruth participated in one of the first joint CPSA-ANC movements, the Anti-Pass Campaign of 1944–45. She was one of 540 delegates at the conference that was chaired by Dr. A. B. Xuma, then president of the African National Congress. The conference elected a National Anti-Pass Council and collected tens of thousands of signatures for Yusuf Dadoo to present to the "liberal," Jan Hofmeyr, acting in the absence of Prime Minister Smuts. Hofmeyr, however, refused to meet with the delegation.

The Anti-Pass Conference was one of many acts of Ruth First's political defiance during her university years. Harold Wolpe recalled that most of Ruth's political work was off campus. Conversely, she was involved in Wits' Students Representative Council and was one of the founders, along with her companion, partner, and lover at university, Ismail Meer, of the Federation of Progressive Students (FOPS). During Ruth and Joe's time at Wits, it was one of two South African universities, the other being the University of Cape Town, that were designated as "open" universities. "Open" is a loaded phrase, since nonwhite students were permitted to do their coursework but were excluded from all social, political, cultural, and athletic activities.

Some students at the university did challenge the racism that existed, while other students protested the presence of black students on campus. An example of the latter was the Afrikaanse Nasionale Studentebond (ANS), an affiliation of the fascist Ossewabrandwag that served as the political base for racist students. Not only did ANS hold protests against black students, the organization petitioned the university to remove black students as well as their fellow travelers, specifically communists and Jews, whom they viewed as one and the same. However, other students demanded an end to social segregation on campus—dining halls, sports, medical laboratories, and more. Medical students were successful in ending some discrimination, including the elimination of segregated anatomy dissecting halls. There were symbolic demonstrations of integrated sports, a tennis match for example, but both the administration and the majority of white athletes kept the fields, pools, and locker rooms segregated. Clearly, there was a fear of black and white students mixing socially. One parliamentarian spoke of the relationship of Ruth First and Ismail Meer: "He said that he had been told that 'there was a very painful love affair between a European girl and one of the non-European students at Witwatersrand . . . 'This state of affairs,' he declared, 'can no longer continue.'"[38]

The student left was an eclectic group with liberals, Trotskyists, socialists, and communists represented when Ruth First enrolled at the university. The glue that kept the activism flowing was a general belief in non-racialism, the goal being South Africa as a democratic society. There was reason for some hope with South Africa's entry into the Second World War, ostensibly, a battle between democracy and fascism. In spite of the bolstering of already existing racist laws by the South African government in 1936, there were those who believed that through institutions like the Institute of Race Relations and politicians such as Jan Hofmeyr, a liberal, non-racial society might soon be a reality in South Africa.

Ruth was involved in the founding of the Federation of Progressive Students (FOPS), a radical student organization. Although FOPS included socialists and liberals, and was not directly related to the CPSA, many of its leaders were also members of the Young Communist League and there was often a thin line between the actions of the two groups. According to Bruce Murray:

> FOPS developed into a tight-knit coterie of student politicians. Dismissed by its detractors as FLOPS, or as simply a noisy irritant, FOPS was vocal, active, and well organized, attracting to it a fair number of radical and even liberal students who never contemplated joining the CPSA, and it exercised an influence on the SRC far beyond that warranted by its actual membership.[39]

Ruth and Ismail Meer were joined in FOPS by future leaders of the South African Indian National Congress such as Meer's close friend J. N. Singh, future ANC leaders including William Nkomo, and Party members Harold Wolpe, Tony O'Dowd, Mervyn Susser, and Ruth's close friends, Myrtle Berman and Zena Stein. The CPSA viewed FOPS as an inroad to the university and Ruth First, who was elected to FOPS's first executive board, was the perfect conduit. Although FOPS claimed progressivism and never communism, the Trotskyists and others quickly shunned it as a Communist organization. In the early stages the group was unable to claim the African National Congress Youth League (ANCYL), the new party of Nelson Mandela and others, as its ally. Ironically, both the Trotskyists and the campus conservatives were most critical of FOPS when the organization gained control of the Student Representative Council (SRC). The conservatives used stolen documents in an unsuccessful attempt to connect FOPS to Moscow, but it was the Trotskyists, in the student newspaper, *WU Views*, who publicly accused the organization of manipulating the SRC elections for the Communist Party. Because the paper lacked evidence, it was discredited and forced to issue a public apology. Soon after, however, a similar paper, *Mamba*, ran a satire that represented Ruth First as "Truth Last."[40]

Ruth First continued her work in FOPS and the SRC during her Wits years, including proposing an SRC motion condemning the racist ANS newspaper *Spore*. Yet a preponderance of her time was spent on Party politics. Possibly the most essential part of her university experience was her relationship with Ismail Meer, both socially and politically. Ruth never wrote nor spoke publicly of Ismail Meer during her lifetime; and in Meer's posthumous autobiography, *A Fortunate Man*, he only writes about Ruth First as one of a collective of political activists. Other people who were close to Ruth viewed her and Ismail as lovers.

Ismail Meer arrived at the University of the Witwatersrand in 1942 to continue his studies when the law school at Natal University was closed to nonwhite students. Meer's family owned a leftist newspaper, *Indian Views*, and he was politicized at an early age. He wrote for the family paper and periodically contributed to the national leftist paper, *The Guardian*, whose Johannesburg office was subsequently managed by Ruth from 1946 to 1963. Along with First, he was one of the founders of FOPS and he joined the Communist Party in 1943. Myrtle Berman remembers Ismail Meer as "very charismatic, very bright, very able. He was a leader who stood out."[41]

Meer's flat was the meeting place for young leftists at the University of the Witwatersrand, "dreary, badly furnished, bloody depressing. . . . But it was awash with activity, always it was a hive."[42] The flat was located at 13 Kholvad House on Market Street in Johannesburg, and it has been described by Nelson Mandela, Anthony Sampson, and Mary Benson as the meeting place for young leftists between 1943 and 1946. Mandela, who was a law student with Meer and eventually Joe Slovo at Wits, recalled staying at the flat when the discussions and parties ran late into the night. At the time, Mandela was living in Orlando, a district of Soweto. Late-night travel was both difficult and dangerous even though Orlando was a planned township for "the better class of native."[43] Mandela's list of struggle activists who came to the flat besides Ruth First and Ismail Meer, also included Joe Slovo. "There we studied, talked, and even danced until the early hours in the morning," wrote Mandela, "and it became a kind of headquarters for '*young freedom fighters*.'"[44]

Both Ruth and Joe later reflected on their perceptions of Nelson Mandela at Wits. Ruth remembered him as "good-looking, very proud, very dignified, very prickly, rather sensitive, perhaps even arrogant. But of course he was exposed to all the humiliations."[45] "A very proud, self-contained black man, who was very conscious of his blackness,"[46] recalled Joe Slovo.

As one of the "young freedom fighters," Ruth participated in numerous political actions, both before and after Joe Slovo returned to South Africa in 1946. While the Communist Party was publicly calling for a non-racial society, debates continued within its ranks. Ruth's relationship with Ismail and the people at 13 Kholvad House placed her in a non-racial world that did not exist for most white students. Concurrent to the 1943 Anti-Pass Campaign, Ruth worked with Ismail Meer on a socioeconomic survey of Fordsburg, an impoverished area of central Johannesburg. In connection with the survey, they assisted women in the area to develop food cooperatives and initiated actions against merchants they believed were gouging local residents. Different types of merchants were targeted, though the events were usually referred to as food raids, and they continued throughout the 1940s and beyond. The food raids were examples of "Robin Hood" socialism, that is, taking from the rich and giving to the poor. Meer was arrested during one of the early raids and was acquitted through the court defense by Bram Fischer, who himself participated in food raids alongside of Joe Slovo:

> I have two fond memories of this episode: Bram Fischer with a crowbar in his hand opening a box of Sunlight soap which he had removed from a recalcitrant storekeeper and was selling at controlled prices to a queue which had formed, then meticulously accounting for every penny to the irate shop owner.[47]

Both Bram Fischer and his wife, Molly, were born into longtime prominent Afrikaner families, but together they joined the Communist Party in 1942. During the struggle years Bram became an SACP leader, and it was fortunate that he was not arrested with Nelson Mandela and others in 1963. Instead of being on trial, he was one of the defense lawyers in the now infamous Rivonia Trial in 1964. Bram was a lifelong comrade of both Ruth and Joe, and, like Ruth, he paid for his political stands with his life.

When Joe Slovo finally returned to Johannesburg after the war, his transition was eased by his membership in the Springbok Legion. The organization was founded in 1941 as a non-racial body for South African soldiers and veterans. A predominantly white group, it included Joe Slovo, Wolfie Kodesh, Cecil Williams, Bram Fischer, Jack Hodgson, and Rusty Bernstein, to name a few. Its mission was stated in the "Soldier's Manifesto":

> The Manifesto called upon its members to realize in civilian life the "unity and cooperation among races" that had formed

on the battlefield. The Manifesto also pledged to oppose any entity that sought to undermine democracy, and, foreshadowing future alliances, pledged to support any individual, party, or movement "working for a society based on the principles of Liberty, Equality and Fraternity."[48]

During the war, the legion propagandized to white soldiers, comparing Nazi Germany and fascist Italy to racist South African extremism. At home, Springbok Legion went from an organization securing funds and tending to the needs of veterans to one that was clearly connected to the CPSA and acted politically, first against oppression, and later against apartheid.

Joe Slovo's membership in the Springbok Legion helped facilitate his seamless reorientation into the Communist Party of South Africa. Although he had never matriculated from high school, circumstances allowed him to enter the University of the Witwatersrand on a five-year scholarship to study law. At the time the University was making a concerted effort to open the school's doors to veterans, and that effort dramatically changed the entire culture as the university doubled in size and admitted older students and some non-matriculants such as Joe Slovo. In 1946, as Ruth First was going through a tumultuous final year at the University of the Witwatersrand, Joe Slovo began the studies that would culminate in a law degree with distinction in 1951. Their paths would cross at Ismail Meer's flat, at meetings of the Young Communist League, and at other political demonstrations. Slovo referred to the period as "perhaps the happiest of my life. The joy of relaxed discovery of knowledge, the excitement of sharp but safe student politics and the finding of new friends."[49] He continued by sweetly describing the beginning of his friendship with Harold Wolpe, who was his fellow law student and from university years forward his best friend. Joe relates some of the story of their friendship; the beginning is notable even though Harold Wolpe insisted that it was mythical:

We had actually first met in 1938 on a football field adjacent to the Yeoville Boys School where we were both pupils. Harold was a year ahead of me and was a star sportsman. One day when I tried to join a football kick-around, Harold warned me off the field on the grounds that the game was for senior boys only, and not for pip-squeaks like me.[50]

Joe Slovo did not feel positive about all of the people he met at the university and was critical of some on the left. He directed especially harsh words at the Trotskyists, whom he viewed as armchair politicians. "It enabled them to exude an aura of revolutionary charisma but, in practice, to surround themselves with an ideological cocoon which protected them against actual involvement in confrontations with the powers-that-be."[51] More interesting, however, were his initial perceptions of Ruth and her friends. It is unclear if his recollections were of SRC meetings, FOPS, the Young Communist League, or encounters at 13 Kholvad House. What is clear is that Joe Slovo identified a divide that appeared to correspond to social class.

Ruth and Joe partook in fierce political arguments throughout their lives together. But possibly, culture, economics, and upbringing also contributed to their disagreements. Wolfie Kodesh, who was a friend to them both, spoke of their different qualities. After talking of Joe as a funny, down-to-earth workingman, Kodesh spoke of Ruth. "She didn't have a rapport with ordinary working-class blokes. She needed the better-educated or bigger thinker, you know. She couldn't bring herself to be one of them. And yet she would give her life to protect them and their rights—*of course she did give her life*. I'm talking about the ordinary working-class, black person."[52]

Joe quickly joined FOPS and became the editor of the group's newspaper, *Progressive Student*. Both Ruth and Joe were part of the organization's core and helped arrange lectures and meetings, all connected to FOPS's non-racial mission. Ironically, the appearance of Springbok Legion veterans at the university transferred leadership roles in FOPS from women like Ruth to men like Joe. Joe also became chairman of the Law Society, and his appointment necessitated an all-night CPSA branch meeting to decide if he would be permitted to give a toast to the King at the society's annual dinner. The vote was yes.

It was also at the University of the Witwatersrand that Joe Slovo first became acquainted with Nelson Mandela, at Ismail Meer's flat and at the law school where both were students. "I met Joe Slovo and his future wife, Ruth First," recalled Mandela. "Then as now, Joe had one of the sharpest, most incisive minds I have ever encountered. He was an ardent Communist, and was known for his high-spirited parties. Ruth had an outgoing personality and was a gifted writer."[53]

Still a student at Wits, Ruth departed on her initial international political mission just prior to her final year of undergraduate studies. Traveling with Harold Wolpe, she went to London to attend the

World Federation of Democratic Youth Conference. She continued on to Prague for a meeting of the International Union of Students and then to France, Hungary, and Yugoslavia, speaking to local groups about South Africa and learning about revolutionary movements in Europe. Ruth briefly mentions the trip in *117 Days*, and wrote a descriptive and detailed, though not reflective, article on the London conference in *The Passive Resister*, a publication that was edited by Ismail Meer.

In 1946, still involved with Meer, Ruth was enrolled in four classes to complete her studies at the university and began a position at the Social Welfare Department of the Johannesburg City Council. Hired as a researcher, her job was to document city life for the 60th Jubilee of Johannesburg. The work included providing survey data on the numbers of park supervisors for white children, beggars, and centers for people disabled or handicapped. As Ruth described it, "I had to produce a sycophantic account of work which bored or disgusted me."[54] When the now famous black miners' strike approached in August 1946 Ruth quit her job to do, as she said to her supervisor at the Social Welfare Department, "political work."

Ruth and Joe became involved in the 1946 miners' strike as participants in the emergency committee. Black mine workers had begun to state their grievances regarding working conditions, food, and pay in 1944 through the African Mine Workers' Union. Its president, J. B. Marks, petitioned the Chamber of Mines and the government appointed a commission, the Lansdowne Commission, which ignored the evidence and ruled against the workers' grievances. The report also condemned the influence of the CPSA on the union. J. B. Marks was an active Party member and the Communist Party supported the strike when it was called in August 1946. Joe and Harold Wolpe distributed leaflets and hung posters. Ruth, who later reflected on the strike and government oppression in *117 Days*, made posters and protested with black workers when 74,000 black miners brought the digging in eight mines to a halt demanding increased minimum wages and better working conditions. The government killed twelve people, and the strike was quickly suppressed. In spite of the failure of the strike, Dan O'Meara referred to the action as the Soweto of the time: "Most obviously it profoundly affected the direction and thrust of African opposition; patient constitutional protest by an elite rapidly gave way to mass political action and passive resistance."[55] Subsequently, union leaders, Johannesburg Communist executive members, and editors and writers from *The Guardian*, the newspaper that Ruth First would join a few months later, were all arrested and charged with assisting the strike and with sedition. Acquitted of the latter charge, some were convicted of assisting the workers and were fined. Ruth later wrote in *Fighting Talk*: "The miners' strike was one of those great historic incidents that, in a flash of illumination, educates a nation, reveals what has been hidden, destroys lies and illusions."[56]

Joe and Ruth continued to work through the Party, and their paths would soon merge. For Ruth, in addition to completing her course-work, working and quitting her first job, becoming more involved in the CPSA, and beginning her seventeen years as the editor of the Johannesburg edition of *The Guardian*, this was also the final year of her relationship with Ismail Meer. They had both joined the Young Communist League in 1943 and helped launch FOPS at the university. Meer remained deeply committed to Indian causes and became secretary, under the presidency of Yusuf Dadoo, of the Transvaal Indian Congress, which, with the African National Congress, South African Coloured People's Organization, and the Congress of Democrats, was central to the early struggle against apartheid in the 1950s.

Neither Ruth nor Ismail wrote about their liaison. Gillian Slovo chooses to categorize the relationship as myth, but concludes her analysis with a sentence true to Ruth's friends who viewed the First-Meer romance as loving and authentic: "Ruth and Ismail parted: he returning to his hometown of Durban and she, so goes the myth, after much soul-searching, staying behind in Johannesburg."[57] One could argue that Myrtle Berman was Ruth's closest confidante at Wits. She spoke of Tilly First's disapproval of the relationship. Tilly did not believe that the relationship was good for opposition politics. There is also reason to believe that the Meer family disapproved of their son's involvement with Ruth. In a succinct statement, Berman captured her memories of the time: "Tilly really had an enormous influence on Ruth, on her and Ismail. Because Ruth at one stage was going to marry him."[58] Many years later Wolfie Kodesh asserted:

> Well now, you see this was the great love of her life, in my view. I heard at the time that she sent him an urgent telegram saying look, we've got a chance to get married before the Immorality Act comes in. . . . But his roots were much more involved with the Indian tradition. Not enough for him to break away from his traditions to marry Ruth.[59]

Thus, Ruth First was no longer involved in a relationship and ready to begin her work as a radical journalist. Joe Slovo remained intensely involved in his studies, the Law Society, and the Communist Party of South Africa. They regularly attended Party meetings and there is a photograph showing a hammer-and-sickle banner, posters of Lenin and Moses Kotane, and Ruth and Joe on the stage with comrades Bram Fischer and Rusty Bernstein. Joe reflected many years later: "I was a blind defender. I'm deeply ashamed of it now. I feel very angry that I was taken in by what I now consider to be anti-socialist conduct in the name of socialism. You can't have a cult without worshippers and I was a worshipper."[60]

Joe and Ruth would not become a romantic couple until 1948, but they worked together on at least two events—squatter rights in the townships outside of Johannesburg, and the defense of the Basuto Peasants' Organization in Maseru, Basutoland. By 1946 over 25 percent of black South Africans lived in the cities, even though urban residency was illegal without a pass. In Johannesburg, as well as other cities, there was a large squatter movement. Approximately 90,000 squatters built living quarters out of discarded metal, wood, and even cardboard on the outskirts of Johannesburg. Ruth First, now a chronicler of black South African life for *The Guardian,* was reporting on squatter camps throughout the Transvaal and Orange Free State. Joe Slovo worked with her on at least one occasion, one of many spurred by the Reverend Michael Scott, a frequent participant at 13 Kholvad House. The story of the squatters' actions as told by Joe Slovo speaks as a warning of the viciousness that was to emerge with even more ferocity when the Nationalist Party won the 1948 election and initiated the apartheid regime. The squatters were led by Schreiner Baduza of the Communist Party, and he supported a critical mass of black people who were determined to take over property even though there was certainty of violent reprisals by the state. The Party dispatched Joe, Ruth, and Rusty Bernstein, who would later be acquitted in the Rivonia Trial, in an attempt to convince Baduza and the people in the township that a massacre was probable if they followed their plan. The police arrived at the scene and many people were beaten. It was illegal for Joe, Ruth, and Rusty to be in Moroka Township and Joe described how the police addressed them as they were leaving:

He asked us what we were doing so late at night in the veld. Suddenly it seemed to dawn on him. Even before we could stutter out an answer, he leered at Ruth from top to toe, gave Rusty and me a winking look and giggled out: "Jesus, and with all those natives too, next time you's better find a safer spot. *Weg is julle* (On your way)." [61]

While there really was no humor in the situation, it does illustrate the tenor of the time, as government forces on the ground could not even fathom white people being in a black township let alone fighting against racism and oppression. The fight, however, was also part of Joe and Ruth's 1948 work in Basutoland. Ruth reported on the sedition trial of brothers Josiel and Maphutseng Lefela, leaders of the Basuto Peasants' Organization, also referred to as the League of the Poor. The organization was part of the radical political party League of Commoners and was affiliated with the CPSA. Joe Slovo, still a law student, was sent by Jack Leviton's Johannesburg law firm to assist one of the firm's lawyers in the case. Joe wrote that the Lefela brothers fired the lawyer, but he did not write about the trial or the verdict. More important, he tells readers that it was in Basutoland, in early 1948, that he and Ruth First began their relationship.

We learn about Ruth and Joe's relationship before they married in August 1949 in Gillian Slovo's memoir, *Every Secret Thing*. She retells Wolfie Kodesh's story of Joe coming to him to make sure that he and Ruth were not an item. When Kodesh assured Joe that he and Ruth were just friends, Joe confessed his love for Ruth First. They moved in together as a couple in 1949, the first year of the apartheid regime, with the blessings, as well as the financial support, of Julius and Tilly First. And in August, with Ruth pregnant with Shawn, they were married. In *Slovo: The Unfinished Biography*, Joe deemphasizes the ceremony: "We started living together at the beginning of 1949, and eight months later we each took off half an hour from our respective offices to get married."[62] Joe did tell Gillian late in his life that his wedding saw Tilly joyful and Ruth crying, but there is no further explanation. And when Gillian searched through a box of her parents' possessions, she found the invitation to Joe's and Ruth's wedding, which was held at Julius and Tilly's home in Kensington. "It was just surprising to us that they had a wedding," recalled Ruth's friend Zena Stein, "that a respectable wedding was going to take place."[63] Though it is advisable to be cautious when citing a novel,

Gillian Slovo's *Ties of Blood* describes the wedding of "Rosa and Jacob," characters at least somewhat resembling Ruth and Joe, that might, at the very least, correspond to reality. In the novel the couple are married in the bride's parents' home with blacks and whites enjoying the celebration. Rosa is nine months pregnant so dancing is not inviting. As Jacob turns up the music and people begin to dance, he kisses Rosa and gently professes his love, telling her: "Let's slip away, nobody will notice."[64]

3—Apartheid, Children, and the Beginning of the Struggle

CHARGED WITH TREASON in 1956, Ruth and Joe were still not totally aware of the vicious, vulgar, racist, oppressive capabilities of the apartheid regime. To be sure, Ruth uncovered government racism and repression from the beginnings of apartheid to the time of their indictments and beyond. Indeed, Joe defended black workers as well as his SACP comrades who were charged for the most part with being black in South Africa. But even Ruth and Joe's understanding of the oppressive nature of apartheid in 1956, when they faced trial, did not enable them to be cognizant of the price that they and other people who fought against apartheid would suffer for challenging the regime. South Africa was clearly a racist state prior to the election of the Nationalist Party in 1948 and the initiation of forty-five consecutive years of apartheid rule. Although Gillian Slovo referred to her parents' lives in the 1950s as the "Camelot" years, the Nationalist Party election created an even more harshly racist society in South Africa. Joe Slovo was not unique in his analysis at the time that the election of the Nationalist Party meant more of the same—meaning the continuance of the racist state. In fact, just after the election the Johannesburg branch of the CPSA produced a pamphlet titled *Mala-nazi Menace*: "What is the much publicised policy of apartheid? It is not a new policy. All they propose is to make the non-European more of a slave, an outcast and a third-class citizen in the land of his birth."[65] It is possible that no one could have imagined that the Nationalist Party would win eleven straight national elections between 1948 and 1992 or that the apartheid government would so vehemently and viciously pass and enforce laws that strengthened and magnified the segregation in South African society of white, Indian, black, and coloured people, with whites of course in a superior position.

South Africa's first apartheid prime minister, D. F. Malan, was overt about the Nationalist Party's intentions as the apartheid plan was presented to the South African public during the 1948 election campaign. Besides explaining that the Natives Representative Council, an advisory body of black representatives, which one member called a 'toy telephone,' would be disbanded, and that segregation of blacks—now to be called Bantus—would be exacerbated with enforcement of reserves or homelands, new punitive measures for blacks in urban areas were introduced. In addition, the Nationalist Party campaigned on even greater separation of Indians and coloureds. A multitude of apartheid legislation passed, and many of the promises proffered by the Nationalist Party were fulfilled by the mid-1960s. Early in the apartheid years, legislation not only classified people as black, coloured, Indian, or white, but also designated where individuals were allowed to live, work, or attend school because of the color of their skin. In many locales, black, coloured, and Indian people were literally removed from their family homes and forced to relocate to designated areas, often far from city centers and workplaces. Education laws assured that children attended segregated schools with only people their own color. The apartheid regime was committed to a totally segregated society—politically, socially, economically, educationally, and culturally.

Neither Ruth nor Joe had cognizance of the extreme price they would pay for challenging the apartheid regime. Joe later spoke of his early thoughts on fighting apartheid: "I think we were sort of euphoric about prospects and a bit blind as to what would eventually happen. There was some basis for being a bit reckless because you know we had a security apparatus which was pretty poor at that point of time, on the other side, and we just got away with murder."[66] When they were married in 1949, Joe was still studying for his law degree at Wits and working with attorneys on political cases like that in Basutoland. Ruth was deeply involved in her work at *The Guardian*, and together they had been elected to the Johannesburg District of the Communist Party of South Africa in 1946. Years later, Ruth spoke with John Heilpern about joining the Party: "I became a communist because it was the only organization known to me in South Africa that advocated meaningful changes. And because it wasn't just a policy, but something positive. They wanted to do something. They were immersed in the struggle for equality. They were committed."[67]

At home, daughters Shawn, Gillian, and Robyn, were born between 1950 and 1953. Their family lived dual lives throughout these "Camelot" years and beyond, similar to other white activists. Ruth and Joe had parties, as did their political friends, such as Saturday night music evenings at Percy Denton's house. Joe shared a close relationship with Harold Wolpe. Ruth had two intimate friends, Myrtle Berman and Zena Stein, the latter a physician. Stein, with her husband, Mervyn Susser, also a physician, were members of the CSPA. They had been active in politics at Wits, and during the 1950s worked in a clinic in Alexandra Township with fellow Party members Margaret Cormack and her husband, Michael Hathorne. Zena recalled that Joe would visit the clinic every couple of weeks to discuss Party issues. Similar to most people who knew Joe Slovo, Zena, Mervyn, and Myrtle commented on his great sense of humor and his wonderful storytelling. However, Myrtle was quick to add that Ruth was also "witty and fun."[68] Although Ruth, Myrtle, and Zena did not see each other daily as they were all extremely busy and lived in different neighborhoods, they did speak often and traded children's and maternity clothing. Within this same intimacy, Myrtle was having lunch with Ruth, three weeks after Shawn's birth, when she went into labor with her first daughter. Myrtle also recalled Tilly and Julius, who lived close by, often helping with childcare. In an interview for the book *Cutting Through the Mountain: Interviews with South African Jewish Activists*, Shawn Slovo reflected on her grandmother Tilly as she spoke of the relationship of Joe's communism to his Jewish cultural identity. "I remember my grandmother's food was quite Jewish even though she was a real rabid communist, a Stalinist down the line. But she did chopped herring, and chopped liver, and it wasn't on the Sabbath or any kind of celebration."[69] Shawn recognized the sacrifices made by both of her grandparents in support of Ruth, Joe, and she and her sisters:

> She was very important to us because she picked up the slack, to put it quite simply. Her support was one of the reasons my parents could do what they chose to do. That's why my mother was able to work full-time and commit herself in the way that

she did. . . . When she was arrested or had to go into exile or had to go into hiding in those dark days, my grandmother and my grandfather were around. . . . They were very key to our childhood.[70]

Myrtle Berman also remembered Ruth's frustration in response to Joe's lack of participation in the mundane aspects of family life. "Ruth would say that Joe was bourgeois. He would come home and expect Ruth to do everything. He wouldn't be involved in the kids' homework or anything. I have to say when they got to the UK Joe really turned up."[71]

They lived in a suburban home, partially due to the generosity of Julius and Tilly First, took Cape Town beach vacations, sent their children in pressed uniforms to private white-only schools, and had black domestic workers cooking, cleaning, and taking care of the children. However, they also worked intensely for social justice through Ruth's writing, Joe's legal work, and public and underground resistance in the SACP, ANC, and Congress Movement. In addition, unlike almost all of Shawn, Gillian, and Robyn's classmates, they often had black South Africans visiting their home. Gillian Slovo described her parents' lives then:

> Young, talented, passionate, they had broken out of the constraints of the South African colour bar. While the rest of whites-only South Africa looked for its entertainment either to classical European music, or to the naive folk songs of the Afrikaner veld, they danced to township penny whistles and to *kwela* and drew the rest of their music from the wider world: from America and the civil rights movement, as they were swept up in Paul Robeson or Harry Belafonte crazes, or from Europe and the latest cult movie. . . . Perhaps they played harder than others because they knew how close to the edge they were living. But the shadows had not yet closed in: they also felt, black and white together, that they were making history in a world that was going their way.[72]

Stephen Clingman also portrays the dual lives of communist families in his biography of Bram Fischer when he describes Sunday afternoons at the Fischers' swimming pool:

The Bernsteins, the Slovos, the Hodgsons would be regulars, but there were many others, of all colours, as well. In a world of apartheid's fetishisms the pool at Beaumont Street was in the most easy way multi-racial, so that its liquid absolutions would combine the amniotic with the amnesiac, and the scandal of varied skins immersed in the same lazy water could simply be forgotten. There, together in that pool, a new kind of South Africa could be represented, all the more outrageous to white puritanism for its refusal to be anything more than ordinary.[73]

The Slovo daughters have frequently discussed what the family surrendered as a result of their parents' commitment to the struggle against apartheid. Dan O'Meara recalled Joe telling him of the family sacrifices when they spoke in the early 1980s in Maputo. Joe also broached the topic when he was interviewed for Donald Pinnock's research on Ruth:

> I think we just kept our kids in ignorance and, therefore, they were bewildered and isolated from their own society. Because it's not like a black kid. In a sense, they suffered more than black kids at some level. They had no support, you see. A black kid whose parents get arrested becomes a hero in the school. A white kid, whose parents get arrested, is a subject of derision — communist scum.[74]

Clearly, Ruth and Joe's family was not typical in white South Africa. Joe and Ruth were each products of their individuality, ideology, infidelity, and intensity. Throughout their lives, they both asserted that they made each other better as they worked for the end of apartheid in South Africa. Joe commented on their marriage shortly after the apartheid government assassinated Ruth:

> But, taken broadly, I would say (however smug and complacent it sounds) that we enjoyed a stimulating companionship and mutuality through most of our period together. It was certainly not without friction, competitiveness and phases during which our political disagreement reached threatening proportions. Nor was it free of other, more or less serious involvements. But the basic fabric of our relationship stood up to all this and

more, including many forced separations connected with our duties in the revolutionary movement.[75]

Because of their participation and commitment, Ruth and Joe were both involved in two of the most important revolutionary decisions of the early Anti-Apartheid Movement—the dissolution of the CPSA and the emergence of the SACP, and the alliance of the South African Communist Party and the African National Congress. The literature on the CPSA, which is deftly analyzed by Allison Drew in *Discordant Comrades*, is derived mostly from the Party itself. The CPSA was launched in 1921 and went through various phases before its dissolution. The Party was immediately faced with the 1922 white miners' strike, and the Party's membership at the time was predominantly white. The early racism and the anti-racist struggles of communist leaders David Ivon Jones and Sydney Bunting, and possibly Ruth's parents, were simultaneous with their attempts to foster an integrated Party. Racial divisions clearly still existed in the Party in 1950, but the recruiting efforts of Jones and others in the Party did lead to a sharp rise in black membership in the CPSA by 1930. Moses Kotane and J. B. Marks, future leaders in the SACP-ANC alliance, became members of the CPSA at the time. In the 1930s Party policy was deeply connected to the Soviet Union. Decisions were taken in concurrence with Comintern dictates, causing schisms and harsh reprisals within the Party. The crucial decision at the time was the mission of ending South African racism. During the Second World War, Party numbers grew. However, by the time the Nationalist Party took office in 1948, the CPSA, in spite of what Joe, Ruth, and their comrades might have thought, was largely impotent. Writing in 1971, under the pseudonym "Lerumo," Michael Harmel argued that the Party was gaining power just as apartheid struck it down. Although his evidence was weak, he referred to Party efforts as "rallying the people."[76] However, Drew explains that though the Party listed approximately 2,500 members nationally, fewer than 1,000 had paid their dues. At the CPSA's final national conference in January 1950, dissolution was never mentioned. The pre-apartheid government had obtained the names of Communist Party members in 1946, and when the apartheid government passed the Suppression of Communisim Act in May 1950, the Central Committee voted to dissolve. Citing Jack and Ray Simons, Drew explains that the Party's lack of strategy to go underground was both organizational and psychological. Harmel also addressed the weaknesses of the CPSA:

Despite the open threats of the Nationalist Party to ban the C.P., no effective steps had been taken to prepare for underground existence and illegal work. A hastily convened Central Committee meeting held in May 1950, when the terms of the new law became known, decided by majority vote and without consulting the membership to dissolve the Party. It was suggested, among other things, that the rank and file would not be prepared or able to face dangers and difficulties of underground work.[77]

Harmel praised the people on the Central Committee who viewed dissolution as temporary, and they would subsequently be essential to the underground launch of the SACP in 1953. However, Joe Slovo and Ruth First were caught totally off guard by the dissolution. Joe commented about dissolution in his autobiography: "Many of us assumed that it was merely a ploy and that behind-the-scenes preparations for underground revival were in hand."[78]

Joe describes conflict and tension between some of the rank and file and the Executive Committee. He recalled the origin of small underground meetings that would eventually lead to the SACP. At the time, there was a "liquidator" appointed by the Minister of Justice whose job was to seize Party assets and compile and confirm a list of South African Communists. Joe's memory of the government process in naming Communists was typical of his, Ruth's, and many of their comrades' bravado: "They believed that being on the liquidator's list was a 'call of honor'![79] And a letter signed by Joe, Rusty Bernstein, Yusuf Dadoo, Moses Kotane, Eli Weinberg, J. B. Marks, Michael Harmel, and Edwin Mofutsanyana said, "Your tyranny will not survive the judgment of the people."[80]

As the Communist Party of South Africa was dissolved, the African National Congress, still a legal organization, began radical reorganization. The ANC's rebirth was initiated in the decade prior to apartheid. Dormant in the late 1930s, the organization began to rebuild membership when it elected American- and British-trained physician Alfred Xuma as president in 1940. Because Smuts had eased pass laws, there was a growing number of blacks moving to South African cities. With them came the migration issues of poverty and resistance. In Johannesburg, both the Soweto and Alexandra townships were growing each day. The ANC protested against discrimination, but the organization was conflicted just as it had been in the 1930s. Ruth First had noted that the ANC was quiet except just before and after their national conferences.[81]

In the mid-1940s the beginning of a radicalized ANC emerged within the newly created ANC-Youth League. Nelson Mandela, Oliver Tambo, and Walter Sisulu won leadership of the ANC in 1949 as the apartheid era began. At a celebration of Walter Sisulu's seventieth birthday in 1982, Ruth commented that because of Walter Sisulu, "We have an ANC in direct and continuing contact with the masses, leading political strikes and mass disobedience campaigns. . . . We have a policy of unity in action in the ANC."[82]

The new ANC was definitely a black organization. Black leaders including Kotane and Marks maintained longtime memberships in both the ANC and CPSA. Ruth and Joe were involved in uniting people from both organizations. Ruth, who would later edit and write with Mandela, Govan Mbeki, and Oliver Tambo, had become well acquainted with the new ANC leaders from the meetings at Ismail Meer's flat. In the beginning, Mandela and most of his ANC colleagues viewed resistance as a nationalist struggle with a goal of black emancipation. While Mandela and others in the ANC later altered their course, the Pan Africanist Congress (PAC), after their secession from the ANC, became the organizational voice of Black Nationalism.

The Communist Party of South Africa's position stated that a nationalist movement could not end oppression because it did not address the essential issues of world imperialism and a class-divided South African society. But Ruth and Joe, and people like Rusty Bernstein and Jack Simons, worked hard to build an alliance, as did ANC members Walter Sisulu and eventually Nelson Mandela. In *Long Walk to Freedom*, Mandela writes that his friendships with Moses Kotane, Ruth First, and Ismail Meer helped him to reconsider his position. Elinor Sisulu writes that Ruth had an impact on her father-in-law when he first heard her speak in 1945. The understanding between the ANC and SACP was that South Africa represented a unique struggle referred to as "colonialism of a special type." Jack Simons reflected that it was the commonly shared understanding of the organizations that there was a direct relationship between the "national libratory struggle and the struggle for socialism" that brought the SACP and ANC together and nurtured resistance politics and actions throughout the struggle against apartheid. Almost fifty years ago, South African historian Mary Benson concluded that the alliance of white communists and the ANC led "to a large extent [to] the refusal of so many African leaders to turn racialist."[83]

The SACP and the ANC worked in unison to fight apartheid beginning in the 1950s. Actions included the 1952 Defiance Campaign and the 1955 People's Congress that led to the adoption of the basic program of the movement, the Freedom Charter. Eventually, because of their actions against the apartheid regime, 156 people, black, white, coloured, and Indian, were arrested and tried in the infamous Treason Trial. Ruth and Joe were in and out of underground meetings after the government enactment of the Suppression of Communism Act (1950) that led to the dissolution of the CPSA. The Communist Party was reconstituted as the South African Communist Party and six underground party conferences took place between 1952 and 1962. Ruth traveled to the Soviet Union in 1951 and then China in 1954. Although Ruth and Joe led public lives, of necessity they did underground political work throughout the 1950s and until they left the country in the early 1960s. They were banned from political meetings and gatherings and occasionally from meeting with any people other than family. However, during the 1950s they still did not appear overly fearful. An example of both personal and political conflict is documented in *Rivonia's Children*:

> Rusty Bernstein and Ruth were often at loggerheads. Ruth treated him as one of those dreary, conventional ideologues whom she found so predictable and deserving of scorn. Still, every Monday evening, after arguing at the district committee meeting, the Slovos would join the Bernsteins for a late supper at one of their houses.[84]

Ironically, Glenn Frankel wrote of the SACP as a "family":

> The Party was like a family—the ties of mutual belief and affection that bound were strong. Even its squabbles were family-like— some of the younger activists complained about the "Northern Suburbs Clique" of the Fischers, Bernsteins, Slovos and Harmels in the same way teenagers complain about their parents. Indeed, over the phone and in conversation, comrades began to refer to the Party as "The Family." The code name was a way of misleading those who were listening in but also a recognition of how many of the members felt. The party was their home.[85]

Concurrent with the passing of the new apartheid laws, Joe and Ruth, along with both their SACP and ANC comrades, were involved in various anti-apartheid actions. There were trade union strikes after the Nationalist Party took office; black people throughout the country boycotted work on June 26, 1950 (subsequently Freedom Day) when the ANC declared a day of National Protest and Mourning. Ruth and Joe were both involved in the Defiance Campaign in 1952. Led by Nelson Mandela, whom Joe referred to as the "Volunteer-in-Chief," black South Africans protested against pass laws and other racist affronts. The ANC ended the campaign in 1953 when over 8,000 people were arrested, many of whom were flogged during their detainment. Ruth and Joe also represented the alliance in their professional lives: Joe in his legal representation of black South Africans and Ruth in her work as a journalist and managing editor of *The Guardian*.

Beginning her work at *The Guardian* at the end of 1946, Ruth served as the manager of the Johannesburg bureau. There were many articles that connected her journalism and politics during her long tenure at the newspaper. The paper was launched on February 19, 1937, with a twelve-page edition. The masthead read, "Presenting the Truth to South Africa about Events Within and Without," and most of the articles were initially international. Modeled after *The Daily Worker* in England, *The Guardian* was not officially part of the CPSA, but it was clearly the unofficial organ of the Party. Just before Ruth joined the newspaper, Moses Kotane and Jack Simons admonished the staff stating that it was imperative for the paper to represent black voices and issues. The representation of black voices and articles on black issues was initiated intensely when Brian Bunting became editor and brought Ruth in to manage the paper's Johannesburg office. James Zug reported on Ruth in his book on *The Guardian*:

Spearheading the charge into African life was Ruth First. In her first four weeks at the *Guardian*, the twenty-two-year-old reported on a tin workers' strike, opined on the royal visit, visited a Sophiatown squatter camp, and interviewed Yusuf Dadoo, Michael Scott, H. M. Basner and Anton Lembede. Two months later, she illegally crept into municipal workers' compounds and took photographs at night while holding a flashlight in her free hand. She sent three African employees of the *Guardian* to secretly investigate a price-fixing racket in the sugar industry. She ventured into squatters' camps and

African townships across the Transvaal and Orange Free State, and datelines as scattered as Pietersburg and Harrismith bore the name of Ruth First. She cultivated close relationships with many political figures, ranging from Youth Leaguers, to the British priest Father Trevor Huddleston, to Walter Sisulu, to Indian leaders like Ismail Meer.[86]

"Ruth began her writing career as a journalist, and as a campaigning journalist,"[87] said Gavin Williams, one of Ruth's closest colleagues. Appropriately, Williams was speaking at the twenty-fifth anniversary of the assassination of Walter Rodney, the Guyanese socialist revolutionary. Williams continued his introduction to Ruth First with a concise homage to her work as an activist and writer:

> She was concerned first of all to get the facts and to get them right, as far as she could. The facts are out there. But they won't speak up for themselves. You have to get out and find them out—from interviews and documents, from books and personal observations. Facts have to be interpreted and communicated. Ruth always wrote to reach the widest possible audience. This required the interpretive skill of the essayist. Arguments must be built on evidence, but are also presented through illustrations. . . . However, for Ruth, it is not individuals who make history or, at least, when they do, it is the context which makes this possible. She insists that social explanations must go behind the actions and motives of individuals to institutions, interest groups and social classes.[88]

Another close friend, Ronald Segal, onetime editor of *Africa South* and then Penguin African Library, celebrated Ruth as a journalist at the London memorial after her assassination:

> She was a remarkable journalist: wholly concerned with identifying and exposing the various horrors of racial rule; with reporting and encouraging the course of struggle against it. She was not indifferent to the risks, the costs that were involved. She simply recognised them as the necessary consequences of her choice. Those investigations and reports of hers—into forced labour on the farms, the workings of the pass laws, conditions in the gold mines; on demonstrations,

boycotts, campaigns—are classic examples of committed journalism. They do not peddle abstract phrases. They depict the
real suffering of the individual victim; the real complex mood
of collective defiance.[89]

Ruth wrote weekly editorials in *The Guardian* from the time of the
Nationalist Party's election through the 1955 launching of the Freedom Charter and beyond. Banned numerous times, the newspaper
always seemed to reappear under new names and new incorpora-
tions—the *Clarion, People's World, Advance, New Age,* and finally *The
Spark,* until final closure on March 28, 1963. The first raid on *The
Guardian* occurred in November 1950 when the government entered
the paper's offices in Cape Town, Johannesburg, and Durban. Ruth
immediately called attorney Vernon Berrange to come to the office
to deal with the intruders. The paper was first banned in May 1952.
Coincidentally, Joe and Ruth were on holiday with the Buntings.[90]
Gillian painted a detailed picture of the office in Johannesburg:

> For a start the noise was incredible: Telephones rang, dupli-
> cators churned, and staples clicked. But it was the occupants
> who raised the level to an all-time high as they shouted down
> phones, at each other, to the air. And as for the mess—well, its
> proportions were mythic: Piles of leaflets teetered precariously
> on desks, banners jostled with collection boxes, old clothes col-
> lected for rummage sales spilled from their boxes. But none of
> that made the office either unfriendly or difficult to negotiate.
> For the place was buzzing with exhilaration.[91]

Ruth wrote her most famous story in 1951 on the enslavement of
Bethal farm workers. She also exposed government seizure of black
land and other land rights issues, township conditions, and political protests including the train boycotts, bannings, and a series on
how pass laws affected the lives of black South Africans. One of her
land rights articles was titled "Africans Turned Off the Land." Ruth
reviewed a number of cases from different regions of the country and
used the voices of people whose land was taken by the apartheid government. "My grandfather woke one morning in his own kraal and
found a white man who said: 'You are living on my farm and must
work for me,' "[92] an informant told her. A second individual provided
an even more graphic account:

The police broke down the people's houses, loading them and all the other possessions on to lorries. For three days six lorries moved the village, against the people's will. Their crops were left standing in the fields, their pigs and chickens remained behind, and they found themselves on poor Trust Farm land with little water, almost penniless and without food.[93]

Ruth provided the same kind of reporting on the townships of Johannesburg:

Placing new burdens on the Africans—the city's poorest, hardest hit by the soaring cost of living, at the lowest end of the cost of living allowance scale, the most fleeced by profiteers and black-marketeers in every shortage, carrying the heaviest burden of transport fares, because they are pushed into the furthest locations—can only cause trouble.[94]

The *Rand Daily Mail* first published the Bethal exposé, but it was Ruth, with the activist Anglican pastor Michael Scott, who had investigated and exposed the slave-like conditions. First and Scott passed the story to the *Rand Daily Mail* because *The Guardian*'s Thursday publication deadline had already passed. In addition, publication by the larger, national paper meant a much greater audience as well as broader acceptance than *The Guardian*. Ruth would expand on the story in several articles and ten years later would report when slave-like conditions were rediscovered at the area's farms. Although Bethal was known as an Afrikaner town, there were also some Jewish families who had immigrated at the turn of the twentieth century and settled as farmers in the area. H. M. Basner, a Communist, Jewish member of Parliament, although aware of the conditions, had suppressed the information, because, ironically, he was afraid it would exacerbate anti-Semitism. First and Scott visited Bethal, the place where police supplied forced labor to local farmers. They were hosted by Gert Sibande, a farm laborer, lay preacher, and local ANC leader, and who, like Ruth and Joe, was later a defendant in the 1956 Treason Trial. Sibande revealed to Ruth and Scott the unsanitary dwellings where workers were forced to live with little food or water. They were paid twelve pounds for six months of labor. Ruth wrote about the conditions in *The Guardian*:

It is not every day that the Johannesburg reporter for the *Guardian* meets an African farm worker who, when asked to describe conditions on the farm on which he works, silently takes off his shirt to show large weals and scars on his back, shoulders, and arms. . . . We saw not a single blanket in any of the compounds. Food consisted of a clod of mealie meal and a pumpkin wrapped in a piece of sacking, each man taking a handful at a time.[95]

Ruth published a series of *Guardian* articles under the headline, "There Are More Bethals." The Prime Minister ordered an investigation that was at best a whitewash, something Ruth had predicted in *The Guardian*. Michael Scott and Ruth First continued their investigations in spite of the government's inaction. They reported on government-farmer collusion and photographed police incarcerating black people fleeing Rhodesia and transporting them to farms in Bethal. Joe went undercover and also helped in the investigations after accompanying Ruth to observe black people being taken from the courts to the farms. "The statistics I managed to gather reinforced our own observations during the so-called pass law trials that this was not a court of justice but a slave-labor bureau."[96]

Concluding this series was a February 1950 article titled "The Worst Place God Has Made—A State of Terror in Bethal." Beata Lipman, one of *The Guardian* reporters, recalled a specific incident at the office between Ruth and the police. Two plainclothes detectives arrived there and asked for Ruth who was out of the office. The detectives decided to wait for her. When she arrived forty minutes later and saw the two men waiting, she said to Lipman: "Has Miss First come in yet?" Lipman said "no," and before turning and walking out the door, Ruth replied: "That's all right, I'll catch up to her later."[97]

Along with her writing, sometimes sixteen articles per week, Ruth was deeply involved in the Defiance Campaign, the Freedom Charter, and the rebirth of the Communist Party. Amid this activism, her narratives were always connected to her politics. Joe, who had begun his rather eclectic law practice, was soon known as a leading advocate. Although Ruth was always identified with her pen, Joe also wrote, his writing becoming quite voluminous in the mid to late 1960s. One of his first articles appeared in 1954 in the radical journal *Liberation*, about the Queenstown Conference of the ANC calling for a "Congress of the People." In the article, he critiqued police state oppression and spoke of the power of the Defiance Campaign and struggle from the ground, stating: "There is a simple and immediate solution to our 'complex and insoluble' race problem: allow each South African to say for himself what he desires in life."[98]

In Joe's practice, he often defended blacks who were detained under the apartheid regime. He contended that he was ill-prepared for the courtroom when he completed his Wits degree, but that law as a tool provided him with a venue for "creativity and some scope for self-expression."[99] Two of his colleagues at the bar, Julius Browde, a later member of the Progressive Party (founded in 1959) who was later lauded by President Mandela, and struggle lawyer George Bizos, Nelson Mandela's longtime attorney, have descriptive memories of Joe as a practicing lawyer. Interestingly, they have conflicting recollections of Joe discussing politics with fellow lawyers. Browde recalled Bram Fischer as very political, trying to convert colleagues, while Joe was not. Bizos tells an opposite story. Both men agree, however, that he was an excellent advocate, appreciated by his colleagues for his skills, sociability, and humor. A young colleague, Denis Kuny, spoke of Joe's collegiality and congeniality, but also referenced his courtroom competence. "He was a good lawyer. What struck me about him was how tough he was in court. Joe was really tough."[100] Browde viewed Joe as the leader who was also Everyman. "He brought everyone down to the same level as himself. Which wasn't a bad level, by the way, it was a good level. Joe was first of all a fine human being. He liked people from all walks of life and all shapes and sizes—all colors, made no difference to him."[101]

Browde and Bizos both recollect Joe's friendship with Gert Coetzee, an Afrikaner Nationalist who became a leading South African judge and in the early 1960s wrote a book titled *The Republic: A Reasoned View*. Browde and Bizos agree that Joe's friendship with Coetzee is an example of his humanity. Browde provided a portrait of the day of Coetzee's appointment as a judge:

Joe knocked on the door and went in and the new judge was sitting with his feet up on the table. He had no work yet, it had not been allotted to him. And Joe said, "Ja, Gert, I see what you're thinking, the working class can kiss my ass, I've got the foreman's job at last." Gert had a good laugh.[102]

Joe had fond memories of camaraderie with fellow lawyers:

> The advocates constituted a community, all housed in one
> building and sharing administrative staff. Teas and midday
> meals were taken together in a common room. The conver-
> sation rarely touched subjects other than bar and courtroom
> gossip. To reinforce the illusion that law is above politics, lead-
> ing and well-known communists, such as Bram Fischer and I,
> shared tables and exchanged formal pleasantries with leading
> Nationalist politicians such as John Vorster.[103]

He was quick to add that collegiality did not extend to the three
black lawyers included in the 120 members of the bar. Joe represented
Duma Nokwe, the first black person admitted to the bar, in his quest
to use the changing room at the Supreme Court in Pretoria. In a move
representative of apartheid's racist gentility, the court provided Nokwe
with his own dressing room in order not to "sully" the white changing room.[104] Joe was also clear on how judicial fairness and decorum,
though somewhat admirable, enhanced the racist, apartheid state:

> Ironically, the honesty and integrity of many of the old-style
> judges, which made possible the occasional redress of griev-
> ance even against white authority, also helped maintain the
> illusion that equal social justice for all might eventually be
> attained through the existing framework. In this sense the
> touching and naive faith in the judiciary of many among the
> racially underprivileged played no small part in reducing the
> disturbances against the status quo.[105]

Joe's initial case was a housebreaking and theft trial. His primary
memory is of an intimidating judge. His book chronicles a handful
of cases with humor and great description. His own courtroom spirit
appears to be clever, creative, and somewhat cunning. Joe was well
aware that his position as a lawyer assisted him in terms of his political mission: "If one was an advocate, as I was, whose practice became
more and more dominated by cases with a political aspect, access to
prisoners, and the broad freedom which still remained to hit hard at
authority in open court, was a great opportunity."[106]

Joe describes numerous cases, but most of these directly correspond to the racist reality of apartheid South Africa. Sometimes he

won, and sometimes he lost, but he understood that black South Africans usually lost. Joe wrote about the death penalty:

> In South Africa the form of punishment is even more repugnant because it contains a racial dimension. In all its history South Africa has hanged six whites for the murder of blacks whereas hundreds of blacks have gone to the gallows for murder of whites. The cheapness of black life also often protects the perpetrator. When a capital crime has been committed against a black, the investigation is usually shoddy and the prospects greater for the accused of an acquittal.[107]

In this particular case, Joe describes a judge as having a courtroom "like Chaplin's *Modern Times* production line,"[108] where he continually lessened charges against blacks who had killed other blacks from murder to culpable homicide:

> My initiation into this judge's style came in a murder trial when he interrupted my flow of cross-examination with the whisper: "Mr. Slovo, if you change your plea to culpable homicide your client won't go to jail." His show of lenience did not stem from a belief in penal reform, but rather from a relaxed, casual attitude towards violence if it did not involve the white community.[109]

Joe Slovo also represented teachers who were directly involved in the defiance of Bantu Education—the law that segregated black children to inferior government schooling. Rebellious teachers had been fired and numerous black people boycotted government schooling and started alternative schools that were quickly deemed illegal by the apartheid regime. Joe defended those who were charged with "the crime of teaching." His description of his questioning of a policeman would be comical if the stakes had not been so high. The testimony included:

> We took cover behind some rocks and bushes. Soon after the sun rose I noticed groups of children aged between six and 13 converging on a spot near the big tree.

> The accused proceeded to suspend the blackboard (Exhibit A) from a nail which protruded from the tree. He then proceeded

to write on Exhibit A with white chalk and the children appeared to be writing.

I approached the accused, told him he was under arrest for conducting an illegal school.

The accused was still holding a piece of white chalk when I apprehended him, I confiscated and now hand in as Exhibit D.

I asked some of the children in the front row, in the presence and hearing of the accused, what the accused had been doing prior to our arrival, and one of the pupils stated that the accused had been teaching them the five times table. The accused made no attempt to deny this.[110]

In addition to the cases that might be defined as defending "Everyman," Joe began representing struggle comrades as early as 1954 when Walter Sisulu was detained for breaking his banning orders. Sisulu had attended a meeting in the Orange Free State that the ANC tried to disguise as a simple luncheon. He was convicted on a unique charge: "Attending a gathering in order to partake of, or be present while others partake of, refreshment in the nature of tea and/or edibles and/or a meal."[111] Sisulu was sentenced to three months of labor, but Joe got him out of jail with a low bail and the case was overturned on appeal. Finally, there was the case that Joe did not accept, representing George Bizos in his attempt to join the bar. Because Bizos was Greek there was some question as to whether he would be permitted to claim allegiance to the British monarchy, a requirement in South Africa at the time. Bizos remembers Joe's response when he asked him to take his case: "George, for a Lithuanian Jew and a communist at that, to tell the judges that there is nothing wrong with the Greek to take an oath of allegiance to the Queen is not the best way of doing it. I will ask Bram to ask one of the leading Anglo-Saxons to do your application."[112]

Ruth First's writing and Joe Slovo's defense of black South Africans increased throughout the decade. Ruth, directly involved in the Defiance Campaign from its inception, reported for *The Guardian* on the 1951 African National Congress meeting in Bloemfontein. This is where Walter Sisulu presented the ANC's resistance plan, in cooperation with Indian, coloured, and white organizations. The plan solicited the government to repeal a litany of racist laws. Further, if the government refused to act, the Defiance Campaign would begin. This joint effort, led by the ANC, but in camaraderie with the South African Indian Congress (SAIC) and the South African Coloured People's Organization (SACPO), somewhat corresponds to the ANC-Communist alliance discussed earlier in this chapter. In fact, it appeared that Nelson Mandela changed his views, moving from what has sometimes been referred to as an inward-looking nationalism to a more inclusive revolutionary nationalism as noted in his speech at the Bloemfontein meeting.

Following the ANC conference, various meetings were held, and a committee consisting of Mandela, Z. K. Matthews, Ismail Meer, and J. N. Singh drafted a letter to Prime Minister Malan that was signed by ANC president James Moroka and the secretary, Walter Sisulu. The letter asked the government to retract "unjust laws which keep in perpetual subjection and misery vast sections of our population."[113] Predictably, the Nationalist Party government rejected the demands to repeal racist apartheid laws. Rejection, of course, meant it was time for "defiance," which in 1952 was for the most part defined as passive resistance. Sisulu, Moroka, and Dadoo appealed for action at a public demonstration at Freedom Square in Fordsburg, at the time Johannesburg's largest Indian neighborhood. Placards read: "Votes for All," "Malan, Remember How Hitler Fell," and "Away with Passes." While no one in the ANC or the other groups could predict the results, they were certain of the need for action challenging the apartheid regime. In his reflections, Joe explains that even Nelson Mandela "did not harbor any illusions about the ultimate possibility of converting the ruling class without a tough revolutionary struggle."[114] There was strategy, however, in the timing of the campaign. In May 1950, the Defend Free Speech Convention called a general strike to protest apartheid oppression against liberation organizations. Although the "stay-away" was peaceful, police opened fire on protesters, killing eighteen people. In response, the ANC announced another general strike, and a day of mourning on June 26, 1950, which was then designated as Freedom Day in South Africa. Joe accompanied Ruth to Alexandra Township where she covered the event for *The Guardian*. "When the police began their baton charge to break up the demonstration on the football field, Ruth rushed to the center with her camera, faced the police and stood squarely taking photographs of them charging toward her."[115] Thus, in May 1952, the coalition decided that the Defiance Campaign would begin on June 26 using non-cooperation and nonviolent actions of civil disobedience.

The campaign began in Port Elizabeth in the Eastern Cape, when Raymond Mhlaba, who was later convicted in the Rivonia Trial and spent over two decades in Robben Island Prison, led thirty-three people into the Whites Only section of the local railway station. On June 27, protests ensued in Johannesburg and other cities. Between June and December, over 8,000 resisters had been imprisoned. Ruth First was involved as both a participant and journalist. She attended various meetings and reported on the scene in Boksburg near Johannesburg for *The Clarion*, one of the early reincarnations of *The Guardian*. The July 26 headline read, "Campaign of Defiance Under Way—Thousands Ready to Break Unjust Laws," and July 3 followed with "Defiance Campaign Unites All Races—150 Volunteers Go Into Action." Ruth and Joe, as well as Myrtle Berman, Yusuf Cachalia, Walter Sisulu, and Oliver Tambo, were all participants in the meetings designed to promote white support of the resisters. Tambo and Sisulu told the group that the silence of white liberals toward the Defiance Campaign was creating a sense of white versus nonwhite South Africa in the black community.

It was at these meetings that Mary Benson, who would later become friends with Ruth, first became aware of her presence. Interestingly, the schism between white radicals and liberals also became transparent. In addition, the meetings probably helped to forge the Congress of Democrats (COD) and ease the alliance of the ANC and soon-to-be SACP. They were held at Darragh Hall, on the campus of the private all-boys school, St. John's College, in Johannesburg, and continued even after the Defiance Campaign came to an end. In 1953, the group launched itself as the Johannesburg Discussion Group and published a newsletter, *Viewpoints and Perspectives,* that was edited by Myrtle Berman.

The ANC ended the Defiance Campaign in December 1952. Mandela, Sisulu, and J. B. Marks, from the ANC, and Yusuf Dadoo, Yusuf Cachalia, and Ahmed Kathrada, from the SAIC, were all arrested and convicted under the Suppression of Communism Act as leaders of the resistance, but their sentences of nine months of hard labor were suspended. During the campaign, membership in the ANC grew rapidly, to an estimated 100,000. The Defiance Campaign helped lay the groundwork for the launching of the Congress of Democrats and the beginnings of the ANC-SACP alliance. Writing in *Viewpoints*

and Perspectives, Ruth argued that the campaign was of major political importance because blacks had entered the "consciousness of
the European population."[116] At the time, Ruth also responded to an
attack on black militancy in *Liberation*:

> The non-European political movements do not scorn argu-
> ment and organisation. They are daily engaged in these tasks.
> But there comes a time in the growth of every political move-
> ment when consistent organisation produces militant people's
> actions in defence of rights under attack or for improve-
> ments in conditions. . . . Political campaigns are not carefully
> rehearsed theatrical performances in which the stage man-
> ager orders. . . . Provocateurs and the government don't take
> their cues from the producer.[117]

What the Defiance Campaign did not facilitate, however, was the
repeal of apartheid laws or a gentler and kinder Nationalist Party
government. In essence, the struggle was just getting under way, with
Joe and Ruth very much involved.

Ruth First and Joe Slovo's political action lists included the South
African Peace Council, the underground re-formation of the Communist Party, the launch of the Congress of Democrats, writing and
promoting the Freedom Charter, and being named as defendants in
the 1956 Treason Trial. They were two of many political activists who
were banned by the government in 1954; however, their orders did
not deny Joe the privilege to travel for his law practice nor Ruth her
right to write. They were also raising their daughters, the newborn
Robyn, Shawn, and Gillian. Ruth was writing predominantly for *The
Guardian*, but also for various other resistance publications. Joe was
appearing in court representing black defendants. They were living
in a house that Gillian remembers as large and spacious, but Mary
Benson recalls as rather modest and anything but bourgeois. Joe and
Ruth were sometimes away for extended periods, and Tilly and Julius
First and the family's black nanny spent a great deal of time with the
children during the "Camelot" years.

Gillian has written of her grandparents Tilly and Julius's generosity, but also Tilly's intensity. In *117 Days*, Ruth speaks of Tilly in
the same context. All three of the Slovo daughters provide a sense of
the family's dual lives—feelings of abandonment, but also family time
and traditional middle-class experiences: Joe and Ruth listening to

American radio shows, Shawn creating plays and games for her and her sisters, and car trips with Joe to the townships where he met with people like Mandela and Sisulu. Shawn often shared alone time with both of her parents on the weekend: "On Saturday mornings I had Spanish dancing and would go to work with Joe in the car. Then after I would be taken to the newspaper office and would get to hang out with Ruth. I would bribe my sisters not to make demands to come along. I'd give them things to shut up—books, money, sweets."[118] Each year, at Christmastime, the family would vacation on the beach at Cape Town. Joe would drive his Chevrolet all night singing and joking, while Robyn, Gillian, Shawn, and Ruth slept through most of the journey. They would meet with other political families and on Christmas Day there was an annual *braai*[119] at Clifton Beach.

Julius Browde, one of Joe's law colleagues, spoke of him as quite a game player. He enjoyed sports, especially soccer, and he played tennis. When comrades, friends, acquaintances, and his brother-in-law Ronald First talked about Joe, they all mentioned poker, a game he played in Johannesburg and London, at a well-known Sunday night game at the home of the ex-*Drum* editor Sylvester Stein. Even though Joe was known to be smart and clever, it was said that his friends welcomed him to poker games, not just for his sociability and humor, but also because he often tipped his hand. He did not bluff well. The people around the table in Johannesburg with Joe included Harold Wolpe, Ivan Sola, Mockie Friedman, Mannie Brown, Tony O'Dowd, and George Bizos. The game alternated among players' homes and Bizos cited a specific night when Joe Slovo hosted:

> Their dining room, living room, and study were an open plan. We were playing on the dining room table, which was elevated, a couple of steps down was the lounge, and the deep part of the lounge was the study. We were playing poker and Ruth was busy typing. It was a habit to stop at eleven o'clock for tea and hot dogs and finish at about 12, 12:30. Joe looked at the time, it was nearly eleven o'clock, and he shouted out, "Ruth." She said, "yes." "It's tea time, please make it." And came back the response, "There are seven of you wasting each other's time. Stop, make it, and make sure I get some."[120]

Beginning in the 1950s Ruth and Joe traveled a great deal—Ruth for *The Guardian* and Joe for his cases, both of them for their political

Ruth in China (courtesy of the Ruth First Papers Project,
Institute of Commonwealth Studies)

involvement. Ruth took an educational trip to the Soviet Union and
China in 1954, just months after Robyn was born. The South African
Peace Council, an organization launched in 1953, had close ties to the
Friends of the Soviet Union, and sponsored the excursion.

Ruth held a position on the Peace Council's executive committee with Helen Joseph, Hilda Watts (Bernstein), Yusuf Cachalia, and
Douglas Thompson. In the Soviet Union and China, the study group,
which also included Walter Sisulu, was shown the successes of Communist development. In China, Albie Sachs and Ruth were presenters
at the planning conference for the next World Federation of Democratic Youth meeting. Albie Sachs had not yet met Ruth First before
this conference:

> Ruth was already legendary in our youth movement as a revolu-
> tionary intellectual. There were a number of women who were
> already in the fifties famous as speakers, as orators, as public
> personalities. But Ruth had the added thing. She was firm on
> theory and she could challenge the men on theory and more
> than hold her own. And that gave her an intellectual cachet and
> respect and admiration that was special. She was very gracious
> to me. I was like the young comrade from Cape Town whom
> she hadn't known very well.[121]

Ruth with Albie Sachs (left) in China (courtesy of the Ruth First
Papers Project, Institute of Commonwealth Studies)

During their first meeting, Ruth helped Albie prepare his presentation and nurtured his stay in China: "She was very friendly. She
was warm. She was fun. Interested in cultural things, a bright person
to sort of be around and I felt sort of elevated being in her company
and being associated with her because she was like the leader."[122]
When she returned to South Africa, Ruth edited a pamphlet for the
Peace Council titled *South Africans in the Soviet Union* that included
contributions from Walter Sisulu, Brian Bunting, Paul Joseph, Duma
Nokwe, and Sam Kahn. She also wrote a three-page article, "Building, Building, Building," which celebrated progress in the Soviet
Union. She told Joe, however, that she was most impressed with the
changes she witnessed in China.

Multiple questions revolve around the privilege of Joe, Ruth, and
many other white people involved in the struggle. Not to diminish
their commitment, passion, or the risks they were taking at the time,
they were still young adults whose advantages affected their dispositions and actions. For example, much has been made of Ruth's love of
fine clothes, shoes, and a near obsession with her hairstyles. Gillian
and others have written of her shopping days at one of Johannesburg's premier couturiers, Eric Pugen. In addition, Gillian reflected
on Ruth's life in the 1950s:

A woman she might be, but she would never let anyone stand in her way. Not for her the support role that had been her mother's fate. Even though she paid lip service to fashion by producing her three girls within the then prescribed two-year intervals, she refused to let motherhood slow her down. Her mother had sacrificed everything for family: Ruth, well in advance of her time, wouldn't even surrender her surname. As a friend would later comment, "The only two people who ever called her Mrs. Slovo were her hairdresser and the prosecutor in the treason trial."[123]

No matter how much Joe and Ruth fought to end apartheid in South Africa, they could never totally escape their privilege.

BY THE MIDDLE OF THE 1950S, Joe's life had become more secretive than Ruth's. He attended meetings at night and functioned on a need-to-know basis. Ruth was still very involved at the newspaper, which by 1953 was called *New Age*. She was also writing for *Fighting Talk* and *Counter Attack* and other journals. Although the *New Age* office was newspaper-centric, Rusty Bernstein recalls it as a place to see comrades and catch up on underground politics. Ruth's spirit directed the work at *The Guardian* Johannesburg office. She initiated endless meetings with people including activist minister Trevor Huddleston in Sophiatown "to keep her finger on the pulse of the townships."[124] She had conversations with ANC leader Walter Sisulu, whom she would call or visit daily. In addition, Ruth mentored young black writers. In the fifties, the list of young writers included Willie Kgositsile, Alfred Hutchinson, and Joe Gqabi. Kgositsile spoke about working with Ruth First:

I found that Ruth used to encourage me a lot. She would say, "Look, I'm going to talk to you about such-and-such, and I need you to point out some of the problems which you see out of what I'm saying. I will try to be as simple as possible so that you must understand, and if you disagree with me, don't be shy—speak." She was one of the white people who really made me feel that she wants me to know as much as she does.[125]

In 1955, Ruth broke a major political story in *New Age* that corresponded to the actions called for in the Freedom Charter. Although

black women had often protested ominous "pass laws," they were not
obligated to carry passes like African men. Ruth discovered that the
government had begun issuing and charging for passbooks that were
required for women in the Transvaal and Free State. The change in
the law implied that women would now be subject to arrest in cities
throughout the country if they did not purchase passbooks. Ruth's
article led to ANC-organized rallies where women joined men and
burned their passbooks in protest, another harbinger of things to
come, both from the government and the resistance. Anthony Sampson, onetime editor of *Drum* magazine, and later author of numerous
books, including *Mandela: The Authorized Biography*, said, "Ruth
First had the aura of *New Age*."[126] Zug's history of *The Guardian* cap-
tures her spirit:

> Ruth First was at the center of the storm. Colleagues had a
> Xhosa phrase for her: "Yimazi ephah neenkati"—a mare that
> holds its own in a race with stallions. . . . A cynosure of the
> political scene on the Rand, First whirled through her days.
> She rushed into Commissioner Street, yelled orders, made tele-
> phone calls, dashed off telegrams, dictated letters, and then
> hurtled down the stairs and jumped into her slope-backed
> Citroën that sped through the streets like a black torpedo.[127]

The government, concomitantly, viewed *New Age*, as well as its
predecessors, as the organ of the outlawed Communist Party. And
indeed Ruth and Joe were integrally involved in restarting the Party
as the new South African Communist Party. The new Party met at
six underground conferences between 1952 and 1962. The first conference was held at Julius First's Anglo-Union Furniture Factory;
Joe remembered Julius watching for police. Ruth and Joe joined the
founding central committee of the SACP that included Brian Bunting,
Fred Carneson, Bram Fischer, Michael Harmel, Rusty Bernstein,
Yusuf Dadoo, Jack Hodgson, Moses Kotane, J. B. Marks, and Hilda
Bernstein—clearly a Johannesburg-led group. Yusuf Dadoo led the
first meeting and Michael Harmel spoke intensely about the struggle—past, present, and future. Fred Carneson stated the need for
greater care and security in the new organization, and some members,
like Rowley Arenstein, who later joined the Inkatha Freedom Party,
bemoaned the changes. "The leadership tells you basically what to do,
and if you don't listen to the leadership you're an enemy of the people.

People who were sort of lesser people in the Party were quite scared of people like Ruth and others."[128]

It might be that Arenstein's comments reflect both personal distaste for Ruth as well as political differences with Joe's connections to the Soviet Union. Regarding the former, it would be fair to say that many friends perceived Ruth as tough. The views of Hilda and Rusty Bernstein are interesting because their reactions to Ruth's disposition are different even though they both viewed her as somewhat stern. Hilda also added how much she loved Ruth:

> I think that Ruth had the kind of arrogant impatience that a lot of very, very clever women have. She was an extraordinarily quick thinker and she was able to shout the attentions from anything, almost anything, political discussions and so on, even when we were discussing books and things, she'd get the core of it very, very quickly. I always felt as though I had cotton wool in my brain when we used to have discussions of that kind because she was so sharp about these things. And I think that leads to a kind of impatience with people. The not suffering fools gladly, that was a phrase, but more or less it was part of her character.[129]

"Well, I mean she was very, very sharp," added Rusty. "I just found her too abrasive for my liking. I mean not suffering fools gladly. I thought I was one of those fools she didn't suffer very gladly!"[130]

Even to this day, people have an obsessive interest in Joe Slovo's ties to the USSR, or more specifically, his loyalty to Stalinism. In 1953, when Stalin died, although Joe was publicly silent, some of his comrades were not. Moses Kotane, who was secretary of the Party for more than thirty years, wrote that Stalin believed in racial equality and added, "In the death of Comrade Stalin the working people of the world and the cause of freedom and peace have suffered a grievous loss."[131]

Stalinism was to become a divisive issue between Ruth and Joe. They disagreed on the Soviet invasion of Hungary in 1956 and many other actions taken by the USSR and GDR. Many years later, in an interview with Stephen Clingman on his relationship with Bram Fischer, Joe spoke to their ignorance regarding the Soviet Union:

> There was a real debate over Soviet-China split. Bram [and] me among those who refused to endorse statement on Soviet

side—20–30 years blind adherence. We felt we couldn't take sides at that stage. Eventually we did endorse the Soviet stand. And swallowed the so-called facts from one side. As time went on, more and more filtered through. But to be quite frank, we didn't reach the point till much later on where we really grasped what was going on. We easily lapsed into an acceptance that the problems were being dealt with after '56.[132]

Ruth and Joe participated in underground meetings, both together and separately. Aboveground, their political work was through the Congress of Democrats (COD). In October 1953, at the Trades Hall in Johannesburg, COD was launched as a white political organiza-tion to correspond and work with the ANC, South African Indian Council (SAIC), and South African Coloured People's Organization (SACPO). Nine months earlier, Ruth had written of the coming of COD in *Advance* (then the name of *The Guardian*). Eighty-eight del-egates attended the conference. Pieter Beyleveld, who had been the vice chairman of the Springbok Legion but would later testify for the government against Bram Fischer, became the first president with Jack Hodgson as secretary. Joe Slovo and Ruth First served on the executive committee. Norman Levy recalled Joe speaking elegantly at the meeting, crediting him with keeping the police at bay. Govern-ment Special Branch members who were spies were expelled from the meeting. They offered no resistance. According to Levy, the lack of repression was directly connected to Joe Slovo's petition to Judge Blackwell for a court order for the right to assemble. COD provided a legal organization for SACP members. Joe explained to Luli Callini-cos that though the alliance was important as a legal entity, "most of the actual political initiatives were processed in sub rosa meetings."[133] Although COD was criticized by white liberals, the Pan Africanist Con-gress, and Troskyist organizations for its multiculturalism (as opposed to non-racialism), it was the embodiment of an organization that the African National Congress, the South African Coloured People's Orga-nization, and the South African Indian Council were willing to work with at the conclusion of the Defiance Campaign. Donald Pinnock described part of Ruth's role within the Congress of Democrats:

The formal acceptance of the white Congress into the Alliance was to catapult Ruth into the role of a key "liberation publicist" for the mass movement. She was called on to assist with and write COD's publications and particularly its news sheet *Counter Attack*, which lasted for about three years. She was also to take over editorship of *Fighting Talk*, the Springbok Legion journal which was to become firmly Congress-oriented under her guidance.[134]

The Congress Alliance—ANC, SAIC, COD, with the ANC as the senior partner—initiated, nurtured, and compiled the 1955 *Freedom Charter*. Professor Z. K. Matthews actually proposed the idea in 1953 in his presidential address at the Cape Congress of the ANC in Cradock. Matthews, an ANC elder affectionately referred to as Prof, was notable for the many firsts connected to his name. In 1923 he was the first black person to graduate from Fort Hare College. He also received a master's degree from Yale University, writing on "Bantu Law and Western Civilization," and studied anthropology with Malinowski at the London School of Economics. Building on Matthews's public proposal, Walter Sisulu organized a conference of the ANC, SAIC, SACPO, and COD. The conference was held in Stanger, a small town in Natal where the then-banned Chief Luthuli lived, thus allowing him to attend the meeting. Ruth and Joe were directly involved, and according to Joe, so was the SACP, albeit surreptitiously. Joe was a member of a delegation, with Oliver Tambo and Yusuf Cachalia, that attempted to convince the Liberal Party to participate in the Freedom Charter. They were rebuffed. Joe and Ruth also participated in a small committee that included Yusuf Cachalia, Duma Nokwe, Pieter Beyleveld, Rusty Bernstein, and Walter Sisulu to accrue and organize the demands of people from throughout the country via regional meetings. Ruth then organized the ideas of the people, presented them to the committee, which used the demands to create the Charter. "Literally tens of thousands of scraps of paper came flooding in: a mixture of smooth writing-pad paper, torn pages from ink-blotched school exercise books, bits of cardboard, asymmetrical portions of brown and white paper bags, and even the unprinted margins of bits of newspaper."[135]

Even before the meeting, named the Congress of the People, was held, Joe spoke with a similar kind of optimism that Ruth had exhibited about the Defiance Campaign. At the 1954 Congress, he asserted that the Freedom Charter would end "the feeling of isolated defeatism which is the result of disconnected and sporadic acts of political struggle."[136] Ironically, when 3,000 people representing the

Congress movement gathered in the black township of Kliptown, just west of Johannesburg, on June 25 and 26, 1955, to endorse the Freedom Charter, most of those who had done the work could not attend because they were restricted under banning orders. This included Ruth and Joe, who had been banned the previous year. Banning aside, Joe described the scene in *Slovo: The Unfinished Autobiography*: "I remember lying on a tin rooftop with some of my comrades some 150 meters from the main square, observing through binoculars this festival of democracy, and hearing the cheers and the singing which punctuated the adoption of each clause of the Freedom Charter. A great day indeed!"[137]

With Norman Levy's assistance, Ruth reported on the Congress of the People in *New Age*. The police terminated the meeting and recorded the names of the attendees for possible later bannings. The Freedom Charter, which began with the words "We, the people of South Africa, declare for all our country and the world to know: That South Africa belongs to all who live in it, black and white, and that no government can justly claim authority unless it is based on the will of the people," became the foundation of the constitution of the new democratic nation of South Africa in 1994.

After the public declaration of the Freedom Charter, the government became more dogged in claiming Communists controlled organizations like the ANC and intensified surveillance and raids on those people they suspected as opposition. The apartheid regime wanted the "free world" to know that Moscow was controlling the efforts of resistance in South Africa. On December 5, 1956, the government began arresting leaders of the Congress movement. Ruth and Joe were arrested shortly thereafter and joined 154 of their comrades as defendants in what became known as the Treason Trial.

4—The Treason Trial
and Underground Action

FOR RUTH AND JOE, the government's crackdown on blacks and other apartheid opponents throughout the country following Kliptown did not represent a great change in Nationalist Party politics. In reality, it was the first of a handful of apartheid escalations that led to Joe's exile in 1963 and Ruth's in 1964. Before leaving the country, both would spend time in prison, Joe in 1960, and Ruth with a much harsher detention in 1963. In 1956, just after the Congress of the People, the couple was still living their dual lives in "Camelot" as well as underground. Secret Party meetings were a constant. Ruth was writing for both *New Age* and *Fighting Back*. Joe continued to represent blacks who were oppressed by the racialism that Bishop Tutu later referred to as "pigmentocracy." Their activities did not abate, except for approximately two weeks when they were detained preceding the Treason Trial. Though neither Ruth nor Joe was obsessed by a fear of the government, they had become somewhat cautious. Alan Paton described his experience flying with Ruth to Johannesburg. He was traveling from the United States but does not reveal where Ruth joined his flight:

> She nodded to me perfunctorily, but she had more pressing things on her mind. Her face was tight and strained. . . . She spent several hours of the flight tearing pieces of paper to pieces, each about the size of a fingernail. The plane was half

empty, and she occupied a seat on the opposite side of the aisle from myself. She made no attempt to hide what she was doing, probably because she knew that it was highly unlikely that I would go to the security police to tell them how Ruth First had occupied herself. I was, like so many other liberals, useless but decent. . . . When she had accumulated a small pile of paper fragments she would go to the lavatory and get rid of them.[138]

Ruth and Joe were affected when two of Ruth's close friends in the South African Communist Party made life-altering decisions. Physician friend Zena Stein, and her husband, Mervyn Susser, emigrated to England in January 1956. Ruth had other friends, of course, and it was not as if she and Zena saw each other often or spoke each day, but they shared an intimate connection. They had children the same age, and besides the impact of their physical departure, there was symbolism in their leaving the country at that point in the struggle. Also in 1956, Myrtle and Monty Berman were expelled from the SACP. It was in February of that same year that Nikita Khrushchev made his condemnation speech of Josef Stalin. Inevitably, the news reached Party members in South Africa. In addition, the Soviet Union invaded Hungary in November, brutally squashing populist resistance and establishing a new USSR-backed government. Though both Myrtle and Monty were relieved when they were dismissed from the Party, they were concerned about their denunciation by some members of the SACP. Myrtle's reflections of the time are ironic in that she alludes to Joe Slovo's ideological breadth, even though it is Joe who was commonly described as a South African Stalinist:

I never felt such enormous relief when we were kicked out of the party in '56 over Hungary and for meeting with Baruch Hirson [Hirson was a Trotskysist]. There was no way that I wanted to get back, you see—categorically no. It was a problem being part of the doctrinaire. Bram and Molly were contacts and so rigid. If we could have had Joe, for example—who was much broader in vision even though outwardly he adhered rigidly to the line. He must have known, but no one was in the position to bite the hand that feeds them.[139]

The Bermans scheduled meetings with both Joe Slovo and Oliver Tambo when they were expelled from the Party. According to Myrtle, they received assurances that they would not be "rubbished" and that both men knew that they would continue to work in the struggle against apartheid.

This might have been the time when some of Ruth and Joe's arguments became public, corresponding to Khrushchev's declaration condemning Stalin and the Soviet invasion of Hungary. Various friends and colleagues, both in print and verbally, commented on the intensity of their arguments, which never dissipated over the years. Both Rusty and Hilda Bernstein remembered them well. For Rusty, "It could be embarrassing. We were having supper with them and they would start a political argument and he or Ruth would get up and walk out."[140] Hilda remembered more context: "Something would spark it off and they'd be going at it. . . . They weren't personal, basically political, but very, very fierce. Joe thought that Ruth was unduly influenced by all the liberal academics in the world. . . . And that this was probably a kind of dilution of . . . our main purpose."[141]

Police throughout the country raided over 10,000 homes in the months following the enactment of he Freedom Charter. Most of the raids were on black people. In July, the six-foot-six Minister of Justice, "Blackie" Swart, announced that he would soon arrest 200 people for treason. The first arrests occurred on December 6, 1956, but Joe and Ruth were not among the detainees. Joe met with his colleague, resistance lawyer Vernon Berrange, and the prosecutor, J. C. van Niekerk, to discuss bail for the detainees as well as to learn about a timeline for the preliminary stage of the trial. Slovo and Berrange were assured that the trial would not begin until mid-January, and van Niekerk, with subversive intentions, wished them good holidays. The gesture was more than cynical, as he was surely aware that both Ruth and Joe would soon be arrested. Indeed, that same night Joe and Ruth went out to dinner with Hilda and Rusty Bernstein, and not surprisingly were somewhat bewildered as to why they were still free. Their freedom, however, was short-lived.

People were arrested all over the country and escorted by Special Branch officers on trains and planes to Johannesburg's central city prison, The Fort. In his book, *The Treason Cage*, Anthony Sampson reflected on the people who were detained:

> The arrested people came from every class and corner of South
> African life. They included an African professor, a white
> bookmaker, a Member of Parliament, three clergymen, two

lorry-drivers, eight lawyers and seven doctors. They lived in the swarming black locations round the gold mines of Johannesburg, or in small country villages in the primitive tribal reserves, or in luxurious houses in European suburbs. They had only one thing in common: they were all members of the African National Congress or its three sister organisations, which were united in their opposition to white supremacy in South Africa.[142]

The Treason Trial, officially named *Regina v. Adams and 155 Others*, began on December 19, 1957, with a preliminary hearing. Ruth and Joe's codefendants included Nelson Mandela, Lilian Ngoyi, Moses Kotane, Oliver Tambo, Walter Sisulu, Gert Sibande, Rusty Bernstein, Z. K. Matthews, Ahmed Kathrada, Paul Joseph, Jack Hodgson, Helen Joseph, Chief Luthuli, and many others. Of the 156 people charged, 105 were black, twenty-one Indian, seven coloured, and twenty-three white. Racialism even determined making bail—blacks paid 50 pounds, Indians and coloureds 100 pounds, and whites were charged 250 pounds. All of the people charged were released on bond within two weeks of arrest. Nonetheless, Shawn, Gillian, and Robyn Slovo stayed with their grandmother because both Ruth and Joe were required to be in court throughout 1957 and 1958.

Van Niekerk predicted that the first stage of the trial would last about two months. It ended nine months later. The prosecution charged that the Freedom Charter was communist and that the defendants were part of an international plot to overthrow the South African government. There was also a claim that as communists the defendants were attempting to nurture discord between whites and blacks. Though the detainees spent only a short time in jail, the experience, said Joe, mirrored the racialism that they were fighting against:

The 17 white men accused had larger accommodation and more exercise space than was allocated to more than 120 of their black comrades. We each had a mattress and they had to make do with rope mats on a concrete floor. We had a cushion and newly laundered blankets, and they had to cover themselves with filthy lice-ridden ones.[143]

Despite prison conditions that imitated South African societal racism, Nelson Mandela described the experience as "the largest and longest unbanned meeting of the Congress Alliance in years."[144] In addition, Joe, with Rusty Bernstein and Walter Sisulu, asserted that the trial nurtured trust and camaraderie between black and white activists. The black prisoners conducted political seminars and sang ANC songs—"Come Back, Africa" and "God Bless Africa." There were also personal moments. Prisoners as well as guards sought out Joe for legal advice. At one point, Joe, Rusty, and Jack Hodgson were taken to the visitors' room and greeted loudly by twenty friends, including Rusty and Hilda's newborn son, Keith.

Blacks and whites sat alphabetically, shoulder-to-shoulder in the dock (an ironic touch, in an apartheid environment). Ruth First was forced to sit in the S section, as Mrs. Slovo, although that was not her surname. People who were under banning orders and forbidden to meet spoke freely at the original trial site, the Johannesburg Drill Hall on Twist Street, a military recruiting and training center in the apartheid era. Mary Benson described the scene in *The Struggle for a Birthright*:

> The prisoners, all races together, looked like delegates at a conference; after all, they had the subconscious certainty that ultimately their concept of justice would prevail. Immediately behind them on identical rows of chairs sat the public. During the breaks in proceedings, prisoners, friends, the Press and the lawyers all mixed freely together—smoking, talking and sucking peaches.[145]

At five in the morning on the first day of the trial, people began to gather outside the Drill Hall. Because it was December, a time for traditional Christmas factory closings in Johannesburg, many blacks were not working. People from all over the country gathered, including a group from the Orange Free State led by past ANC president James Moroka to honor and support leaders they viewed as people's heroes. Leaflets were distributed and placards read, "We Stand By Our Leaders." Singing and chanting went on throughout the trial days, and if anything, the crowds increased during the nine months of the trial's preliminary stage. The people who gathered were clearly angry, yet there was still a celebratory spirit that was also shared by the defendants. Nelson Mandela, Rusty Bernstein, and Walter Sisulu, as well as Joe Slovo, described laughter and singing as they were driven to and from the Johannesburg Drill Hall in gray prison vans. Joe served as one of the defense lawyers even though he was a defendant, and witnessed the disorganization and incompetence that guided the beginning of the trial. He equated the continuing mishaps as directly corresponding to the farcical nature of the charges and the trial.

On the very first day court was delayed three times. Initially, the sound system did not work and then because there were no interpreters despite the fact that defendants spoke different languages—of which there are eleven in the country. Finally, the first day concluded with an adjournment when defense lawyers protested that black people were not allowed to view the trial. Although the courtroom had segregated areas, only white faces were present. The second day was more absurd as the defendants were forced to sit within a fenced cage. Joe recalled that detainees posted placards on the cage—"Dangerous Animals, do not feed." The defense lawyers left the trial in protest and the cage was removed. Joe Slovo's role as an attorney in the case allowed him to sit at the attorneys' table rather than with his fellow defendants. At some point he got into a dispute with the magistrate, Frederick Wessels, and was charged with contempt. Immediately, the other defendants began to shout, protest, and move toward the magistrate until they were halted by Chief Luthuli. They stopped instantly. The next morning Joe was fined 20 pounds and relegated to his seat in the dock rather than at the lawyers' table. During the cross-examination of a government witness the magistrate addressed Joe, who was still sitting in the dock, as both defendant and advocate:

> "Yes, Mr. Slovo, any questions?" I rise slowly to my feet, do a cinema walk over knees and legs, and, with deliberation, walk down the long passage to the lawyers' table, gravely look at the witness and then, leaning my head close to the microphone, I say: "Your Worship, no questions," and I immediately proceed to make the long return journey. To his credit, Wessel joins in the burst of laughter, and after the next tea adjournment he announces that I may resume my former place at the lawyers' table.[146]

Clergy, socialist, and liberal South Africans began raising money to support the defendants. The trial meant that many of the accused were not able to work and those who lived outside of Johannesburg were forced to find lodging in the city. The Bishop of Johannesburg, Ambrose Reeves, a man who would work with Ruth First ten years later in England, the liberal novelist Alan Paton, Labour Party Parliamentarian Alex Hepple, and others volunteered. Through the funding of Canon John Collins and Christian Action in England, they provided support through the coordination of Mary Benson and Freda Levson. Rica Hodgson, the wife of Jack Hodgson, also a defendant, was one of the primary fund raisers. Ruth's brother, Ronald First, was at one point the fund's treasurer. Daily volunteers included Tilly First and Ruth's future friend and publisher, Ronald Segal, editor of *Africa South* and a chief organizer in Cape Town; he wrote of prominent businessmen donating money after assurances that they would remain anonymous.

The preliminary phase of the trial started with Van Niekerk's presentation of the charges for the prosecution and Vernon Berrange's response for the defense. What was to become nine laborious months of the prosecution's case, witnesses, cross-examinations, and final statements began with the state presenting a document taken when the house of Joe Slovo and Ruth First had been raided. As Stephen Clingman notes, it was no small irony that "with a certain Kafkaesque circularity—an account of the initial raid for treason became evidence of treason in the monumental Treason Trial."[147] Joe commented on the listings of court documents and speaking in his own defense said: "This is something that I as an accused feel with deep resentment. . . . We have to listen to a report that a speaker said: 'Comrades, we are serving two sandwiches and a cup of tea for sixpence.' "[148]

Vernon Berrange referred to the testimony as "the mass of illiterate nonsense" and he found himself, and his colleagues, constantly questioning and disproving state witnesses. One detective read his notes from an ANC speech and quoted: "It is time to kill Malan." When defense lawyers pointed out that his notes said, "check," not "shoot," he was forced to admit his mistake.[149] Another witness testified that he heard a revolutionary speech at an ANC meeting. The defense tested his hearing acuity in court and revealed that he had fabricated the words of the speech. A third witness misidentified one of the defendants. Three state witnesses, Josiel Mokwena, Joel Camane, and Solomon Dunga, testified that Congress policy was nonviolent and non-racial. Who were they testifying for? Joe questioned those who testified against himself. One police officer, Kunene, stated that he had heard Joe speak in an insurrectionist tone at a farewell party for the Assistant Indian High Commissioner. When asked if he could identify Joe as the speaker, he said nothing more about his being the speaker, but rather said that he could easily identify Mr. Slovo because "Slovo is a very popular man in Johannesburg. We Africans always talk about him. He is always ready to assist the Africans."[150] Joe Slovo's cross-examination of Jeremiah Mollson, a Special Branch detective who testified that he had exact recall of subversive ANC speeches, depicts Joe's work as a lawyer:

SLOVO: Do you understand English?
MOLLSON: Not so well.
SLOVO: Do you mean to say that you reported these speeches in English but you don't understand English well?
MOLLSON: Yes, Your Worship.
SLOVO: Do you agree that your notes are a lot of rubbish?
MOLLSON: I don't know.

This last response caused an outbreak of laughter from the defendants. The magistrate scolded us for laughing, and said, "The proceedings are not as funny as they may seem."[151]

In the fourth month there was important testimony that would be repeated during the second stage of the trial when Professor Andrew Murray, a "scholar" of communism at the University of Cape Town, testified as an expert witness for the prosecution. Vernon Berrange prompted him to admit that the Congress speeches he labeled as communist corresponded to the speeches of Abraham Lincoln. During the second stage of the proceedings, Issy Maisels's questioning, in what might have been the key moment of the trial, pressed Murray even further on communism and the Lincoln orations. As the preliminary stage of the prosecution's case reached the halfway point and slowly began to move toward completion, the witnesses continued in the same vein. The prosecution had coached the black people they had arrested for various crimes to present preposterous stories of ANC radicalism. At one point, Joe was so frustrated within a cross-examination of a witness who had rambled about events that had nothing to do with the charges, that he exclaimed, "We could be here permanently, for the rest of our lives."[152] The daily reality was that Ruth, Joe, and their fellow defendants made themselves as comfortable as possible in the courtroom. They brought in soft chairs and food, as well as books and work, so that they could spend much of the time ignoring the continuous drone of the prosecution's case. According to all accounts, Magistrate Wessels turned a blind eye to their actions—or lack of actions, as the case might be. Throughout the trial, the Defense and Aid Fund supplied money, food, and clothing to defendants in need. Various organizations set up tables and served lunch outside the courthouse each day. Tilly First was involved in the actions of the Defense and Aid Fund and the organizations that brought lunch to the courthouse. She appeared at court daily and helped to make sure that the needs of the defendants were met.

Finally, the first stage of the trial ended in January 1958. During the magistrate's deliberation about the continuance of the case, the government announced that charges against sixty-five of the defendants had been dropped. Almost all of the people whose cases were dismissed were relatively unknown, but ANC leaders Oliver Tambo and Chief Luthuli were no longer indicted. The only explanation was that they were both famous throughout the world as Christian leaders, but this is rather flimsy logic in that others who remained charged had the same credentials.

When the second phase of the trial began in August 1958 Ruth and Joe were among the accused. The trial was moved to Pretoria, quite a burden for many of the defendants whose lives and work were in Johannesburg. The government converted an old Jewish synagogue into a courtroom. The state was represented by Oswald Pirow, the former Minister of Justice, whose organization, the New Order, had in the 1940s promoted National Socialism, and who was known to admire Adolph Hitler. Ironic, that he would prosecute in a Jewish house of worship, maybe less so that he would die of a stroke during this brief second stage of the trial. Ruth and Joe's lives were not focused on religion; in fact, there is not one reference to them ever entering a synagogue except for their required attendance at the Treason Trial. Joe spoke about the setting: "Appropriately enough, the judges sat where the Torah would have been kept and the accused faced them as they would have done had they been taking part in a religious service."[153]

The well-respected Issy Maisels and Bram Fischer joined Berrange for this phase of the trial. After the defense team crushed the state's indictment, Maisels broke open the case in his second cross-examination of Andrew Murray. Again Murray identified work by Lincoln as communist, but this time he did the same with the writings of Woodrow Wilson and Prime Minister Malan. Finally, Maisels

Ruth and Joe during the
Treason Trial (courtesy of the Ruth
First Papers Project, Institute of
Commonwealth Studies)

read a piece that Murray himself had published in the Afrikaans family magazine, *Die Huisgenoot*. Murray did not recognize the article
and stated that it was communist theory. Joe referred to Maisels and
his colleagues' court presentations as Talmudic. The court ruled for
the defense on October 13, 1958, when Judge Rumpff stated that
Congress was peaceful and nonviolent and that there was no evidence
proving that the organization was communist. As Joe noted in *The
Unfinished Autobiography*, Ruth spontaneously announced that they
were having a celebratory party that same night.

In his 1958 book, *The Treason Cage*, Anthony Sampson wrote
about Ruth and Joe in biographical chapters as leaders in the movement against apartheid. Interestingly, Sampson did not do the same
for Nelson Mandela. In Sampson's subsequent book, *Mandela: The
Authorized Biography*, he explained in a rather tongue-in-cheek manner that at the time he believed that Mandela was too detached to be a
future leader. He wrote that the names First and Slovo "were often on
African lips,"[154] and noted that "Ruth First, though only thirty-two,
was already part of South African history."[155] Sampson concluded,
acknowledging the importance of both Joe and Ruth to black people
and the struggle:

They were attractive, definite people, who epitomised what
Africans required from Europeans: they gave large, expansive

parties in their low modern house near Sophiatown, where all the races came together in a pocket of racelessness, and they worked with a sense of common purpose which helped to obliterate any resentment of domination or bossiness. Joe Slovo had what Africans most admire—a sharp and fearless legal brain which could bully police witnesses and open up the cracks in the law, and the dislike of the workings of the state that Africans instinctively feel. Ruth First was the Johannesburg representative of *New Age* which voiced the scandals so discreetly hushed-up elsewhere. In its foreign policy *New Age* was as obedient to Moscow as the *Daily Worker*, but in its home reporting it reflected what all Africans were saying, and what many white Liberals would have said if they dared. Ruth First had the aura of *New Age* about her.[156]

Walter and Albertina Sisulu attended Ruth and Joe's October 13, 1958, party as did many of the other defendants and people from the Treason Defense Fund, including Ambrose Reeves, the Bishop of Johannesburg. According to Sampson, one of the attendees was an American named Millard Shirley who was later identified as a CIA operative. Notably missing was Nelson Mandela, who immediately went into hiding after the verdict. If later reports are correct, it was Shirley who provided the tip to the Special Branch that led to Mandela's arrest in 1962. The party was a grand celebration. Joe wrote that they had expected a visit from the police. On cue, at around midnight, "South Africa's finest" climbed through windows and ran through doors grabbing any black person who was holding a glass. Black people at the party were well schooled in the liquor laws that made it illegal for them to possess alcohol. So they had already disposed of their drinks in sinks, toilets, the garden, and a large vase Joe had purchased for Ruth with his poker winnings.

None of Ruth and Joe's guests had alcohol in their glasses and no charges were made. The police, however, had alerted the press. One Afrikaans paper, *Die Burger*, titled their article, "Many Colours at Party," and wrote that "whites and non-whites" drank together even though no one was charged. In addition, clearly with incendiary motivation, the paper reported, "In many of the motor cars white women rode with natives."[157] Reporter Chris Vermaak, from a second newspaper, *Die Vaderland*, jumped on Ruth and Joe's dining room table to photograph the rainbow crowd. Joe sued the paper and Vermaak,

Joe with Johannesburg tennis group. Standing from left to right:
Harold Wolpe, Wilf East, Julius Baker, Ben Arenstein, and Hymie Barsel.
Kneeling: Joe and Rusty Bernstein (courtesy of UWC Robben Island–
Mayibuye Archives)

who was intimate with the Special Branch, eventually agreed to a
£300 settlement.

In addition to parties, gatherings with family and friends occurred
on the weekends. Ruth sometimes prepared her duck specialty and
friends brought their own favorite feasts. George Bizos cooked a
whole lamb on a spit in the Slovos' garden. Parties that Joe and Ruth
hosted are also portrayed in both Gillian Slovo's memoir and Shawn
Slovo's film, *A World Apart*. Rica Hodgson reflected on her interaction with Ruth:

> When I first met her she was a real bluestocking, she had no
> style, her hair was curly, she hated it like poison. She subse-
> quently straightened it and spent her life straightening her
> bloody hair. I remember a party at her house. It must have been
> the early treason trial. Ruth had the most wonderful eyes and I
> said to her, "You know, Ruth, you don't do anything to enhance
> your looks. Why don't you use some green eye-shadow?" But
> she was quite shy about it all. Not long afterward she was
> thinking about makeup and she went to get the best makeup
> there was, the most expensive. I think I had some influence on
> her in a way.[158]

Infidelities became known in the mid-1950s. It might be more
accurate to say that Ruth and Joe lived out some version of an open

marriage. Gillian wrote about her parents' affairs and in an interview Robyn Slovo broached the topic as well. Joe, while commenting on how he and Ruth were devoted to each other, acknowledges their political debates, and goes on to say of their relationship: "Nor was it free of other, more or less serious involvements."[159] Ruth confided to Myrtle Berman:

The late '50s you know their relationship started being bedeviled by infidelities. And I remember Ruth saying to me that Joe started it and she was really hurt when she discovered. And she probably flung herself into the fray. It was like I remember pilots in the Second World War thinking they may not be around and hectic, feverish partying. And Joe and Ruth felt that things were about to go sour which in fact did happen. Their behavior: Well they used to party and drink too much— go off with people. It was not in that way a good thing. I mean Ruth had one real hard time with a man whom she met that she really fell for. And I think he got frightened and broke it off. And she was—she used the word "thrashed."[160]

Though it would be well beyond substantive historical data to assert that infidelity was the norm in the CPSA, there has been similar discussion in portrayals of leftist struggle groups throughout the world. The questioning of capitalism, racism, and bourgeois social structures, and the rejection of these ethics, has also meant flouting the sexual mores of oppressive societies. Viewing infidelity from a leftist sociological perspective does not address the human hurt that often accompanies the practice. When Gillian Slovo asked her parents' friend Wolfie Kodesh about the issue, he explained that there was "a lot of that sort of thing."[161] Kodesh observed that when you get older you realize that who slept with whom was not very important.

During the Treason Trial and afterward, Ruth and Joe's political work intersected; Ruth continued writing articles on apartheid racism and resistance and Joe defended black South Africans. Besides *The Guardian*, Ruth edited and wrote for *Fighting Talk* from 1955 to 1960, when the magazine discontinued because of the State of Emergency. Ruth took over the editorship of the monthly sixteen-page publication from Rusty Bernstein. During her five years as editor she was able to attract an incredibly eclectic group of writers. The list of South African struggle stalwarts is impressive in itself—Mandela, Tambo, Kotane, Luthuli, Matthews, Mbeki, and Dadoo. But she also attracted from afar—Kenyatta, Ben Bella, Nkrumah, Touré, and Nyerere. Never before had there been a list of revolutionary African leaders who wrote for the same publication. *Fighting Talk* also published Father Trevor Huddleston's farewell to South Africa in 1955 and letters from South African writer Eskia' Mphahlele, who at the time was in exile in Ghana. In a response to a somewhat caustic request for an article, Ruth's comrade, Lionel Foreman, who sadly died from a heart condition while a defendant in the Treason Trial, penned the following response as a humorous limerick:

> There was a young liberal called Ruth,
> An Absolute Stranger to Truth
> Whose temper was bad
> (I know it—By Gad)
> A temper most sadly uncouth.
> And of young Miss First
> This was not the wirst
> For she spoke so fast
> She left you aghast
> And when she was puzzled she curst.[162]

Brian Bunting spoke of Ruth's skills as an editor:

Ruth had the capacity to dig out facts and talent, to harness not only her own energies but also those of others. Nor was she content merely to propagandise or sloganise. She believed the best propaganda was the facts and editors and readers knew they could rely on every word she wrote. Nothing was left to chance, nor was any stone unturned. She worried and worried at a problem until it was solved.[163]

These same traits, of course, were evident in her work at *New Age* (*The Guardian's* name at the time). The women's campaign against the government forcing black people to carry passbooks that Ruth wrote about in 1955 continued with vigor the following year. Concurrent with the Treason Trial arrests was the apartheid regime's determination to make separation of the races even more ubiquitous than it had been in the past. In August 1956, over 20,000 women, under the auspices of the Federation of South African Women (FSAW), marched on the Union Buildings in Pretoria. They were led by Lilian Ngoyi, Helen Joseph, and Rahima Moosa. As Ruth reported in her article in *New Age*, upon arrival the three women took anti-pass petitions to Prime Minister Strijdom's office where they left the papers with an assistant. The government ignored the petitions. The march was followed by a conference in Johannesburg and additional women's protests through 1959. Ruth covered FSAW events, both rural and urban, from Johannesburg to the Free State. In much of her political writing, she was more participant-observer than documentarian. Also, working with Hilda Bernstein, and relying on the sensibilities and organizational skills of Rica Hodgson, she hosted meetings and banquets for FSAW women. Her reporting provided both motivation and ground rules for future women's actions. She exposed police violence against the protesters in Sophiatown, Zeerust, and Winburg. Unsurprisingly, Ruth was chastised for inciting "natives" by other newspapers: *Die Burger*, *The Star*, and *Die Transvaler*.

"Ruth was the most important in the fifties because her journalism kept the spark alive," Joe reminisced in a 1990s interview.[164] It is notable to emphasize how central Ruth First's role was in the decisions of the content that *New Age* published. Mary Benson represented a good number of progressive South Africans in her criticism of the paper: "I think the worst thing the communists did in the *New Age* and the various papers was to totally put across the Soviet line in foreign affairs. It was the biggest waste of energy and it just antagonized us." She chastised Brian Bunting because he worked for a Soviet news agency, but Benson stressed Ruth's value because she was "more open and followed her instinctual leads."[165]

As the 1950s waned, "openness and following her instinctual leads" meant reporting on issues of racism, class disparity, and apartheid oppression. Locally, Ruth wrote about apartheid racism in Soweto, Sophiatown, and Alexandra. Mary Benson's critique is significant, though, because Brian Bunting and other staunch Party members were continually pressing for international Party-line articles. Though Bunting had hired Ruth at *The Guardian* and respected her greatly as a journalist, their relationship would later deteriorate in exile as he, probably more than anyone else in the Party, toed the Stalinist line. Ruth, however, wrote extensively about the 1957 Alexandra bus boycott, where people in the township protested an increase in fares and boycotted bus service. The boycott spread to other townships and Ruth reported that bus ridership dropped from approximately 45,000 riders each day to close to zero. In Ronald Segal's magazine, *Africa South*, she chronicled the masses of people walking to work, of white citizens offering rides, of Johannesburg newspapers demonizing the boycott leaders, and of police harassment. Ruth also reported the boycott victory in *New Age* when an agreement was made with the Johannesburg City Council to reverse the fare increase. She continued to expose the horrible conditions of poverty in Alexandra, ironically the very township of Zena Stein's medical clinic—same people and for the most part the same issue, disparity and apartheid racism. While she wrote on poverty, gangs, and lack of police, she also questioned a government proposal:

> Native Affairs Department "clean-ups" are suspect and the people live in fear of them. In the Western Areas slum clearance meant the abolition of freehold, the death of a long-established township, the *forcible removal* of an entire community. In Evaton the clean-up meant the vicious imposition of influx control. Will it be the same in Alexandra?[166]

Although not the term used by government, *forced removals* became the mid- to late-1950s version of segregating the "races" in South Africa. Though it occurred throughout the country, the largest of the many horrors took place in Sophiatown in Johannesburg, a neighborhood close to Roosevelt Park where Joe and Ruth lived with Shawn, Gillian, and Robyn. Writing about Sophiatown, Ruth described the inhumanity of apartheid oppression, "Old people, children, even new-born babies sleep each night in the open, while daily demolitions go on in Sophiatown and even more families are turned out of their homes."[167] Unfortunately, in Sophiatown and other cities throughout the country, neither Ruth First's articles nor the protests of the masses ebbed the tide of forced removals. In an act of ultimate arrogance, upon completion of removals and the transforming of Sophiatown into a white-only neighborhood, the government renamed it Triomf, the Afrikaans word for triumph. Joe Slovo commented on how the destruction of Sophiatown affected his family:

> Our house was barely a mile from Sophiatown, and its disappearance deprived Ruth and me of the late-afternoon and weekend company of many of our friends who, on their way

home, paused for a snack, an illicit drink, or, like Patrick Malao, for a relaxed hour or two with us and our children. Gone too was yet another place where we could visit our friends without a special permit from the Native Affairs Department.[168]

Two other *New Age* stories portray Ruth First's intensity and humanity. Before she returned to Bethal, she traveled to the Cape to find an African chief who had been banished by the government. In some ways, the story is less important than her encounter with Wolfie Kodesh prior to her journey. Friends since youth, Kodesh worked with Ruth at *New Age* where he did a little bit of everything. He tells of Ruth requesting his accompaniment on the assignment to find the missing chief. When Wolfie refused, Ruth asked him to go to the Congress of Democrats office and get Ben Turok to accompany her. Kodesh replied, "What, am I your servant?" Ruth turned a "cold shoulder" and told him that he had a chip on his shoulder. Two weeks later, Wolfie Kodesh went into Ruth's office with an actual potato chip on his shoulder:

And she's concentrating like hell, typing away there, you know, and I came in. I saw her looking up once, down again, puzzling, and then she . . . looked up again, looked at the chip and said, "Oh, you bastard!" started laughing—and that's how we became friends. This chip on my shoulder. And it was as though we'd never had the two weeks of silence.[169]

Kodesh stopped laughing as he continued talking about Ruth: "Because once she got her mind onto a story—oh-oh, there was nothing that would stop her. She would dig deep into a story and go into any location, day or night, if necessary, to follow up a story."[170] Ben Turok did join her on the trip. They drove for miles and miles over dusty roads with Ruth occasionally wiping her face while still wearing "her normal smart city clothes, high heels, and permed hair."[171] At one point the gas tank sprang a leak that Turok plugged with soap. Eventually they found the chief who willingly related his story to Ruth who then wrote about him in *New Age*. Turok had been on committees with both Ruth and Joe, and he had personal experience of Ruth's reputation as a forceful and intense woman. Recording their journey, he said, "I found her to be a vulnerable and warm person with a fine sense of humour beneath the brittle exterior."[172]

Ruth's tenacity was clearly apparent in her return to Bethal, almost ten years after first breaking the story with Michael Scott on farm labor atrocities.Wolfie Kodesh told the story first to Donald Pinnock, but also to James Zug and Gillian Slovo. Gillian Slovo begins her description in *Every Secret Thing* with the memory of her mother coming into the driveway and beckoning her to celebrate as she pulled out a bag of potato chips. It was a potent moment because the ANC, meaning also their family, had boycotted potatoes due to slave-like working conditions. The story was of a black farmworker appearing at the offices of *New Age* to tell Ruth, Kodesh, and the younger Joe Gqabi who was apprenticing with Ruth, his tale of escaping from a labor farm where workers were beaten and some even killed. Local authorities, in cooperation with farmers, provided black people to work the farms as twentieth-century slaves. The escapee told of a friend who had been seriously beaten and could not escape. Immediately, Ruth had Kodesh drive her and Gqabi to the farm, where they witnessed workers being tortured surrounded by mounds that appeared like graves. They were forced to quickly escape when the farmer's son recognized what they were doing. Back in Johannesburg they were able to convince the courts to investigate the farmer. Subsequently slaves on numerous farms were freed. In addition to Ruth's articles, a court case that was brought against the farmworker by the farmer helped initiate the investigations. He got the worker charged with perjury, claiming that Ruth First had fabricated the story. Ruth turned to George Bizos, who then defended the farmworker successfully, also exonerating Ruth.

In the late 1950s, Ruth was bold enough to write about issues that arose within the ANC. It must be emphasized, however, that most of her venom was directed toward the break-off Africanist faction that was to become the Pan Africanist Congress (PAC) in 1959. When the faction left the ANC, the *New Age* headline read "Good Riddance." Ruth's criticism of the ANC was much less acerbic. When they banned *Bantu World*, a conservative newspaper, from a conference, Ruth used the pages of *New Age* to remind ANC leaders of her own paper's constant harassment and bannings from the apartheid regime.

As the "Camelot" decade neared conclusion, Ruth First and *New Age* were being observed more closely by the apartheid regime. Comrades would try to meet clandestinely, but they were not always cautious. For example, Joe met almost weekly with Bram Fischer in one of their law offices, clearly places that the Special Branch was monitoring. Reflecting in 1992, Mary Benson spoke to the issue:

> I'm always fascinated at how, for all their politics, they never, either the CP or the ANC or liberals or anyone, sufficiently allowed for how ruthless Afrikaner nationalists were. They took it all much too lightly, I think, in the fifties. Their security was always desperately lacking in any real feeling of the potential cleverness or cruelty of the police and state. So they were continually caught out.[173]

When Ruth was confronted in 1959 by a *New Age* reader, a Mr. Nkambule, about a Special Branch officer working undercover at the paper, she apologized and also viewed it as a warning:

> Apologies for having Oliver Mti on staff who turned out to be special branch. I regret greatly that it was through our office that you were put in touch with a man doing the work of the special branch. But it just shows how all in the Congress Movement must be on their guard against such informers. Yes, as you write, it surely makes you think.[174]

At the time the Special Branch, through harassment and arrests, attempted to turn *New Age* reporters into spies like Mti. Ruth even wrote an article, "The Facts behind Verwoerd's Spy System," in which she described the system as being part of the Department of Native Affairs. And after workers at the newspaper were rejected once again in 1958 for membership in the Commonwealth Press Union, she worked with Robert Resha and Alex La Guma to launch a non-racial trade union—the National Union of South African Journalists.

Although both Joe and Ruth had been served their first banning orders in 1954, Joe was still allowed to travel for work, just as she was permitted to be a journalist. He took cases throughout the country and they were often reported on in local as well as Johannesburg newspapers. The East London *Daily Dispatch* covered one such trial in King Williamstown. Joe represented 254 black people who were originally charged with disturbance and obstruction for congregating on sidewalks. Joe argued that they were bystanders and asked the judge to recuse himself because he had shown bias. The judge did not acknowledge Joe's motion, or his many objections during the trial, though he did dismiss the disturbance charge and convicted the defendants of obstruction, sentencing them to a fine of £3 or a month of hard labor. Joe objected to the presence of armed police in the courtroom. According to the *Daily Dispatch*, he used the courtroom to voice a political statement when he argued that the "armed camp" nature of the courtroom was prejudicial to his clients.

Joe followed this case with three acquittals. The first case took place in East London where he was able to get 132 black workers cleared for illegal striking; there was insufficient evidence, as the prosecution could not prove that there even was a strike. He also successfully defended labor leader Arnold Selby and ANC activist Lampton Dwane, who were charged with raising money for strikers and intimidating workers. Representing 4,000 Indians who were being forcefully removed from their homes in Ladysmith, Joe told the Group Areas Commissioner that the actions were equivalent to genocide and that if the decision was taken by the commission he would be comparable to a social criminal.

Although they were both susceptible to arrest by the Special Branch, neither Ruth nor Joe veiled their political liaisons and both continually attended meetings. Rusty Bernstein writes of ongoing conversations with Joe throughout the 1950s even though their banning orders prohibited them from seeing each other. Ruth did not hide her conferences with Walter Sisulu or Trevor Huddleston or the many other people she would call upon. Beginning as a student at Wits, then in exile in Dar es Salaam, London, Luanda, Lusaka, and Maputo, visiting friends in the struggle was Joe Slovo's common practice.

For Joe, but less so Ruth, the Party was ever present. Although Joe described Moses Kotane as hard and tough, he also thought that it was Kotane's relationship with Chief Luthuli that nurtured the SACP-ANC alliance:

We had always been taught that the Party was the vanguard of the struggle. But it was the late 1950s which gave real meaning to this maxim in revolutionary practice. The Central Committee (to which Ruth was elected at an underground conference in the late 1950s) through its Johannesburg-based Secretariat often functioned on an almost daily basis. There was no major event which was not subjected to analytical scrutiny. Long before any of the campaigns waned, the question of "what next" had already been the subject matter of many agendas. And we established our position in the liberation movement by persuasion and example—not, as our detractors allege, by caucus and manipulation.[175]

In his memoir, *Memory against Forgetting*, Rusty Bernstein describes Joe, Ruth, and Harold Wolpe as being part of a group that initiated meetings to reconstitute the Communist Party even before the ink was dry on the Suppression of Communism Act. The meeting to relaunch, albeit underground, was held in 1952 in the rural Transvaal. There were twenty-five attendees and the organization was officially named the South African Communist Party. Joe and Ruth were at that meeting as well as future SACP assemblies at Julius's factory, hidden suburban cottages, and rural sites. Over the next forty years they would both serve on the Central Committee, and Joe would be both Chairman and General-Secretary of the SACP.

Though political work directly through the Party remained underground throughout the 1950s, above-ground activity filtered through the Congress of Democrats. Interestingly, Michael Hathorn, who with his wife, Margaret Cormack, and fellow physicians Mervyn Susser and Zena Stein, operated a medical clinic in Alexandra, remembered Joe as relatively silent at Party meetings. Hathorn and the others were well acquainted as a result of Joe's frequent visits to the clinic to talk with them about the SACP and political issues. On at least one occasion, Hathorn drove Joe to a meeting and remembered Joe waiting until everyone else had spoken before publicly presenting his position. Hathorn viewed Joe Slovo as a bit too much of a politician. At the 1959 conference, held at Julius First's Industria factory, a motion was made to publicly announce the existence of the SACP. From the 1952 clandestine reignition of the Party, the silence had been so total that not one member had been convicted as a communist. Rusty Bernstein wrote that supporters cited Lenin and argued that a party of the working class needed to be public. Those who opposed the motion believed that open knowledge of the Party might ruin the SACP-ANC alliance. The membership was closely split on the issue, with a slight majority favoring the status quo. Joe Slovo preferred to go public, but as a compromise the conference voted to publish a journal, *The African Communist*, with no affiliation appearing on the publication. Secrecy, of course, would soon become moot, but the 1950s, even 1959, were still part of the "Camelot" years.

Ruth and Joe (courtesy of the Ruth First Papers Project,
Institute of Commonwealth Studies)

Things would change dramatically for Ruth First, Joe Slovo, and their compatriots as the decade progressed into the 1960s. When Ruth and Joe's house was searched by police in the 1950s, they would take copies of Stendhal's *The Red and the Black* solely because of the title. There were still light-spirited moments as Joe recalled asking one policeman who was searching their house what they were looking for and the policeman replied, "Politics, man, politics."[176] Joe also told a prescient story of arguing for the removal of police who had illegally shut down a labor meeting. In his ruling against the state, Judge Blackwell said, "This is not *yet* a police state."[177] A year later that statement would have been difficult to make in apartheid South Africa.

5—Sharpeville, Prison, and Exile

"BYE-BYE, BLUE SKY," mocked the guard when Ruth was led into prison in late 1963. Joe had been detained earlier and by the time Ruth was arrested he had been forced to remain outside of the country. Their plight, as well as the fate of other anti-apartheid activists, corresponded to South Africa's becoming more like a police state in 1960 in the aftermath of the Sharpeville Massacre. The Pan Africanist Congress, under the leadership of Robert Sobukwe, a thirty-five-year-old instructor at the University of the Witwatersrand, had preempted the ANC in calling for a national protest with black people turning in their passbooks at police stations under the slogan "No Bail, No Defense, No Fine." The day was March 21, 1960, and in Sharpeville, a township south of Johannesburg, the police attacked the demonstrators killing sixty-nine people and wounding 186, the majority shot in the back as they ran from police fire. Shortly afterwards, more protesters were killed in Langa, a Cape Town township.

Hurriedly, an ANC and SACP joint committee that included Sisulu, Mandela, Nokwe, and Joe convened at the Slovo home in Roosevelt Park to plan a nationwide general strike memorializing the murders at Sharpeville and Langa. They decided to forcefully proceed on an anti-pass campaign. Chief Luthuli publicly burned his passbook in Pretoria. There were demonstrations throughout the country and for a moment some government ministers appeared to realize that a relaxation of apartheid oppression might be necessary to avoid revolution. In addition to the mass demonstrations, the United Nations, the U.S.

State Department, British Parliament, and the Dutch condemned the South African government. Members of Parliament publicly blamed the victims. A week later both the ANC and PAC, like the SACP, were banned as the government declared a State of Emergency. Police followed with pre-dawn raids arresting 19,000 members of the SACP, ANC, PAC, Congress Movement, Non-European Unity Movement, Liberal Party, and others who challenged, or who the government believed challenged, the apartheid state.

One of Gillian Slovo's memories is of her grandfather, Julius First, contacting people and alerting them in Yiddish that the raids had begun. Joe, not Ruth, was among the first wave of people detained. At the time, Joe was involved in a court case representing the families of 430 miners who were killed by the collapse of the Clydesdale Coalbrook mine in the Orange Free State. The tragedy was the worst mine disaster in South African history and Ruth sent her colleague Joe Gqabi to cover the story. Gqabi worked on the story for almost a month and his article facilitated the ANC's call for political action. When Joe Slovo tried the case, he asked for and was granted a temporary adjournment in order to meet another defense obligation in Ladysmith. The plan was for the miners' case to restart on March 31, but Joe Slovo did not return. He was arrested early in the morning of March 30. Ruth, Joe, and their comrades had been warned that arrests were imminent. By Joe's account, he and Ruth responded without urgency. He did make a nighttime ride past the Grays, the Johannesburg Special Branch headquarters, as the common belief was that if the top floor was alight, arrests were forthcoming. As Joe recounted the story, the lights were on, yet neither Joe nor Ruth was too concerned. When the Special Branch arrived, they arrested only Joe. They conducted an extensive search of the house, but left with little evidence. They were unable to find documents hidden in a special compartment that Rusty Bernstein had designed for a desk for Ruth, which was built in Julius's factory.

After Joe was detained, Ruth, with her three young daughters in tow and disguised in a red wig, went into temporary exile in Swaziland. Her parents joined them with the help of Ruth's brother, Ronald, and the girls were enrolled in school in Mbabane, Swaziland's capital city. Other activists had also migrated to Mbabane, including Jack Hodgson, whose wife, Rica, had been arrested in the sweep. Swaziland is a country that is surrounded by South Africa with the exception of an eastern border shared with Mozambique. It was governed in 1963 by the British Colonial Office. The country also had a king, Sobhuza II, who had attended the founding conference of the ANC in 1912, but later in the 1970s allowed the Special Branch free access for search and seizure of apartheid opponents. In 1960, Swaziland continued to be viewed as a short-term haven. Gillian remembers a fairly seamless transition and also mentions that her parents had planned for Ruth to leave with the children if he was imprisoned. In his book, however, Joe states that it was a decision of the Central Committee.

Ruth First, her daughters, and her parents spent most of the period of the State of Emergency in Swaziland. Comrades in Mbabane included Jack Hodgson, Harold Strachan, the Bakers, the Levys and their children. Adelaide Tambo later joined the group while waiting to reconnect with her husband, the most prominent ANC member in exile, Oliver Tambo. Various sources, including Rica Hodgson, in her book *Foot Soldier for Freedom*, described Ruth traveling back and forth into South Africa for underground meetings of the Central Committee of the South African Communist Party. Harmel, Kotane, Turok, Fischer, and Dadoo were usually present. Ben Turok remembers Jack Hodgson attending with Ruth. They wanted Ruth to remain in South Africa but relented because she felt that she needed to stay with her children in Swaziland. One topic of discussion was a continuance of the earlier debate that Joe had referred to as "rough discussions" regarding whether the SACP should become public. The decision was a fait accompli and SACP leaflets were distributed leading to criticism in both the English and Afrikaans press. Some of the people in Mbabane questioned elitism at the core of the SACP and argued that Party leaders were more entitled than ordinary comrades in exile. Harold Strachan's book, *Make a Skyfe, Man!*, provides a rather idiosyncratic critique of Ruth and other people, particularly Jack Hodgson, whom he refers to as an elitist. Norman Levy touched upon the elitism that existed among the Johannesburg left in the fifties, corroborating Strachan's assertions with a less eccentric analysis:

It soon became a typical exile community, fraught with tensions, real and imagined, that stretched the tolerance of the more senior exiles who served on the "cheery refugees committee" and eroded the harmony of everyone. Ruth First, Jack Hodgson, Pieter Beyleveld, Julius Baker, Phyllis Altman and Issie Rosenberg, to name only the most influential among them, should have given better leadership to this distraught group. . . . These were partly based on economic differences and status in regard to their influence and the length of time they had served in the movement. For the most part, the two groups lived in different quarters, the first enjoying a very different quality of life from those who struggled to subsist on very limited resources.[178]

Ruth returned home to South Africa before the children and their grandparents as the emergency eased. AnnMarie Wolpe found her a place to stay underground, first in the home of an architect who "was a very attractive man, bearded, with an incredible home and this very earthy wife who made wonderful vegetarian foods and salads."[179] Gillian Slovo writes that Ruth initially moved into the home under the alias of Ruth Gordon. Once she got to know and trust the architect, whose wife already knew Ruth's real identity, she confided in him. Shawn Slovo recalled her grandmother taking her to visit Ruth during this underground period and, according to Gillian, Ruth had an intimate relationship with the architect. Julius and Tilly First returned to their Johannesburg home with Robyn, Shawn, and Gillian while Ruth remained in hiding in the northern suburbs. She did not rejoin her family until shortly after Joe's release.

Joe Slovo, as documented in *The Unfinished Autobiography*, became somewhat of a prison ethnographer during his six months of detention. He first spent time at Marshall Square, then The Fort, and finally at Pretoria Prison. It was at The Fort that he had his only contact with Robert Sobukwe, the leader of the Pan Africanist Congress, whom Joe and his comrades had intensely criticized for PAC's "ill-organized and second-class"[180] planning that led to the Sharpeville Massacre. Both were awaiting medical attention and simply acknowledged each other's presence. In early 1963, Sobukwe contacted Joe hoping that he might file an appeal in his case, something that was impossible, as the time limit had expired. Joe Slovo spoke of a great bonding among the prisoners and wrote Ruth descriptive, but also cryptic, letters describing his prison life. Highlighting the "Keystone cop" actions of warders, he noted the privileges of living with his comrades. In fact, Joe had a benign view of how he and other whites in the resistance were perceived at the time:

We were looked upon as oddities rather than as enemies. The passionate hatred and fear of "commies and liberals" had not yet become so deeply embedded in the popular white imagination; the menace of liberation still seemed too distant and the challenge to race rule was still contained within fairly innocuous bounds of studied non-violence.[181]

Joe Slovo's 1960 imprisonment yielded multiple tales portraying his life with fellow detainees. One of his codefendants in the Treason Trial, the Reverend Douglas Thompson, held Sunday services that were more political than pious. Joe wrote Ruth about a service celebrating May Day and described working as a jailhouse lawyer for non-political detainees, but also warders. He was thrilled by Monty Berman's cooking, intrigued by Eli Weinberg's stories, and astonished by the numbers of non-politicos who were locked up as "communists" under the State of Emergency. He participated in a political prisoner choir and theater group performing *A Midsummer Night's Dream* under the direction of Cecil Williams, who was with Nelson Mandela when he was arrested in 1962. In his correspondence with Ruth, Joe wrote of another, original production that portrayed Treason Trial lawyer Issy Maisels as the hero.

More important than the activities, Joe's relationships with his fellow detainees became deeper and closer. Norman Levy writes of "Joe's Throne," the outdoor toilet from which Joe sometimes held court. Ruth summed up the camaraderie in a letter: "By the sound of it your wonderful company have the best brought out of them by confinement; though it's largely the company, not the confinement."[182] Choir activities were led by John Lang, the Bermans' comrade in the African Resistance Movement, and Eli Weinberg, with whom Joe had worked in the SACP. Each day at Marshall Square, walking together four miles (seventy-two times around the yard), Joe had the privilege to learn Eli Weinberg's story. In a letter to Ruth, Joe shared the story of one of his elders, Archie Lewitton: "We have a cynic among us—an excellent chess player—who wallows in his reputation of hardness, but we all recognize that he is one of the most gentle of souls."[183]

A relatively long hunger strike occurred at the Pretoria jail, started by the women political prisoners and joined by the men. Joe communicated with Ruth in the midst of the strike explaining the view from inside the prison. He began the letter with the rather odd sentence, "I feel hilarious," and then continued with comments on how the fast was affecting people, sharing his outrage because the minister had denied the strike's existence. Distrusting the prison authorities, the men received word directly from the women that they had indeed ended the fast and the men began to eat on May 23, 1960, Joe Slovo's thirty-fourth birthday. Black prisoners, who of course were imprisoned in a different section of Pretoria prison, serenaded Joe and a birthday cake was smuggled into the cellblock to complement Monty Berman's celebration dinner. Joe referred to prison meals as "Chez Monty" and his entire tone, while writing about Monty Berman twenty-three years later, was both gentle and critical; the former in a genuine affection for the man, and the latter because, in Joe Slovo's evaluation, Monty Berman and his movement exemplified undisciplined revolutionaries.

Letters between Joe and Ruth continued to flow. A visit from his children left Joe in awe, and he portrayed them sitting on his lap and of Robyn teasing the guard. "There is little in this world which gives one such a feeling of optimism as a child's smile," is one of his concluding lines.[184] The response from Ruth was appreciative of their daughters as "natural and at ease and not obstreperous like so many others."[185] Silently acknowledging the possibility that she and Joe might soon be forced underground, she asserted that she and Joe relinquishing their possessions would not be problematic.

Reflecting on his prison experience, Joe was quick to add that his was the white experience, as blacks and whites were segregated in South African prisons. Because he was a lawyer, he was sometimes allowed to visit the cells of his black comrades. His description contrasts black and white prison accommodations and accentuates white privilege:

They slept on coir mats on the concrete floor covered by blankets which smelt of prison. The cell walls were dark in color and the single bulb gave off a candle's light. A tin bucket in the corner provided the night toilet. The light was switched off at an early hour and I was then escorted back to our white men's prison palace, to our beds, mattresses, white sheets, bedside tables, a separate ablution block, our own control over the lights and generally all the mod cons usually advertised in the "To Let" columns.[186]

Joe continued his recollections with sensitivity to black consciousness and African nationalism. It is also important to note that civility provided to white political detainees in 1960 was obsolete by 1963, when Ruth, as well as those tried in the Rivonia Trial, were imprisoned by the apartheid state.

Throughout their lives, younger colleagues and comrades were attracted to the couple. One of those younger friends, an American named Danny Schechter, met Ruth at the London School of Economics (LSE). He was over twenty years younger than Ruth and Joe, and wondered how Robyn, Gillian, and Shawn perceived their parents' younger friends. Ronnie Kasrils recalled Ruth's generosity when he first became involved in the struggle. At the suggestion of then Party stalwart Rowley Arenstein, the young Kasrils sent Ruth a political poem he had written. Ruth responded positively and provided him with a reference to the *Daily Worker* in London.

Joe and Ruth also befriended Denis and Hillary Kuny. Denis was a young lawyer who became connected with Joe in the courts. When he told Hillary about Joe, she suggested that they invite Joe and Ruth for dinner. According to Hillary, the couples soon became friends and the Kunys volunteered to become involved in the struggle. "We will do anything we can as long as it's very low profile. So in the beginning people didn't know us. We were very young. Our house became a safe house. We gave the house for meetings."[187]

Joe and Ruth stayed at the Kunys' house for a short time in 1962 when they thought their arrests might be imminent. On another occasion, Hillary arranged for them to stay at the poet Lionel Abrahams's home. According to Hillary, Ruth and Joe gave her and Denis permission to have fun, to enjoy life. Joe told her, "Listen, you have got the wrong idea of Marxism. You think that Marxism means that everyone's got to be without. I'm telling you that Marxism is about giving lots to everyone."[188] Joe and Ruth served as friends as well as political, professional, and cultural mentors. Reflecting on Ruth, Hillary said:

> We talked a lot about books. She read a lot and I remember her coming to the house with a book for me, Stendhal. She said, "Hillary, this is a very, very special book and I am giving it to you because I really think you will value it." We did a lot together. You know people always say she didn't suffer fools. She could put you down if she didn't like you. But she also had enormous warmth and enormous sweetness.[189]

Albie Sachs accompanied Ruth and Joe on a holiday to Plettenberg Bay in December 1962. Interviewed many years later, he still
viewed the invitation as akin to a rite of passage. His reflections speak
to apartheid white privilege—even for revolutionaries:

> It was like a last halcyon wonderful holiday of playing bridge at
> night, going out into the lagoon and eating oysters, and having
> fun and joking and part of the contradictions of South African
> life. That white people, even those deepest in the under-
> ground—Joe we know now deeply involved in Umkhonto we
> Sizwe—have this holiday at a pleasure resort. So I became
> quite friendly with them and it was a sign that I was allowed
> into their intellectual company even if we did not discuss hot
> politics or anything. I was just seen as somebody up with them
> in terms of style and wisecracks and doing things of interest
> and so on. It was very enjoyable and great fun to be with them
> and relaxed. And I thought about it because later in the next
> year I was in solitary confinement and I would try and imagine
> happier days and also thinking all of us who were in Pletten-
> berg Bay at that time was either in jail or outside the country.[190]

Ruth continued writing for both *New Age* and *Fighting Talk* and
her articles were as fiery as before the State of Emergency. *New Age*
and the Non-European Unity Movement's newspaper, *The Torch*,
were banned during the State of Emergency, but were unbanned after
the five-month period. Even though repression in South Africa had
escalated, Ruth viewed *New Age*'s mission as bridging the borders of
journalism and politics. "Sometimes our columns reflected what was
happening; sometimes we initiated exposures that prompted new
campaigns and gave our staff a reputation and a keenness for being
first on the spot to write the news that no one else had the courage
or will to print."[191] However, with continuing arrests, activists leaving the country, the banning of the ANC, and accelerating police
surveillance, it was becoming much more difficult to cover stories
of government oppression, especially outside of Johannesburg and
Cape Town.

In 1961, Joe Slovo was directly involved in the forming of Umkhonto
we Sizwe (MK), the underground military operation, that though
formed by ANC and SACP leaders, initially claimed itself an independent organization, a distinction that Joe referred to as a "necessary

fiction."[192] He called MK "the people's war."[193] Nonviolence as a tactic
was criticized in a paper by Michael Harmel, a member of the SACP
Central Committee, as being unrealistic at a time when the government
treated passive resistance as treason. Using this paper as a foundation,
leaders in both the ANC and SACP agreed that it was time for armed
struggle. Thus, with some funding from African states and Communist governments, Umkhonto we Sizwe was secretly launched, with
Nelson Mandela and Joe Slovo as the High Command. Their deputies
were Govan Mbeki and Jack Hodgson. Contacts made previously by
the SACP enabled cadres to be sent to China for six months to train as
soldiers. The extended plan was to station the cadres in other African
states for further training and planning for armed struggle against
the apartheid regime. Tactically, Mandela and Slovo chose to initiate
the mission with a sabotage campaign within the country. Regional
commands were formed throughout South Africa to engineer local
acts of subversion. The plan was to bomb government buildings and
infrastructure—with no attacks on places inhabited by people. Even
within this campaign a small bit of hope remained that the oppression
might end without all-out armed struggle. The apartheid regime did
not agree.

In 1961, Ruth and Joe helped organize the purchase of Lilliesleaf, the property that the government raided in 1963, leading to the
infamous Rivonia Trial in 1964, when top ANC leaders, including
Nelson Mandela, Govan Mbeki, and Walter Sisulu, were convicted of
sabotage. At the conclusion of the trial, except for Bram Fischer, the
leadership of both the ANC and SACP was either incarcerated or in
exile. Despite valiant attempts, the struggle inside South Africa was
moribund. As Gregory Houston writes, "It was one of the most severe
blows that MK, the ANC and SACP underground would suffer."[194]

In 1961, Arthur and Hazel Goldreich and their children moved
into a 28-acre estate that was utilized as the underground headquarters of the ANC and SACP as they planned the sabotage campaign.
Julius First provided some of the funds and Nelson Mandela at times
lived at the safe house under an alias and disguised as the caretaker.

In spring 1961 while he was underground, Ruth arranged for a
television interview with the future president and British reporter
Brian Widlake. It was in this interview, much to the dismay of some
of his ANC brethren, that Mandela publicly broached the possibility
of moving past nonviolent resistance. "If the government reaction is
to crush by naked force our non-violent demonstrations we will have

Ruth with Walter Sisulu and others (Photograph by Eli Weinberg courtesy of UWC Robben Island–Mayibuye Archives)

to seriously reconsider our tactics. In my mind, we are closing a chapter on this question of non-violent policy."[195]

MK commenced the sabotage campaign on December 16, 1961, an Afrikaans holiday celebrating the 1838 Battle of Blood River. Walter Sisulu and Moses Kotane sought the approval of Chief Luthuli, who agreed to the plan only after being assured that Joe Slovo, Bram Fischer, and Rusty Bernstein were the Party members who were involved. Ironically, Luthuli accepted the Nobel Prize for Peace in Norway just one week prior to the beginning of the sabotage campaign. Though there were some early successes, there were also many foibled instances of MK as the "Keystone Cops." It should be remembered, as Joe noted in *The Unfinished Autobiography*, "Among the lot of us we did not have a single pistol."[196] A bomb factory was set up in Rica and Jack Hodgson's flat. Amazingly, police never conducted a raid, even though they were "visiting" the homes of most of the other people involved on a regular basis. Rica Hodgson spoke of her kitchen being overrun with homemade timing devices, pens with transparent ink, medicine jars filled with condoms that were used to make the bombs.

Joe participated in one of the first failures, but no one was hurt. He took a bomb to the Johannesburg Military Hall, the same building where the Treason Trial began, to discover, to his surprise, a group of black workers cleaning the building. As he was leaving, a soldier stopped him, but he was successful in exiting the building with the bomb intact. He felt somewhat vindicated when that same evening Jack Hodgson and Rusty Bernstein blew up a manhole that housed telephone wires connecting Johannesburg and Pretoria. Acts of sabotage were documented weekly in *New Age* with both photographs and articles. The paper published MK's original manifesto and further statements. Photographs of the first subversive strikes were featured in a front-page article portraying a destroyed pylon set next to an image of someone planting a Tanzanian flag on the peak of Mount Kilimanjaro in celebration of independence.

Joe Slovo's stories from the sabotage campaign range from spy-like intrigue to successes and failures, but none are of killing innocent people. One tale illustrates the danger and seriousness of the war between the resistance and the government after the State of Emergency. A comrade in Cape Town, Jack Tarshish, had requested that explosives be sent through a courier. Since the SACP in Johannesburg had no security information on the courier, they delivered the explosives to his hotel before their arranged meeting time. Later the same day, it became imperative to deliver a different message to Cape Town so they again contacted the courier in order for Joe to meet him the following morning. Joe had car trouble and missed the meeting. When Tarshish met the courier, he was arrested by the Special Branch, and from the courier's testimony, Tarshish served twelve years.

In his leadership capacity in MK, Joe traveled throughout the country engaging in clandestine meetings. Ronnie Kasrils remembers meeting him for the first time on one such occasion. Ronnie was living with Rowley and Jackie Arenstein and Joe stayed in their house on this particular trip to Durban. Kasrils was somewhat surprised because the Arensteins, people he viewed as hospitable and warm, acted coldly toward Joe. As a young man just becoming involved in the struggle, Kasrils was disappointed that comrades would treat each other without warmth. What he did not know, of course, was that there was a history of tension between Jackie Arenstein and Ruth First from when they lived in Swaziland during the emergency. For Ronnie Kasrils, the evening was the beginning of a very important relationship as a comrade of Joe Slovo:

So there's Joe coming solely on clandestine purposes to Durban and I really like this man—warm, witty, interesting to talk to. So I consequently spent quite a bit of time talking to him. Joe was always a highly sensitive human being who could be easily hurt through social rebuff and I could sense that he was a little bit down and unhappy. Joe's a mensch, a highly

sociable, interactive person who likes nothing better than relaxing and chatting. So I just find this guy, I'm twenty, so Joe's
just thirty-six when I meet him and he is a household name in
the movement, leading force, leading advocate, brilliant man.
I just found him so engaging and it created the seeds of a lifelong friendship and closeness. So I chatted with Joe the whole
night. I recall it was generally about the ANC and the Communist Party and the international situation. I can remember
there was a very funny joke he told me that evening. And I can
see Joe laughing in this mischievous way. But talk was mainly
about the politics of the day.[197]

Joe as the co-commander of MK signified his coming of age, a
confirmation of his role as one of the most important struggle leaders.
It was a responsibility that would increase at each stage of the fight
against the apartheid regime.

At *New Age,* in spite of government crackdowns, new reporters
and office people were hired including Ruth's friend Rica Hodgson,
an accomplished fund-raiser from the Treason Trial Defense and Aid
Fund. Ruth continued attending Central Committee meetings as well
as underground summits with ANC people. In March 1962, when
newspapers in South Africa capitulated to the new Publications and
Entertainment Act that among other dictates demanded media self-
censorship, Ruth directly addressed their acquiescence in *Fighting
Talk*: "They have traded their freedom to write as they please and
they have retired from the battle before it is half fought, and in doing
so they have thrown all other publications to the Nazi wolves—*Fighting Talk, New Age, Contact* and many more. This is not surrender; it
is treachery."[198] Ruth First established the position of *Fighting Talk*
with the juxtaposition of articles on South Africa and the struggles for
independence throughout the continent. However, the situation would
only worsen for *Fighting Talk, New Age,* and every South African who
was involved in the resistance. Police expanded their repression and
began to question employers, friends, relatives, and acquaintances of
those people involved in the struggle. The government motivation
was the creation of fear. In November 1962, both of the papers Ruth
wrote for were banned, terminating the publication of *Fighting Talk.*
Hilda Bernstein commented, "A part of us died with it."[199] Continuing
The Guardian tradition, *New Age* reappeared under a new name, *The
Spark.* The new publication, however, was short-lived. In February

1963, the South African government prohibited people who were currently banned, who had ever been banned, or belonged to groups that had been banned, from working for any printing or publishing company. This was the death of *The Guardian* family of newspapers. In addition, and certainly not a surprise, having copies of any newspaper that the government ruled subversive was also a criminal act, a law that was soon to greatly distress Ruth.

Joe was still consistently called upon in his legal capacity to defend African ANC leaders in court. In 1961, he defended Walter Sisulu who was charged, like Mandela, for his ANC activities. When Sisulu was found guilty in March 1963, the magistrate ruled against bail even though it was not within his discretion. Slovo argued stridently that the Supreme Court offered the judge no authority to deny bail to Sisulu. Joe presented the case to the Supreme Court and the magistrate was then ordered to set bail. Joe was also part of the defense team that tried, unsuccessfully, to argue for the acquittal of comrade Ben Turok, who had been charged with sabotage. In December 1961, police discovered a dud bomb in the Rissik Street Post Office. The bomb was actually wrapped in a paper bag in the offices of the Native Divorce Court located in the post office. There were fingerprints on the bag, but the police were unable to identify them. In May of 1962, Turok was arrested in a general sweep and his prints matched those on the bag. Joe argued the possibility that someone else had appropriated a bag that Turok had previously handled. The defense was unsuccessful, of course, but Turok had a shortened sentence of only three years despite the fact that he was convicted of sabotage.

During the Turok trial, Joe had an exchange with Ronnie Kasrils, whom he would not see again until 1966 in London. Kasrils attended the trial and on one particular day he accompanied Joe returning to his chambers. They spent about an hour together. Joe talked about the trial and Kasrils realized that Joe was acting as a mentor:

> The thing that I realized was that he was warning me about possible mistakes. I'm in MK, he's a leader in MK, he would know I'm in MK but we're not connected and are not going to reveal anything. But he starts talking about Benny and the errors that had been made and how the Special Branch got on to Benny. I remember Joe, he tells you something like this and is very simpatico to Benny, but he sees the humor of it but it's

an error that leads to the man's arrest. His mind's so lively that he sees how you can take precautions and then be forgetful about some other piece of paper that you previously had that's in the back of his car. So he's telling it to you as an insight into how mistakes are made and like a good communicator, it's with a smile on the lips. It shows his humanity, you see.[200]

Operation Mayibuye, the second stage of the armed struggle, was introduced in a plan written by Joe Slovo and Govan Mbeki. Many in the movement viewed the sabotage campaign as futile. The government began to pass even harsher laws and sent army and police personnel abroad to learn more psychological, vicious, and "effective" detainment and interrogation methods. In addition, the boundaries were encroaching on known members of the SACP, ANC, Congress Movement, Non-European Unity Movement, and even the Liberal Party. The ANC and SACP had already sent Oliver Tambo and Yusuf Dadoo out of the country to perform organizational functions without the threat of government interference or arrest. In addition, after living underground, Nelson Mandela was again arrested. The rationale for Operation Mayibuye, which means "The Return," specified that guerilla warfare would serve as the spark that would lead to South Africans, over 80 percent of whom were oppressed by the apartheid regime, to rise up in revolt. The plan called for 7,000 soldiers and an unimaginable number of weapons as Joe and his comrades believed that overthrowing the government was the only option.

Most of MK's High Command approved of Operation Mayibuye, but strong dissent arose from Rusty Bernstein, Walter Sisulu, and Bram Fischer. Rusty Bernstein argued that Operation Mayibuye was unrealistic, romantic, and irresponsible. Joe referred to Fidel Castro as an example of such a successful approach and countered that MK had already sent many people for military training in China, Ethiopia, and Algeria. Bernstein and the other dissenters realized that Operation Mayibuye was a fait accompli. Many years later, Joe Slovo admitted that Operation Mayibuye was not a realistic plan; "It does seem crazy now, doesn't it?"[201] He also argued that hindsight is easy and then described the mission:

Hundreds of activists would leave the country to be trained in the techniques and art of organizing and leading a guerilla struggle. At the end of their training they would, with the help of some of the newly independent African states, return with the minimum necessary armed equipment to a widespread set of strategic areas which had already been selected. In the meantime a network of full-time organizers was to be appointed to prepare these areas both politically and organizationally, more especially to ensure a relatively speedy integration of the local populace into the armed struggle. All these organizational preparations would be accompanied by intensive national campaigns of mass mobilization including a national anti-pass campaign. The precise timing of guerrilla action would depend on the implementation of all these preparatory steps.[202]

Clearly, to most people in the struggle by 1962, Nelson Mandela was the leader of the resistance. The future president's underground freedom ended on August 5, 1962, after he had gone to speak at a meeting in Durban. Anthony Sampson wrote that Mandela's whereabouts were probably revealed to the Special Branch by Millard Shirley, the CIA operative who attended Ruth and Joe's Treason Trial party. Knowing that Shirley was at the party and that he was the person who exposed Nelson Mandela is one of many events that justify using "Keystone Cops" as a descriptor of some resistance actions— before, during, and after the early 1960s.

Following Mandela's arrest, Joe Slovo was not only one of Madiba's lawyers; he was also fully involved in a strategy to assist in his escape from The Fort. A working committee that included Joe Modise, Harold Wolpe, and Joe met at Rivonia where they reviewed various schemes. Most of them were unrealistic. For example, one proposal was for Arthur Goldreich, nominal owner of Rivonia, and in the not too distant future a prison escapee with Harold Wolpe, Abdulhay Jassat, and Mosie Moola, to devise a mask so that Mandela could impersonate a fellow prisoner. After much discussion, Wolpe, Modise, and Joe agreed on an intricate plan to facilitate the escape during Mandela's trial.

The plan became moot. On the eve of the trial the South African government transferred Nelson Mandela to Pretoria to face his charges. Not only was the escape strategy defunct, Joe was no longer able to serve as Mandela's attorney due to his latest banning order restricting him to Johannesburg. He appealed to the court in hope of being permitted to travel to Pretoria for the trial. Joe's request was denied. This virtually ended his vocation as an attorney; he no longer could represent the people he had served throughout the country. Joe Slovo has written on how banning orders affected his life and how he eluded his restrictions for clandestine political meetings. Joe also wrote about two different attempts to encourage Minister of Justice Vorster to rescind his bannings. George Coleman, the chairman of the bar in Johannesburg, made the first attempt. He prompted Vorster to offer a repeal of the banning order if Joe vowed to curtail subversive activities. Coleman interpreted this as meaning that all Joe had to do was repeat his attorney oath to the laws of the country. Joe, of course, had a different interpretation: "I had a completely different understanding of the meaning of subversive, and that he would undoubtedly exploit such an undertaking to the detriment of the cause in which I believed."[203]

Shawn Slovo's 1988 film *A World Apart* shows Joe, whose fictional name is Gus Roth, leaning over her late at night to kiss her good-bye. Shawn's character asks her father where he is going and when he will be home. He answers that he will return soon. The scene follows Shawn as she watches her father and mother kissing outside their home before he drives off. In reality, it was supposed to be a short trip with J. B. Marks to assure both the ANC and SACP in exile of Operation Mayibuye's merits. At the time, Joe never guessed that he would not set foot on South African soil for almost three decades. As previously noted, life was increasingly more risky for the people actively struggling against apartheid. Joe and Marks were set to leave early in the morning, June 3, 1963. The evening before, Ruth and Joe had dinner with Joe's best friend, Harold Wolpe, and his wife AnnMarie. They met at a small restaurant near Zoo Lake and AnnMarie remembered the scene:

All our attempts at light-hearted chatter sound false. There is an air of quiet tension, and even foreboding, as we eat our peppered filet steaks with round blobs of garlicky breadcrumbs on top. Joe and Ruth have a warm but undemonstrative relationship. Tensions arise from their political differences, but they avoid any altercations tonight. I wonder how Ruth is feeling, but she isn't the sort of person you can ask that question.[204]

The next morning, Joe Slovo and J. B. Marks traveled by car to Bechuanaland, what is now Botswana. Joe took a flight with multiple stops to Tanzania, but not before relinquishing his seat on the first flight out to Samora Machel, the future president of Mozambique. In Dar es Salaam, Joe conferred with Oliver Tambo to seek approval for Operation Mayibuye. Meeting at the Palace Hotel, Slovo presented Tambo with a draft of the plan. Oliver Tambo's reaction still delighted Joe thirty years after the event:

> I don't know if you have ever been with OR at a meeting where he really becomes passionate and excited. . . . He had the most remarkable eyes. His eyes used to just physically dart from one side to the other as you were looking at him and you could see he was terribly taken with excitement. . . . [He] was sitting there reading this document and his eyes started darting and . . . I have never seen him do that before or since. He actually got out of his chair and did a dance round the room. It seemed to everyone at that stage that, you know, we were now in business. That now there were possibilities and serious plans for beginning to meet the other side—on its own ground.[205]

Before leaving the continent, Joe wrote a twelve-page letter to his oldest daughter Shawn trying to explain the importance of his mission while professing his love for the family.

Although Joe's travels were initially viewed as a temporary absence, it was quickly apparent to Ruth that he could not return to South Africa. In addition, the final issue of *The Spark* was published on March 28, 1963. One article listed political prisoners, titled "Remember the Men and Women in Jail." The banner headline read, "We Say Goodbye but We'll Be Back" and there were biographies and front-page photographs of Ruth First, Brian Bunting, Fred Carneson, M. P. Naicker, and Govan Mbeki, the paper's editors. The truth was that *The Guardian* newspaper would never return. But the government ban on her writing would not deter Ruth First. She traveled by train to Windhoek, the capital of South West Africa, later liberated as Namibia, to research and report on control over the territory after South Africa had defied a United Nations request for an exploratory visit. The research trip eventually led to Ruth's book, *South West Africa*. She recalled four days of anonymity in which she was able to study government records, do research in the state archives, and interview local people about their oppression under South African rule. She did not find the security forces as intense as they were within South Africa's borders, but she was continually monitored:

There was even an uncomfortable air worn by the more intelligent of the detectives, as it became obvious that talks to White town councillors and Herero Chiefs, businessmen and administration servants, with walks down main streets and to historical monuments, constituted a normal enough programme for a visiting journalist. But the scrutiny never faltered: the trail to the dry-cleaner and the shoemaker, the skulking next to the telephone booth, both ends of the road and every exit of the hotel patrolled, detectives following me to the airport, to the post office to buy stamps, watching me at breakfast, interviewing people I had seen—"What does she want from you?"[206]

The government archivist made it clear that he would determine what Ruth accessed. After four days, with blacks still very much willing to talk, the archives were closed to Ruth First. In addition, visits from the Special Branch frightened blacks and silenced whites:

Interviews were conducted on street corners, in motor-cars, under a tree, in crowded shops; some had to be cancelled: for this is a community where passers-by look askance at any conversation between a White and an African. Where flimsy cords of communication between colours are spun, intimidation severs them instantly.[207]

Ruth First discovered two countries in South West Africa. One was a dominant white colonial country with an ideology that blacks were inferior but were also to be feared for they might seek reprisals against the oppression of colonialism. In the black community, however, she found strength and ideological distrust of anything white, especially South Africa. Similar to her country, South West Africa was an apartheid state, an apartheid imposed by the South African government. Ruth's book described the history of colonialism in South West Africa, beginning with German occupation and moving to the South African occupation at the time. She carefully introduced the different black and "coloured" tribes and analyzed the complex tensions that existed between the Afrikaners and Germans during the Second World War. After providing introductions to what she called the antagonists, Ruth chronicled a detailed historical, political, and economic description of the exploitation, oppression, and resistance in South West Africa that eventually ended with SWAPO's revolution and an independent Namibia:

South Africa's administration of South West Africa has not changed much in the forty-odd years since she took possession of the mandate. Migrant labour remains the cornerstone of policy. The crowding of Africans into small Reserves has undermined their subsistence economy, while taxes have increased only their impoverishment. Labour regulations decree that a tribesman may enter a labour area and earn a cash wage, to pay his tax and tide his family over a short period in their rural slum, but that he must return home at the end of his labour contract. In this way, land and labour are inextricably linked in the mechanics of South West African society; and administrative policy has given the force of law to the silent inducements pushing tribesmen out of the Reserves to work in White-dominated South West.[208]

In her conclusion, Ruth connected race and class, described other African countries that were approaching independence, and argued that South West Africa remained an extension of South African apartheid. She wrote of both the government and press in South Africa, assuring white South Africans of their superiority over blacks. She noted that decades of broad "education" had made the project successful. White people in both South Africa and South West Africa were more racist than anywhere else in the world:

Only in South Africa does government policy march steadily backwards into the past, offering tear gas instead of conciliation, entrenching itself in power with guns instead of votes, denying Africans the last shreds of their parliamentary representation and promoting despotic chiefs as their rulers instead, encouraging Balkanization with dreams of small, separate tribal Bantustans. It is cruelly ironic that the richest, most developed country in Africa should adhere to feudal labour relations and the most outworn political ideas. A modern industrial state, it is built on the colonial subjugation not of a territory across the seas, as in the classic imperialist pattern, but one that exists everywhere within its own boundaries. In South Africa colonizers and colonized live side by side, and apartheid is the state machine which balances them in their uneasy relationship, close and mutually hostile.[209]

South West Africa was smuggled out of South Africa after Rusty
Bernstein critiqued it for Ruth. Mary Benson read the proofs, and
the book was published by Penguin in London in 1963. It was immediately banned in South Africa. Authorities in South Africa viewed
Ruth's writing and then smuggling the book out of the country as
evidence of subversion prior to her arrest later that year. After Ruth's
assassination, South African historian Shula Marks asserted that the
book was a "pioneering historical and political account"[210] and that
"in a field which has been notoriously neglected by scholars it remains
one of the best and most readable books."[211]

Shortly after Ruth returned home, in January 1963, she was subjected to further retribution in the form of two new banning orders:
one restricting her to Johannesburg, and the second from attending
any political or social gatherings. In spite of her new constraints, Ruth
visited Rivonia almost daily and was central to Umkhonto we Sizwe
strategy meetings. She also worked with Govan Mbeki to edit his
manuscript, written partially on toilet paper during detention. The
manuscript was to become *The Peasants' Revolt* after it was smuggled
out of the country and published in London. Because Ruth was unable
to travel or write as a journalist, she enrolled in a library science program at the University of the Witwatersrand and assumed part-time
work in Jack Levitan's law office. Donald Pinnock cites interviews
with Walter Sisulu and Robyn Slovo in his analysis of Ruth First;
the quote provides an interesting comment on the complexities and
intersections between revolution and family:

> According to Walter Sisulu she was during that period, "one of
> the most dynamic personalities in the movement. . . . She was
> moving in circles of the ANC, the Indian Congress, the trade
> unions and as editor of *New Age* in Johannesburg she was cen-
> tral to nearly everything." Her daughter, Robyn, remembered
> that "none of us (children) ever knew what was going on. It
> was at times very fearful—a huge amount of insecurity. It was
> considered better not to tell the children anything."[212]

Ruth was integral to all the important underground political
decisions, and with Joe gone and the government increasing its
surveillance and harassment, her stress was intensifying. What the
children understood was that family days at Molly and Bram Fischer's
pool were no longer the norm. They were cared for more and more by

their grandmother and were being shipped on vacations with friends of their parents who did not share the same level of banning orders from the apartheid regime. Gillian Slovo acknowledged the fear and secrecy that were part of their everyday lives, but she also wrote about their attempts at normality:

> In the brightness of each new morning we ate our breakfast and were driven to school. With Shawn already at secondary school, Robyn and I turned up brightly in our short-sleeved blue and white gingham dresses, surreptitiously donning our reviled white panama hats as we moved through the school gates, ill-matching brown shoes polished to a gleam by our Elsie at home.[213]

Few moments were typical for Ruth. After Joe's departure, she often escaped to the movie theater. She would meet theater impresario Barney Simon, to whom she had been introduced by Hillary Hamburger, and who came to love her deeply as a friend:

> We became close friends in that period. The things that were most marked about her were obviously her fantastic mind, her fantastic clarity and her intelligence. And her generosity. I mean, I know a lot of people were scared of her, but her generosity, her care, and her laughter—her laughter was such a remarkable thing.[214]

All "normality" collapsed on August 9, 1963, when Ruth First was arrested under a 90-day detention order with no formal charges. She was taken into custody, just twenty-nine days after the raid at Lilliesleaf that led to the Rivonia Trial. She was anticipating the arrest. At the time, there had been over two hundred acts of sabotage and Ruth had been a daily visitor at Rivonia. Her absence there during the raid was a matter of luck. Gillian Slovo recalled a 1963 visit:

> At the farm she beeped the horn and a black man appeared. He peered into the car, smiled in recognition and opened up. . . . Walter Sisulu came out and hugged us and then he took Ruth off to one side and started talking urgently into her ear. And all the time, we hung about, unable to understand a word of the conversation going on around us, only sensing that our fates were tangled up in that makeshift place.[215]

Ruth playing herself in Jack Gold's film on her imprisonment
(courtesy of the Ruth First Papers Project, Institute
of Commonwealth Studies)

It is reasonable to wonder why Ruth stayed in South Africa, fully involved as she was in the events at Lilliesleaf. As part of the new laws, the government could essentially detain anyone without criminal charges for up to ninety days. Even the time limit was a misnomer. Prisoners, including Ruth, were often immediately rearrested when their terms expired. In a letter Ruth wrote to Joe just five days before her detention, she chronicled lists of comrades who had been detained saying, "People disappear behind barred doors."[216]

Ruth was arrested at the Cullen Library at the University of the Witwatersrand.

Two Special Branch officers drove her to The Grays, the headquarters of the Special Branch. Before she left the library, however, she was able to ditch a note that referenced a new clandestine meeting place. The Grays was a cement block building on the border between commercial and industrial neighborhoods. Special Branch offices occupied the sixth and seventh floors at the top of the building. After being searched at The Grays, Ruth was driven to her house to collect some clothes while government agents spent three hours searching the premises. Ruth was upset for her daughters, and she blamed herself for carelessly leaving out a copy of *Fighting Talk*, a banned publication at the time. The authorities retrieved it in their search and could have used it to charge her under the Suppression of Communism Act. These facts were part of her reflections in various moments throughout her days in prison as she fully expected to be indicted with her comrades who were facing the Rivonia Trial. The Special Branch, however, was again unable to discover her desk's secret compartment. Gillian Slovo remembered every moment of the day of Ruth's arrest. Her grandfather, Julius First, picked up her and her sisters at school but dropped them off at the street because the gate was open and a stranger was guarding the driveway. Then she and her sisters witnessed Ruth packing her bag and being driven away by the security police.

As she was led into the prison, through the Europeans Only entrance, one of the Security Branch lackeys who arrested her laughed as he said, "Bye-bye, blue sky."[217] Inside she was stripped of many of her belongings. But Ruth was clever, and also a middle-class white woman, so she was able to retain things that were never usually allowed in prison. However, she was often placed in solitary confinement and was seldom allowed to have visitors. The diary of her imprisonment, *117 Days,* is only 144 pages, but the story and analysis is quite dense. Ruth chronicles the early days, her daily schedule, her feelings, giving her different warders aliases, brief exciting moments with her friends AnnMarie Wolpe and Hazel Goldreich, visits from Tilly, Shawn, Gillian, Robyn, and her sister-in-law Clarice.

Condemned to solitary confinement, Ruth inhabited a six-by eight-foot cell that was meager at best. The graffiti on the wall included "Magda Loves Vincent Forever," and "Mayibuye i'Afrika (Let Africa Come Back)." Her body was forced to adjust to lumps in the bed and the noise was often overwhelming. She spent the first few days planning how she would manage the imprisonment and how she would learn from her interrogators rather than help them. She believed, at that point, that her strength would sustain her and she would be able to reverse things with her captors by insisting that she could not communicate with them until she was informed of her charges. However, she also realized that she was lost within the prison walls. Inevitably, Ruth's spirit changed during her almost four months of detention. Shortly after arriving, she was buoyed when AnnMarie Wolpe was placed in a cell across from her. Ruth knew before she was imprisoned that there were plans for a jailbreak of Rivonia detainees Harold Wolpe, Arthur Goldreich, Abdulhay Jassat, and Mosie Moola. With AnnMarie in prison, it was clear that they had successfully escaped. Actually, AnnMarie Wolpe had been brought to Marshall Square for only one night after fourteen hours of interrogation at The Grays.

During the first week of Ruth's detention there was a sweet but sad visit at which Robyn offered her mother chewing gum before they were told that visiting time was over. "There are things written on the inside of the paper, something for you to read,"[218] said Robyn, before her and her sisters' visit ended. In a later visit, this time with her mother, the guard was preoccupied and Tilly was able to speak seriously, telling Ruth that she had been informed that there would be charges after ninety days for possession of illegal literature. Again, Ruth would brood over her own carelessness and *Fighting Talk*. On the same visit she also learned that her father had successfully left the country.

Like Joe during his detention in 1960, Ruth, unsurprisingly, was a prison ethnographer. She created nicknames for her guards that connected with their dispositions—raucous, shrill, pained, and competent. She wrote of attempting to get the news by tiptoeing on her bed to see the newsstand across the street from her cell window. She read the scribbling of many of her comrades on the walls in the exercise yard. Wolfie Kodesh wrote, "W.K. loves freedom forever."[219] Most poignantly, with her political, journalistic craft, Ruth reflected on racism, as it existed in the prison within the context of her privilege, even as a political detainee:

I, a prisoner held under top-security conditions, was forbidden books, visitors, contact with any other prisoner; but like any white South African Madam I sat in bed each morning, and Africans did the cleaning for the 'missus.' Should a spot appear on the floor during the day the wardress would shout to the nearest African warder 'Gaan haal my 'n kaffer' (Go and get me a kaffir), and once again all would be well in South Africa's forced labour heaven.[220]

It was not until the second week in prison that the Special Branch even began to probe Ruth about her political work. At that point the questioning was very mild. Initially there were two interrogators, Nel and Smit, but the latter was silent. Nel presented Ruth with the 1963 law under which she was detained and Ruth was dismissive of the questions that were asked. They visited Ruth weekly for a few weeks and the dialogue was always similar. Each time Ruth was asked to make a statement, she said that she could not possibly make one unless she was charged with a specific crime. Nel and Smit would simply leave. During the second month, the interrogation changed, first with the coming of Special Branch officer Swanpoel whose partner was Van Zyl. "Swanepoel was squat, bullfrog-like. His face glowed a fiery red that seemed to point to a bottle, but he swore that he had never drunk so it must have been his temper burning through, for Swanepoel's stock-in-trade was his bullying."[221] Swanepoel was harsh with Ruth, but she responded to his questioning with a mixture of teasing and disdain that appeared to entertain Van Zyl. Swanepoel suggested that Ruth might need to be moved, and then said, "You're an obstinate woman, Mrs. Slovo. But remember this. Everyone cracks sooner or later. It's our job to find the cracking point. We'll find yours too."[222] Swanepoel, as well as the other Special Branch interrogators, was effective at dropping hints of possibilities that they knew could impact Ruth. Would her mother be detained? What about her non-political brother? Comrades were talking! Then at times the tone would change as when one of them told her that she would not be charged in the Rivonia Trial. In actuality, from Ruth First's book alone, it is evident that psychological methods of interrogation, although initially seemingly harmless, had begun the day she was arrested.

She was not talking to the Special Branch. Colonel Klindt, the commander of those who had interrogated Ruth, and the person whom Tilly and others would see for permission to visit imprisoned family members, came to Marshall Square to speak directly to Ruth. Although Klindt was bad-tempered, he appeared to be accessible to the families of political prisoners. He received the same answer that Ruth had given his men. She could not speak because she had not been charged. He told her that she would be charged, although she never was, and she was transferred to the women's prison in Pretoria. Her cell in Pretoria was larger and cleaner than the Johannesburg cell. In addition, she was the only person in her section of the prison where the general population consisted of black women. Rather than viewing a newspaper stand from her cell window perch, she now observed the swimming and recreation area for white prison personnel. It was a time of pronounced loneliness. She read the Bible, and in her book she refers to two passages that stood out within the context of her Special Branch questioners: (1) A fool's mouth is his destruction and his lips are the snare of his soul, and (2) Confidence in an unfaithful man in time of trouble is like a broken tooth, and a foot out of joint.[223]

Ruth was at the Pretoria prison for close to a month. She spent much of the time feeling totally isolated, but also reflecting on how facile the Special Branch was in alienating her from everything she loved and knew. Solitude was interrupted by the weekly visits from officer Nel that Ruth referred to as perfunctory. He tried to engage her and also lectured her on the merits of apartheid. She confronted him about her health, reminding him that it was too hard for her mother to get her healthy food in Pretoria. She also chided him because the Special Branch had arrested her brother. Ruth and Nel continued to trade barbs. Then, about a week before Ruth's ninety-day sentence was to end, when she was called to interrogation, it was her mother, rather than Nel, who was there to see her. Tilly told Ruth that she had learned from Klindt's deputy that Ruth would be charged for possession of *Fighting Talk*. This proved to be misinformation. The next day, two different Special Branch men came to move Ruth back to Marshall Square for the last days of her 90-day sentence.

One of the Special Branch officers who drove Ruth back to Johannesburg, Johannes Jacobus Viktor, though not as blustery or overtly violent as Swanepoel, would prove much more dangerous. He immediately informed her that he knew Joe well, and that he had saved Joe from a group of angry prostitutes that Joe had exposed as snitches in a magistrate's court trial. Joe wrote about the trial in depth in *The Unfinished Autobiography*, referring to it as the "fucking police" trial.[224] He also acknowledged that Viktor had in fact saved him, unfortunately providing the detective with a future inroad into Ruth's life. Viktor was flirtatious with Ruth and she responded. She referred to their relationship as hostile, saying that he was "provocative" and she was "waspish."[225] What she did not know at the time, but is portrayed clearly in James Kantor's prison diary, was that Viktor was also an unapologetic anti-Semite. Ruth went after him and the Special Branch vigorously in their early conversations. "The Security Branch followed me, opened my letters, tapped my telephone, compiled a dossier on me. Then they had me arrested. They were my jailers. They were my prosecutors and my persecutors. I trusted no undertakings of any kind by the Security Branch, I said. I simply did not trust them."[226]

Viktor was expected to get Ruth to make a statement, hopefully before her first 90-day detention expired. Two days before its completion, Ruth's mother and children came to alert her that her release might not be forthcoming. She presented a positive energy, implying that she would be home in time for Robyn's ninth birthday. As they were readying to leave, Tilly whispered that someone was talking to the authorities, making Ruth even surer that she would not get out of jail. The Special Branch behavior later the same day could not have been more insidious. Nel came to tell Ruth to pack her belongings because she was being released. She balked and confronted him: "I don't believe you . . . You're going to re-arrest me."[227] The charade was taken further. Ruth was checked out of the prison and given her valuables; but then as she walked to a pay phone to call Tilly, she was re-arrested. Even though she was intellectually well aware of Special Branch psychological tactics, she immediately found herself in a tail-spin of emotional stress.

With Ruth feeling defeated, Viktor was ready to take advantage of her vulnerability. The day after Ruth was re-arrested, Nel asked her if she was prepared to answer questions. As awful as Ruth felt, she had thought intensely the night before and believed with conviction that she could make a statement without implicating anyone, and perhaps that would satisfy her tormentors. It reminds one of Melville's *The Confidence Man*. Can a con con a con? Ruth was driven to The Grays and taken to an interrogation room on the seventh floor. She recalls feeling semi-dazed as she entered the room: "I hardly heard. I was packing my mind. Into a strong-room section labeled 'Never to be divulged.'"[228] She reminded herself that she would only speak about things that were already in the public domain and people who were in exile. As Ruth looked around the room, she realized that she had entered a new stage of her detention and interrogation. All of her accusers were present—Van Zyl, Van der Merwe, Nel, Swanepoel, and Viktor. Ruth refused to speak when Swanepoel set up a tape recorder, so Viktor directed him to remove it from the room. For the most part, Ruth spoke autobiographically. Both Swanepoel and Viktor took notes and everyone in the room seemed rather bored. In the mid-afternoon, after Ruth had offered nothing about Rivonia meetings, Viktor decided that they had done enough for one day. But at that point, Ruth knew that her interrogators were not going to provide her with any information. After Viktor left the room, Swanepoel became more aggressive. With the hindsight of other interrogations, Ruth understood that this was Viktor's and Swanepoel's plan. They were playing good cop, bad cop. Swanpoel ranted violently that they knew all about her involvement in Rivonia from an informer and that she was absolutely worthless and had told them nothing. Before Swanepoel could finish his rage, Van Zyl intervened and stopped the session. Van Zyl ending the conversation is intriguing because according to AnnMarie Wolpe, he and Joe Slovo had an amicable relationship. Swanepoel, however, had clearly had an effect on Ruth when he said:

> You're deep in it. You can count your lucky stars that we still have respect for women in our country. You could have been charged in the Rivonia case. But we didn't want a woman in that case. . . I know you Communists by now, I've dealt with dozens of your kind. And I've learnt that they have to be put against a wall and squeezed, pushed and squeezed into a corner. Then they change and talk.[229]

Ruth decided that night that she would make no further statements. When Viktor came to Marshall Square the next morning, she informed him that she was finished talking. They continued on to The Grays, however, because Klindt had granted Tilly a visit with her daughter. Viktor sat in on the visit, and Tilly was able to see that Ruth was struggling. She hugged Ruth good-bye and whispered, "We're depending on you. Keep your courage up."[230] Viktor continued to play his part, as Ruth was allowed to visit with her sister-in-law, Clarice, the following day. He also kept telling her that it was in her best interests to provide a full statement and he arranged a meeting for Ruth with Klindt the same day. Klindt apologized for Swanepoel's behavior, and then repeated Viktor's encouragement about making a statement while Ruth answered with her own refusal. Then, before she left his offices, he gave her a puzzle book that her mother had brought for her long before this visit. He also gave her two pencils that said "Property of the South African Administration."

When Ruth returned to her cell she deliberated, sadly, over whether she had betrayed the cause and her comrades. "I was appalled at the events of the last three days. They had beaten me. I had allowed myself to be beaten. I had pulled back from the brink just in time, but had it been in time? I was wide open to emotional blackmail, and the blackmailer was myself."[231] Not sleeping, feeling nauseous, and clearly depressed, Ruth stressed over what she might have told her interrogators. She worried deeply that Joe and her comrades would never be able to forgive her and she pondered if it had been her own arrogance that had caused her to talk at all, remembering that "Joe had always told me that my weakness was my extreme susceptibility to acceptance and fear of rejection and criticism."[232] Ruth wrote a suicide note on the inside cover of the puzzle book Klindt had given her. When her warder left prescribed sleeping pills in her cell, she decided to try to kill herself by taking an overdose. Her suicide was unsuccessful. Her doctor had provided very low-dosage pills. One has to wonder why the medicine was left in her cell.

Viktor continued to solicit a statement from Ruth. He brought her books, but he did not reveal that the courts had said that 90-day detainees had to be allowed reading material. He presented himself as her friend and reminded her that she could easily get out of prison. In spite of her reflections on psychological torture, and living through her suicide attempt, Ruth continued to converse with Viktor. Her motivation for this continued connection is questionable. Finally, even though she had not made a further statement, Viktor arrived to take her home with the parting words that he would be watching her. In reality, Ruth First's release had nothing to do with the Special Branch, but rather was due to the work of Helen Suzman, who at the time was the only member of the Progressive Party in Parliament. Suzman had been Joe Slovo's professor at Wits. She worked against apartheid for the thirty-six years she was in government and was first approached by Violet Weinberg, Eli's wife, and asked to intervene because of Ruth's poor health. Tilly First almost sabotaged the plan, but Bram Fischer interceded and Suzman was able to get Prime Minister Vorster to facilitate Ruth First's release.

When Ruth was freed from prison in late November, Joe and her father, Julius, were living in London. Joe wanted Ruth and their daughters to join him as soon as possible. Although Ruth knew that she had to leave South Africa, she did not want to be perceived as having deserted the cause. She felt isolated and lonely; her movement was banned and she had sent the girls on a trip with Hilda Bernstein and her children. Ruth had hoped to holiday with them but her request to leave Johannesburg had been denied. Hilda was allowed to travel, as Rusty was in jail awaiting the Rivonia Trial. Although Ruth was thrilled that her daughters would be able to go on holiday with the Bernsteins, she was still struggling with her imprisonment and her future. It is interesting that she executed her day-in-day-out tasks even though she was in the midst of recovering from the trauma of her jailing and the atomization of the movement. For example, she had taken her car to a shop to be repaired so that Hilda could use it for the trip. She even commented to Joe how good the car looked after it was fixed. About the children, she wrote him: "The kids are lovely. Talk quite often about settling and living in London so to them it's an easy proposition."[233] Ruth pondered leaving and was given both Hilda Bernstein's and Bram Fischer's blessing. Fischer's approval was especially potent because he himself was adamant about staying in South Africa, though it eventually led to his nine-year imprisonment and an early death from cancer.

At the time, Ruth and Joe were writing to each other, sometimes more than once a day, and their correspondence reveals both their love and their tensions. They were also speaking on the phone, even though it was surely tapped. Gillian recalled changes in Ruth's frame of mind after some of the calls. Ruth's complexity is expressed through the letters she wrote to Joe. She told him about daily events and concerns and he responded, at least as far as was noted from within her letters, by telling her to drop everything and come to England. While the letters were being exchanged, Ruth applied to the government for a passport. The application was rejected but she was given word that if she applied for an exit permit it would probably be granted. She wrote Joe that there were issues and difficulties in her leaving and that she was afraid of a new life in England. She also reassured him of their lives together:

> I need to talk to you. There are things I must tell you because you are you and I can tell no one else. And when will I see you to tell you. Some will fade and recede with time, which is just as well I expect. Look, I'm not given to expansive declarations or ecstasy. I know you hold that against me. Not now perhaps, but at times. And I was always more inhibited than you. But don't worry about me and you. It's the best. Always. And will be the best ever in time.[234]

In addition to her declaration, Ruth struggled with her own political and professional needs and was very worried about their future economic position in England. Subsequently, she was also trying to arrange to take exams so that she could complete her library degree. Ruth begged Joe to understand that leaving was imminent, but also complicated:

I'm in a state of indecision, difficulty, dither. There are so many difficulties, Joe. You must see this from my end as well as yours? I need more time to think about what you write. These problems are not solved as fast as you wish. This letter won't satisfy you but I want to save you the worry about whether it has reached me. Give me time to think and plan. . . . You might think I am being bogged down in a trivial matter like exams. But I can't suspend myself here in limbo while you and I work out plans for a new life. I have to face the fact that my earning capacity is nil at present, in spite of what you say about so-called talents. I admit that survival in a place like London terrifies me. You don't seem to share my apprehensions . . . I can't climb out of commitments so lightly and I've tried in this letter to explain how committed I am.[235]

Gillian Slovo writes that Joe continued pressuring Ruth to come quickly and that there was probably some blame in his words. At one point Ruth wrote to him: "THERE ARE NO FACTORS OF WHICH YOU ARE UNAWARE." Ruth continued to go to the movies with Barney Simon, who also encouraged her to leave the country. Mostly, she was confused and scared for the next step of her life journey. Some letters were about other family matters. Themes included her mother's fears about money and her worries about how her brother was handling her father's business affairs. Perhaps this was part of her own concern regarding her and Joe's financial situation:

I have been taking the line with Ron that if he is going to invest all the Anglo-Union capital the least he could do is talk it over with my Dad as so much is at stake. A flight to London for concentrated talk and planning would not be amiss. But it doesn't appear to be necessary. The die with Anglo-Union is cast or the link broken or however else you'd like to put it and my Dad doesn't seem to react violently against Ronnie's business plan.[236]

Finally, the exit permit arrived on March 9, 1964, informing her that she was approved "to leave the Republic of South Africa permanently." With Shawn already on a boat to England with family friends, Special Branch officers followed Ruth, Gillian, and Robyn from their home as they drove to Jan Smuts International Airport to leave South

Africa. It is customary in South Africa for families and friends to see people off at the airport. Because of the banning orders, things were different in March 1964. Hilda Bernstein, who had just watched the prosecution close its case in the Rivonia Trial, still came to the airport to see Ruth off. They were not able to talk to each other as Special Branch officers were ever present, but there was a quick good-bye in the women's bathroom. With Rusty Bernstein still imprisoned and on trial, Hilda recalled, "I felt I had a stone in my heart; and knew I could not go."[237] She reflected even further:

> I was deeply affected by Ruth's departure. She was a close friend; I knew of the prison agony that brought her near death, and believed she should go. At the same time I felt I was being deserted. It was not just a personal matter. She had been an intimate part of the years of struggle, and now she was forced to relinquish it; South Africa would be the poorer. It seemed a personal loss, and something much bigger. So many had left, so many more would have to go.[238]

Tilly First left South Africa a few days later to join Julius First and Ruth's family in London. Incredibly, Ruth First was to never see her birthplace again.

6—The Initial Exile: Living in London

FANFARE WELCOMED RUTH and her daughters Robyn and Gillian when they arrived at Heathrow Airport. Joe and friends were there, but so were British television reporters who treated Ruth as an international celebrity. The struggle against apartheid that had become Ruth and Joe's lives was, to use a boxing metaphor, on the ropes. Three months after her arrival in London, Nelson Mandela and seven other defendants were convicted in the Rivonia Trial and sentenced to life in prison. For the next twenty-six years, both blacks and whites were imprisoned, beaten, and murdered by the apartheid regime. The government had virtually paralyzed the ANC and SACP as well as the other organizations fighting for a democratic South Africa. Hilda Bernstein and Bram Fischer attempted to reconstitute the SACP Central Committee in the country, but the banned organizations were impotent. The beginning stages of their family life in London were both sad and difficult. Initially, Ruth clearly believed that the cause was lost. But she rebounded, and Joe, after a short time, continued his clandestine political work. They both valued their freedom out of prison and their family was together. London was unfamiliar for Shawn, Gillian, and Robyn, but the family was happy that they were no longer in South Africa, as 1963 had been torturous.

Shortly after Ruth, Robyn, and Gillian's arrival in London, Shawn landed by boat and Tilly by air. Ruth's letters to Joe portrayed both her economic and professional anxieties. Joe shared her concern. Although he no longer wanted to practice law, he did consider

Ruth speaking at Trafalgar Square
(courtesy of UWC Robben Island– Mayibuye Archive)

enrolling in the London School of Economics to prepare himself for a United Kingdom license to practice. He never enrolled. In 1965 the entire family moved to a permanent residence in Camden Town. Julius and Tilly purchased the house and lived in the home's ground-floor flat. Julius and Tilly had shares in Anglo-Union and they asked their son Ronald, who was still living in Johannesburg, to arrange a cash buyout. Unfortunately, Julius's brother, Louie First, had died, and his son-in-law, who now managed the business, refused the Firsts' request. Ronald First asked one of the prominent Johannesburg law firms to provide pressure, and Tilly and Julius received their payment within two weeks. The money was used to acquire the house in Camden Town as well as other London properties.

Joe Slovo began working full-time for the ANC and was provided a small salary and a stipend for the family's housing. Although Ruth worried a great deal about family expenses, neither her domestic responsibilities nor her family's economic issues prevented her from diving into her political writing, books as well as articles. Both were involved in anti-apartheid demonstrations, and Joe, with comrades such as Yusuf Dadoo, was often on the front lines at South Africa

House protesting the Rivonia Trial. Ruth was focused on her writing while simultaneously making anti-apartheid speeches throughout the country. The only woman orator at Trafalgar Square, her speeches were smart, fiery, and creative. Her provocative messages triggered disdain from some in the Party for not toeing the Soviet line.

Ruth's friend Ronald Segal gently prodded her to write books that he wanted to publish in the new Penguin Africa series. Ruth took the challenge. She published *South West Africa* in 1963 and initiated writing *117 Days* in 1964. Both Segal and Joe encouraged her to construct her prison memoir, which she completed in the quiet of Cecil Williams's London flat. *117 Days* is a personal and revealing work, much different than her political writing contesting oppression in Africa. Segal, and almost all of the people who knew Ruth, had no clue of her attempted suicide until they read the manuscript. Ruth confided her concerns to South African poet Lionel Abrahams:

> I didn't want to wallow in self-discovery and write too explicitly but a description of what happened makes it all, alas, too clear, and there is space to read between lines. . . . Old habits die hard. In the future I shall stick to facts, like land ownership and mission schools and annual general meetings.[239]

Although Ruth First had reservations about sharing her own story, the book was appreciated. Albie Sachs, who authored his own account of being a prisoner in South Africa, felt buoyed by *117 Days*, and Rica Hodgson corresponded with Ruth about her reaction to the book:

> Your sheer guts is to be commended. But this would come better from those who did not previously know of your courage. And lastly, but for me much more importantly, it is your incredible honesty and integrity that moved me most of all. How anyone with your sensitivity could bare yourself as you have done is nothing short of heroic. If you have any qualms about belittling or lowering yourself in the eyes of your friends and comrades, let my small insignificant voice hasten to reassure you. On the contrary! You emerge from your book a bigger and better person than I ever thought you before, and in some inexplicable way—by being able to share your revelations—I have a deeper understanding and a stronger sense of humility and tolerance—for which many thanks.[240]

117 Days was published in 1965 and the British Broadcasting Corporation contracted with Ruth, through Jack Gold, to adapt it for a television movie, *90 Days*, that aired in 1966. Ruth portrayed herself. In Barbara Harlow's thoughtful profile of Ruth, she explains how the film prompted Ruth to reflect even more deeply on her interrogations than she had when she was writing her book. After the broadcast the South African government lodged a protest, emphasizing that BBC publicity had been dishonest about Ruth's life. In part the letter read, "She was involved in a plot to overthrow the legal government of South Africa by violent means." [241] There was also a radio program and a play relating the story.

Very fortunate in terms of representation, Tony Godwin, the executive editor at Penguin, referred Ruth to one of London's most celebrated agents, Jonathan Clowes. Clowes served among others Doris Lessing, and he represented Ruth until she moved back to Africa in the mid-1970s. Ronald Segal's 1964 letter to Ruth obliquely portrays Clowes's skills as an agent:

> You don't know how lucky you are. Your advance from Penguin is almost double the normal—it's your eyes of course—and there are few publishers of such standing—dead seriously—who would touch the subject. Memoirs, except from retired field marshals or top diplomats, are treated with doubt by the hard-back publishers let alone by the paperback boys. So count your blessings.[242]

Jonathan Clowes remembered Ruth First as totally committed to the cause of African liberation and did not hesitate in admiringly labeling her a propagandist. Selling her work to publishers was no easy task, he admitted.

During the final stages of her work on *117 Days*, Ruth also helped to complete Govan Mbeki's book, *The Peasants' Revolt*, as well as a collection of Nelson Mandela's writings and speeches, *No Easy Walk to Freedom*. Mbeki's book was published in 1964 and *No Easy Walk to Freedom*, like *117 Days*, appeared in 1965. At the time of printing, both Mandela and Mbeki were beginning their decades of imprisonment on Robben Island. Ruth would never see them again. In addition, these three books were banned in South Africa. The preface of *The Peasants' Revolt* includes the following sentence: "This book has had a painful birth."

The preface to *No Easy Walk to Freedom* was brief. Ruth explained the book's process and reminded the reader that some of Mandela's speeches were unavailable because their only home at the time was in the South African police archives. The book includes Mandela's voice between 1953 and 1963. Oliver Tambo, who would subsequently work closely in exile with Joe Slovo in the underground struggle, wrote the introduction. Tambo, the leader of the ANC during the organization's exile, collaborated with Ruth on various projects. For example, during the early London years, he asked Ruth to be the ghostwriter of a paper that he would present to other African leaders. She promptly sent him a draft. Ruth continued producing articles including one about her imprisonment that appeared in *The Western Mail*. A piece appeared on South West Africa in the journal *New Africa*, and she had an article on Bram Fischer rejected by the *New York Times*. Ruth viewed rejections both personally and economically. Radio and television interviews included appearances on Radio Moscow and Swedish television. She also put great effort into correspondence with people throughout the world regarding her writing and issues in Africa. Ruth would continue to be an avid letter writer throughout her lifetime. Although she had an exemplary agent, a portion of her correspondence included administrative tasks for *117 Days*. For example, she communicated with Jacques Bost in Paris about a serialized version of *117 Days* and met with editors from Sweden, Denmark, Holland, and Japan about publishing the book. In January 1965, Ruth First wrote to Ruth Lazarus, also a South African expatriate and the director of UNESCO's Literacy Activity Section in Paris, asking her to approach Jean-Paul Sartre about writing an introduction for the Penguin publication. There is no evidence, however, that he ever received the request.

Shortly after *117 Days* was launched, Winifred Courtney, a member of the American Committee on Africa and a United Nations observer on the continent, reviewed the book. Courtney corresponded with Ruth in 1962 when both were researching South West Africa. In the review, Courtney signified three types of South Africans—those who believed time would change the country, those who were loyal to the country in spite of their discomfort with systemic racism, and heroes and heroines. Naturally, Ruth and Joe were members of the third group. Interestingly, Courtney points out that the group's factions acted in independent ways. In conclusion, the review emphasized that while Ruth was a heroine in the struggle against apartheid, it was black heroines that suffered an even harsher price for their actions.

Ruth First's association with the United Nations as well as Amnesty International began in 1964. Initially, it centered on prison conditions in South Africa, a subject that was also included in her lengthy correspondence with Carrie McWilliams, editor of *The Nation*. Working with Bishop Ambrose Reeves, who was now leading the student Christian movement in England, and Bram Fischer in South Africa, Ruth petitioned the International Commission of Jurists, part of the United Nations in Geneva, regarding the treatment of prisoners on Robben Island. She adopted this action on behalf of Fischer who hoped to make the world more aware of apartheid oppression. Just as she was persistent in her journalistic work in South Africa, Ruth's determination led to a United Nations Special Investigative Commission. She had also copied the petition to E. S. Reddy, the same United Nations official who nurtured the ANC's petition for apartheid sanctions in 1959. Ruth's correspondence with Reddy would lead to a relationship with the United Nations for the next decade. One of the people Ruth would include in her future United Nations work, in addition to Pallo Jordan and her daughter Gillian Slovo, was Ros de Lanerolle, who worked for Ronald Segal's journal, *Africa South*, and became Ruth's friend and confidante.

Ruth continued her familiar nonstop pace during her first years in London. Worried about money, she was unconvinced that she could earn a living as a journalist and writer. She applied for an academic fellowship at the University of Manchester, but was informed by Peter Worsley, considered in the United Kingdom one of the founders of the New Left, that they felt they needed to continue to support fellow South African Jack Simons, who already held the appointment. Ruth responded with great understanding as she was truly happy that Jack Simons had the position. She also spoke of her own, somewhat displaced life:

> And though it's a year since I got here I've been feeling more unsettled than ever. I had a false settling in year with a little bundle of work commissions that kept my nose to the grindstone, and only when I'd worked my way through the pile did it really hit me that I'm now back at starting point and must plan what to do and work at.[243]

Amid speaking engagements, journal submissions, and media appearances, Ruth also invested time in 1965 on a writing project for a proposed anthology edited by Lionel Abrahams and Nadine Gordimer. The book was also to include chapters by Athol Fugard, Eskia Mphahlele, Lewis Nkosi, and one of Ruth's mentees at *The Guardian*, Alfred Hutchinson. Penguin undertook the project with full understanding that it would be banned in South Africa. On January 13, 1965, Ruth sent a letter to Gordimer that spoke to apartheid and her own exile:

> I'd be grateful for a prompt acknowledgement: I have an uneasy feeling every time I post to South Africa that the envelope might never get to its destination. I'm writing you in the hope your address is not interfered with! Please give Lionel my warmest regards. I know he'll write when he can. And my best wishes to you too. I was so envious of you the last time we met because you were staying behind and I was leaving. And I still feel the same, though this is living in a dream world pre-90-day detention and Rivonia Trial and all that.[244]

Ruth submitted her contribution and Abrahams responded positively while reminding her of the "intense importance of yourself in the story." Unfortunately, the project never came to fruition.

The years 1964 and 1965 marked the beginnings of Joe's clandestine work in exile. He settled into one of the African National Congress's ramshackle offices on Goodge Street in London, also the unofficial headquarters of the South African Communist Party. There was an office across the street that housed *The African Communist*, and another around the corner on Rathbone Street where Reg September and M. P. Naicker worked for the ANC. Joe's shared workspace with Yusuf Dadoo is intricately described by Ronnie Kasrils:

> Three desks, a couple of odd chairs, nondescript carpeting, book shelves and a battered filing cabinet were the furnishings. Photographs of Mandela, Sisulu, J. B. Marks and Kotane hung imperfectly on the walls under a ceiling that sagged. A bust of Lenin and piles of Party journals from Australia, Cuba, Czechoslovakia, the USA, Nigeria, Vietnam and the like, testified to our international links. The pleasant aroma of Dadoo's pipe pervaded the otherwise unremarkable setting.[245]

Joe and Dadoo in London
(courtesy of UWC Robben Island– Mayibuye Archive)

Jack Hodgson and Stephanie Kemp also worked with Slovo and Dadoo. Kasrils joined them in the latter part of 1966.

By the end of 1965, Joe and Yusuf Dadoo would meet at the office each day to respond to queries from the ANC in Tanzania and Zambia and comrades remaining in South Africa. They also planned actions within their homeland. Dadoo would informally chair the daily meetings, Joe would add humor, and Stephanie Kemp's job was to decode and develop correspondence written in invisible ink. They worked cautiously, as if both the office and phone were bugged, and often the meetings would continue over lunch at Dadoo's favorite pub, The Valiant Trooper.

In 1964, Joe attended the SACP Central Committee meeting held in the Soviet Union. It had been in Prague the previous year. Vladimir Shubin wrote about the occasion in *ANC: A View from Moscow*:

Specialized training in guerilla warfare was also organized for the higher levels of the ANC and SACP leadership. One of the flats in the well-known apartment blocks of Moscow (close to the Kremlin) was occupied for several weeks in 1964 by a strange group: a number of black people of various ages, some even grey-haired, and a young-looking white man. . . . Their faces were known to hardly anyone in Moscow, and even those dealing with African affairs would have had difficulty recognizing them as the top ANC and MK leaders: Oliver Tambo, Moses Kotane, Duma Nokwe, Joe Modise, Joe Slovo and Ambrose Makiwane. They came to Moscow for "consultations" on the organization of the armed struggle (the word "training" was not used for the leadership).[246]

Early in 1965, Joe traveled to both Dar es Salaam and Lusaka for meetings with Oliver Tambo and other ANC leaders in exile. Despite the excitement brought from the London work and visiting Africa, the spirits remained low, with comrades in prison while others were on trial and being sentenced. Amid planning and actions, a tremendous sense of impotence prevailed. Joe reflected on the situation some years later: "The post-Rivonia successes of the enemy had created demoralization that without the beginnings of armed activity, without a demonstration of our capacity to hit at the enemy, it was difficult to conceive of people getting together in any large measure to reconstitute the political underground."[247]

A substantial number of MK cadres had already been sent by 1964 to Odessa on the Black Sea to receive military training, with the goal of future excursions back into South Africa. Soon after being in the Soviet Union, Ronnie Kasrils and his wife, Eleanor, came to London to work with Dadoo, Hodgson, and Joe. Kasrils recalled serious work, but he also remembered both Ruth and Joe reaching out and assisting him and Eleanor settle into their new environment. They were invited to one of the famous Sunday lunches that Ruth and Joe often hosted. Joe picked up Ronnie early so that he could be briefed about military training in the Soviet Union. They drove the streets of London and Joe spoke at length on the dire conditions in South Africa and mistakes the movement had made. He also cited strategies for moving forward in the struggle. Joe tutored Kasrils on the need to bring MK soldiers home and also of their mission to create propaganda, both at home and throughout the world.

Although Ruth was never particularly close to the Kasrilses, Ronnie recalls her kindnesses during their first years in London. She offered Eleanor advice on where to buy clothing and food, referred her to her own doctor when Eleanor was pregnant, and helped them locate furniture for their flat, which in Ronnie Kasrils' words was "shabby with almost no furniture."[248] Because the Kasrilses were new to London, and their flat was anonymous, the Central Committee of the SACP held meetings in their living room to discuss how to maintain the Party. Ruth expressed concern for their living conditions.

All the while, Ruth was involved in her daughters' lives. Robyn has clear memories of spending time with her mother and some of her friends, of being taken shopping and of her own friends adoring Ruth. "Not what a mother was supposed to be like—movie star-like."[249] Shawn, however, cherished a bond with her father. "I was playing piano. Music was my strongest link with Joe. We sang together. He played guitar."[250] All three daughters, as well as Joe and Ruth's friends, also noted that the arguments in South Africa continued in London. Robyn has focused memories:

> She was determinedly of the bourgeoisie. And Joe really wasn't. I think Ruth found all those relaxed habits of Joe's and perceived lack of sophistication as a source of discontent for her. Don't nosh. Don't eat peanuts in bed. He would crack jokes that she thought inappropriate. He was chubby. Got bits of food stuck on his face. Very affectionate to us. She used to feel that wasn't always okay. Joe used to actively embarrass her. I remember an incredible argument over the way to cut tomatoes. Ruth felt French cut.[251]

Ruth confided in Rica Hodgson:

> Sometimes her and Joe had terrible rows in front of me, in front of other people. And she said to me, I think she was ashamed. "You know Rica, we might shout and scream at each other, but we have a huge respect for each other's intellect. And don't forget we have three daughters, that means we love each other." And she did love her girls.[252]

All five family members began to develop their lives in London, but Ruth and Joe's hearts never left Africa. Although their days were filled with work, they also found time for friends. Joe ate lunch with his fellow workers at The Valiant Trooper and other places in the Goodge Street area. Ruth enjoyed luncheons with academics, literary people, and old friends like Myrtle Berman and Rica Hodgson, and new ones, including Ros de Lanerolle. Hodgson tells of picnics as well as Sunday and Christmas dinners at Ruth and Joe's house. During the early years, Joe and Ruth would sometimes dine out with Monty and Myrtle Berman, who preceded them into exile in the United Kingdom. Myrtle recalled the spirit of those evenings. "It would be kind of light politics with Joe's wit setting the style of the conversation. And very much Monty and Ruth connecting on recipes and cooking."[253]

Often, Myrtle and Ruth made specific plans to meet at Sylvester and Jenny Stein's well-known Friday-night salons. Sylvester Stein was the brother of Ruth's friend Zena Stein and had been intensely involved in the arts and literary scene in Johannesburg before exiling to London. Corresponding to his cultural verve, he had been the editor of *Drum* magazine before leaving South Africa. South African exiles as well as Europeans and Americans often attended the weekly event. At various times one might find writers Doris Lessing, Eskia Mphahlele, and Lewis Nkosi present. There were musicians, artists including South African exile Albert Adams, and Americans: the actor Zero Mostel, peace politician Eugene McCarthy, Stokeley Carmichael, Sarah Vaughn, and the incomparable Paul Robeson. Ruth found the mixture of people and the conversations exciting, yet Berman recalled that when they were both in attendance, they would spend much of the evening connecting about each other's lives:

> I always remember Ruth being there because she would come looking lovely and elegant and beautifully dressed. She and I would sometimes spend the entire evening together because we didn't see each other a lot. So when we used to see each other at one of these we would often get into a corner, but we always had some time just catching up and just talking—family talk.[254]

Joe's life also intersected with Sylvester Stein. Stein treated Joe to Chelsea soccer matches, and Joe became a devotee of the team. Not necessarily a salon regular, Joe often attended Stein's Sunday-night poker game, a weekly event until Sylvester quit gambling of all kinds in 1970. If anything, Joe and Ruth's networks expanded in London. What differed was the extensive travel that soon ensued, Ruth for her writing and Joe for his work in the African National Congress.

Initially, Ruth traveled to Africa doing research for her books. Soon Joe was on the road organizing and planning for both the ANC and SACP. They negotiated travel, making sure in the early years in

London that at least one of them was home. But most of the domestic responsibilities appear to have fallen to Ruth. She was clearly resentful of this division of responsibility. Inevitably, the ANC and SACP were still no less sexist than the rest of the world at the time. Gillian Slovo wrote of her parents' lives in the 1960s:

> Those first years in England were stormy times for Ruth and Joe. Her life was a round of new ideas, of her growing confidence in the world, of international conferences and late night exchanges and of new ideas. His was full of secrets and of disappointments, of trips to the Soviet Union for "consultations" or abortive attempts to kick-start the rebellion in South Africa. At home they argued passionately, fiercely, bitterly. They argued about money, about why his only contribution to the household's domestic labour was to make the salad dressing, about his continuing and urgent calls away which disrupted almost every holiday we took, but most of all they argued about politics.[255]

Excursions in and out of London became a pattern until Ruth took an academic position at the University of Manchester later in 1972. This period, for Joe, entailed working in the Goodge Street office and traveling to the German Democratic Republic, the Soviet Union, Angola, Zambia, and Tanzania. By the end of the decade, Ruth's travel included research trips to Egypt, Kenya, Tanzania, Nigeria, Ghana, Sierra Leone, Sudan, Ethiopia, and Libya. Ruth had numerous projects, yet much of her work in Africa was researching for her future book, *The Barrel of a Gun*. She was besieged by speaking engagement and writing requests, continued to do work for the United Nations, enrolled in graduate studies at the London School of Economics, and initiated a long list of book projects. In 1966, she traveled to Nairobi to help the Kenyan revolutionary Oginga Odinga work on his memoir, *Not Yet Uhuru*, which was published the following year. As a side note, the Kenyan government ordered Ruth to leave Kenya shortly into her stay. Ruth's articles on Africa began to appear regularly in newspapers, magazines, and academic journals. In 1966 alone, she published an article on Kenya in England's *National Guardian*, wrote on South West Africa in *Labour Monthly* and the *National Guardian*, wrote on Soviet women with Olga Ushakova, and penned a *Sunday Times* piece on Nigeria and Biafra titled "Only the War Lords Can Win."

Ruth's writing was political, sociological, and also ideological, and engendered controversy that was focused on more than just her political views. Her worries about money and her own insecurity were also factors. Joe commented on her lack of self-confidence:

> Ruth was terribly inhibited about all her talents. She projected the confidence and arrogance and all that, but she was the most inhibited, insecure, in the sense of never feeling that she was on top of things. That she could do better. She was very shy but it manifested itself in the kind of thing that people often resented and that is sharpness, and assertiveness and so on.[256]

One example that was political, economic, and personal was a dispute with Colin Legum in 1966. Legum was a South African expatriate who had been a journalist and a member of the Labour Party in South Africa. He was a harsh critic of communism and was later chastised by Joe Slovo as being responsible for "the postwar assault on the homeless and the hounding of city blacks"[257] in his role as the Johannesburg Labour Party's chairman of Non-European Affairs in the 1940s. At the time of his dispute with Ruth, he was an editor at *The Observer* in London. First had written Legum, asserting that he had criticized her as a communist in a lecture he gave in Sweden. He apologized for her discomfort and closed saying that "in none of my speeches or conversations did I at any time indulge in criticisms of you in any way. Although our politics have always been at sharp variance, I have always respected your integrity and, latterly, your courage."[258]

Ruth responded immediately, accepting Legum's explanation. However, she did not stop there and added, "Those reports from Scandinavia were pretty insistent, and detailed."[259] She continued explaining that her interpretation of his message was that she was hiding her real politics when she was in Sweden. Ruth countered stating that in fact she was being true to Amnesty International's request for her to speak on political prisoners in South Africa. There was no further communication between Ruth and Colin until December 1968, when the tone became much more harsh.

In 1966 Ruth began attending graduate seminars in political sociology at the London School of Economics and political science at the Institute of Commonwealth Studies (ICS). She met scholars from throughout the world and was open to the ideas of the New Left, an ideological perspective that was not welcome among some people in the South African Communist Party. Stalwart intellectuals like Tariq Ali and Ralph Miliband respected Ruth First. She had the honor of studying with Miliband, a onetime student of Harold Laski, and one of the leading anti-Stalinist theoreticians of New Left politics. Ruth took Miliband's courses at LSE, and they spent time in each other's homes engaged in conversations that were usually political. Miliband had great admiration for Ruth First:

> She was the least "utopian" of revolutionaries; but she was not in the least "disillusioned"; she never gave the slightest hint of doubt about the justice of her cause or about the urgent need to strive for its advancement. She deplored the shortcomings, stupidities and crimes of her own side. But this never dimmed her sense that there was a struggle to be fought against the monstrous tyranny that is South Africa. . . . Beyond all disappointments and setbacks, it was [the] sense of the reality of oppression which moved her.[260]

One of her friends at LSE was Danny Schechter who returned to the United States in the late 1960s and launched a news organization called the African Research Group. He and Ruth often corresponded, exchanging information of events on the continent. They also collaborated from afar on research on the CIA. Later known as "Danny Schechter, The Media Dissector," a radical critic of journalism in the United States, his first memories of Ruth First are instructive:

> At LSE in my class I saw this really attractive woman who was clearly older, professional, not sort of the student culture and when she spoke and asked questions she was extremely compelling, very brilliant. Ruth was also interested and intrigued by the American New Left. So here's this woman who is very intimidating to me initially—didn't take any shit. Being a student was the last thing she wanted to be but she was cut off from the struggle she had been part of and in exile.[261]

Schechter provides an insightful analysis of Ruth's time in England, saying, "She was not playing the revolution; she was making the revolution, or trying to."[262]

Although Joe Slovo's writing is never acknowledged to the same degree as his wife's, he too was publishing articles during their early

Joe and Brian Bunting (courtesy of Helena Dolny)

years in the United Kingdom. By 1966, Joe's energy was directed to reviving the struggle in South Africa. Yet he wrote numerous articles for the *African Communist* using the alias Sol Dubula. Topics included a tutorial on Marxism, a review of Brian Bunting's *The Rise of the South African Reich*, South West Africa and the upcoming United Nations decision on condemning South African colonialism, pseudo-socialism in Kenya, a condemnation of the writing of Pan Africanist Congress leader Matthew Nkoana, and news briefs on countries throughout the continent.

Joe's primary mission, however, was attempting to reconstitute the underground struggle. This was a complex and convoluted task, combatting the near fatal harm done by the Rivonia Trial and other tortuous activities of the apartheid regime. Even though he was working for the African National Congress, the time period between 1964 and 1969 found Joe Slovo and his South African Communist Party comrades even more alienated from the ANC than they had been before coalescing around the Congress of Democrats and then Umkhonto we Sizwe. Simultaneously, Joe was working closely with Rusty Bernstein and other exiles to reestablish the SACP in London. Actually, the foundation of the SACP base in London had begun a decade earlier when Ruth, on a short trip to the United Kingdom, asked Simon Zukas, a Zambian communist in exile, and Vella Pillay, a young South African exile working as an economist for the Bank of

China, to form a unit at the same time the Party was reestablishing itself underground in South Africa. But at this point in the mid-1960s, the critical mass of the Party was in the United Kingdom. Between 1965 and 1967 the Party was working to stabilize London cells.

Bram Fischer's final visit to London portrays the desperation as the Party worked to revive itself. Fischer was one of the lead lawyers in the Rivonia Trial yet was subsequently harassed by the Special Branch. He was arrested on July 11, 1965, but was only held for three days with minimal government interrogation. At the time, he explained to his daughters that he thought that the apartheid regime was inviting him to exit the country forever. Bram Fischer had no intention of leaving. As expected, he was soon rearrested. His September arrest was not under the 90-Day Detention Act as in July; instead, together with eleven others in the underground, he was charged under the Suppression of Communism Act. Two days later, quite unbelievably, Fischer was granted bail and given a passport, on his oath to return for trial when he completed his work on a case in England.

Fischer's trial moved quickly and he had a month in London prior to his expected date of return to South Africa. He met with people in the United Kingdom who he hoped might be of assistance in the struggle against apartheid. For example, corresponding to the work he was doing with Ruth First on prison conditions, he visited with Lord Caradon, the British ambassador to the United Nations. Fischer also met with Ruth on the same subject as well as other issues while he was staying at Grosvenor House. Most powerful, and deeply connected to the struggle, were his discussions with family and SACP comrades about whether to return to South Africa. Joe Slovo was directly involved in those conversations. Joe had a special place in his heart for his longtime friend, as did many other people. The Slovos and Fischers began vacationing together at the same time that the Nationalist Party came to power, and Joe told Stephen Clingman about meeting Bram's mother and father when Bram took him fishing at their family farm near Bloemfontein. Joe remembered sitting on a park bench with Fischer, Dadoo, and Harmel and discussing whether Bram should return to South Africa. Fischer, however, had already made a decision to go home:

I was in charge of corresponding with Bram in London. He was anxious we weren't doing enough to send people back. We tried desperately to get him to stay outside. I recall sitting with him on a bench in Regent's Park and spending hours on the question-and-answer combination of pure personal loyalty and political judgment. He had given his word. But he also felt confident he would be able to go back and play a role.[263]

Bram Fischer's decision to return to South Africa and the knowledge that he would have to go underground and probably spend the rest of his life in prison affected Joe to the very core of his being. Joe was already sensitive to the fact that he was sheltered from the dangers that were faced by people who remained underground in the country. He continuously struggled with whether he was avoiding being in South Africa where the struggle needed to be waged. Joe was also aware that some of his comrades, both inside and outside South Africa, were critical of the safety he enjoyed in the United Kingdom. Ronnie Kasrils was working closely with Joe when Fischer came to London:

He was clearly torn and it was Bram who was the one remaining senior leader. It must have weighed heavily. I would say the early stage, post-Bram's arrest, more and more we discussed him and myself going back. And we even had lessons in disguise from some woman in the theater in London whom he knew.[264]

It was twenty-four years later when Joe returned. In the 1960s, Joe, Ruth, and Dadoo and Harmel had been designated as prohibited immigrants by the Tanzanian government. Ghana and Kenya were adamant in their insistence that the ANC conform to an African nationalist party line. The nationalist stands of these newly independent African countries brought back memories of the intensity of Mandela and other ANC "Young Turks" in their resolve to keep communists out of the ANC in the late 1940s. The Party organized into cells in London and Joe's cell included Rusty and Hilda Bernstein, Julius Baker, the Seppels, Eleanor and Ronnie Kasrils, and Barry Feinberg.

Ruth's London cell included Paul Joseph, Reg September, Harold Wolpe, Thabo Mbeki, and Jack and Rica Hodgson. Interestingly, though there is no actual evidence of Ruth being suspended or expelled from the Party, Joe did state that Brian Bunting had wanted to remove Ruth from the SACP because of her New Left tendencies, positions that were magnified in 1968 with the Soviet invasion of Czechoslovakia. It is also possible that Ruth's continuous harmonious relationships with Oliver Tambo and other ANC leaders were at least in part because she was critical of the Soviet party line. As previously implied, this was not the case for Joe and other members of the SACP in London. The ANC did have representatives in London, but even though Joe had traveled in 1966 to meet with Tambo and other ANC leaders in Africa, he believed that he and the Party were being rejected. They were not welcome in Africa nor were they full participants in the struggle as the ANC succumbed to the importance of African nationalism. Referred to by some as the "African Image," Joe Slovo addressed the issue in Tanzania: "They were also infected by narrow black nationalist ideology which made them suspicious of the ANC's traditions of non-racism and its links with a communist organization."[265]

Joe's 1966 journey to Tanzania was precipitated by Oliver Tambo, who traveled to London in September 1965 to meet with members of the SACP. He appointed a committee that included Joe, Yusuf Dadoo, and Joe Matthews to draft a plan that would strengthen the ANC-SACP alliance. The committee sent a proposal to the ANC in Dar es Salaam in November but there was no response. Instead, the ANC asked them to write a new report on the conditions of the struggle in South Africa. The second committee report featured the ANC-SACP schism as well as the necessity of a strong alliance, even a war council, for armed struggle within South Africa. Tambo immediately asked ANC stalwarts, but also SACP members Moses Kotane, J. B. Marks, and Duma Nokwe, to respond to the proposals. The dynamic is especially interesting. While Marks appeared to support SACP involvement in Africa at the time, Kotane, who was one of the African leaders of the SACP, clearly believed in the "African Image." Ironically, Joe Slovo had initially left South Africa with J. B. Marks on a mission to convince other African countries to support armed struggle in South Africa. Ronnie Kasrils commented, "There had been tensions already between Kotane and Slovo back in South Africa. I think that Kotane regarded Slovo as this arrogant white intellectual, not in a racist way, and I think Joe found that Kotane could be bloody arrogant."[266]

The period of time spanning Oliver Tambo's September 1965 meetings in London and the Morogoro conference (an ANC conference) in late 1966 was very difficult for Joe Slovo. While Ruth was writing, making new contacts, and studying at the London School of Economics,

Joe was dispirited by the apparent shunning of the SACP by the ANC. When Ronnie Kasrils arrived in London he found Joe extremely concerned about the struggle against apartheid and the security of people still in the country. Kasrils spoke of Joe's primary mission:

> But the overwhelming commanding concern is how to get the struggle back on track. Inherent in that is how to reestablish the Party and its role and its alliance with the ANC where it is finding for the first time in a decade that the Party is shut out from the mainstream of the liberation movement.[267]

In late November 1966, Oliver Tambo called for a Consultative Conference in Morogoro, Tanzania. It was the first official meeting of the Congress Alliance in exile and a tense dialogue ensued. Robert Resha, who not so kindly referred to Joe as "lefty," argued against a war council and others in the ANC questioned the trust of the SACP in the leadership of the ANC. Twenty-two people attended the conference and many of those in the ANC remained committed to the "African Image." A displeased Yusuf Dadoo challenged the ANC leadership saying, "We are being told to subordinate ourselves. . . . If it is the considered view of this meeting that the ANC can go it alone then let it be so."[268] Joe Slovo offered the group a compromise system, with each of the alliance groups actively participating in the struggle within the leadership of the ANC—no more "African Image." The conference did not totally resolve issues of participation, but a steering committee was elected from the alliance, including the SACP, to help shape the politics and actions of the struggle in exile. The members of this committee included Joe, Dadoo, Harmel, Tambo, Nokwe, La Guma, Naicker, and Matthews. Tambo also created a Cooperation and Coordination Committee whose job was to help integrate Indian, coloured, and white comrades into the work of the ANC.

Joe Slovo returned to London with hope that the SACP and ANC would again be partners. He knew, however, that it was necessary for the cadres in London to exhibit their value to the leadership of the ANC. Bolstered by the Morogoro meeting, and with great resolve, he and his London group set out to continue the struggle in South Africa. However, they were fully aware that there were still great difficulties among the cadres in the frontline states.

Approximately 1,000 people had left South Africa by this time with the goal of returning as part of the armed struggle. When Joe returned to London from Morogoro, some 500 were in the Soviet Union or the German Democratic Republic for training, and another 500 were stationed in camps, mostly in Kongwa in Tanzania, awaiting the call from the ANC/MK to return to South Africa as soldiers. Ironically, neither Joe Slovo nor his London comrades were included in any of the ANC decision making within Africa. But Joe and his comrades in the SACP office did connect their charge for armed struggle to covert operations within South Africa. Joe still met daily with Dadoo and together they planned clandestine efforts with Hodgson, Kasrils, Kemp, and Ronnie Press. He was also involved with further invigorating the SACP in exile, as cells were expanded and further connections were made with the Party in England as well as various other countries. Ronnie Kasrils described his London cell and work on the *African Communist*:

> We had such outstanding minds there it was just wonderful to discuss and debate, considering the situation back home. It was usually Hilda Bernstein who kept very up with the news at home. She would give us the news breakdown and then we would discuss developments in the international communist movement or Black Consciousness in South Africa or a topic of that nature. And a third element would be some logistical aspect—solidarity in Britain, raising funds for the party. We produced the *African Communist* every three months and there would always be an evening when the unit would put leaflets into envelopes and would stamp those envelopes with addresses. Joe Slovo was always very happy to participate in licking stamps. And again, you're doing something as mundane as that and if you have Joe present you're hearing the latest Yiddish jokes. You'd have tea and cake, sort of a social event.[269]

A decision was taken that the Party needed to find non-South Africans who were willing to enter South Africa to covertly distribute political propaganda materials. There were connections with English trade unions as well as the local Communist Party, and Ronnie Kasrils was assigned to recruit students at the London School of Economics, where he was enrolled. However, the London group was delivered a blow, at least in terms of its own place within the struggle, when they were not consulted on a military operation. In August 1967, shortly after the death of Albert Luthuli, and not long after Joe Slovo and

Yusuf Dadoo's return from Morogoro, MK launched a joint military operation called the Wankie Campaign. Umkhonto we Sizwe joined the Zimbabwe African People's Union (ZAPU) freedom fighters and entered Rhodesia with the hope of reaching South Africa to begin the military struggle. Though the effort was a disaster, it eventually led to soul searching and finally substantive discussions and actions between the ANC and SACP in 1969. At the time, however, Joe was even more disheartened than he had been before the 1966 Morogoro meeting. Kasrils remembered Joe's reaction—distress yet determination:

> In '67 I remember Joe's shock that the ANC was launching armed combatants across the Zambezi into the then-Rhodesia—the famous ANC-ZAPU Alliance. In August it is announced there is fighting in Wankie. It comes like a bolt out of the blue for us. Joe's concern was on his face and he was deeply upset. This is something that he and Dadoo should have been involved in and they were kept out of it, and that hurt him deeply. And it made him very concerned about the question of being sidelined. We worked on sending people into the country as soon as possible. It was in the meeting with him and Dadoo saying, look, we've got to do what we can now that this has taken place. It is very important. It doesn't matter that we weren't part of it. We've got to get propaganda material back in the country. We've got to get the message across to our people about support and how important it is. The first time since Rivonia the ANC is showing its fist. It's showing the struggle continues. It is of inestimable importance.[270]

In retrospect, it is almost impossible to comprehend that Joe Slovo was not consulted on a military operation. In his travels to the Soviet Union and the German Democratic Republic, he interacted with and taught MK trainees and he was one of the leaders of MK. Yet the only source that suggests he was consulted is Janet Smith and Beauregard Tromp's biography of Chris Hani.[271] Books like Luli Callinicos's *Oliver Tambo*, Vladimir Shubin's *ANC: A View from Moscow*, and Ronnie Kasrils's *Armed and Dangerous* make no mention of consultations with Joe. Callinicos's book quotes Chris Hani on how Oliver Tambo was involved in every detail of planning the operation. But only Shubin addresses the issue of the London SACP group's lack of involvement, citing Tom Lodge's hedging, first saying that

"Communist Party leadership was 'totally unaware' of the develop-
ments in Zimbabwe," but then claiming that other SACP leaders, like
Kotane, "would have known in detail about the preparations."[272]

What is certain is that Joe and his small group of colleagues accelerated their pace after the announcement of the Wankie Campaign.
Alliances were made with British unionists, young Communists, and
students from throughout the West. The plan was to forge a political
propaganda campaign within the borders of South Africa using leaflets and broadcasts to advertise that the struggle was alive and well.
British dock workers, some of them communists, packed leaflets into
ships destined for Cape Town, and fairly crude "bombs" were devised
to shoot pamphlets onto city streets from the roofs of urban buildings.
These devices were developed through the ingenuity of Jack Hodgson and Ronnie Press. At some point, Press also invented a way for
tape recordings of ANC messages to be played in the central business
districts of South African cities. Arriving by ship, leaflets were also
carried by recruits, in false-bottom suitcases that were constructed by
Hodgson. Joe recruited intensely and one of the recruits was Ruth's
friend Danny Schechter. Ronnie Kasrils approached Schechter after
he discussed him with Ruth First:

> I wanted to find out from her what she thought of him because
> I had in mind recruiting him and she said he is very political.
> Then very typical of Ruth in her unconformity with the Soviet
> line and the South African Communist Party line, she made a
> remark. I can just see her telling me this while we sat having a
> meal. She said, "You know, Ronnie, one thing you must under-
> stand is that Marxism is not the crust of the earth for Danny."
> That's the way she would say it. That's word for word.[273]

Schechter's task was to deliver some messages, send some post-
cards, and to publicly set off a leaflet bomb in downtown Durban. He
described the last undertaking:

> It took a real effort to get it right. I had to place it in the appro-
> priate location which would give the very subversive (and
> certainly illegal) fliers the most public visibility. That required
> reconnoitering and finding a point of entry and egress. I found
> a parking structure over a busy street. . . . Once I found the
> right place, I had to arrange the device, set the time, turn the

clock-like meter, and then disappear. In short order the leaflets would be dumped out in a public street, picked up by some, noticed by pedestrians and probably the police and demonstrate that the ANC was in the country and appealing for anti-apartheid activism and denunciations of the government.[274]

Not directly involved in the SACP operation, Ruth was still clearly aware of Joe's work and Ronnie Kasrils's recruiting role at LSE. Her response to Kasrils about Danny Schechter and Marxism is potent as it contextualizes her ideological and personal changes throughout the 1960s. Ruth's work ethic and the multiple spheres of her undertakings enhanced the breadth of her work. Ruth appeared to be juggling multiple responsibilities—researching in Africa, writing books and articles, making speeches, doing United Nations reports, academic studies, and caring for her daughters. In addition, she continued to be anxious about her family's economic concerns. In 1967, John Heilpern interviewed Ruth for *Nova* magazine:

> When I first came over to London and traveled on the tube I'd panic because I kept thinking black people would get into trouble for travelling with white. It was an automatic reaction. In South Africa you can't even talk openly to an African without creating a scene—you're supposed to walk past people you know and like because they're black. I remember once talking to Nelson Mandela outside the post office in Johannesburg—I've known him since I was a student—and as we talked everyone began to stare. Well, the more fuss there was, the more that proud handsome man kept on talking. But the fact, just the fact, that we were talking as equals was creating a sensation.[275]

She was always somewhat uneasy in the United Kingdom, but to cope as in the past, Ruth leapt into her work. Her research trips to Africa had begun in 1964 and the interviews and observations for *The Barrel of a Gun*, which was published in 1970, lasted until 1968.

Working intensely during her African journeys, Ruth was in constant correspondence with Joe. She wrote to Joe about her research, African heat, and shared her guilt for being away from the family. Both her drive and insecurity are apparent throughout the correspondence. She sent letters from Cairo and Khartoum in 1967 and from West Africa in 1968. Writing from her hotel in Cairo's Opera Square, she asked Joe, "I am talking to too many veteran politicians and not enough ordinary people . . . Who will read a dull political book...? People want to read stories."[276] Ruth noted the same challenges from Khartoum and then again from Nigeria and Ghana the following year. One letter from Sudan, where she was staying at the women's hostel at the University of Khartoum, illustrates her guilt and insecurity— both domestically and professionally:

> Time flies horribly, but I wonder if for you, laden with all the chores I should be doing. You said stop worrying, and I did for a while, but now to begin again. Have I got what I need? I begin to doubt. When I get back you must BULLY ME TO TAKE TIME OFF ALL else except you & the kids to sort material & write something up.[277]

Upon Ruth's request, her literary agent, Jonathan Clowes, secured several advances to help pay for her travels to Eygpt, Sudan, Ghana, Nigeria, and Libya. Research costs as well as family expenses were also augmented through her research for the United Nations. In 1967, she agreed to do reports on South Africa and Namibia in collaboration with South African trade unionist Alex Hepple. She was to receive just over a thousand pounds for her work. Oliver Tambo's friend E. S. Reddy, secretary of the UN Special Committee against Apartheid, wrote to Ruth in October 1967 thanking her for taking on the projects. Though there is no record of Ruth's letters to Reddy, his thank-you letter must have followed her questioning the value of the United Nations fieldwork:

> I agree with you that the testimony of the witnesses on the reserves was very weak and you will need to do the work as if there was hardly any investigation. But that is the way these committees are. You cannot blame them alone. I find that some of my friends went to the committee, without preparing a thing, as if that was a junket.[278]

Reddy concluded the letter with a suggestion that Ruth refer to Julius Lewin, Jack Simons, and Sholto Cross as sources. He then offered her £3,000 to write a report on the South African economy.

Ruth First continued her work as a United Nations consultant through 1973, relying on the help of her daughter Gillian, her friend and colleague Ros de Lanerolle, and Pallo Jordan to assist her as researchers. There is a remarkable resemblance between the African country reports that Ruth produced for the UN and the country reports that were later published under the auspices of the South African Communist Party.

Ruth's documents on South Africa were vast and included topics like capital punishment, massacres, deaths in jail, forced removals, treatment of political prisoners, bannings, strikes, Bantu homeland policy, African transit camps, the farm labor system, black workers, the student movement, and the black family. Corresponding to her past journalistic role at *The Guardian*, sources included newspaper articles, scholarly publications, and policy reports. Unlike many UN publications, description and analysis blend just as they did in Ruth's articles and books. The South African reports were followed by publications on Namibia and Rhodesia before Ruth ended the affiliation as she entered academia.

During 1968, Ruth was also finishing the research for *The Barrel of a Gun*, beginning her work on two other books, *The South African Connection* and *Libya: The Elusive Revolution*, and writing articles on issues throughout Africa. The latter included an article on Biafra that was published in the American radical magazine *Ramparts*, which caused Ruth a great deal of aggravation when they cut her piece down from 4,300 words to 800 words without any consultation. Ruth explained to the *Ramparts* editor that they had changed the meaning of the article, but the damage was done as the item was already in print. A second confrontation for Ruth in 1968 was a continuation of her 1966 struggles with Colin Legum. Ruth was upset because an article on Ghana that she had submitted to *The Observer*, where Legum was an editor, was rejected. Much like her letter to him in 1966, she said:

> You persist in your efforts to undermine my reputation, and, in this instance, to damage my work prospects and career in the only field for which I am equipped, namely journalism. Do you really not think it time that I could be judged by my professional merits when submitting articles for publication?[279]

Ruth also asked her friend Mary Benson to speak with Legum, with whom she was also a friend, and Benson wrote to him the following day:

I remember you expressing to Ernie Gross and on other occasions, about Ruth's writing being roundly suspect because of her communism, then all I can do is to appeal to you to try to look at it frankly and with generosity. I can't understand your block—but somehow anything I tell you of Ruth's fine qualities gets nowhere . . . Are we really still back in the age of Joe McCarthy? However, I won't go on—and indeed now I come to think of it Isaac Deutscher used to write for the *Ob* and he too was a Marxist. So what's the answer—should we all get together and have a shindig—I of course find it depressing and distressing that there should be such a gulf between people who have so much potential for understanding.[280]

Colin Legum responded to Mary Benson on December 18 and to Ruth the following day. He told Benson that he would be very angry with her if they were not such good friends, but he wrote vindictively about Ruth: "I hope you will agree that I have at least been frank with Ruth—something which we have never found to be true of her.... But I promise you that no strictly personal considerations are involved."[281] Legum's admission to Ruth was longer and even more pointed. After explaining that he voted against her article because it offered nothing new on Ghana, he added that the editor rejected the piece because he felt it was too sophisticated for the paper. Yet he could not finish without a lecture:

I utterly fail to see how referring to a well-known and ardent communist as a communist can undermine her reputation.... Certainly you have no special knowledge of Ghana, especially when compared with other writers willing to write for us. As for political judgment—you and I disagree fundamentally in our assessment of political situations in Africa and elsewhere. I don't expect you ever to commend my political judgment to those whom you are ever called upon to advise; and I cannot see why you should expect me to commend your political judgment, which is central to expert analysis on African situations. There is nothing underhand or "singular" about this approach. It is quite open and responsible—and, in fact, reflects the nature of our own relationship over a period of roughly 30 years.[282]

Ruth waited six weeks to respond to Legum's scolding. She could not resist the opportunity to lecture back:

> First, on the approach I use. You may not believe me, but I am loyal fundamentally to my craft. I do not strain or select evidence to justify an ideology. I have always tried to do careful and thorough research, and though journalism, in your hands, or mine or anyone else's does not always give the space and opportunity to fully display the evidence, I try scrupulously to reflect it. I have, I think, some considerable experience of gathering evidence and information under difficult and what might be thought specially African conditions. I ask only that each article, or book, that I write be judged by what I say. . . . The only way to judge an opinion, or an ideology for that matter, is in its statement. Any other way, using an ideology for a category, judging people not by what they say or do, but by a history of past commitment, and you're not that far off—though you won't like this—from McCarthy (Joseph, not Eugene!)[283]

It appears that the conversation between Colin Legum and Ruth First ended with Ruth's reference to Joe McCarthy.

In the late 1960s, Ruth and Joe traveled together within the United Kingdom and Europe. Sometimes it was with Susan and Ronald Segal to the house the Segals owned in Switzerland. They also visited with Kader and Louise Asmal at their home in Dublin. Kader was on the faculty of the University of Dublin and both he and Louise were active in the Anti-Apartheid Movement. Ruth would give talks in Dublin while Joe had meetings with Irish socialists, and the spirit in the Asmal home was usually light and friendly. Louise remembers when the two couples went to a sea cottage on the coast of Ireland and Ruth convinced the fishermen, who only sold lobsters to commercial brokers, to allow them to buy lobsters for dinner that particular night.

But good food and good company did not preclude politics for Joe Slovo or Ruth First. Joe involved these friends in recruiting Irish leftists for political propaganda forays into South Africa. In addition, in Kader Asmal's posthumous memoir, *Kader Asmal: Politics in My Blood*, he writes that Joe wanted him to return to South Africa, claiming it was safe because Asmal had dual citizenship.

Tilly First (courtesy of the
Ruth First Papers Project, Institute
of Commonwealth Studies)

Ruth and Joe had a full social life in London. They continued hosting parties and socialized, both together and separately, depending on the occasion. Friends and family visited from South Africa, and the visitors' memories of Ruth and Joe are social, not political. Hillary Hamburger recalled accompanying Joe to see *Fiddler on the Roof* during a 1967 visit, and Denis Kuny went to the movies with Harold Wolpe and Joe at some point during the same holiday. Ruth's brother, Ronald, spent time with both their parents and Ruth and Joe in London. "We went to the theater together, with Joe and Ruth. We never clashed on any situation and we got on very well. And Clarice was enamored with both of them, absolutely enamored."[284] Ruth and Joe were also a vital part of a community and although much of it was based on SACP and anti-apartheid affiliations, it often transcended the political. Rica Hodgson remembered one such moment when her husband, Jack, was in the German Democratic Republic and she was concerned about their son Spencer who was not attending his high school:

I phoned Robbie Resha and Joe to please come and see Spencer that evening and I must say that Joe was really good because he knew about a polytechnic up the road not far. And he said to Spencer, "You only need to take two courses." And Spencer opted to go to the polytechnic. And Joe said, "You will get your credentials to get your scholarship to go abroad"—that meant the GDR.[285]

Once when both Ruth and Joe were traveling, they relied on Rica to stay in their house with Shawn, Gillian, and Robyn. In addition, Ruth appealed to her to supervise a birthday party for Shawn. Rica remembers that evening very well:

You know, Ruth thinks if she makes a list everything is fine. It's all down on a list. It will all happen like that. So she gives me this list, it's Shawn's birthday on such and such a day, please Rica, see that she has a party. Just make sure they don't get any booze. She doesn't lock anything you know. Her wardrobe's open, her cupboards, and so on. But she can have a birthday party and she can invite kids from her school. I had never been to a kids' party in London, had no idea.[286]

The party, of course, was a disaster, with Jack working hard to send the boys home after midnight. Rica recalled Ruth's response when she admitted that the party had gotten out of hand. "When I spoke to Ruth when she came back she told me I'm old-fashioned."[287]

A public, political schism between Ruth and Joe in 1968, reenergizing arguments that friends had first witnessed around 1956, surfaced when the USSR, through the Warsaw Pact, deployed tanks to crush the attempts initiated by Alexander Dubcek to democratize the government and Communist Party in Czechoslovakia. Other friends also experienced the political divide. Hilda Bernstein had rifts with Rusty over the Soviet invasion of Czechoslovakia. She even banned him from their bedroom. She viewed Ruth as her compatriot:

I suppose the way I feel about Ruth mostly is that as I drew away from the attitudes of the party towards the Soviet Union and various other things, Ruth was also drawing away. And she was the only person that I could talk to who understood why I felt that way and yet was not able to make any kind of break with the party. She knew, she understood.[288]

Antithetical to her kinship with Ruth, she spoke critically about Joe: I developed a kind of resentment to Joe. I suppose it dates from

Julius First (courtesy of the
Ruth First Papers Project, Institute
of Commonwealth Studies)

1968 onwards, at the time of the Soviet invasion of Czechoslovakia. I decided that moment that I'm not going to stay in
the Communist Party. And attended a party group meeting at
which I said I was resigning. The next day Joe took me out
to lunch and had a long argument about the question of the
party and he said, "You realize that you're opting out of our
struggle."[289]

Events in Czechoslovakia and the ideological rift between Joe and
Ruth emerged at a time when both were facing crossroads. Joe was
still feeling marginalized in Africa as he continued leading the political propaganda campaign and Ruth was moving further and further
toward a New Left perspective. In publications that would not appear
in print until after the 1969 Morogoro Conference, Joe was writing
more intensely on the need for the struggle to move home. Ruth,
of course, continued her torrid pace of writing, including speeches
and media work. She produced a special on Frantz Fanon for ATV
Network television in London, titled *Power from Beyond*, and she
planned on writing a book on Fanon until her New York editor,
André Schiffrin, squelched the idea. After finishing the research and
drafts of *The Barrel of a Gun*, she received a congratulatory letter from
Ronald Segal: "You have broken away from the comfortable corners

of a Southern African situation that you know. It needed guts. And that, I am beginning to think, is more important to the serious writer than anything else."[290] Ruth was to live, write, and teach with "guts" throughout the next decade, as her life changed politically, ideologically, and professionally. Partially because of the failure of the Wankie Campaign, and reactions on the ground from some of the defeated soldiers, including Chris Hani, Joe's life would also change, and from his perspective quite positively, beginning in 1969.

7—Academics, Writing, and Activism: Moving toward Africa

THE RECEPTION OF *The Barrel of a Gun* catapulted Ruth into the world of academics. Ronald Segal, whom Albie Sachs referred to as Ruth's intellectual brother, shepherded the book through Penguin. In the United States, Segal, Ruth, and literary agent Jonathan Clowes corresponded with the young publisher André Schiffrin to shape the book for American readers. Ruth provided in-depth case studies of military coups in Nigeria, Ghana, and Sudan within the context of colonialism and the decolonization of Africa. She was completing the manuscript for publication as Joe worked tirelessly to meld a substantive partnership between the ANC and SACP and penetration of Umkhonto we Sizwe back into South Africa. Joe and Ruth were often in different locales at this time in their lives, committed to their mission to end apartheid and fight for a democratic South Africa.

Ruth acknowledged Joe unequivocally in her introduction, but he clearly questioned her foray into work that did not focus on South Africa. The book, however, was groundbreaking in that it provided a description and critique of post-colonial African leaders by an African socialist. As Ruth First stated at the outset of the book, "Harsh judgments are made in this book of Africa's independence leaderships. Yet this book is primarily directed not to the criticism, but to the liberation of Africa, for I count myself an African, and there is no cause I hold dearer."[291] She emphasized the point in the first chapter of the book. "Power lies in the hands of those who control the means of violence. It lies in the barrel of a gun, fired or silent."[292] In the same section she graphically described the un-revolutionary African revolutionary:

> What independent Africa has not herself experienced, she does not easily recognize. She can be only too careless in her ignorance, and smug in her superiority. Men who still struggle for independence are considered unrealistic, for all the advice that they should struggle onwards. They should know better than to espouse hopeless causes or to fight for goals beyond the reach of the manipulating politician or the coup-making officer. I cannot forget the remark of a young Nigerian politician, who not long before had enjoyed a reputation for radicalism and had even been imprisoned for his politics. He and a friend were discussing the then recently reported death of Che Guevara at the hands of the Bolivian army and the CIA. "What could he expect if he went messing about in other people's countries?" he exclaimed. In Britain, the United States and Cuba, Black Power advocates declare: "We will hook up with the Third World. We will go for the eye of the octopus, while our brothers sever its tentacles." Many in Africa have not yet recognized eye or tentacle.[293]

Similar to New Left icon C. Wright Mills, Ruth possessed the uncanny ability to ask questions that combined societal, biographical, and political issues. In the case of *The Barrel of a Gun*, her queries were about Africa and foreign intervention, during both colonial and post-colonial times. The book's themes dealt with who actually rules, the elements of instability, economics, people on the ground, coups, power and oppression, and the representation of coup leaders. She argued that foreign intervention was about economics, power, and control. The first sections of the book broadly address colonialism and independence and later chapters offer more specific case studies on Sudan, Nigeria, and Ghana.

Ruth was masterful at connecting colonialism and post-colonialism to the failure of progressive/radical change throughout the African continent. She uncovers the co-opting of African elites by the West, including the United States, but in the final analysis her writing in *The Barrel of a Gun* confronts independent African regimes:

The government of Africa, in the hands of the politician-manipulators, or the less flamboyant but infinitely more parochial soldier-rulers, is not on the whole tyrannical, but bumbling. Time and again it makes false starts, and spreads false hopes. Condemnation there must be; but compassion too, for those who talked so boldly about freedom but had so little freedom of maneuver. The soldiers illuminate the foundations and the failures of the new states of Africa. Those who have usurped government to consolidate the political system have been driven openly to reveal the armature of state power that supports them; the more it is revealed, the more puny it is shown to be, for its essential supports are not inside but outside Africa. As for the soldiers who seize government reform or radicalize it, their success or failure will depend on the popular forces for change that they release within Africa; not on the force of armies or the power that flows out of the barrel of their guns.[294]

Most of the reviews of *The Barrel of a Gun* were positive and credited Ruth for breaking new ground in understanding post-colonial Africa. Kader Asmal, writing in the *Irish Times*, said, "Only someone who loves Africa and knows its hopes and aspirations could write with such honesty and enlightened criticism."[295] The book was also recognized in academic journals, as well as *The African Communist*. Critical readers were genuinely positive about her use of case studies that covered the breadth of each country's population.

Two of the several critiques of Ruth's work emerged in the *African Communist*. The most scathing review, however, was by Jeffrey Butler, a historian at Wesleyan University in the United States who was born in South Africa and was viewed by the left much like Colin Legum. Writing in the *Journal of Interdisciplinary History*, Butler asserted that the book was bad scholarship that vacillated from narration at best to pamphleteering using "conspiracy theory" at worst. The "conspiracy theory" accusation is especially interesting since both Communists at the time and academics shortly thereafter argued that *The Barrel of a Gun* exemplified Ruth First breaking with internal colonialism and Party-line Marxist theory. In his 1973 review, radical sociologist Immanuel Wallerstein wrote: "The book is a critique of these coups from the left, but one that happily rejects a conspiracy explanation as a substitute for analysis."[296]

Preceding the publication of *The Barrel of a Gun*, Ruth was back at home while Joe was traveling, including a trip to Tanzania for the ANC's historic Morogoro Conference. Staged the last week of April 1969, the conference was a direct result of discontent among MK cadres as well as the continuing marginalization of Slovo and other SACP comrades in the United Kingdom. During the Wankie Campaign, the MK attempt to get cadres into South Africa, Chris Hani and six other MK fighters crossed into Botswana, hungry, thirsty, and defeated. Instead of a welcome from the country's first democratic government and President Seretse Khama, Hani and his fellow soldiers were imprisoned. They were released through the efforts of Oliver Tambo and the Organization of African Unity and then returned to Lusaka and ANC headquarters. Disappointed with what they viewed as corruption within the ANC leadership, influenced by the restlessness of fellow Umkhonto cadres, and finally displeased by what was now considered the incompetence of the Wankie Campaign, a memorandum, subsequently referred to as the Hani Memorandum, was submitted to the leadership of the African National Congress. The document made accusations such as Joe Modise caring mostly about his entrepreneurial endeavors, Moses Kotane of nepotism, Duma Nokwe of cynicism toward the rank and file, and even Oliver Tambo of turning a blind eye to the problems. Reaction from the ANC leadership was swift. Hani and the other signees were confronted and suspended from the ANC by an ANC Military Tribunal in March 1969. The tribunal is said to have voted the death penalty for treason, although that is not entirely clear. Struggle stalwarts, ironically including hard-liner Mzwandile Piliso, along with Ray Simons, Yusuf Dadoo, and Joe Slovo, called for a calming period and further discussion. Despite being extremely upset by the memorandum, especially its characterization of Kotane, Oliver Tambo finessed the discontent into an appeal for the consultative conference.

The calming period culminated in the Morogoro Conference where seventy delegates representing MK, ANC, and the Congress Alliance met to review various documents which were submitted to the ANC office in Lusaka. For Joe Slovo, the conference brought hope on two fronts: first, it would reassert the alliance between the ANC and SACP. Second, and most important, it would accelerate the mission of sending Umkhonto we Sizwe cadres back into South Africa to fight in the revolution against apartheid. Shortly before the conference, at a meeting of the Central Committee of the SACP and the National Executive Committee of the ANC, Joe bemoaned what he viewed as the void:

> To our shame there have, in recent years, been too many exam-
> ples of backward political postures (including tribalism) of
> some of our members and other conduct which is foreign to
> our ideology and stands in conflict with standards of behav-
> ior which our Party has always insisted upon. The absence of
> organized contacts has also encouraged all sorts of so-called
> revolutionaries or so-called Marxist-Leninists to fill the gap
> and to use the mantle of revolutionary doctrine for intrigue.[297]

The mood of "shame" appeared to dissipate at the conference. In a letter written while struggling to finish *The Barrel of a Gun*, Ruth reminded Joe that it was he who was at the core of the action— "you're the one on Limosin and the magic carpet."[298] Ruth was right. Joe Slovo was an important participant and was directly involved with two documents, "Strategy and Tactics" and "The Revolution-ary Programme." The degree of Joe's participation in "Strategy and Tactics" varies depending on the source, but it can be stated unequiv-ocally that he was involved. In fact, a draft of the document dated March 1969, cites his name as the author and the edits are notated in his handwriting. In addition, Ronnie Kasrils recalls Joe's efforts on the draft:

> We had discussions and Joe was doing a lot of work on strat-
> egy and tactics and had long discussions with Jack, myself, and
> Yusuf Dadoo on the question of how the underground should
> develop, its relationship to the politics in the country, and to
> MK. So it was invaluable for him to have us who were involved
> in these processes as part of this discussion. You know, he was
> a guy who didn't claim all the glory himself.[299]

According to both Luli Callinicos and the SADET volume, the document was presented to the conference inviting serious discussion and debate. In actual fact, three documents were presented to the conference that was chaired by J. B. Marks. "Strategy and Tactics," referred to as the keynote policy document, was given by Joe Slovo. The first paragraph read:

The struggle of the oppressed people of South Africa is taking place within an international context of transition to the socialist system, the breakdown of the colonial system as a result of national liberation and socialist revolutions, and the fight for social and economic progress by the people of the whole world.[300]

"Strategy and Tactics" corresponds directly with other SACP documents. It describes the long history of oppression and resistance in South Africa, with emphasis on the 1950s, building up to MK and the necessity of armed struggle. Guerilla warfare and the Cuban, Algerian, and Vietnam struggles are all cited, and there is a long discussion on the importance of the marriage of the political and the military:

When we talk of revolutionary armed struggle, we are talking of political struggle by means which include the use of military force even though once force as a tactic is introduced it has the most far-reaching consequences on every aspect of our activities. It is important to emphasise this because our movement must reject all manifestations of militarism which separates armed people's struggle from its political content.[301]

There is also some irony in "Strategy and Tactics." Within the issue of the political and the military, the document reads as if it is an extension of *The Barrel of A Gun*. "Above all, when victory comes, it must not be a hollow one. To ensure this we must also ensure that what is brought to power is not an army but the masses as a whole at the head of which stands its organised political leadership."[302] On the other hand, the document emphasizes "colonialism of a special type" and describes internal colonialism in both economic and racial terms. Thus the assertion is that government is colonialist in the context of capitalism, except that it colonizes and oppresses black people within South Africa.

In its conclusion, "Strategy and Tactics" describes all the roles that groups and individuals that are part of the struggle must play in the emancipation of South Africa. Though not discounting the total racism of the apartheid regime, the document clearly emphasizes the connection between class and race and the struggle:

Our drive towards national emancipation is therefore in a very real way bound up with economic emancipation. We have suffered more than just national humiliation. Our people are deprived of their due in the Country's wealth; their skills have been suppressed and poverty and starvation has been their life experience. The correction of these centuries-old economic injustices lies at the very core of our national aspirations. We do not underestimate the complexities which will face a people's government during the transformation period nor the enormity of the problems of meeting economic needs of the mass of the oppressed people. But one thing is certain—in our land this cannot be effectively tackled unless the basic wealth and the basic resources are at the disposal of the people as a whole and are not manipulated by sections of individuals be they Black or White.[303]

The heated debate that followed Joe's oration connected the issues in the Hani Memorandum and Joe's historical and political look to the future. Resolutions were adopted that reduced the size of the National Executive Committee of the African National Congress, adding younger members, including Chris Hani. In addition, a new body, the Revolutionary Council, was launched. While the former still included only blacks, the latter was multiracial and its leadership comprised of Tambo, Dadoo, Matthews, and Slovo. At one point in the conference, Tambo, in a gesture of democracy and solidarity, stepped down from the leadership and left the meeting. When he returned at the urging of J. B. Marks, he was overwhelmingly confirmed as ANC president. At the time Joe told the conference, "What happened today is that we lost a great president—and gained an even better one."[304]

In Joe's view, the Morogoro Conference set the stage for energizing the struggle. The resolutions had given credence to the demands of MK cadres who sought to return the fight against apartheid back to South Africa, and the South African Communist Party, in its entirety, had been invited to rejoin the leadership of the struggle. In a 1983 *African Communist* article, Joe reflected on the importance of the conference:

Looking back on it, comrades, it could be said that there were moments at that Morogoro Conference when the very future of our whole movement seemed to be in jeopardy. But it was J. B.

Marks's skill as chairman and the greatness of comrade President Oliver Tambo, who was then Acting President, which pulled us through and laid the basis for what we are today.[305]

Upon his return to London, following Morogoro, there was vitality in the discussions between Joe, Dadoo, and Kasrils. Joe briefed those who were not in Tanzania about J. B. Marks's patience and thoughtfulness within a very challenging and tense setting. As usual, Joe relayed humorous moments:

> There is this guy Problem, do you know Problem? He was there as an interpreter, you know you've got to have that. Someone's speaking Zulu, someone Sotho, guys don't really understand English. I said I know Problem and he says, well I didn't and there I am sitting there and I see this guy sitting next to me, he's got a very thick file, and on it is written Problems. And Joe thought, My God. And he could so laugh at himself, he said, I didn't know the guy was named Problem, I was so relieved that he was an interpreter.[306]

Beyond the humor, of course, was Joe emphasizing the importance of the mission that was now finally corresponding with the ANC in Africa. Training was needed and Kasrils witnessed an enormous change in Joe's demeanor:

> Of course it was so profound, this change out of Morogoro, and you could see how delighted Joe was because it's always on display with Joe and I saw in this the contrast to Joe with ants in his pants. The guy with angst in his face from 1965 when I arrived in London to Joe now where the way ahead is assured.[307]

Joe began to travel back and forth between London, Moscow, Berlin, and various sites in Africa. He and his London comrades procured even greater opportunities for training to send cadres into South Africa. Perhaps this was somewhat ambitious, but at the very least, propaganda forays continued in the early 1970s. Connections were made throughout South Africa to utilize people in the struggle who were unknown to government authorities. They were taught about locating places to stay, purchasing supplies, as well as lessons in the technology that they would depend on to operationalize the spread of struggle propaganda. Though Joe totally believed in the value of the military training that was offered to MK soldiers in the Soviet Union and the GDR, he was also convinced that cadres needed to learn lessons specific to South Africa. "Joe was always keen on having people at the Lenin School for a year but he was always saying to me we've got to get these guys afterwards just to refashion their minds for the unique aspects of our struggle through courses with Rusty Bernstein or Mick Harmel."[308]

While Joe maintained his connection to the Soviet Union, he was clear on the significance of local politics. This is evident in his emphasis in "Strategy and Tactics" of the importance of politics and the role of the South African working class in the struggle. As he was constructing "Strategy and Tactics," he was working on various articles and essays that corresponded to his presentation at Morogoro. Joe's writing quickly became vital to the struggle. Just before Morogoro, he published an article on Régis Debray, Che's comrade in Cuba and Bolivia, in which he was highly critical of Debray for minimizing the importance of politics in revolutions. A second article in *The African Communist*, "Che in Bolivia," articles in *The Socialist Register* and *Marxism Today*, and most important, his essay "No Middle Road," part of the book *South Africa: The New Politics of Revolution*, connected directly to "Strategy and Tactics" and had significant influence on the struggle throughout the 1970s and '80s. "Che in Bolivia" was published just after the Morogoro Conference advocating the necessity of working-class political commitment in revolutionary situations. Joe praised Che Guevara and the importance of guerilla warfare, referenced armed struggle and the revolutions in Vietnam and Algeria, and analyzed the difficulty of predicting the perfect revolutionary moment, all directly related to words in his Morogoro report. The essence of the article is found in Joe's analysis of Che's Bolivian diaries to illustrate how fundamental politics and local people are to successful revolutions.

In criticizing Che Guevara, Joe begins with a thoughtful refrain. "At the end of the day it is our capacity to build on the positive foundation and to reject the negative features of revolutionary thinkers, which will spell success."[309] Relying on the diaries, Joe explains that Che's murder and the failure of the revolution was caused by Che's "failure to win popular support and its almost complete and utter isolation from the Bolivian masses—peasantry and workers alike."[310] Joe writes about the joint military operations of MK and ZAPU in Rhodesia as an introduction to his discussion about the coming of armed revolution in South Africa. Similar to his motivation in "Strategy and Tactics," the words are directed at his comrades: both leadership and the masses. He refers to Che's lack of engagement with Bolivians and specifically of the distrust of "outsiders" in Africa, and concludes by connecting politics and struggle. The final paragraph of the article quotes Amilcar Cabral: "The political and military leadership of the struggle is one."[311]

Upon her completion of *The Barrel of a Gun*, Ruth transitioned directly to other writing projects. She contacted Jack Simons, who was living in Lusaka, asking him to author a chapter in a book she intended to edit for the general public on "the vulnerability or predicament" of African independence. Correspondingly, she also stated her desire, similar to Joe, to return to Africa. "I envy you the chance of living down there on the African ground, and working close to it; on the other hand I suspect I couldn't undertake to live semi-permanently in Africa right now, not for a little while anyway until our kids are older and really independent."[312] Simons responded, a month later, suggesting that the book address national goals, economic determinants and dilemmas, functions and structures of government, and international relations. Finally, Ruth continued the conversation in November 1971 by asking Jack to be her co-editor of the book, which was to be published by Granada Books.

Although the collection never reached fruition, Ruth began manuscripts that became the books *The South African Connection* and *Libya: The Elusive Revolution*, the former referencing some of her prior writing on South African capitalists. By the early 1970s, she worked collaboratively with Ann Scott on what was to become their book on South African writer Olive Schreiner. In addition, she was besieged by invitations to speak about apartheid and the Anti-Apartheid Movement. The list of organizations was long including multiple universities, synagogues, Jewish organizations, and even Rugby Africa, in addition to the many anti-apartheid groups in the United Kingdom. The rather lengthy list does not include the lectures she gave abroad in the Netherlands, Norway, Denmark, and various African states. Ruth First was unable to meet all of the requests, but she was generous in accepting invitations. Anti-apartheid activist Polly Gaster, with whom Ruth became more acquainted during her years in Mozambique when Gaster was working in the Ministry of Information, recalls Ruth's efforts at the time:

When we'd been through the liberated areas of Mozambique—this would be '72 and then we came and we organized a slide show out of the pictures and took it around England showing life in liberated areas. One time I had to go to Manchester and I did three meetings in two days at different colleges and universities and Ruth came to every single one. Now that's what I call solidarity. This must have been incredibly boring for her to sit in three slide shows but she just told me I was getting better as I go along.[313]

The respect that Ruth First received from her LSE professors extended beyond politics and academics. Ronnie Kasrils reflected on the perception Londoners had of Ruth First:

So there was this whole range of people in Britain, right from the most conservative types who highly respected her and her bearing and learning and her background. The fact that she had been a foremost leader of the struggle in South Africa, had been in detention, and had written this book on her detention that the BBC had filmed. I saw the incredible respect in a cartoonist. We were producing a comic book on the struggle. I went to see this artist and that morning there was a wonderful article on Ruth in *The Guardian*—a full page with wonderful photographs. This guy said to me, "Do you know this woman?" I said yes, and he asked me to tell him about her. This was your ordinary middle-of-the-road-type Brit. Not exactly left wing politically, though a guy who would be sympathetic to the ANC, and so engaged with the article on Ruth. But you see, she made this impact on such a wide range of people from some of the Tories who would be sympathetic to hearing about anti-apartheid, but right through the whole middle ground, center ground, liberal, socialist, Communist Party, academic intelligentsia, and the New Left. She was a most profound person and a fantastic figure in Britain.[314]

In July 1970, Ruth and Rica Hodgson attended the "Solidarity for the People of the Portuguese Colonies" conference in Rome. Ruth had worked closely with the conference organizer, Dina Forte, helping in the planning. Polly Gaster remembered Ruth as "meticulous and prepared" in all of her solidarity work. The keynote addresses of the conference were delivered by Amilcar Cabral, of the African Party for the Independence of Guinea and Cape Verde (PAIGC), Agostinho Neto of the People's Movement for the Liberation of Angola (MPLA), and Marcelino dos Santos of the Liberation Front of Mozambique (FRELIMO). Ruth and Joe considered all three men as friends, and Joe wrote of the links between the three liberation organizations and the struggle against apartheid in his 1973 article, "Southern Africa: Problems of Armed Struggle." One of the others who traveled with Ruth and Rica was Alan Brooks, once a member of the African Resistance Movement with Monty and Myrtle Berman, but by this time an ardent member of the SACP based in London. In fact, it was Brooks, albeit unsuccessfully, who had been adamant about expelling Ruth from the Party. Pallo Jordan commented on Ruth's political commitment:

> Ruth was sort of what you would call a dissident communist. She didn't break with the CP but she couldn't identify with many of the views and I think she felt very much constrained to keep her opinion to herself that she was on the wrong side of certain people. As it is one was aware that some of the more dogmatic elements of the CP wanted to have her excluded and isolated in the Party. So she felt very constrained by things like that but of course, being a political person, she was always politically engaged.[315]

Ben Turok referred to Ruth as "one of the leading lights" of the conference and Rica Hodgson described her as hectic as she organized meetings and spoke at a press conference. She and Ruth enjoyed Rome, visiting the legendary Trevi Fountain, and dining and drinking with international comrades.

Joe nurtured the Morogoro decisions and the propaganda actions in South Africa as he continued to travel to the Soviet Union and the German Democratic Republic from his London base. Delegations from the ANC and SACP met in the Soviet Union following the Morogoro Conference. Yusuf Dadoo and Joe Slovo were both part of the SACP delegation. Joe spoke to the sensitivities of the ANC regarding the broadly held view, intensely supported by South African media propaganda, about the ANC being pawns of white Communists:

There was more than one occasion when the views, mood and arguments of ANC leaders radically influenced the formulation of Party policy and the other way as well.... We have all been "captured" by the ANC and it is right that this should be so. Only the vulgar or those who wish to make mischief see in our collaboration a white-anting process. They cannot understand how two political parties can work so closely together without stabbing each other in the back.[316]

After declaring the SACP's loyalty to the ANC and the struggle against apartheid, Joe addressed the necessity of scheduled clandestine meetings so as not to compromise the public image of the ANC, but to collectively aid the struggle. Tambo reacted with warmth, but also with caution, and J. B. Marks affirmed Joe's statements. The meeting concluded by avowing the importance of the alliance, with a proclamation that the leaderships of both organizations would maintain consistent non-public contact to address common problems.

At the South African Communist Party meeting in 1970, an opinion was voiced that the agreement was not as inclusive as the Party would have preferred. The importance of this meeting, however, was that in spite of Morogoro not offering everything the SACP wanted, it did supply renewed hope to the Party. In addition, the Soviet Union provided facilities that enabled not just the Central Committee but additional members of the SACP to attend the meeting. This was the first time since the Rivonia Trial that a critical mass of Party members were able to congregate. At the meeting, held at Stalin's dacha outside Moscow, the SACP reenergized itself and asserted participation in the struggle. There was an appeal for additional cells and younger blacks; ironically Thabo Mbeki and Chris Hani, whose past and future differences were well known to other struggle leaders, were elected to the Central Committee. Joe, of course, attended the subsequent Central Committee meetings, in the GDR in 1972 and again in Moscow in 1973.

With Joe's resolve strengthened, he helped lead one of the most adventurous, albeit failed missions that came under the auspices of Umkhonto we Sizwe, "Operation J." Interestingly, despite his messages of caution, Oliver Tambo was very much Joe's partner in this attempt to send soldiers into South Africa via the sea. Local newspapers in South Africa were beginning to report on the propaganda campaign, and though the government wanted to emphasize the

"Communist threat," the reports were simultaneously revitalizing people on the ground in South Africa. Subversive pamphlets with misleading titles like "Meet the Cape Wines" were sent into the country disguising revolutionary documents. Another example was an Automobile Association brochure titled "Handbook: 1977–1978." The first page listed phone numbers in eight small South African cities; the second page was titled "Emergency Action" and the third "Accidents and the Law." Past page three, however, one could read Joe's classic proclamation, "No Middle Road." The idea for Operation J had been first broached by Rivonia escapee Arthur Goldreich in 1963. Then in 1967, Joe Slovo reinitiated the conversation with Moscow and in 1970 the Politburo agreed to fund a boat, supplies, and training for the soldiers who would enter South Africa. Slovo, Tambo, and Moses Mabhida planned the mission and Somalia offered its ports and support. A boat, aptly named the *Adventurer*, was purchased by the USSR for £75,000, and the soldiers traveled to the Soviet Union for quick training sessions. Alex Moumbaris, one of the leaders of the expedition, had already done reconnaissance along the coast. However, there were a number of false starts and though the ANC suspected that the crew had sabotaged the plan, Joe reported that they simply got "cold feet."[317]

Even though the plan to enter South Africa from the sea proved impossible, there were people underground in the country awaiting the arrival of the MK cadres. Tambo, Mabhida, and Joe Slovo decided to send some of the soldiers into the country by land. Moumbaris and the others flew to Swaziland, but there one of the soldiers was apprehended and informed on the others. According to Shubin, the disappointment was so great within the Soviet Union that some Russians even suspected Joe as a possible spy. The spy was actually a Soviet-U.S. double agent. At the time, Joe and other leaders were not happy. However, Moumbaris's trial, known as the trial of the "Pretoria Six," became a symbol of creativity and bravery for the young South Africans who would leave the country to join Umkhonto we Sizwe shortly thereafter. Reflecting, Joe wrote:

This went on till 1976 I would say with one project or another, with none of them really succeeding. But our failures, although one does not plan for them, have some kind of impact. It could be seen by everyone that the ANC was persisting in its efforts without end despite enormous difficulties. People were becoming aware that here was a committed and dedicated group which was just going to continue knocking their heads against the wall until somehow there was a crack in it. I think that was a very important side-product of the efforts, most of which ended in failures. But one wonders where we would have been without these stubborn attempts to find the answer.[318]

Newspapers in both South Africa and abroad began to increase their coverage of the propaganda campaign. Much to the South African government's dismay, the articles demonized the country more than labeling the freedom fighters as "evil Communists."

The complexities of life that Ruth and Joe were juggling at this time were astounding. Their books and articles represented some of their most important written work. Traveling abounded for both people and she was in the public eye in the United Kingdom. Ruth visited Libya four times to work on her book on the Gaddafi regime. She was continually besieged by correspondence. Some of the letters she received represented political and intellectual conversations, such as a 1971 letter from Idris Cox, a longtime member of the Communist Party of Great Britain and an editor at both *Workers' Weekly* and the *Daily Worker*. In reference to *The Barrel of a Gun*, Cox apologized for not contacting her sooner. He explained that he had to wait for the book to become available at the library, as he could not afford to buy a copy. It is obvious in Ruth's response, that she knew and respected Idris Cox, and she appreciated the letter:

Idris, I'm not sure if I've expressed my appreciation of the trouble you took to write. If it merited that attention from you perhaps it did have something to say after all. As with all the books I've ever tried by the time it's finished I'm no longer satisfied with it. But I've always believed books should raise questions so that one moves on to the next topic; I doubt that I've answered your questions satisfactorily but thank you for asking them. All good wishes to you and your wife.[319]

A letter from André Schiffrin, her publisher in the United States, was congenial as he explained to Ruth that although the book was successful in the UK, the American edition did not sell. Schiffrin concluded that he could not offer her a contract for another African book. Though disappointed, Ruth was too involved in her life and work to dwell on American rejections. Her book *The South African Connection* was launched in 1972, and between 1970 and 1974 she published thirty articles and reviews. Many of the articles corresponded to *The Barrel of a Gun*, some were on apartheid, and three articles linked directly to *The South African Connection*. This book was co-written with journalists Jonathan Steele and Christabel Gurney and was reviewed in a dozen journals. The book described and critically analyzed the symbiotic economic and political relationships between apartheid South Africa and the West. The focus was on South Africa's relationship with Great Britain, but the ties between the United States and South Africa were given substantial treatment. As in *The Barrel of a Gun*, case studies were especially powerful. The stories document foreign government and corporate links to South Africa and presented case studies on supposed corporate reform of apartheid by the Polaroid Corporation in the United States and the Oppenheimer empire in South Africa. The book also included analysis of the relationship of apartheid racism to capitalism:

> Britain and the West profit from apartheid without doubt. This is the indictment which is central to this book: British and Western involvement are by now so deeply grafted into the politics and economics of apartheid that attempts to 'reform' business in its relations with South Africa, while admirable from a moral view, must end in failure. It is not a matter of amputating a leg or an arm from business; the whole body of economic involvement is corrupt.[320]

Ruth First and her co-authors reveal the inadequacy of corporate justifications for working with the apartheid regime—the denial of connections between business and politics, and the contradictory assertion that corporations are slowly helping to end apartheid. The authors refer to the need for armed struggle in the introduction and conclude with what was developing into one of Ruth's essential beliefs: the fundamental necessity of taking the struggle back into the country. "Only when forces inside South Africa, aided, possibly, by favourable international circumstances, effect a change in control of the South African system will Western governments perhaps consider changing sides and trying to join the winning one."[321]

Barbara Harlow, a professor at the University of Texas, confirms that the book anticipated the 1980s sanctions and boycotts against apartheid South Africa. The reviews for the book were for the most part descriptive rather than insightful. There is vision, however, in Gavin Williams's essay "Ruth First: A Socialist and Scholar." Williams, who would play a prominent role in nurturing Ruth's appointment at Durham University, wrote years later that *The South African Connection* portrayed Ruth's position on the nationalism versus socialism debate that existed in the struggle against apartheid. While asserting that the book adopted a mechanistic socialist perspective, he built on Ruth's position:

> Far from undermining apartheid, as some liberal economists argued, capitalism in South Africa depends on it and reinforces it. In turn, this new writing gave rise to a variety of theoretical and historical disputes, between Marxists and liberals and among Marxists themselves. These arguments were already present, in a less complete form, in Ruth's own writings. In the first instance they were used to counter the view that foreign investment, by promoting capitalist development, would contribute to the reform of apartheid. But, like the implications of the analysis of *The South African Connection,* they raise deeper questions about the liberation struggle. Was it sufficient to define it as a struggle for national liberation? If capitalism was the source of the problem, wasn't socialism the obvious solution?[322]

Joe Slovo's writing in the 1970s also had significance, both strategically and as an inspiration for future MK cadres. Besides Central Committee meetings in Eastern Europe and more frequent visits to Africa, Joe made an interesting trip to Moscow in 1971. Presented in Mark Gevisser's book, *Thabo Mbeki: The Dream Deferred*, it is preceded by the author's contention that "the relationship between the two men was fraught by intellectual competition and riven by intellectual mistrust, but at the heart of it was a personality clash."[323] Gevisser continued:

> Slovo told several of his confidants that, while Mbeki was in Moscow, the SACP Central Committee received a complaint about the young man's personal conduct in regard to a woman. Slovo was dispatched to Moscow to discipline Mbeki, a task that was particularly difficult not only because of Mbeki's status but because of their budding mentor-protégé relationship.[324]

Ruth First had always been thought of as the more intellectual of the couple, but now Joe Slovo was viewed as the strategist of the struggle. His role would become even more evident when MK began to send more soldiers back into South Africa after the Soweto uprising in 1976. Pallo Jordan noted: "Ruth, I suppose, had always been the one with the much more intellectual bent although Joe was a thinker himself."[325] In addition to Joe's 1973 article, "Southern Africa: Problems of Armed Struggle," his most important contributions at the time were an article titled "A Critical Appraisal of the Non-Capitalist Path and the National Democratic State in Africa," which appeared in *Marxism Today*, and his most famous essay, "No Middle Road," published in 1976. Concurrently, Jordan conversed with Joe about the issues Slovo was raising in his writing when he and his wife dined at Ruth and Joe's home. "I remember this one exchange that we had; he said to me, 'Are white workers, workers—talking about South Africa?' I responded to him that that's a question you've got to put to African workers. I think that came as a shock to him, but he used it in the 'No Middle Road.'"[326] Ronnie Kasrils contends that the *Marxism Today* article distinguished Joe ideologically from some of his closest SACP comrades. He recalled Yusuf Dadoo being very upset with Joe because he felt the article veered away from the Party line. Jordan said, "You could talk and disagree, and we had differences. Joe was far less rigid about issues than his peers. Some say it was because he was married to Ruth. To some of his comrades a difference was a brawl."[327]

The *Marxism Today* article appealed for additional socialist research on development in Africa and asserted that socialism can only occur through a struggle "led by a revolutionary political vanguard guided by scientific socialism; and that none of these objects can be lastingly achieved without overcoming the dependence on the world capitalist economy."[328] The introduction is followed by a historical discussion of Marx, Engels, and Lenin on whether a socialist revolution might bypass the capitalist stage of development. Although there was some equivocation in the theoretical writings of Lenin, Joe Slovo's analysis suggested that skipping capitalism was possible if certain external and internal elements coalesced—broadly stated, non-capitalist society would need Soviet aid for its indigenous revolutionary cadres. Joe inevitably brought some humor to debate on the term *non-capitalism*, a contradiction in terms to some in the SACP. "The negative nature of the term opens the way for an unending Talmudic-type debate on the categorization of state forms, economic formations, etc. which are, so to say, neither fish nor fowl."[329]

The article goes on to discuss various post-colonial African nations—Sudan, Ghana, Tanzania, Egypt, and Algeria. Much of this section appears to correspond to *The Barrel of a Gun* and other of Ruth's publications. For example, Joe writes:

> The conflicting interests (including external ones) in the developing socioeconomic structure, however difficult they might sometimes be to locate, begin to reflect themselves in the state apparatus. In addition to its administrative role it often becomes a vehicle for the creation of a new privileged social community for whom "the aim of the state becomes (their) private aim, in the form of a race for higher posts, of careerism."[330]

Slovo concludes the article with six components necessary for socialist revolution in Africa. His arguments correspond to Ruth's final arguments in *The Barrel of a Gun*:

> It is only when this conflict is resolved in favour of the working people that a new state will have been won in the struggle. Such a state based on workers' and peasants' power will have the capacity to move towards a socialist order, whatever transitional economic and social strategies the specific conditions would then demand. As yet no such state has been won in Africa.[331]

Reviews of *The Barrel of A Gun* began to appear in scholarly journals and Ruth, after receiving the disappointing news from André Schiffrin's Pantheon Books, accepted an invitation to enter the world of academia. The University of Manchester, where Gillian Slovo was a student, awarded her the Simon Research Fellowship for the 1972–73 academic year. Thus, she was to receive a monthly paycheck to continue her writing. During the year Ruth worked on *Libya: The Elusive Revolution*, which was published in 1974. The book was prescient of the 2011 overturning of the Gaddafi regime.

At Manchester, Ruth First began a collegial/political relationship with Gavin Williams, a South African-born sociologist who was on the faculty of Durham University. Williams had read Ruth's work and gotten to know her at academic conferences and political meetings. He encouraged her to apply for a position in the Sociology Department at

Durham. Ruth was initially reticent, as she did not have a PhD. The head of the department, Phillip Abrams, however, was very positive about Ruth's candidacy for the position. Williams wrote a recommendation as did Thomas Hodgkin, Ronald Segal, Sir Robert Birley, Peter Worsley, and a number of Manchester professors. Williams's letter of support read:

> Last term she gave a lecture at Durham on the military in underdeveloped countries which in my view was a model of clarity of exposition of complex and unfamiliar material to my undergraduates. Tony Barnett prescribed *The Barrel of a Gun* as one of the key books in the course on sociology of developing societies, which is of course the one we would be wanting her to teach if she were appointed.[332]

Ruth was appointed to the position and was on the faculty at Durham University from 1973 to 1978. She taught numerous courses, including the Sociology of Developing Societies, during her first year. The syllabus was rather typical of the new orthodoxy and relied heavily upon "dependency theory." Ruth's course notes include analysis of the writings of Gunnar Myrdal, Max Weber, Karl Marx, and Erving Goffman. According to Williams, her experiences as an activist and journalist brought richness to the course:

> Ruth did not engage with the dialectical controversies of the 1970s, when intellectuals were concerned to elaborate definitive versions of Marxist theories. Ruth made use of, and at Durham University, taught theories of development and underdevelopment not for their own sakes but to explain historical events and institutional structures.[333]

During her second year at Durham, Ruth helped develop a team-taught course on Sociology of Industrial Development. Students studied industrialization during their second year and development in the third year. Ruth was primarily responsible for the development section. She also taught Political Sociology, Third World Social Movements, and Sociology of Gender. The Sociology of Gender course is notable in that Ruth has been credited with pioneering the subject, as part of a shift to feminist scholarship. The most noticeable sign of that shift came a short time thereafter in her work with Ann

Scott on a biography of nineteenth-century writer Olive Schreiner. The gender course took the form of a student-initiated seminar, with Ruth as instructor. She also introduced the "women's question" in her political sociology course, believing that the subject nurtured more involvement from female students.

Similar to the responses to *The Barrel of a Gun* and *The South African Connection*, there were multiple reviews of *Libya: The Elusive Revolution*. In it, Ruth describes and analyzes tribal and colonial history, Cold War "independence," the 1969 revolution, and finally the Gaddafi regime. She describes his ambition, his condemnations of both the West and the Soviet Union, and his changing positions on the United States. She also draws parallels to the countries she wrote about in *The Barrel of a Gun*. Finally, Ruth concludes that the Libyan revolution:

> is characteristic of this style of statist, technocratic planning. The state is actively to intervene in production, and to dominate it. Planning and execution are to be the responsibility of technicians and experts. The masses of people are to be beneficiaries of an authoritarian paternalism; there is to be no participation or mobilization from below.[334]

The reviews criticized the lack of depth in her understanding of the importance of Libyan tribal history, but she was also praised for writing a readable analysis for generalists. Warren Clark, later Ronald Reagan's appointment as ambassador to Gabon, believed that her Marxism affected her analyses; whereas Charles Bertrand argued that the book did not address issues of class. In retrospect, the book's relevance for contemporary affairs in Libya is remarkable.

Ruth First was a well-prepared and dedicated teacher. She never promoted herself as a fashionable academic. Gavin Williams related this characteristic to her intensity and formidable work ethic:

> She certainly never had a sort of fan club in a way that some star academics do. You know a group of people who associate themselves very closely with an academic star. It was a very small department. I think she was too acerbic for that to be feasible. But also it wasn't her style. She was getting on with things—doing things. She had no interest in having that sort of set of followers. It just didn't fit.[335]

However, she did have a powerful effect on some students, both formal university students and others she mentored just as she had done during her time at *The Guardian*. She was able to hire some of her students from England when she left Durham to work at Eduardo Mondlane University in Maputo. Included in that group were Judith Head, who was subsequently a member of the Sociology Department at the University of Cape Town, and Chris Gerry, who taught at the University College of Swansea. Gerry recalled being Ruth's student at Durham:

> As a young research student, I was introduced to her at Durham University and she played a very important role in sorting out some of the inevitable clumsiness and errors in the first academic article I submitted for publication. The legacy Ruth leaves in the university and outside is bigger than the sum of all its parts—bigger than Ruth herself, because she caused so much to develop in others and demanded as much from those around her as she did from herself.[336]

Head worked with both Ruth and Gavin at Durham and she had vivid memories of being Ruth's student:

> She was a very intelligent woman, an amazing woman. Very, very penetrating eyes and you could see her marvelous intellect shine through her eyes. I was a bit scared of her. She was a bit intimidating, or at least I found her intimidating and I'm quite a bold person. She was a great supervisor. She didn't interfere but she gave feedback on stuff you had done and advised you. She would give me very sharp, very condensed paragraphs full of very useful advice. And terse little comments in the margins and so on.[337]

Judith would go to Ruth and Joe's home in London for meetings and her memories speak to the hectic nature of Ruth's life:

> Camden Town was a mixture. Part of it was very working-class immigrant and part of it was not really posh but middle class. But it was a lovely place to be because it was this mixed community. It was a lovely house. We were having a meeting there one afternoon and I can remember it very well because she

gave me, and it was the first time I ever had it, an Italian liquor called Amaretto Sorrento, an almond liquor. What I remember most about that meeting was that her phone didn't stop ringing and it was irritating because you'd be sitting there and she'd have to leave the room and have these lengthy conversations. I just thought it must be ghastly to be her daughter because how do you ever get a moment with her. It was much easier in Durham, actually.[338]

Ruth cultivated some close relationships with other women in London. In the 1960s, she became close to the younger Ros de Lanerolle who worked with Ronald Segal at Penguin Books. They were friends for twenty years and de Lanerolle's memories include the personal and political. She remembers kindness as Ruth and Joe stayed with her on a New Year's Eve after her husband had told the children that he was leaving the family. She was an editor on Ruth's books and collaborated with her to launch a news features clipping agency, South Africa and Its Features. She commented on Ruth making a personal commitment to women's rights, especially black women:

> Many, many African women spoke about sister Ruth with great love and affection. And I think in the study classes which she led, particularly with African women or women with working-class backgrounds, a much less academic, much less competitive, a less hard analytical side of Ruth would come out. And this would be seen very much to support her role of empowerment. She saw the importance of empowering women in the women's section of the ANC. Not simply through academics, but she certainly paid a lot of attention to helping black women in particular to empower themselves, to gain confidence, to ask hard questions, to deal with the questions they were maybe timid about raising in public.[339]

Ros de Lanerolle shared stories of Ruth organizing social time for them together, even when Ruth was only in London for weekends during her appointment at Durham. They talked a great deal about their children and Ruth's worries. Ruth was especially critical of Robyn's boyfriends. And it must be said that Robyn presented a challenge for her parents. It appears that Ruth was the one who dealt with family issues. Robyn later commented: "Ruth felt she should do

something about me. She didn't understand that she couldn't participate in making me better. She kept feeling she needed to do more."[340]

As noted by other friends, de Lanerolle witnessed the battles
between Ruth and Joe. Ruth was very private in terms of her marriage—she did not talk about Joe. Gavin Williams also remembered
Ruth being "discreet and private" about her life. They talked academics and politics. But like many other people who knew Ruth and Joe
well, Williams was present during one of their infamous arguments.
It was during a weekend when Joe visited Ruth in Durham. The
couple took a road trip to the coast with Williams and his wife, Gill,
to visit *Review of African Political Economy* colleague Chris Allen and
his wife, Frances. On Sunday, Joe had to catch a train back to London
from Newcastle. Gavin Williams recalled the afternoon:

> So we drive back and it is wet and Joe's insistent that he's got
> to get the train back from Newcastle to London. So I'm driving
> quite fast in a car with wet wheels and this is not a pleasant
> thing to do. Gill is in front and Joe and Ruth are going hammer
> and tongs at the back and it is about Portugal. And it's about
> the relation between the Party and liberation movement. And
> Joe was very close to that as a loyalist. On the one hand you
> could say this is a political argument, there's more edge to it
> than that. I was driving the car so I didn't see the looks on their
> faces, but it was pretty aggressive. So I think it was personal
> as well as political.[341]

Ros de Lanerolle said that Joe assumed the domestic slack when
Ruth was teaching in Durham—odd, because Shawn, Gillian, and
Robyn were young adults then. Ruth's brother Ronald, and the couple's
friends, Myrtle Berman, Hillary Hamburger, and Denis Kuny, viewed
Joe as the housekeeper in the early 1970s, just as they did when they
visited London while Ruth was doing research in Africa. Whatever
his domestic responsibilities, Joe continued writing, traveling back
and forth to the Soviet Union, and moving toward his journey back
to Africa. In 1975, while in the company of other SACP and ANC
leaders, Joe visited the Soviet Union to honor Moses Kotane's seventieth birthday. As Kotane's prognosis was poor, this was something
of a sad celebration. The SACP-ANC delegation also met with Soviet
emissaries during this August visit and discussion topics included
black consciousness, South African government military involvement

in Angola, and the possibilities of MK invading South Africa. All of the issues discussed would soon be central to Joe's life.

Joe's clandestine work in London was peaking. South African comrades David Rabkin and Ray Suttner made contact with Joe and his London Goodge Street comrades and were sent back to South Africa to continue the propaganda campaign. One of the books they read, as preparation, was *117 Days*. Unfortunately, they were among the people who were betrayed by struggle traitors resulting in their imprisonment in South Africa. There was also a betrayal in London when a small group within the ANC again challenged having whites as part of the struggle. They became known as the "Gang of Eight," and were ousted from the ANC. The Western and South African press used the upheaval to renew the "issue" of communism leading the struggle against apartheid. Joe had a strong voice at Morogoro and wrote the SACP's official condemnation of the Gang of Eight. In the document, "The Enemy Hidden under the Same Colour," Joe condemns the South African regime and press for citing the traitors' charges as fact in propaganda against the struggle. In addition, he meticulously rebuts each of the Gang of Eight's accusations. "The Enemy Hidden under the Same Colour" introduces the document as the SACP's statement "on the racist and anti-communist activities of the group of eight."[342] Joe concludes the report:

> And now the wedge-drivers who had been working behind closed doors against the whole liberation movement and its policies have come out into the open. They are part of the impure load which every revolution carries and when that load is thrown aside the journey to victory is always a swifter one.[343]

Not surprisingly, Joe was one of the targets of the South African regime and press. But because Joe was then so busy and so directed and committed, there was just too much hope, too many possibilities, and too much to accomplish to compromise his time responding to their criticisms.

In 1974, while on the faculty at Durham University, Ruth became involved with colleagues in launching the academic and political journal, *Review of African Political Economy (ROAPE)*. Gavin Williams was the editor, and the founders included progressive academics— John Saul, Peter Lawrence, Robin Cohen, Chris Allen, Lionel Cliffe, and Ruth First. The journal was dedicated to the progressive analysis of class and politics in Africa. Ruth reviewed articles, planned special issues of the journal, and wrote pieces for it. In 1975 she co-edited a special issue with Gavin Williams on "Classes in Africa." In the intro-duction, Ruth and Williams critiqued post-colonial African politicians and Western academics who disavowed the reality of class society. At the same time, they argued against crass Marxist scholars for refusing to accept specific on-the-ground African realities. Citing Marx, they asserted, "It is essential to consider social classes in a specific society or social formation at a distinct juncture in time."[344]

Integrated as a member of Britain's academic world in the mid-1970s, Ruth never exited the world of progressive politics. She attended African National Congress meetings and those of the Anti-Apartheid Movement, encouraging young socialists who did not necessarily follow the ANC or the SACP party lines to become involved in the movement. At meetings, she did not hesitate to engage in radical and controversial debate. For example, Gavin Williams recalls a meeting of the Anti-Apartheid Movement where she was attacked after criticizing the movement's support of the Zimbabwe African People's Union (ZAPU) in Rhodesia:

I sat next to Ruth, on her right-hand side, at the meeting. Thabo Mbeki then came up to sit on my right-hand side. He had no love for me. His purpose was presumably to keep an eye on Ruth. Afterwards, at her house over drinks, she said that Thabo was the sort of person who, come the revolution, would put you up against a wall and shoot you.[345]

Williams also remembers Ruth complaining about the South African academic mafia during a meeting of the British Sociological Association. He quickly reminded her that she was also a member. Most important, however, as both an academic and a revolutionary Ruth First supported challenging commonplaces, especially those of her own political camp. Rica Hodgson recalled attending a meeting with Ruth of ANC women in London:

Ruth was not one of the speakers that day. She was on the floor. The chairperson said: "In the Soviet Union 75 percent of the doctors are women." Everybody cheered and clapped, you see. Ruth said: "Excuse me, Madam Chair, have you ever seen a woman up in the presidium with all those double-breasted suits?" She wasn't letting them get away with anything.[346]

Ruth continually questioned why she personally, and the ANC institutionally, were not doing more to return home and continue the struggle. She took a leave of absence from Durham in 1975, spending one semester on the faculty of the University of Dar es Salaam, at the time one of the most vibrant institutions of higher education on the African continent. Phillip Abrams worked on the logistics of the exchange, and though he questioned whether it was timely for Ruth academically, he was certain that it was important for Durham to establish relationships with universities in Africa. It also appears that he knew it was critical for Ruth, personally and politically. Although she spent only a semester in Dar es Salaam, her tenure there coincided with lectures and teaching by Walter Rodney, Terence Ranger, Mahmood Mamdani, Archie Mafeje, Jacques Depelchin, and John Saul. Ruth was excited by the conversations and debates with colleagues, but was also taken aback at how vicious some of the debates became. She wrote to Joe on one occasion after an academic seminar, "But even my stony heart was moved by Ranger's plight."[347]

Ruth stayed at the Kunduchi Beach Hotel during her time in Tanzania. Upon arrival, the department chair informed her that she would teach the course he was teaching. She had the weekend to prepare. Ruth was elated to be back on African soil. She wrote to Gavin Williams, telling him how exciting it was to be teaching about issues that were directly relevant to her African students. Thus, despite a great lack of supplies, the ambush by the department chair, and colleagues from the German Democratic Republic with whom Ruth never got along, she was thrilled and determined to teach and interact with students. She taught second-term economics and the syllabus topics included theories of underdevelopment, strategies of development, industrialization, rural development, rural cooperation in Tanzania, and class and development. Ruth's notes capture the essence of the course. Especially instructive is her concern for student feedback:

Hope you'll speak up, even dissatisfaction, complaints. Lectures pack too much? Too thin? Coming over too fast? . . . Interruptions (questions) during lectures? You must judge. Break continuity—danger. Throw me off my balance? On the other hand sometimes helpful to ask for clarification. And if I can't give it at the time I promise to go away and think about it for the following time. As for seminars, these are to be "working sessions," she emphasizes to the students. YOU to do the work.[348]

Ruth was excited about her students throughout her semester in Tanzania and shared this with Joe. She was pleased that the university appeared to be serious about enrolling older students: "I'm amazed at the level of my students, though I'm sure there are duds and conservatives among them too. . . . From the looks of it numbers of older people, experienced people have got in, and their commitment is very earnest, even if only for careers."[349] She questioned students who were motivated by "fixed ideological positions," and wondered out loud whether they were going to use their university credentials to become bureaucrats above other callings. Yet she was aware that there was diversity amongst her Tanzanian students and she shared this perspective with Joe:

My course hit a few good high spots—and some low—but they're hipped to the analysis of under-development, and it's really intriguing how they react when they have to apply their method to Tanzania. This is when the divide comes. The radicals persevere with the analysis; the nationalists take refuge in statements about exceptions. Or something even less tangible.[350]

At the end of the semester Ruth returned to England and her position at Durham knowing full well that it would only be a short time before she went back to Africa, which she believed was her academic and political home. In England she divided her time between London and Durham, continuing her heightened pace of writing, public speeches, and lecturing. Appearing on the BBC World Service whenever the topic was Africa, she was interviewed about Mozambique, Egypt, and Libya, and at one point confronted administrators at the network concerning the ideological tone of some of her interviewers. Finally, she interacted with colleagues and students at Durham, worked studiously on the *Review of African Political Economy* as well as her book on Olive Schreiner.

One of the major turning points in the struggle against the apartheid regime—the Soweto Uprising—began on June 16, 1976. Students in Soweto Township gathered for a march to Orlando

Stadium to protest the inequalities of Bantu education in general, and more directly, the imposition of Afrikaans as the language of instruction in black schools. The protest entailed a great deal of planning. The black consciousness movement was gaining traction in the country for high school and university students through the leadership of Steve Biko. Just as it did during the Sharpeville Massacre in 1960, the government overreacted, shooting into crowds of fleeing students and killing over one hundred people. The photograph of the limp-body of Hector Pieterson, a thirteen-year-old student, being carried through the crowd was published throughout the world, visually exemplifying the horrors of apartheid to everyone in the universe. Soweto became the spark for young South Africans; following it, large numbers of young people made the choice to join the struggle. For Ruth First and Joe Slovo, the aftermath of the senseless and shameless massacre, at the very least, magnified their quest to take the struggle back home.

While Ruth was investigating ways to return to the continent, Joe's departure was inevitable: scores of youth were moving to Zambia and Angola to join Umkhonto we Sizwe. Joe's 104-page essay "No Middle Road" had been published in a book, *South Africa: The New Politics of Revolution*, and clandestine copies were being smuggled into South Africa as pamphlets under pseudo-titles. Companion pieces to "No Middle Road" were "The Politics of Armed Struggle: National Liberation in the African Colonies of Portugal" by Basil Davidson and Anthony Wilkinson's "From Rhodesia to Zimbabwe." Joe built on the SACP's conceptualization of colonialism of a special type/internal colonialism to emphasize the need for a political-military revolution that combines issues of class and race. He underscored the necessity of armed revolution on South African soil because the government was making any type of negotiation or liberal reform impossible through its oppression and violence toward the South African people:

> But the new society in South Africa will only come through a successful revolutionary assault by the deprived, in which increasing armed confrontation is unavoidable. To counsel otherwise is in fact to counsel submission. . . . There is no other path to the winning of majority rule over the whole of South Africa, for the simple reason that all other routes are permanently barred.[351]

Joe Slovo analyzed revolutions and guerilla warfare in Africa and throughout the world. He illustrated that he had studied both theory and practice, and had learned from elders such as Oliver Tambo, as well as younger people, specifically Pallo Jordan, with whom he discussed the essay at length prior to its publication. Near the end of the essay, Joe linked workers and students in the country to the revolution:

> The current resurgence of black political militancy within the country, particularly amongst the workers and youth, is primarily a response to a whole set of changing objective factors, including (in the case of the workers) the growing gap between wages and prices. But the revolutionary tradition perpetuated by the liberation movement's actions not only played a part in this resurgence but serves to inform it with more radical aims.[352]

Many responses were elicited from Joe's essay, with citations in *The African Communist* in the 1990s and in the first decade of the twenty-first century. The only academic review on the entire book, written by Patrick Wall who was a member of the House of Commons, appeared in *African Affairs*, the house journal of the Royal African Society. Although Wall chastised the authors for ignoring the role of southern Africa in world politics, he referred to the book as essential reading. He made sure that his readers understood that Joe and Ruth, even though Ruth did not have an essay in the book, were communists, but he then praised the history presented in Joe's essay.

Joe had little concern for academic reviews when he wrote "No Middle Road." If there was a goal for the essay, it was to facilitate an acceleration of on-the-ground struggle in South Africa. Though it would be an overstatement to designate "No Middle Road" as the blueprint for armed struggle, the essay provides a theory-praxis foundation. Joe's words echoed Ruth's continual criticism of herself and the struggle in exile—why are we not taking the struggle home?

8 — Academics and Revolution:
Taking the Struggle Home

"THERE WAS JUBILATION everywhere, especially in the camps in Angola. Joe Slovo said afterwards that he couldn't sleep that whole night. He stood on the balcony of his flat in Maputo, hoping to see the explosion."[353] Joe's elation came June 1, 1980, after Umkhonto we Sizwe's successful attack on the SASOL oil refinery in South Africa. Early in 1977, Joe returned to Africa to help lead the mission to take the struggle home to South Africa. He lived in Luanda, then Maputo, and finally Lusaka, Zambia's capital, which had become the base of the ANC in exile by the 1980s. Later in 1977 Ruth moved back to the continent, landing in Maputo. Holding various titles within the struggle between 1977 and the end of exile in 1990, Joe's initial role was co-director of Umkhonto we Sizwe with Joe Modise. Ruth's was to do research, which culminated in her posthumous book, *Black Gold: The Mozambican Miner, Proletarian and Peasant.*

Joe spent 1977 traveling between the United Kingdom, Angola, Tanzania, Mozambique, the German Democratic Republic and the Soviet Union. He made one trip to Cuba. Ben Turok recalled that "he was all over the place, always on the trot."[354] Teaching at Durham University when Soweto exploded, Ruth began to plan her journey back to Africa. Even though she had begun her collaboration with Ann Scott on the Olive Schreiner book and had commitments to her graduate students, and still felt great responsibilities toward her daughters, albeit now young adults, she knew that her place was in southern Africa.

Because of her prior research, journalism, and activism, Ruth was very close, as was Joe, to the new leadership in Angola and Mozambique. At the invitation of Aquino de Bragança, a Goan journalist who was an advocate and freedom fighter for the Portuguese colonies, Ruth visited the newly liberated Mozambique just after her 1975 semester at the University of Dar es Salaam. In March 1976 she wrote to de Bragança: "Beside a revolution, doing a teaching job is mediocre stuff."[355] He had published articles by Ruth in *Afrique-Asie* and he responded with an invitation to come to work on a research project at the Center of African Studies. Ruth arrived in Maputo in 1977 to direct a study on black miners, and she returned the following year, taking an appointment as Assistant Director and Director of Research at the Center of African Studies. Although it took her another five years to formally resign from Durham, she was firmly placed in Mozambique from 1977 onward.

After the Soweto uprising, one of the ANC's slogans was "Don't Mourn, Mobilize." Joe Slovo and Joe Modise were chosen by Oliver Tambo to lead the combined military/political struggle. High school as well as university students began leaving the country en masse after the Soweto Uprising, with hundreds ending up in Luanda. They were afire with the hope of being armed by the ANC to take the struggle back to South Africa. In the years that followed, Joe's primary base was Luanda, the capital of Angola. Still experiencing counterrevolutionary incursions, the prime minister, Lopo de Nacimiento, announced, "Angola was going to be the base for Marxism-Leninism in Africa."[356] He welcomed the ANC as well as other liberation groups into his homeland. Luanda was a city that the Portuguese had attempted to destroy as they fled when colonialism ended. Ronnie Kasrils described the accommodations in *Armed and Dangerous*: "The ANC residence was a mixture of seaside boarding-house, back-street garage and military encampment. Our house was a moderate size, double-story building with a palm tree dominating a small front garden and a couple of tents and a vegetable patch in the back."[357] Pallo Jordan, who was then the ANC director of communication, arrived in Luanda approximately at the same time as Joe. He is much less generous than Kasrils in his description of the ANC residence:

When I arrived there it didn't seem like they had a firm grip on things. One of the things that was really bothersome in the premises that we were using was an infestation of flies that was intolerable. I couldn't understand why people were putting up with it, for God's sake. We were human beings; we can't be dominated by flies. But it was a function of the fact that the municipal government did not have a firm grip on things. One of the big problems was an alleyway that was filled with garbage, and of course that's where they were breeding. And then in our own premises we kept the garbage cans next to the kitchen door, which of course is not a clever thing to do. You should put things like that some distance from you. Those were the things one did. That first week I was there we moved the garbage away and set the garbage in the alleyway on fire. It was rather amusing, because it wasn't as if you were working with people who didn't know. You were always coping with that sort of thing. No water pressure because the Portuguese ruined the pipes before they left.[358]

Ruth visited Joe at his new Luanda home on her journey to Maputo, and she too described the surroundings, including exotic plants where Joe lived with Sowetan generation students "all glowing with rebelling," and he "misses his telly, hot baths and other London luxuries but is looking happy enough and is too busy to notice much else."[359]

Besides multiple trips to Maputo to see Ruth, Joe was often on official business in Moscow, Berlin, London, or Dar es Salaam—or meeting with ANC, SACP, GDR, and USSR comrades in Luanda. Teaching, organizing, and strategizing the armed struggle with new young recruits was the other aspect of his work in Luanda and various MK camps throughout Angola. This is to say nothing of the fact that it was Joe, in collaboration with Cassius Maake, who actually opened the Luanda ANC office in April 1977. In the Soviet Union, Oliver Tambo reintroduced Joe to Soviet leaders as a member of the Revolutionary Council and the new Deputy Chief of Operations. It was at this meeting that Joe spoke of the time as favorable for armed struggle within South Africa. While in the Soviet Union, Joe also continued to participate in the teaching of South African cadres who were undergoing military training and consulted with Soviet contacts for even greater aid. In his Umkhonto we Sizwe memoir, James Ngculu quotes a July 1977 letter from Yusuf Dadoo to the Soviet

Union asking for fake passports and other forged documents. He begins the letter: "We request for you to forward the following items to Luanda as per agreement for delivery made by Comrade Joe Slovo with Comrade Makarov."[360]

In April, the same month in which he opened the Luanda office, Joe traveled to the German Democratic Republic for a meeting of the SACP Central Committee. Here the Party adopted a document titled "The Way Forward from Soweto," which reemphasized the necessity of systematic and planned armed struggle within South Africa. In addition, the SACP voted to name a Politburo that included not only Joe Slovo, but Moses Kotane, Yusuf Dadoo, Moses Mabhida, and Thabo Mbeki. In his own book, *Slovo: The Unfinished Biography*, Joe describes being part of a delegation headed by Oliver Tambo that visited Cuba that same year. He writes of meeting Fidel Castro, but there is no thick description regarding the trip.

An important NEC meeting in Luanda convened to address individual armed incursions into South Africa by sometimes renegade, but often just impatient, Soweto-generation cadres. This meeting took place prior to the September 1977 murder of black consciousness (BC) leader Steve Biko by the South African security police. Mention of Biko is significant because many of the young people who were leaving South Africa to join MK were devotees of, or at least greatly influenced by, the black consciousness movement. In the years preceding Soweto, and even in its aftermath, the ANC was critical of BC as a diversionary movement. Joe and Ruth counseled the organization to be cautious, positively noting that it was young BC supporters who were infected with the revolutionary "spark." Rusty Bernstein recalled that Ruth sensed the coming of BC long before other friends, including himself and his wife, Hilda. Indeed, it was Joe's essay "No Middle Ground" that served as the "spark" for many of the new cadres. James Ngculu, Terrence Tryon, Mohammad Timol, and Keith Mokoape, MK veterans who worked with Joe in Maputo and Lusaka in the 1980s, all gave credit to the essay as having great influence on their joining MK after the Soweto Uprising. Mokoape noted Joe's sensitivity to young BC cadres' initial skepticism of the ANC and remembered taking "guidance from Joe" when he left South Africa. Pallo Jordan and Albie Sachs suggest it was Joe's influence that brought BC to MK. Jordan mentioned that the essay "would have an electrifying effect on young black South Africans who would soon become part of the struggle against apartheid."[361] Sachs has detailed memories of Joe's position, influence, and even humor regarding black consciousness:

After '76 and the Soweto Uprising and the emergence of black consciousness there were many black leaders in the ANC who said we don't like this black consciousness, and saw it as a threat to revolutionary consciousness. Joe was the one who said it's fantastic—they're expressing their revolutionary consciousness through black consciousness, and they're going to give enormous energy and strength to the armed struggle. So here was the paradox of the white person in the movement embracing black consciousness and blacks in the movement seeing themselves as old-time, non-racial, socialists.[362]

Joe's writing, his view of black consciousness, and his general humanity had a great impact on the new MK recruits. This is apparent in his work with cadres in the camps throughout the years of the armed struggle.

Though the ANC had moved its offices to Lusaka, Joe often frequented Tanzania for meetings despite the fact that he had not been welcome there since leaving South Africa in the early 1960s. Ben Turok hosted him on at least one occasion. This was an interesting scenario as the two men were clearly not fond of each other. Turok recalls that they argued about Joe's carelessness. There were dinners with Pam and Marcelino dos Santos, who later became friends with Joe and Ruth in Maputo. Marcelino would emerge as Samora Machel's vice president in Mozambique. Pam, though much younger than Ruth and Joe, was a South African who left the country in the 1960s. In Tanzania, Joe would usually stay in the home of Dan O'Meara, the nephew of his early mentor, and Linzi Manicom, O'Meara's partner at the time. Dan and Linzi were members of the African National Congress. He was teaching at the University of Dar es Salaam, and Linzi was working for the ANC. Dan and Linzi's memories of Joe visiting in Dar es Salaam highlight Joe Slovo's humanity. In fact, Dan remembers that it was Joe who came to Linzi's and his defense when a faction in Tanzania wanted them removed from the ANC:

People tried to have us kicked out of the ANC because we were depicted as being anti-CP. Joe didn't mind as long as we didn't attack the SACP directly. He wouldn't allow that in public.

But in private, he and I had this amazing conversation one day when he said, "What are your problems with the SACP?" And I said very frankly, "Here they are,'" and he said to me, "You know, you're probably right but I've just been in it too long and I am going to stay until the death and try to change it." And I absolutely respected this. This was a man who joined the Party in the 1930s. But he could have a conversation. He didn't feel personally attacked. He was clear in his own ideas and he was open to changing them.[363]

Manicom and O'Meara recalled the Joe Slovo they first came to know in 1977 in Tanzania. Linzi wrote of "late nights around the dinner table, talking, joking, debating, with bottles of Konyagi and Dodoma wine to take care of the tropical thirst."[364] Dan spoke in depth of Joe's humanity:

Joe was depicted as the rabid Stalinist. Joe was the only person in the SACP leadership who would read the stuff that these white intellectual Marxists were writing in London. Some of whom were fairly strong critics of the ANC and the SACP. He would read it. He would take it very seriously. He wouldn't regard them as enemies. He wouldn't denounce them as enemies. He would engage with them. All the other members of the SACP leadership were busy denouncing people left, right, and center. He was really interested in what the academic left people were producing. And I think there Ruth had an impact on him. The thing about Joe, unlike most other South African communists, Joe had the best sense of humor of any human being I have ever met. Here he is the man who is essentially the key person of the SACP and he's telling these anti-Soviet jokes. He sort of put all my stereotypes into question. So Joe had this wonderful sense of humor and he could laugh at himself. He had this wonderful human touch. Everybody loved Joe. He was a mensch and everybody knew him as a mensch.[365]

Travel consumed much of his time, but Joe's main role, beginning in 1977, was working with Joe Modise to organize training and planning for military incursions into South Africa. This work gained much more urgency in 1978 and the years that followed. However, Dan O'Meara and others remarked that no matter what the safeguards Joe and his compatriots in leadership positions enacted to control renegade acts, the South African regime, as in the 1960s, continued to demonize Joe Slovo and Ruth First. In December, after an unauthorized attack by Soweto-generation exiles at the Carlton Centre in downtown Johannesburg, the right-wing journalist Aida Parker wrote in *The Citizen*:

> The police remain convinced that the masterminds behind the new onslaught are former Johannesburg attorney Joe Slovo and his authoress wife, who writes under the name of Ruth First. Slovo, the ANC's chief guerrilla tactician, is based at the ANC's Luanda terrorist camp. His wife is supposedly working at Maputo University. Both named communists, they are readily acceptable to the Marxist governments in Luanda and Maputo.[366]

Living between Durham and London at the beginning of 1977, Ruth's immediate work and life was ever demanding. She was in the midst of her project with Ann Scott and consulting for a United Nations ad hoc committee convened by E. S. Reddy to document human rights violations in South Africa, Namibia, and Zimbabwe. Ruth expounded on the treatment of black women under the apartheid regime. At the same time, she was diligent in her role as an editorial board member for the *Review of African Political Economy* and would become involved, somewhat controversially, in an article that appeared early in 1978.

After correspondence with Aquino de Bragança earlier in the year they decided that Ruth would move to Maputo to work at the Center. Ruth clearly wanted to be in southern Africa, but she initially only committed for one year. She still struggled with leaving her daughters. De Bragança was nicknamed "The Submarine" because he seemed to instigate action in the Mozambican revolution while submerged just below the surface. He met FRELIMO leaders in 1961 while representing the Goan People's Party at a meeting of Portuguese colonial liberation fighters. Then, just after Mozambican independence, he founded the Center of African Studies at Eduardo Mondlane University in Maputo. Aquino's concept for the Center was similar to the institution of the same name that existed in Lisbon: a "hearth for the development of nationalist thought in the 1940s and 1950s, Frelimo leadership wanted the CEA to exist once again, this time located within independent Mozambique and with a new focus on the liberation of Southern Africa."[367] Aquino envisioned the Center as a place where the best minds would congregate, think, talk, and write while concurrently supporting Frelimo and the new Mozambique. He also knew that Ruth First, who he sometimes said "worked like a locomotive," would be an exceptional partner in the Center. She would help turn ideas into action.

Ruth traveled from London to Maputo with an initial mandate to study Mozambican mine workers in South Africa. When she arrived, Maputo was a city that had suffered a great deal of damage from the Portuguese colonialists before they exited the country. Ruth stayed with her good friends Moira and Zé Forjaz. Moira had helped Tilly care for Shawn, Gillian, and Robyn in 1963 when Ruth was in prison. Ruth had other friends in Maputo, Pam dos Santos and Albie Sachs, and through Pam's connections she subsequently rented a two-bedroom flat on Julius Nyerere Street, overlooking the Indian Ocean. The project that de Bragança had brought her to work on that year was in many ways a demonstration of the collective research that Ruth would facilitate in the years that followed at CEA. Aquino had assembled a staff of history graduates, and although the composition of the Center would change greatly in 1978, Ruth's 1977 research group included Aquino's staff as well as a number of expatriates who were on the faculty of the university—specifically Marc Wuyts, who taught in the Economics Department; the historian Alpheus Manghezi; and David Wield, who was in Engineering. In total there were fourteen researchers supervised by Ruth and Wuyts. The study consisted of surveys and fieldwork. Fernando Ganhão, the Rector of Eduardo Mondlane University, gave Ruth only seven months to complete the project.

The 1977 CEA study was published after Ruth's death as *Black Gold*. In 1978 it became the theoretical, methodological, and substantive model for Center studies. The CEA librarian Colin Darch's participation in the project illustrates the collective nature of work at the Center of African Studies. Research from the study had been presented at a 1978 conference in Zambia, and the report was printed in Portuguese. Ruth wanted the study published in English. However, she believed the report required further work, and she assigned Darch to write a chronology and a section on health and safety in the mines. When he explained that he knew nothing about mines, Ruth replied, "Well now is your chance to learn."[368]

In Maputo that year Ruth spent time with Moira Forjaz, colleagues from the Center, and had visitors, including, of course, Joe, who often came to Mozambique. Zé Forjaz recalls that Ruth was in their house almost daily during her years in Maputo. They considered her family. There were also trips back to London to visit her daughters, as well as her parents and friends. In fact, she returned to London just a month after moving to Maputo to celebrate Ronald Segal's fiftieth birthday. She would often eat lunch at Moira and Zé's spacious house in the city, and she and Moira would occasionally have drinks on the veranda at the famous Polanna Hotel looking out at the sea. Pam dos Santos recalls having tea with Ruth at Club Navale, a place where Ruth, and then later Joe, had their daily swim. There was also a celebration with friends at a local tavern for Joe's fifty-first birthday. Ruth took time for small gestures of friendship; she was always thoughtful, remembering people—whether bringing clothing back to Maputo from London for colleagues' children or bringing African artifacts to London from Mozambique for friends in the United Kingdom. She wrote to Jack Simons when his daughters were being harassed by the apartheid regime, and he responded:

> It was good to receive your card and to learn your concern about Mary and Tanya. Thank you—you are one of the very few comrades who have done so—some comrades might think that to express concern and sympathy with other comrades is petty-bourgeois—how else can one explain their behavior.[369]

In 1977 Ruth hosted Walter and Albertina Sisulu's daughter Lindi, who had just been released from prison in South Africa. She asserted that Ruth's prison experience made staying with Ruth "the best thing for me at the time,"[370] adding, "Ruth knew exactly how to treat me. She never overfussed, but at the same time she was empathetic."[371] Ruth was comfortable, confident, and happy in Maputo. Living again in southern Africa, doing work that was valued politically, was akin to coming home, or at least almost home, for Ruth First.

The previously noted controversial incident at the *Review of African Political Economy* (ROAPE) occurred in late 1977. Unity Movement member Archie Mafeje had submitted an article on the Soweto Uprising, "Soweto and Its Aftermath," to the journal. Mafeje was a lecturer at the University of Dar es Salaam in 1975 when Ruth taught at the university, and later taught at the Institute for Social Studies at The Hague, the University of Cairo, and the Council for the Development of Social Research in Africa in Dakar. When Mafeje's article was accepted for publication, Ruth demanded that she be allowed to write a rejoinder in the same issue. Having an editorial board member critique an article in a journal issue is rare in academia. In fact, it amounts to an intellectual ambush. In retrospect, Ruth's friend and editor of the journal, Gavin Williams, agreed with that assessment. Ruth, however, was demanding and had an influential voice on the board. Peter Lawrence, who has spent much of his academic career at the University of Keele, and was a member of the ROAPE editorial board, recalled that Ruth pushed hard for her positions. Specifically, she wrote "After Soweto: A Response," in which she chastised Mafeje's essentialism, his view of class and race consciousness, his criticisms of the ANC and SACP, and most forcefully, his Unity Movement Puritanism, referring to the group as "armchair politicians." Joe felt antagonistic toward the Unity Movement, and it might be that it was impossible for Ruth, when some in the SACP were questioning her Party allegiance, to allow the journal to publish an article that she perceived to be anti-ANC and clearly anti-SACP.

Ruth and Aquino were now strategizing about her work at the Center of African Studies for 1978. She informed Durham University that she would not return to her position the following year, but Gavin Williams, and even the department chair Philip Abrams, knew that Ruth would never return to Durham. Joining Aquino, she laid plans to expand the staff and begin courses and research for and with FRELIMO administrators and workers. Aquino and Ruth were ideal partners. Ruth was detailed, theoretical, and political. In addition, she could facilitate the success of programs at the Center. She referred to Aquino as not unorganized but rather anti-organized. Aquino, somewhat the absent-minded professor, was political, in the sense that he was well connected in the country and was powerful enough to represent and protect the Center inside and outside the university. The inside protection was especially important because the university's rector, Fernando Ganhão, not a supporter of the CEA, could not contest the friendships and camaraderie that de Bragança had with President Machel and Vice-President dos Santos. First and de Bragança began an exchange about creating a staff of highly trained academics who would not only serve as a think tank and teaching faculty for FRELIMO, but would expand the ideas in the University to include social, political, and economic issues throughout southern Africa. The process would begin early in 1978.

Between 1978 and 1982, although living in Maputo, Ruth visited London often. Joe's travel increased in 1978. However, much of his time, even from the beginning of the year, was spent in the military camps in Angola, where the MK soldiers were being trained. An evolution in the Angolan camps was evidenced by changes caused by the infiltration of traitors and even a massive air attack in 1979 by South African government forces at the main camp, *Novo Catengue*, in south Angola. ANC military camps were found throughout Angola, but most of the training was done at Funda, just outside of Luanda. The commander of the Funda Camp was Obadi (Motso Mokgabudi), an MK cadre who would become extremely close to Joe at the end of the 1970s. Though Joe did not live in the camps like Ronnie Kasrils, he was well known by the MK soldiers training at the camps. Cadres who came out of the black consciousness movement referred to Joe as Ijudi, meaning the non-racial Jew. He was known to have long nighttime debates with both on-the-ground cadres and camp commanders. Kasrils writes of one occasion in which Jabu Nxumalo and Joe discussed the Zulu leader, Chief Buthelezi. Three decades after he spent time in the MK military camps with Joe, Ronnie Kasrils is certain of Joe Slovo's importance in the camps, his rapport with the cadres, and his humanity, whether it be in a tent in the bush, a meeting in Moscow, or in a fine London restaurant:

> Joe became much more relaxed being able to go back to Africa and being absolutely part of the front line—at center stage. I would say he was the most popular person amongst the comrades in Africa. They absolutely adored him. Here is this old guy. Joe's like an uncle and he's very avuncular. He's endearing, more than anyone they encounter. He was a great leveler, Slovo.[372]

Pallo Jordan was also with Joe in Angola. Even though Jack Simons was more well-known for teaching the cadres politics and connecting South African apartheid, racism, and class disparity to the capitalist world, Jordan describes Joe Slovo as a principal teacher:

> Joe would have been sort of the principal teacher in the military at the time, the theoretical, strategy side of things. There

were regular talks, lectures, and discussions that took place. There was interaction between him and the rank-and-file soldiers. That also contributed to the degree of popularity he enjoyed amongst the MK cadres. Because remember, a lot of these new crop of MK cadres, the '76 generation, were people who came from high schools and universities. So there was sort of that inclination anyway. You know, grappling with ideas—the young and exciting new ideas. So he was very attractive to them.[373]

Ronnie Kasrils offers a memory of Joe in the camps that has absolutely nothing to do with the struggle, but it is a classic portrayal of the expansiveness of Joe Slovo. Joe and Ronnie had a spirited rivalry about British soccer, with Joe supporting Chelsea and Ronnie favoring Arsenal:

I'm in the camps in Angola and he had a little radio. Joe was in the camps quite often and he would say it's Saturday, who's playing? And we'd retire to my quarters and we'd tune in to listen to BBC overseas to listen to the football. We had such rivalry. His team was Chelsea and mine Arsenal. The reason why he supported Chelsea was that his friend, the writer that wrote *Second Class Taxi*, Sylvester Stein, very famous in London, typical Slovo lefty-liberal friend, was quite wealthy and he had two season tickets and he would take Joe to see Chelsea. So I was on the Arsenal side. God, the seriousness with this: We had a standing bet and that bet was simply who would be higher in the table, Arsenal or Chelsea. Depending on that you won or lost the bet and the bet was a lunch at our favorite Greek restaurant, George's, off Goodge Street. It was so funny because I never, ever had to buy him lunch.[374]

Kasrils continues, connecting football to Joe and the MK cadres:

I love Joe's mind. It's such an inquiring mind. He really rubbed off on me. What's this intellectual wasting his time with chat and bloody jokes and football? But Joe, after that levity and relaxation, it was such a serious philosophical question. He's fascinated by this, and on football he would say there are these two buggers, we are in a jungle camp in a very deep forest with these young people from Soweto and the townships and we're the only two white guys for miles and miles and he'd say to me, "I can't understand it, wherever I am on a Saturday I am so interested to know what the results were in England and if Chelsea has lost I get very depressed." It shows this man's humanity. That's what the casual observer doesn't understand. It's the elements of the humanity of a person. You're not a machine. This is what these young guys could see in Joe because he talked to them about many things and they loved his jokes. They just loved that warmth and humanity he provided as well. You're recruited into it. You're given the help, the support, the guidance. And this is where the whole aura of Joe Slovo builds up.[375]

As more young people were leaving South Africa to join MK, Joe and other leaders were troubled because, though the young soldiers were ready to fight, few had a sense of South African oppression and racism within a political perspective. Militarism, of which Joe was sometimes accused, was viewed as a major problem. Thus political classes taught by Joe, Ronnie Kasrils, Pallo Jordan, and Jack Simons were offered in the camps. Joe had discourse not only on South Africa, but also on Cuba, Régis Debray, Che Guevara, and how their stories might relate to the struggle against apartheid. Ten years after the ANC committed to addressing these issues, Joe Slovo reflected on the struggle:

> We had to admit that we lacked a clear strategy for internal political mobilization as the foundation for developing the armed struggle—that we had not placed before the people clear short-term and long-term slogans and goals for mass action in the field of popular struggle. We had not paid sufficient attention to the militant political struggles inside the country, to the possibilities of combining legal with illegal actions and relating both to our political-military strategy. We had not given proper weight to the significance of the many mass organisations which had recently arisen; and we had sometimes taken sectarian positions towards them.[376]

In October 1978, Oliver Tambo led a contingent that included Moses Mabhida, Joe Modise, Mzwandile Piliso, and Joe Slovo to

Vietnam to study the successes of guerilla warfare in that country. When the group returned, Tambo strongly urged the leadership of both the ANC and SACP to promote mass political struggle within South Africa. A meeting of the Revolutionary Council was held from December 27, 1978, to January 1, 1979. The council, with Joe Slovo actively involved, appointed a committee, the Politico-Military Strategy Commission, which produced the now famous MK *Green Book*. This document promoted further actions that became the essence of Joe's work for the remainder of the struggle.

The core of *The Green Book* addressed furthering the armed struggle by combining political and military mobilization. According to Luli Callinicos, it was Joe Slovo who authored the document. While the tone was forward-looking and tactical, there were also caveats in regard to strategic and political miscalculations of the past and present. *The Green Book* defined issues while simultaneously strategizing for the politicization of the masses. Joe Slovo's voice is heard throughout the manuscript, and is especially visible in the historical, oft-repeated discussion on the ANC and SACP:

> In the light of the need to attract the broadest range of social forces amongst the oppressed to the national democratic liberation, a direct or indirect commitment at this stage to a continuing revolution, which would lead to a socialist order may unduly narrow this line-up of social forces. It was also argued that the ANC is not a party, and its direct or open commitment to socialist ideology may undermine its basic character as a broad national movement. It should be emphasized that no member of the Commission had any doubts about the ultimate need to continue our revolution towards a socialist order; the issue was posed only in relation to the tactical considerations of the present stage of our struggle.[377]

Another topic that is discussed at length in *The Green Book* is the administrative dysfunction in the armed struggle. Joe referred to the issue as "a logjam at the leadership level," noting that everyone in leadership positions was doing four or five disparate jobs. Joe spoke with Ronald Segal, Ruth's colleague and good friend, and the man who first drove Oliver Tambo across the border in the early 1960s, asking if he might speak with the president about focusing his time. The main emphasis of *The Green Book*, however, was creating a strategy of a "protracted people's war in which partial and general uprisings will play a vital role."[378] The list of recommendations was both long and descriptive, but a partial rendering portrays the tone of the document:

- The maximum mobilization of the African people, as a community robbed of its land and sovereignty, is a fundamental pivot of the alignment of national revolutionary forces.
- The victorious outcome of the present phase of our struggle will create a people's power whose main immediate task will be to put an end to the special form of colonial-type oppression, guarantee democratic rights for all South Africans, and place the main means of production into the hands of a people's state.
- The aims of our national-democratic revolution will only be fully realized with the construction of a social order in which all the historic consequences of national oppression and its foundation, economic exploitation, will be liquidated, ensuring the achievement of real national liberation and social emancipation. An uninterrupted advance toward this ultimate goal will only be assured if within the alignment of revolutionary forces struggling to win the aims of our national-democratic revolution, the dominant role is played by the oppressed working people.
- The strategic objective of our struggle is the seizure of power by the people as the first step in the struggle for the victory of our national democratic revolution. Seizure of power by the people means and presupposes the all-round defeat of the fascist regime by the revolutionary forces of our country. It means the dismantling by the popular power of all the political, economic, cultural and other formations of racist rule and also necessitates the smashing of the state machinery of fascism and racism and the construction of a new one committed to the defense and advancement of the people's cause.
- The character of the South African ruling class and the nature of its state apparatus dictates that national liberation and people's power can only be won by revolutionary violence in a protracted armed struggle which must involve the whole people and in which partial and general mass uprisings will play vital role. Such a people's war can only take

root and develop if it grows out of, and is based on, political
revolutionary bases amongst the people.

The Vietnam expedition and the crafting of *The Green Book* illustrate the urgency and issues within the armed struggle. In addition,
they had a substantial effect on subsequent events for Joe Slovo and
Umkhonto we Sizwe. Shortly after the National Executive Council's
acceptance of the document, Oliver Tambo summoned Joe Slovo for
a private meeting. The two men planned a semi-secretive force called
the Special Operations Unit that would plan and carry out military
excursions in South Africa. President Tambo went back to NEC
and basically sought approval, telling the committee that they would
have no role or responsibility regarding Special Operations. Slovo
was responsible only to Tambo. Luli Callinicos wrote, "A crack team
was selected from the many hundreds of eager cadres in the camps.
Those chosen felt privileged to become part of the Unit."[379] The Special Operations Unit consisted of fourteen members selected by Joe
and his two trusted deputies, the aforementioned Obadi and Rashid,
whose birth name is Aboobaker Ismail. The Unit carried out approximately seventeen missions by April 1980 and consumed Joe's world
throughout the early 1980s.

Because Ruth had committed to living in Maputo at the end
of 1977, Joe also moved to the city, amid all his 1978 travels and
work. Mozambique had easier entry into South Africa than Angola,
and although the camps continued to operate out of that country,
operations were situated in Mozambique, Swaziland, Lesotho, and
Botswana to send MK soldiers into South Africa. Ruth was intensely
committed to her work at the Center of African Studies, as was Joe
in following through on the Special Operations Unit. As a couple
they knew a more informal Maputo. They dined in the city's restau-
rants and taverns, as well as in the homes of their FRELIMO friends.
They hosted visitors and were in constant social as well as political
contact with fellow South Africans and internationals (cooperantes)
that were friends of FRELIMO and the ANC. Although she was a
cultured and sophisticated individual, Ruth is remembered by Albie
Sachs as restricting her activities and not taking advantage of the
cultural richness available in Maputo:

I would go to the cinema and she would listen to BBC—that
was her link to the world. We had great discussions there. I

loved it. It had something to do with the non-British intellectual background. I was telling Ruth one day how much I
enjoyed going to the cinema and she said well what do you see,
there's nothing to see. And I said I saw a fantastic Bulgarian
film. "BULGARIAN films!"—it was like she said the suits of
the Politburo, but with such sort of disdain. That voice, I still
hear it in my head.[380]

With Aquino's support, Ruth began to hire colleagues to work at
CEA. One of South Africa's foremost historians, Shula Marks, conversed with Ruth about the process. They met for coffee in London
and Marks remembers two topics of conversation: Ruth's sadness
in not being more involved in her daughters' lives and the hiring of
faculty for the CEA: "She did at one point confide in me about the
sadness she felt in neglecting her family and although she wouldn't
change what she was doing, there was sadness and I found that very
touching."[381] Ruth asked Shula to review some of the files of people
applying for positions at CEA. Marks believed that the most notable
application was that of American anthropologist Bridget O'Laughlin,
who soon after became Ruth's closest colleague and friend at Eduardo
Mondlane University. Helena Dolny noted their friendship: "Bridget
and Ruth spent hours and hours together and they were kindred spirits. I remember Ruth saying one day after she had been with Bridget,
'The more you talk the more there is to talk about.'"[382]

Besides Bridget, Ruth's other key colleague at the Center of African Studies was Marc Wuyts. Ruth brought in outstanding young
scholars and utilized colleagues who were already on the faculty at
the university: young South Africans and Mozambicans such as Rob
Davies, Alpheus Manghezi, Marco Teixeira, Sipho Dhlamini, and Dan
O'Meara. Other young academics recruited included Colin Darch,
Judith Head, Chris Gerry, Jeanne Penvenne, and Helena Dolny. Intellectuals like Kurt Habermeier, Jacques Depelchin, John Saul, Anna
Maria Gentile, and Albie Sachs worked for the Center. O'Meara did
not join CEA until 1981; he spoke about Ruth's selection of colleagues:

Ruth went out of her way to recruit young Marxist researchers
who had done interesting work that was critical of ortho-
dox Marxism. So there was nobody amongst the people she
recruited who was a hard-line Stalinist—none, including herself. So far as I know, apart from Ruth, I don't know about

everybody, but only one other person was a member of the Communist Party. So on paper she had recruited what intellectually should have been the most congenial group of people.[383]

Life at the Center of African Studies was not always smooth. Each of the people Ruth asked to join her work has multiple recollections that are not limited to academic and political issues. Colin Darch, who was brought to CEA to establish a library and organize documents, recalled that Ruth rescued him when he arrived in Maputo. Initially, Mozambican authorities refused Darch admission into the country, and Darch recalls Ruth arriving at the airport:

> After about four hours Ruth appears. She always wore highly chic shoes and her approach was a clicking on the floor— briskly, she didn't walk slowly. So she sort of marches in and her Portuguese was bad, and I have to say she never really learned it. There was an Institute for Languages and they ran Portuguese courses and Ruth and I signed up for this course and we went to the first lesson. Ruth had an argument with the woman, the teacher was a white Mozambican, and somehow or other the issues of how the Portuguese left came up. We're sitting there wanting to learn irregular verbs and Ruth and this woman get into this ding-dong battle about whether or not the Portuguese ran away and abandoned the country in '74 to '75. Ruth said something like there was a climate of fear and this woman said, "No, no, no; that's not right." And the entire lesson was stalled by this political argument and then Ruth storms out. That was the end of Portuguese lessons.[384]

Dan O'Meara and Linzi Manicom also experienced Ruth and Joe's hospitality when they arrived in Maputo. "Ruth met us at the airport and she drove us to their house and Joe cooked his famous lemon chicken, which is really delicious. He charmed everybody with his lemon chicken. We had a great lunch together."[385] When lunch was finished, however, Ruth took Dan directly to the Center to get acquainted with his colleagues and their political work. In a 2011 talk at Wolfson College, Bridget O'Laughlin reflected on CEA, Mozamibique, and southern Africa, asserting that there was "a millenarian cast to everyday life."[386] She recalled that "stevedores changed out of their ragged work clothes to take a break for classes in the middle of the day, young students went to the countryside for literacy or vaccination campaigns, manual workers, clerks and managers, doctors, nurses and patients called each other comrade, neighbors got together to clean the rubbish from the streets,"[387] and more. Ruth informed Ann Scott that a feminist spirit blossomed with women questioning the male-dominated leadership though at the same time admiring and supporting Samora Machel. Acknowledging the struggles and dangers—food scarcity and safety, including attacks from counterrevolutionaries and eventually the South African government—O'Laughlin linked the millenarian spirit to the work of CEA:

> We felt that we were a part of a process of major historical change, the end of colonialism, not just in Mozambique, but in Africa, the end of a system of racial injustice in which where you lived, the school you went to, the kind of work you did, the kind of medical care you received, how you were served in a shop—everything depended on the colour of your skin.[388]

Ruth's work at CEA provided the opportunity to combine research and teaching with a "direct revolutionary force."[389] As Director of Research, she was often in the office at 7:30 in the morning, took a long lunch, sometimes at the home of Moira and Zé Forjaz and other times at a local café, was back in the office until dinner and would then often write or edit late into the night. Responsible for the daily operations of the Center, her roles included securing funding by writing proposals and corresponding and meeting with donors. She also scrounged for materials, basic supplies like paper and pencils, and was responsible for finances and arrangements, budgeting, arranging transport for fieldwork, and also helping support staff. These obligations were in addition to her managing the development course and teaching. She taught a course titled "Politics of Class Alliances" for which students read Samir Amin, Walter Rodney, Ernest Mandel, Eduardo Galeano, Rosa Luxemburg, and Vladimir Lenin. She also mentored younger colleagues, wrote, and edited, and outside of CEA had political responsibility in her SACP cell.

While she was still writing, Ruth's efforts were focused on the development course. O'Laughlin emphatically noted that collaboration was a ethos of CEA. "Our research reports came out in the name of the CEA rather than individual authors; that reflected something real and important about the way we worked and our collective accountability for the outcomes."[390] Staff at CEA, with Ruth as the leader, worked with cadres of worker-students. Defined succinctly by de Bragança and O'Laughlin, "the course was innovative in its objective—to teach research by doing it."[391] More descriptively, students were employed at different government workplaces; the jobs included a bank credit manager, a director of a port workers' school, army officials, education ministry workers, and more. Staff members, including Ruth, taught collaboratively, and attended the classes with the students even if they were not formally teaching, with the goal of "constructing new forms of socialist agricultural production, state farms and cooperatives."[392] Besides government administrators, the first group of students included Mozambican journalists and newspaper editors who were less than satisfied with the classroom accommodations:

> Our first classroom was a former lab with Bunsen burners and high stools. It wasn't a very comfortable place. The journalists suggested to Aquino that it might be better to hold the course in the journalists' club, a comfortable place with good chairs and sometimes stuff to drink. Ruth ruled this out immediately, insisting that the Development course was an academic course, not a place to exchange opinions. We stayed in that classroom until we eventually got one that could be set up in a roundtable format.[393]

The second course expanded themes to include non-agricultural social production. After addressing both theory and issues in Mozambique, the course culminated with a month-long field project in which students and staff went to live amid and study various sites of production—state farms, cooperatives, mines, and shipping. Students were divided into brigades and usually two members of the CEA staff accompanied them on the field projects. O'Laughlin spoke about the research:

> At the end of each day, people came back to discuss what they had found out, how it related to our research focus, what new questions were emerging, what interesting divergences there were, what was missing. We then decided what notes should be written and who should write them and planned the next day's activities. In note-writing we gave great importance to

Ruth in rural Mozambique
(courtesy of the Ruth First Papers
Project, Institute of Commonwealth
Studies)

including description and examples, not just the researcher's assessment of what was happening. The trained researcher then read the notes written by students and discussed with each one what was missing or unclear or particularly important to follow up on.[394]

Fieldwork did not always go smoothly. Colin Darch recalled accompanying a brigade who were interviewing FRELIMO armed struggle veterans. "The Mozambican students complained like mad. You know, these huts are dirty, it's too hot, there are insects and so on. It's an African village and these are urban students. They didn't have those rural roots."[395] It was Ruth who initiated the field projects, even though she, like the Mozambican students, was totally an urban person. In fact, she claimed that the countryside gave her "a permanent headache."[396] However, she was committed to the fieldwork because she believed that it would lead to the transformation of peasant production, first in Mozambique and then in her native South Africa. Thinking about ANC political-military operations, Bridget O'Laughlin reflected on Ruth's connecting the development course to revolutionary politics in Southern Africa:

Care around operative involvement did not mean that Ruth thought that either she or the CEA were marginal to the struggle against apartheid. Ruth was always concerned with using fully the political space available and pushing the boundaries, pulling back if she had to but hoping that she'd extend the space. These sallies were not always successful. She really did think (as did Joe) that the consolidation of the Mozambican revolution was critical for the struggle against apartheid, that the struggle was a regional, not a national one.[397]

Ruth also wrote of the political, pedagogical, and teaching nexus of the development course. In a letter to South African academic Julius Lewin in late 1979, she explained why students read Lenin: "I'm not for teaching/using Lenin as though he set up a model for all to follow, but his analysis of forms of rural social formation under conditions of early capitalism in Russia, and his theses on co-operation, are highly relevant here and now."[398] She went on to emphasize liberation education:

> Our experience of our course is that so many years of education is only one criterion, and often not the important one for gauging people's capacities to understand politics/strategy/ theory, or whatever. Of course, people have to know how to read and write, and then we have to help them read critically. But the key to that capacity is the relevance of the matters that are raised.[399]

Ruth First considered this period at the CEA as one of the most productive and militant in her life, precisely because political struggle was directly integrated into her everyday work of teaching, research, and writing. She believed her contribution to the consolidation of the Mozambican revolution was directly connected to the liberation of South Africa. This was feasible because she had a strong political vision of her objectives and a sharp analysis of the political context within which she worked. The importance of the development course derived for her not only from what it was in itself, but from where and when it was located—in revolutionary Mozambique during a period of revolutionary conjuncture in southern Africa.

Ruth First designed the course around four principles:

- Implementing revolutionary strategy is a matter of method—of using Marxist method to investigate and analyze the concrete and constantly changing situations that the revolution confronts and directs.

- Promoting a revolutionary context, where the university had to take on new forms of training that took advantage of the experience of cadres and responded to the requirements of everyday practice.
- The struggle to build socialism as a struggle to transform the organization of production.
- The struggle for national liberation in South Africa, which was strategically of a piece with the struggle to build socialism in Mozambique.

Though the development course started with theory, the purpose was application, not memorization or intellectualization. When Ruth discussed theory at the 1982 Social Science in Southern Africa Conference that she organized for CEA, she said, "We're very interested in provoking. If students don't ask questions then we are failing."[400] Core principles were portrayed in the paper Bridget O'Laughlin presented at Wolfson College as she connected pedagogy to politics while celebrating Ruth's mission:

> Didactically we wanted to get across to the students a number of basic points: that understanding cooperatives and state farms within a strategy of socialist transformation meant locating them within the lives of those rural people they pretended to reach; that small-scale peasants in Mozambique were not subsistence producers but people whose livelihoods were systematically related to markets; that politically relevant research consists of listening and observing, not telling people what to do; and finally that such research addresses real questions and thus must be organised to explore counter-explanations and alternative definitions of problems encountered.[401]

Endless discussions ensued between Ruth and her colleagues at the Center regarding the curriculum of the course. They were particularly concerned with promoting their adult students' full involvement and engagement, even though all of the students were employed full-time. Ruth and her colleagues strove to have their students view "social investigation as a necessary part of their work."[402] Their task was not always successful. She addressed some of the difficulties at the 1982 Social Science Conference:

228 / RUTH FIRST AND JOE SLOVO IN THE WAR AGAINST APARTHEID

> The kinds of questions I'm referring to, for instance, are the
> problems of how we teach students who have different histories
> of education, come from a widely different range of structures—
> the university, ministries, mass organisations and so on. And I
> think that whereas we should probably admit that we started
> off rather romantically about this, saying it's so important to
> crash educational barriers and break this elitist monopoly, we
> shall do it with sheer willpower, in the course of teaching we
> have come to acknowledge that there are problems. . . . Now I
> don't say we've resolved it. We struggle with it.[403]

Students and staff traveled throughout the country, setting up
camps and learning about and working with tea workers, harbor
workers, small farmers, and cotton workers. By connecting their
theoretical training and fieldwork, they learned about the colonial
aspects and exploitation of family agriculture, cheap contract labor,
the petit-bourgeois trader class, and technological exploitation. Thus
curriculum, research, and the products they would produce were topics for discussion at staff meetings at the Center. Memories of those
meetings and CEA projects vary depending on which staff member
speaks, and Ruth's perspective is not available except through her
1982 Social Science Conference presentation and, to a lesser degree,
her book *Black Gold*. Ruth and others at CEA emphasized the collaborative nature of Center work, but that perception was not unanimous
among the staff. For example, Dan O'Meara thought that the climate
of the Center included a favored group that Ruth trusted and worked
with more closely than other colleagues. He referred to Ruth's man-
agement style as "democratic centralism," and he remembers long
discussions on issues, with Ruth making the final decision. "We
would discuss everything and once the leadership decided that was it.
Ruth was the leadership."[404] O'Meara came to understand this within
the context of CEA's mission and connection to FRELIMO, and he
credits Ruth with having a total understanding of the economic issues
in Mozambique and facilitating exceptional research reports that were
effective in influencing policy:

> The research reports that Ruth presided over were phe-
> nomenally good and were well received by FRELIMO. Any
> intelligent person reading them could see that they were an
> immanent critique. She didn't come out and say this is wrong.

She said this is what is happening and she allowed the FRE-
LIMO leadership to draw their own conclusions.[405]

However, having been recruited to do research on South Africa, and
then becoming, for the most part, a team member of the development
course, O'Meara and his colleagues in the South African nucleus were
extremely frustrated because they were not doing the work they had initially been requested to do within their academic disciplines. O'Meara's
criticisms were directly related to Ruth's leadership at the Center:

> She was incredibly nervous that we would all do what we
> did in Western society and start denouncing FRELIMO for
> betrayal of socialism, so she put an incredibly tight rein on us.
> Her antennae, which were already very well developed—they
> vibrated for the slightest hint of independence would mean
> there was potentially trouble down the road with FRELIMO.[406]

But despite his questions regarding Ruth's leadership and his role
at CEA, O'Meara offered a powerful conclusion regarding working
with Ruth First: "We admired her, we respected her immensely, but
God, she was difficult."[407]

Colin Darch's perspective suggests Ruth as political and utilitarian:

> She had very little patience with intellectuals sitting around
> debating how many angels can dance on the point of a pin.
> That is not what interested her, which is not to say that she
> wasn't interested in theory. She was really interested in the-
> ory and she believed clearly that theory and practice must go
> together. But the theory must not stop one from getting to the
> point of practice. My reading is that it was the Party activism
> and the journalism together which gave her an awareness of
> the need to get stuff out. We had to produce. We were not
> doing this out of personal interest. If you look at the CVs of the
> people who worked at the Center, in the years they were there
> they published almost nothing in Western academic journals.
> Because everything we did was collectively done.[408]

Ruth served as a mentor to the young researchers who became
part of CEA. Bridget O'Laughlin joined the Center from a post as
an assistant professor at Stanford University. Although established

as a scholar, and already well published, she viewed Ruth as both a teacher and colleague. Judith Head recalled the red marks that covered the pages of her dissertation, for which Ruth served as her doctoral advisor. Helena Dolny pointedly remembers Ruth First critiquing her writing. Of course, mentorship was not always smooth and there were political debates and issues to deal with. Some CEA researchers believed that Ruth First was too ideological and somewhat harsh in her critique of colleagues. This was especially true when the subject was South Africa, rather than workers in Mozambique. Finally, there were colleagues other than Dan O'Meara who believed that Ruth was forcing them into projects that did not utilize their expertise. Criticisms acknowledged, the general spirit that came from the young researchers, as well as from Aquino de Bragança, was that Ruth First nurtured, sometimes intensely and other times gently, the work of other researchers at the Center of African Studies. John Saul was in the Department of Marxism and Leninism at Eduardo Mondlane University, and spoke to this very issue:

> Besides, even when one looked back at moments of interpersonal tension one had had with her it was also with the realisation that such tensions were not arbitrary ones, that almost invariably something important, intellectually and politically, was at stake. The seriousness of her engagement, the intensity of her concern, could never be doubted. Nor, if you were struggling to be as serious yourself, could such moments cast any doubt upon her personal concerns, her compassion, her continuing solidarity in the next round of whatever struggle, public or personal, was in train.[409]

As part of both Ruth First and Aquino de Bragança's commitment, they created a journal with staff members that would bring research to the Mozambican people. Ruth was emphatic that reports first be published in Portuguese, and the journal, *Estudos Moçambicanos*, was a Lusophone publication produced in Maputo. In the inaugural issue, Aquino and Ruth led with an article titled, "Underdevelopment and Migrant Labour," which explained the work of CEA and argued for democratic socialism as the path to a sustainable independent Mozambique.

Seriousness prevailed about life and certainly about the academic/political work at CEA, but Ruth was also happy in Mozambique—there was fulfillment in the work that she was doing. She and Joe were living in the fashionable Sommerschield suburb of Maputo amid the leadership of FRELIMO and the ANC. Ongoing conversations were shared with Joe about issues and events at the Center as well as the South African revolution. Joe confided in Ruth about his clandestine missions and Ruth's work at the university brought her in contact with cooperantes who were sympathetic to the ANC as well as FRELIMO. She would often introduce these people to Joe, and some, like Guido van Hecken, an academic at the university who had once unsuccessfully tutored Ruth in Portuguese, would subsequently work with Joe in the struggle. Cooperantes were never part of the Special Operation Unit, but they did provide safe houses for ANC operatives and sometimes carried propaganda and even guns into the country. Often their roles were not entirely clear. For example, Helene Pastoors recalls Joe telling her that he would ask her to do things that probably were not her responsibility but that it was her duty to set limits. As Ruth was collaboratively building the Center of African Studies, Joe was beginning to organize the Special Operations Unit of the South African underground.

Joe appointed Obadi as the deputy in the Special Operations Unit and soon after, in April 1979, Rashid began his work with the unit. Little is known about Obadi's personal life as an MK commander, except to say that he and Joe were close and that Joe had total faith in him. He was the commander of the Funda Camp when Slovo selected him as his deputy. Rashid, whom Obadi had slated to train the men who were to become Special Operations cadres, had left his native Johannesburg after the Soweto Uprising and was schooled in explosives and military engineering in the German Democratic Republic. He then came to Funda to train elite cadres. It was here where the on-the-ground story of Special Operations began.

At the end of April 1979, Obadi brought around twenty soldiers to Funda to undergo specialist military training with Rashid. The cadres had no prior knowledge of the Special Operations Unit. Obadi told Rashid about Special Operations and also explained that Joe Slovo was in charge of the unit. Rashid was sworn to secrecy. He worked with the soldiers for approximately six weeks with focus on military training that would facilitate going into South Africa to destroy oil refineries, power stations, and possibly military outposts. These types of excursions would soon be referred to as "armed propaganda" with the purpose being twofold: first, to show that the South African regime was not invincible; and second, to engage and energize the masses in the country, both urban and rural. Rashid informed Obadi of the twelve men that he believed should join the unit. He recalled Joe coming with Obadi to Funda when the course was completed at the end of May:

> There was a weekend in which Joe Slovo came to the camp and I gave my recommendations to Obadi. We assembled only the people that had been selected out of group and then Joe gave everybody a talk. He said the names of all of the people and told them that they should be prepared to leave. That they were leaving for the front line. He did not say where exactly they were going to go. And right at the end he said, "You, join the unit." So I was given five minutes. I wasn't expecting it at all. It was the first time I had met Joe. We were then taken off to Luanda from camp and the next day we all flew down to Maputo.[410]

When the Special Operations Unit arrived in Mozambique, they were taken directly to a residence in the suburb of Matola that was subsequently referred to as "the terror nest" by the apartheid regime. This type of group house was very different than the house in which Ruth and Joe lived in Sommerschield. This discrepancy again points to questions regarding class disparity in the revolution. Joe Slovo was often at the Matola residence, and when he was not traveling, he worked almost daily with Obadi and Rashid in the planning of military excursions into South Africa. Joe assigned detailed military and strategic planning to Rashid, and four sites were selected for the initial attacks on three oil refineries—two were Sasol refineries and the third was a Mobil refinery in Durban. In addition, the plan was to attack Fluor's corporate headquarters in Rosebank, since it was the company that built the refineries. As per Oliver Tambo's instructions, the attacks were to transpire when people were not at risk. Under Joe's ultimate command, reconnaissance was done at each of the sites and the Durban operation was abandoned after Rashid reported that gas clouds might cause human deaths.

Even though Joe was clear on the details and knew the cadres well, he also understood that there were always uncertainties in military operations. He had been critical of the ANC for not fighting the revolution in the country, but now this was center stage: the three attacks were the first systematic, official ANC incursions, and he was in charge. The plan was for all three operations to be launched in the early morning hours of May 31, 1980, corresponding to the annual parades celebrating Republic Day in South Africa. It was an odd night for Joe, because he could not reveal to anybody that the operation was even happening. Although he was in contact with Oliver Tambo, there was nothing to relay because he was not informed until the following morning that all three infiltrations had been successful and that none of the Special Operations cadres had been harmed. Nadja Manghezi comments on the moment in her book *The Maputo Connection*:

> The operation was a milestone in the armed struggle. The unit had carried out a major operation against the regime, causing enormous losses in fuel. In Maputo word spread like wildfire that it had been planned from there. There was jubilation everywhere, especially in the camps in Angola. Joe Slovo said afterwards that he couldn't sleep that whole night. He stood on the balcony of his flat in Maputo, hoping to see the explosion.[411]

Joe and Ruth were ecstatic upon learning that the operations were successful and had resulted in great financial damage. Ronnie Kasrils had just arrived in Maputo and talked with Joe shortly after Sasol:

> He was so proud of his structures. So Joe was really hands-on and went to the extent in Maputo of visiting the power stations, visiting anything that could give him an insight into how industry would function—power stations and the like. He explained to me how he had had that access, and how interesting—you know, not having engineering but he would make a study of it.[412]

Joe notified President Tambo, and shortly thereafter they went together to honor the cadres who fulfilled the attacks, meeting with them at their residence in Matola. Rashid spoke of Joe's propensity to interact with the cadres:

> Joe Slovo would come and talk to the cadres himself. He would be part of it. He would listen to it. Even though we did the specialist briefing, he would sit in and talk to the cadres—this

is what we want done, it is very important, and things. Even after, when all the units had returned safely, bringing those people together—they all met with the President—was an extremely critical thing.[413]

The South African press, as well as newspapers and magazines in the United States, demonized the ANC. Vladimir Shubin wrote that the regime quickly stated that the Soviet ambassador in Zambia collaborated with ANC leader Frene Ginwala to plan the operation. He also explained the impossibility of this assertion in that the two people were barely acquainted. In the United States, the *New York Times* and *Newsweek* ran articles on the bombings. Both articles correctly named Joe Slovo as directing the attacks, and the language, with quotes from South African officials, references terrorism and Soviet-inspired revolution. Both articles stated emphatically that Joe was a white man. This, of course, was also the powerful statement by the South African regime. The *New York Times* cited the Minister of Police asserting that Joe's "purpose there was to oversee the operations of terrorists and spies infiltrating into South Africa."[414] The *Newsweek* article was actually titled "Public Enemy Number One," connecting Joe to the Soviet Union.[415]

The South African regime's response to the underground attacks was important for the ANC. Even though the government's plan was to influence the West as well as South Africans, by demonizing the ANC as an organization of terrorists led by white communists, it marked one of the first times that South African newspapers reported the nation's own vulnerability. The South African government maintained more weapons and power than MK, but weakness had been uncovered. Vital for the ANC both inside and outside of South Africa, the success of the attacks was also significant because it supported Joe Slovo's return to President Tambo to request continuing support of the Special Operations Unit. Rashid reflected on the meaning of the Sasol attacks:

It turned the country around. It actually set the entire country ablaze. Because in the camps and everywhere else what were people calling for? They wanted to go into the country and fight. In fact, all of MK wanted to be part of special operations. Everybody would say to us we want to join your units and we had to be very cautious. I think that's extremely important.[416]

Joe with Oliver Tambo on the far right (courtesy of the Ruth First Papers
Project, Institute of Commonwealth Studies)

The ANC's jubilation was not lost, however, on the South African regime. Their reprisals came not only through the press but also through instant attacks. First a safe house in Swaziland was bombed on June 3, and then two days later a car bomb attempt was made on Chris Hani in Lesotho. While these attacks were unsuccessful, they were a foreshadowing of more effective state terrorism in the near future.

Later in 1980, Joe attended a meeting of the ANC's National Executive Committee and Revolutionary Council where he received the support to continue the Special Operations Unit. However, at the same meeting it was decided that the Revolutionary Council would also have a special operations unit, stressing political over military, and led by Mac Maharaj. Mac's appointment and the subsequent rivalry between the two leaders represents the beginning of fifteen years of tension. Although many debated issues with Joe Slovo, there are only a few individuals with whom he appeared to have intense conflict. In 1980, the ongoing political versus military debates were based on false philosophical premises. The two branches had by this time, despite the constant debates, become totally intertwined, to the degree that when the new unit was formed, Mac Maharaj asked Joe

Slovo to transfer Rashid to his unit. Joe refused, but in the name of comradeship, he allowed Rashid to advise Mac. This fact speaks to one of the criticisms that Mac and other commanders made of Joe Slovo. They complained that Joe seemed to have the best people working under his command. Keith Mokoape, James Ngculu, Terrence Tryon, and Mohammad Timol were all MK members and they all worked with Joe in Maputo. In each and every case, they asserted that they preferred to work in Joe's unit.

Sue Rabkin, who was assigned to work with Mac Mahraj even though she was very close to Joe and Ruth, and was in some ways Ruth's mentee, provides the best summary of why young Umkhonto we Sizwe cadres wanted to work with Joe Slovo:

> His ability to analyze and look to achieve what it was to get to where we were trying to get to was luminary. A whole generation of MK cadres was brought up on "No Middle Road." It was their bible. You used to see these dog-eared copies in the residences in the military residences. It was debated over campfires. Comrades knew that book inside out and if you didn't you were looked down upon. There was no one who hadn't read it.[417]

Joe and Ruth in 1980 knew, Joe because of MK intelligence and Ruth because she was politically savvy, that more South African reprisals were yet to come. A personal experience of death, however, was faced in 1980 when Julius, Ruth's father, died. Earlier in the year they had hosted an eightieth birthday party for him at the Camden Town Hall. When Ruth and Joe came to London for the funeral, they stayed with Rica Hodgson and also reconnected with Ruth's brother Ronald, whom they had not seen for some time. Joe spoke at Julius's funeral referencing his love for football and his wife, Tilly. "After the dust settled at the football ground, he saw Tilly and fell in love with her."[418]

At the time of Julius's death, the South African government had begun its reign of assassinations of ANC operatives in both South Africa and the border states. Joe Gqabi, a *Guardian* journalist with Ruth in the 1950s and now an ANC leader, was killed at his house in Zimbabwe. Dan O'Meara recalled Ruth First's speech at the memorial service in Mozambique: "Ruth spoke very eloquently. The woman had a way with words that was quite extraordinary."[419]

In Maputo, on January 30, 1981, the South African government took revenge for the Special Operations incursions in what became known as the Matola Massacre. South African commandos clandestinely entered Mozambique wearing blackface and FRELIMO military uniforms. On the way to the Maputo residences, they killed a Portuguese citizen who was working for Mozambique Electric. Colin Darch, Ruth's colleague at CEA, remembered:

> There was a Portuguese technician who was driving by in the area and they killed him with a machine gun. And the reason was that he was a round-faced white man and they thought he was Joe Slovo. The picture of him if you look at the newspaper reports at the time of the Matola raid—they thought they got Joe Slovo.[420]

The South Africans proceeded to three residences and killed fourteen MK cadres. At the house where the Special Operation cadres lived, there were two survivors and one of them, Matthews Thobela, known as Mabena, spoke with Nadja Manghezi. He was reading *Studying Siege* and Obadi was playing Scrabble with a fellow commander, Soli Mayona, when the attack occurred. Mabena was able to fire on the commandos, killing one, a British national, before he himself escaped.

Obadi and Rashid both resided in the residence that was targeted. Obadi had just returned from Angola a day before the attack. Rashid had been sent to Swaziland to discipline a cadre, thus was not at the house during the ambush. Obadi was not immediately killed, but was shot and received what proved to be a fatal stomach wound. Joe Slovo was emotionally devastated by the attack. He was close to each of the people who had been killed, and was especially despondent at the death of Obadi. He spoke with Obadi's mother when she illegally crossed the border into Mozambique to claim her son's body. "'I told her how sorry I was,' he said. 'And what a great guy her son had been. She didn't cry. She looked at me and quietly said that she was proud of her son, that what he had done was right, that he had given his life for a great cause.' His eyes had misted up. 'She told me to carry on.'"[421]

Joe was also terribly upset that the Special Operations Unit was unable to detect and thwart the attack. They had known that three MK soldiers had been arrested in Swaziland and had been tortured.

There was reason to believe that one of them might have provided the location of Matola safe houses while under duress. When Rashid recalled in an interview being with Joe beside Obadi's hospital bed when their comrade died, he could not refrain from sobbing, even though it was thirty years since the Matola Massacre. Amid the horror, he recounted the pressure and burden, but also the commitment when Joe Slovo said, "We've got to make a success of these operations. We've got to make it work. We owe it to those comrades that died."[422]

"Making it work" meant moving forward with Special Operations incursions into South Africa. This was partially possible because of Mabena, who by injuring and killing South African commandos, foiled any possibility of them finding future Special Operations plans, which were stored on the upper floor of the Matola residence. For Joe Slovo, honoring comrades was essential to sustaining the struggle against the apartheid regime. He also knew that the cadres who had been murdered were exceptional soldiers and were hard to replace. Joe focused on three targets in "Operation Blackout." The first stage was designed to demolish two power stations in the Eastern Cape. One of those stations was at Camden and the other at Arnold. The second operation entailed a rocket attack on the Voortrekkerhoogte military base near Pretoria. This was an extremely important target because if successful, it would magnify the fact that the regime was not impenetrable and would also serve as an example of the capabilities of armed propaganda. Joe was even more intense than when he had prepared for Sasol. After Matola, Joe had moved his commanders, like Rashid, out of the residences and into cooperante safe houses in the center of Maputo. Often in the evenings he would visit Rashid:

> Joe would spend time talking to me. Quite often at 7:30 in the morning we would sit and make a decision, but that would invariably be after we had sat and had drinks the night before talking about these things—he would never make a decision over a glass of whiskey. We would always formalize what we were talking about and make a decision first thing in the morning when we were fresh, when we were ready. His approach to things was always thinking about the concept and what would take the struggle forward. I was the specialist, so he said, what are you going to do about it? We needed someone of Joe's character and ability who had access to the national leadership.[423]

Meeting at various safe houses, but not at the ANC office in a flat off Avenida Mao Tse-tung, Joe and Rashid would sort through the details of plans for operations, with millions of questions from Joe asking for clarifications. They reviewed maps of the country and the power grids. According to Rashid's account, Joe was simultaneously restrained and ambitious:

The next major operations were against the power stations. I remember saying to Joe, if we carry out attacks on five power stations we would have wiped out 50 percent. And Joe would say, Don't you think you're being over-ambitious? Why don't we cut it down to this size and shape? Remember we are a very small command; if we overstretch ourselves now we are at risk. At the same time we had to continue these operations at a rea-sonable pace—it was Joe's expectation. You had to constantly produce results.[424]

The actions at Camden, Arnold, and Voortrekkerhoogte were all successfully completed in June 1981. First the two power stations were bombed and two weeks later Special Operations cadres hit Voortrekkerhoogte. Ed Wethli, who was married to Helena Dolny, transported the rocket out of Mozambique in a large Ford Ranchero for the Voortrekkerhoogte attack. Sue Rabkin recalled Joe coming to see her and reporting that the operations were successful: "Joe arrived and he had newspapers with him—the British newspapers, South African newspapers. We went back to my house, or somebody's house, and he said, 'Yeah, I organized that' and he gave me a few details."[425] Despite Special Operations successes, Joe pondered the cadres' capabilities. He had great trust in Obadi and then Rashid, but he was not always confident in the other MK cadres. Five months after the successful incursion into South Africa, Joe scribbled a short note to Jack Simons: "At home things are bubbling encouragingly. I only wish our structures and style of work measured up to the poten-tial. Well . . . we must find a way to meet the situation."[426]

Besides her work at the Center, Ruth and Ann Scott were com-pleting their book on Olive Schreiner in 1980. Rica Hodgson read the book in manuscript form when she stayed with Ruth in Maputo, where she was working with Dutch filmmakers on a documentary to raise funds for the defense of children in Africa. She noted parallels between Schreiner and Ruth in terms of politics and feminism. Pallo

Jordan made the sharpest connection concerning Ruth's life, feminism, and her writing on Olive Schreiner:

> There was a misperception at the time that women who were successful in that male world were very harsh on other women. I think Ruth used to have a little bit of that. It changed after she started doing the Schreiner biography because, as she used to say in her more candid moments, when it came to the issue of feminism she was a late bloomer. In other words, in a sense, she had always accepted the terms of the male-dominated and male-defined world and she was going to succeed within those parameters. She then began to interact with feminism through Olive Schreiner.[427]

Ann Scott, who is currently the editor of the *British Journal of Psychotherapy*, and Ruth were well-matched co-authors. Scott was a known feminist in the United Kingdom and Ruth was an exiled South African freedom fighter. Olive Schreiner was publicly known for her feminism, anti-racism, and anti-imperialism. In their book, First and Scott illustrate that Schreiner was also a woman who lived within the context of her time:

> We see Olive Schreiner's life and writing as a product of a specific social history. We are not only looking at what she experienced but at how she, and others, perceived that experience; at the concepts with which her contemporaries understood their world, and again, at the consciousness that was possible for her time—after Darwin, before Freud, and during the period when Marx's *Capital* was written.[428]

Scott interviewed Ruth for an article in the grassroots feminist magazine *Spare Rib* in 1974. Ruth had received a contract to write a book on Olive Schreiner in 1973, and she asked Scott to collaborate after that interview. Scott recalled being told by socialist feminist writer Sheila Rowbotham that "Ruth felt she needed to work on Schreiner with a feminist because she didn't feel she understood things that were obvious to young feminists."[429] To paraphrase one of the book's reviewers, American feminist Elaine Showalter, First and Scott wrote a historical, social, political, psychological, and medical biography. They wrote about Schreiner's struggles as a Victorian and post-Victorian woman, her writing, fiction, nonfiction, and letters, and the breadth of her life within the time she lived, both in South Africa and England. The book covered her childhood and highlighted her famous novel, *The Story of an African Farm* (1883), her feminist essay "Women and Labour" (1911), and her critique of Cecil Rhodes, colonialism, and imperialism, *Trooper Peter Halket of Mashonaland* (1897). First and Scott analyzed Olive Schreiner's crusade against racism, at the same time refusing to ignore her use of racist terms and being somewhat patronizing— again, a sign of her times. Living as an adult in South Africa, she resigned from the "feminist" Women's Enfranchisement League because the organization supported only white women voting. Allison Drew documents Schreiner's resignation in *Discordant Comrades*: "It was not a personal matter that made me leave the society. The women of the Cape Colony, all the women of the Cape Colony, these were the terms on which I joined."[430]

Ruth First and Ann Scott, in their holistic account of Olive Schreiner's accomplishments and struggles, commented, "Her creativity and her failure were the expressions of the same struggle."[431] Throughout the biography, beginning in the introduction and reappearing in the conclusion, the co-authors enveloped the public issues that Olive Schreiner championed within her personal struggles—psychological and medical, but possibly more about the times in which she lived.

There were those who wondered if the book was flirting with an autobiography of Ruth. One of those individuals was Ruth's friend Wolfie Kodesh: "I was reading it and it was sort of hazy. It sort of melted into Ruth's character so much when she was writing about Olive Schreiner. It could have been Olive Schreiner writing about Ruth, if you know what I mean, because they had a lot of similarities."[432]

Though it is reasonable to assert that there were similarities between Olive Schreiner and Ruth First, it is somewhat outrageous to compare the two women at this point in Ruth's life when she was happy and politically engaged. As Gillian Slovo writes in *Every Secret Thing*: "She was a woman in a man's world, forced continually to prove her capabilities. Now finally she had found a home that would accept her talents, her brilliant mind, her fierce commitment, her long experience. She felt validated: she could be herself."[433]

As Ruth completed *Olive Schreiner* and worked on *Black Gold* and other Center of African Studies publications, all in a collaborative vein, Joe was also doing a great deal of writing and travel. A trip to the Soviet Union in 1981 was especially notable because Joe was able to visit his birthplace in Lithuania for the first time since child-hood. He had attempted to visit in 1968, but the trip was canceled due to democratic challenges to the Soviet Union in what is today the Czech Republic. In 1981, Joe's comrade Alexei Makarov joined him on the journey. "Alexei has a homely, sentimental warmth so typical of the Russian personality. He was an appealing kind of Communist; his contributions to discussions were not caked over with deaden-ing clichés. His defense of socialism was all the more convincing because there was no utopian pretense that all problems had already been solved."[434] Not only was the trip rushed, to Joe's dismay he was treated as something of a celebrity. Yet he did have the opportunity to see the town where he was born, speak to some of the people who lived there, and then, just before departing Vilna on a train back to Moscow, he was able to meet his two cousins, Sareta and Bela, whose families he would meet on a future visit.

In addition to *The Green Book*, Joe was publishing consistently in the *African Communist*, including two articles under his Sol Dubula alias, and in *Dawn*, Umkhonto we Sizwe's journal. He spoke at the sixtieth anniversary of the SACP held in Maputo in 1981. Joe's voice was broadcast throughout Southern Africa via Radio Freedom, an outlet of the ANC. The anniversary speech was a combination of many talks in one and included history, celebration, ideological rheto-ric, Fidel Castro, the honoring of martyrs, "strategy and tactics," and the steadfast alliance of the ANC and SACP. It also included refer-ences to "people power" that linked directly to the armed propaganda that had been initiated by Joe and other ANC leaders. The incursions into South Africa and "people power" were also the emphasis of Joe Slovo's Radio Freedom interview in 1982:

I think it is true to say that today as never before the ANC and its allies stand completely unchallenged at the head of the lib-eration struggle. And there's no doubt that heroic actions like Sasol, like the attacks on the police stations, on power stations, the shelling of Voortrekkerhoogte, the attacks on refineries, and so on—these have all played a most vital role in raising the militancy of our people and providing them with even greater confidence in carrying on their own mass struggles.[435]

Joe had a practice that he came to refer to as "Route 66," in which he visited numerous comrades and friends for an after-dinner drink. Joe's visits included political discussion, humor, and even music. Rashid recalled one visit when he was reading Lenin's *What Is to Be Done?* When Joe saw what he was reading, he said, "You know what is to be done."[436] For Dan O'Meara, Joe's visits meant playing guitar and singing political and folk songs. "Joe wasn't very good, but he loved playing the guitar. That was one of the grounds of our friendship. He had discovered when he came to Mozambique that I played the guitar and we would spend a lot of time playing."[437]

Ruth was in an SACP cell with Sue Rabkin, Rashid, and Obadi. Rashid got acquainted with her through the SACP and social occasions—dinners and beach outings that Ruth organized. Joe and Ruth enjoyed prawns and chips at the Macaneta Restaurant where they often ate with friends for free because the owner considered them freedom fighters. The restaurant was in great contrast to the upscale Polana Hotel that Ruth frequented with Moira Forjaz. Ruth First was comfortable in both places. Conversations with Ruth and Joe were exciting for Rashid—there was a vibrancy he had not experienced before. He clearly viewed Joe as a teacher who would always ask him to comment on the writing he was working on or just ideas in general. He viewed Ruth as someone who pressured him on his ideas and politics. At one point she challenged him on militarism and armed struggle. He told Sue Rabkin that he felt as though he was being attacked. According to Rashid, Rabkin said:

> What are you so worried about, Ruth thinks you're amazing. She's attacking you because she wants you to think differently—that's what she's about. Because people want to get the ideas across, they want to nurture. They want to mentor. But also it's because you're open to different points of view and people don't have to always agree with you. It doesn't mean because they attack you they don't respect you.[438]

As Rashid came to know Ruth more, he understood her criticisms:

> What Ruth was concerned about was that we shouldn't just think of the military operations, but that we needed to interface between the military operations and the political—how one supported the other and at the same time how all of it went into

Joe and Dadoo (courtesy of the Ruth First Papers Project,
Institute of Commonwealth Studies)

forming this broad approach to the struggle. And this leads to
"people's power" and this notion of "people's power" comes
from Joe and Ruth.[439]

Sue Rabkin acknowledged how provocative Ruth could be, but
added: "My tutelage in the Party was actually done by her. She
challenged us on everything. She was illuminating—very, very illuminating."[440] For Rashid and Sue, these were life lessons and they
treasured Ruth and Joe's "ability to discuss and debate and the ability to take discussions to different levels."[441] Other people were not
so sure. Ronnie Kasrils, for example, still recalls an attack by Ruth.
At this time, at least according to some people in the struggle, Kasrils was considered something of a Soviet true believer. In his own
words, his relationship with Ruth had "soured." Ruth's attack, or the
"blow-up," as he called it, was at a dinner for Yusuf Dadoo at Sue
Rabkin's flat. The topic was the Solidarity movement in Poland. Kasrils remembers tension in the air:

Ruth came straight at me and said in a very unfriendly way,
"And what would you do about Poland?" I said, '"One needs

to know a bit more about it. I said I would defend the revolution." And she retorted sarcastically, "yes, I suspect you
would be sending in the tanks." You could cut the atmosphere
with a knife. Joe was quiet and they were sitting on needles—
nobody opened their mouths. So I came back at her, I think I
was probably rude, I might have said, What are you going to
do? Are you going to just let socialism collapse? I was quite
aggressive and she said to me with quite a snarl, "Why don't
you take another drink!" I said, "And what's yours, Ruth—
sulfuric acid?"[442]

Ruth never accepted Stalinism and was not a true believer. The
Marxist scholars she brought to the Center of African Studies advocated democratic socialism, not Soviet or GDR ideology. Pallo Jordan
reflected on Ruth and the SACP:

Ruth was what you would call a "dissident communist." She
didn't break with the CP, but she couldn't identify with many
of the views, and I think she felt very much constrained to keep
her opinion to herself. She was on the wrong side of certain
people. As it is, one was aware that some of the more dogmatic
elements of the CP wanted to have her excluded and isolated in
the Party. So she felt very constrained by things, but of course,
being a political person, she was always politically engaged.[443]

In 1980 Ruth attended the International People's Tribunal in
Milan that focused on self-determination in Eritrea. This position
was in conflict with both the ANC's and SACP's support of Ethiopia
in this particular struggle. Joe spoke about Ruth's stance within the
struggle and the Party:

She died in the Party. She was in the Party unit in Maputo
and we had units there right until the last moment. You must
remember that people like Brian [Bunting] and others actually wanted to hurl her out of the Party. Well, because during
the time when we were already in England and so on, she,
for example, participated in this Italian international organization, which had hearings on various breaches of human rights.
I don't remember what it was called, but she was a patron of
that and, for example the issue of Eritrea, which we had a very

pro-Soviet point of view. She was out on a limb and, in general, she was regarded as sort of having moved away from the tenets of Marxism by quite a number of people because of her skepticism of the Soviet Union. So there was actually a strong move from among the hardened Stalinists to drop her from the Party and quite frankly, between you and me, if it hadn't been for my role—not that I intervened, but because of my status and position, she would have been hurled out of the Party quite long ago.[444]

In addition to their struggle lives, Joe and Ruth traveled to London, and their daughters visited them in Mozambique as did friends from the United Kingdom and South Africa. Everyone commented on how content and confident Ruth appeared in Maputo. Barney Simon:

She just blossomed in Mozambique. She was very happy there. I saw her twice when we were doing WOZA, and she was really there for the sake of her daughters that visit. And I can remember she came to my room, took off her shoes and put her feet up on a chair, and we just spoke and spoke. I brought the WOZA guys in to meet her, and she was very interested in them. As people, as a new energy that was happening.[445]

Rica Hodgson remembered that Ruth let her hair become frizzy in Mozambique, and Hillary Hamburger recalled Ruth telling her about changes in her dress habits:

Ruth was a different Ruth from the Ruth here in terms of the way she dressed. She once said to me, and I have never forgotten it, "I cannot believe my past investment in clothes and things." She said, "Do you know that I have four dresses now? It's crazy when I think of how much time I spent on clothes." And she said, "It's a liberation for me."[446]

Hilda Bernstein visited in 1982: "I think she was happier there than I've ever seen her."[447] She also spoke about Ruth's work at the Center of African Studies:

All the things she was best able to do came together in the research she was doing at that institute. And I think if you want to find out what really was the best of Ruth it was the couple of years that she worked there, and the work that she produced and she had initiated and started doing. That was the epitome of all her abilities.[448]

Mac Maharaj's wife, Zarina, taught at Eduardo Mondlane University in the early 1980s and she too remembered Ruth First's spirit. She wrote about Ruth dancing to Motown in her book, *Dancing to a Different Rhythm*, noting, "She reveled and was growing in the atmosphere of independent Mozambique."[449] Zarina Maharaj viewed her as something of a mentor in relaxation:

At this point I also started learning from Ruth First, especially about the art of relaxation. On occasional Sunday mornings I would join her on the ferry across to Katembe, where we would swim in the sea, have a late lunch and go for a walk, then return to Maputo to take in a movie. It was instructive to note how she could switch off so totally from work on these occasions, one of the secrets, she told me, of her immense productivity.[450]

But life was still feverish for Joe and Ruth. She spoke in January 1982 at a seventieth birthday celebration for imprisoned Rivonia Trial defendant Walter Sisulu. He was honored with the Isithwalandwe Seaparankoe Award (the one who wears the plumes of the rare bird), the ANC's highest accolade. Joe Slovo was later honored with the same award. Ruth spoke of his humanity and commitment to liberation. Shortly after praising Sisulu from her heart, Ruth traveled to Tanzania where she met with teachers and students at the ANC School in Mazimbu. Spencer Hodgson wrote about the meetings at the school. "In the few days she was here, she made a tremendous impact. Her vitality and uncompromising truthfulness really set sparks flying; her questions about the school, its purpose, cut right through to the heart of the problems. Long after she left discussions were still raging."[451]

After returning from Tanzania in 1982, Ruth began to prepare for a major conference that was to be sponsored by the Center of African Studies At the time, UNESCO had a Social Science Center in Zaire and there was talk of relocating it to Eduardo Mondlane University. According to Bridget O'Laughlin and Colin Darch, Ruth was opposed to the proposal because she thought that it would take away

Ruth seated at left of woman standing at a Maputo conference
(courtesy of Pamela dos Santos)

resources from academic departments and CEA. However, she did agree, albeit reluctantly, when the Rector, Fernando Ganhão, asked the Center of African Studies to host the UNESCO conference on social sciences, where there would be international academic presentations on Southern Africa and a discussion of the relocation of the Social Science Center.

The Social Science Conference occurred between August 9 and 13 and was considered a great success. Ruth and Aquino sent out formal invitations in May, and a letter, in the case of at least Jack Simons, that described Ruth's hopes for the conference:

> We want, in fact, an engaged meeting of social scientists, committed to the liberation struggle and to the transformation of the independent societies; indeed, without saying so explicitly, to the critical rejection of those trends in the social sciences which make for academicism rather than struggle.[452]

Ruth and Aquino spoke at the conference about the Center and the Development course. Other CEA colleagues, such as Jeanne Penvenne, Rob Davies, and Dan O'Meara, read papers, and African and international scholars like Apollon Davidson from the Soviet Union, Immanuel Wallerstein, Aquino's friend from the United States, Pallo Jordan, and Joe's best friend, Harold Wolpe, attended the conference.

Ruth arranged for Abdullah Ibrahim, whose stage name was Dollar Brand, to play with his band in Maputo during the dates of the meeting. The conference was vibrant, and Dan O'Meara recalls that Ruth was critical of his and Rob Davies's paper as well as the one presented by John Saul. Joe questioned his and Rob's thesis and O'Meara had a lively conversation with Harold Wolpe, John Saul, Pallo Jordan, and others debating the thesis of the paper: "The Botha regime wasn't going to scrap apartheid, but they had changed the style of apartheid in ways the ANC was failing to take into account and which could potentially undermine middle-class black support for the ANC."[453] O'Meara also recalls Ruth's criticism of John Saul's paper, which referred to his experiences in the Department of Marxism and Leninism defining two types of Marxism—"frozen Marxism" and "revolutionary Marxism." The former corresponded to the Soviet Union and the German Democratic Republic, and the latter to possibilities in Mozambique. A spirited debate ensued.

With the great success of the Social Science Conference, the Center's staff met for drinks at the end of the final day. Ruth congratulated each person and provided a calendar for time off to honor the hard work the staff contributed for the conference. Though extremely fatigued, she was elated by the participation, and both she and Joe looked forward to a social weekend with Harold Wolpe and other friends who had remained in Maputo after the conference ended. For both Joe and Ruth, times were exciting and filled with possibilities.

9 — Assassination, Grief, and Expulsion from Maputo

AFTER A LONG WEEKEND, Ruth drove her Renault to the Center of African Studies office on Tuesday morning, August 17, 1982. She was wearing a red blazer she had borrowed from Moira Forjaz, white skirt, and her favorite Italian shoes and expected something of an easygoing day. She also planned to return to the office late in the afternoon for a get-together honoring John Saul, who was leaving his post in the Department of Marxism and Leninism and returning to Canada. Joe planned to spend at least some of the day with Harold Wolpe, who was still in Maputo, and they were all meeting Sue Rabkin and Pallo Jordan for lunch at Moira and Zé Forjaz's house. Accompanied by Moira, Ruth then ran some errands for the party. She made a quick stop at home to retrieve a bottle of wine before returning to the office.

Helena Dolny was in her office when Ruth returned to CEA, and she recalls hearing the clicking of Ruth's shoes as she walked down the corridor with Aquino de Bragança. Aquino peeked into Helena's office and asked if she was coming to the reception, to which she replied that she would be down shortly as she needed to finish some work. As it happened, John Saul was late for his own party. Pallo Jordan was in Ruth's office with Aquino, Bridget O'Laughlin, and Ruth awaiting the arrival of Saul and other guests. Aquino, in his half-teasing and half-serious way, told Ruth that people might think that she was the director, not him, because her mailbox was totally full and he got so little mail. Before going to retrieve her letters, Ruth offered the refrain that she had repeated many times: "Well, you know if you want to get mail from people you have to write to them."[454]

When Ruth returned, Aquino was sitting at her desk, so she stood next to it. Pallo was adjacent to her and Bridget stood near the door. The four continued to chat and Ruth began to open her mail. Helena Dolny, still in her office, was startled by a large explosion. O'Laughlin, who was pregnant, heard three blasts and saw Ruth "lying straddled on the floor, facedown and motionless. She was not moving and lying totally still."[455] Pallo Jordan, injured badly in the bombing, holds vivid memories:

> She was reading her mail and chatting away and then suddenly there was this flash. You know in the movies when they show explosives like that and they make everything go into slow motion. That is how you perceive the whole situation. I mean nothing goes into slow motion, but that is how your brain perceives it. It's at the end of that when you try gathering yourself together and you realize that there was a bomb.[456]

Jordan suffered multiple injuries and was hospitalized for an extended period. His left eardrum was blown out, one eye was destroyed, and he had shrapnel throughout his body, fragments of Ruth's bones. Ruth First was dead. She was fifty-seven years old and had been assassinated by the apartheid regime.

Ruth's killing followed the regime's murders at Matola and the killing of Joe Gqabi, as well as the assassinations of Rick Turner, Petrus and Jabu Nzima, and Griffiths and Victoria Mxenge, and the "hanging" of physician and trade unionist Neil Aggett in a Johannesburg prison cell. Undoubtedly, the South African apartheid government had assassinated Ruth First. But it was not until Gillian Slovo's memoir described her interview with South African agent provocateur Craig Williamson, and his testimony before the Truth and Reconciliation Commission (TRC), that anyone in the apartheid regime took responsibility for Ruth's murder. Much has been written about Williamson's life as a spy and his attempts to infiltrate the African National Congress. When the lists of the regime's assassinations orchestrated by Craig Williamson became public, people of the struggle began to talk about mistrusting him when he was supposedly working for the Anti-Apartheid Movement. Correspondence transpired in 1980 between Joe and Oliver Tambo that addressed

Williamson trying to gain the ANC's favor. Joe wrote, "There was no chance of Williamson getting involved in our affairs. We were suspicious of him throughout."[457] Obviously, Craig Williamson did infiltrate Joe Slovo and Ruth First's affairs. In his testimony before the TRC, Williamson admitted orchestrating the sending of the letter bomb. He argued that even though he could not recall if it was addressed to Joe or Ruth, they were both viable targets because they each threatened the sovereignty of the Republic of South Africa.

In Maputo, as well as to friends and comrades throughout the world, the news of Ruth First's murder spread quickly. The South African regime began to spin Ruth's assassination through the nation's press. Joe had seen Ruth an hour earlier and was still at home having tea with Harold Wolpe when he received a phone call from Ruth's colleague Marc Wuyts. He immediately drove the Mazda he was using to Ruth's office. He suspected the worst, and knew that Ruth was dead as soon as he entered the building. After that, the factual sequence becomes blurred, although Albie Sachs recalls going to the mortuary. His words to describe viewing Ruth's body were "terrible and shocking and destructive."[458] Robyn, Gillian, and Ruth's mother, Tilly, were in London. Shawn was in New York. They all left quickly for Maputo. Zé Forjaz was at a conference in Portugal, and he escorted the women on the final segment of their sad journey. People quickly began to gather at Ruth and Joe's house on Rua Azarua. Sue Rabkin had been en route to meet Ruth but was stopped by Mohammad Timol who then informed her that Ruth was dead. Rabkin "shook like a leaf" as she drove to the Sommerschield house where she found Joe, despondent, and Harold. It was not long before ANC women arrived. "The ANC moved into the kitchen and then nobody could bear it because you know what happens at an ANC funeral. The ANC moves into the kitchen and takes over the whole kitchen so you never have to think about a cup of tea or a glass of water and they stay all the time."[459] Friends in Mozambique quickly came to comfort Joe. Dan O'Meara and Linzi Manicom had been on a short holiday but they came back to Maputo when they received the news. O'Meara recalls the overwhelming sadness:

> So we just sat around his house and Joe was absolutely shattered. He was there and not there. Nobody knew what to say and he would make small talk if people spoke to him; he didn't say anything, he just sat. It was important to him that people

were there. He didn't want to go into his room. He wanted to sit with people, but he couldn't talk. If someone asked him a factual question he would answer. The man's world was clearly rocked in a very fundamental sense. I think everybody has said about that relationship that as complicated and as difficult as it was, it was fundamental to Joe.[460]

Meanwhile, Moira Forjaz began to notify Ruth's family and friends in South Africa and the United Kingdom. Barney Simon was staying at Mary Benson's house when they received the news:

Mary was reading in the garden and suddenly she made a sound that I just instinctively knew I didn't want to hear. And I remember that feeling that my back became like a mountain of rock. I didn't want another sound from Mary. I didn't want to know what had caused that sound. And then she told me she'd just heard that Ruth had been murdered. I just said, "Okay, don't tell me. I can't understand it. I'll have to wait."[461]

A month later, Simon added Ruth to other fallen South African freedom fighters—Albert Luthuli, Robert Sobukwe, Bram Fischer, Lilian Ngoyi, and Steve Biko—to the dead heroes scene of his play, *Woza Albert*, then showing in London and Edinburgh, where it was dedicated to Ruth First.

Moira called Hillary Hamburger at 2 a.m. She was so grief-stricken and hysterical that Hillary thought she had said Joe had been killed. Hillary learned from South African Broadcasting that it was Ruth. Myrtle Berman wondered why the regime would kill Ruth and not Joe. Ruth's death was both ironic and unique, because many who knew Ruth First and Joe Slovo imagined that it would be Joe who would be assassinated.

The apartheid regime killed Ruth First because they knew that ideas are important. They killed Ruth First because she organized an international conference that questioned the authority and actions of the South African state. They probably also killed Ruth because she was an easier target than Joe and the regime knew that her murder would devastate Joe Slovo. Since the letter bomb was already in Ruth's mailbox during the conference, one can assume that the apartheid regime wanted her killed during the festivities. Shortly after Ruth was assassinated, Joseph Hanlon, a journalist who had interviewed

Ruth years earlier, explained that though most academics would not understand, the murder of Ruth First was a warning for academics: "They should not attend conferences like the one Ruth organized, and they should not support or practice research or teaching that calls for socialist transformation."[462] The South African government also killed Ruth First because she mentored young people in connecting ideas and actions, with the goal of democratic socialism in South Africa. Her close friend, colleague, and comrade, Gavin Williams, summarized it best in his 2010 speech at Rhodes University:

> Ruth First has come to be an icon of the revolutionary hero. This is to make too much of her. It is also to make too little. There is a danger that her real achievements, her bravery and her integrity, will be hidden behind the mirror. Ruth combined during her life the practical politics of the movement for liberation with commitments to investigating, researching and explaining.[463]

Three events in Maputo followed Ruth's murder: a concert by Abdullah Ibrahim at Cine Afrika, a memorial at Eduardo Mondlane University, and then a graveside service at Llanguene Cemetery where she was buried next to the Special Operations cadres who had been murdered in Matola. Joe visited Aquino, Bridget, and Pallo in the hospital the day after the bombing. He teased Bridget, saying, "Well, at least now they'll stop saying that you're a CEA agent."[464] When Joe went to visit Pallo Jordan in the hospital, Harold Wolpe was in the room; he'd brought a book that he knew Pallo treasured. There was some irony in that Jordan was wearing an eyepatch, was medicated, and not in condition to read. Joe chatted quietly with Pallo, and said to him, "You know, you are one of the people Ruth really respected."[465]

The memorial concert was led by composer Abdullah Ibrahim who began by reading a poem, "Cheap Death," which Bridget O'Laughlin had written in her hospital bed. He then read his own powerful poem, "The Boers Are Not Our Teachers." Dan O'Meara:

> It was clearly an incredibly emotional moment. As he walked onto the stage, the whole hall had gone dark, and the spotlight was on him. He's a tall guy. He was dressed entirely in black. He just started reading this poem in his very thick South African accent and I just collapsed. I couldn't think of a better way

to sum up what I thought the ANC stood for and what I think Ruth stood for and clearly what Joe stood for.[466]

Ibrahim and his band played music, and there were speeches as well as ANC and FRELIMO sloganeering. Albie Sachs, who a few years later survived a car bomb attack by the South African regime, recalls that "the music was a little bit soothing, but we were dismayed, shattered, stunned. It was just awful, incredible."[467]

At the Eduardo Mondlane University memorial, Rector Fernando Ganhão preached that Ruth did not accept "ready-made ideas" and he noted that her revolutionary role was to "disturb when necessary."[468] Ganhão had his battles with Ruth, but on this occasion he asserted, "We had struggles that were salutary because it was through this confrontation of ideas, through dialogue, through deepened debate that she carried out her role as a teacher."[469] Albie Sachs gave the most powerful speech. He spoke in Portuguese and began by noting that there were three contradictions in Ruth First's life: (1) being a white person in a black movement; (2) being middle class in a working-class movement; and (3) being a woman in a male political environment. Sachs explained that Ruth employed the contradictions to further the struggle. She did not fight her own white privilege, but rather "used all the advantages you got as a white person to feed into the struggle for support of emancipation in destroying the barriers between black and white."[470] As a middle-class person in the struggle, she relied on her education, benefits, and style to support the ANC and socialist movement. An example was her loving interactions with the ANC women's group, Albie explained. It was the third contradiction, however, of being a woman in a man's world, that she was never able to resolve. Thirty years after Ruth's murder, Albie Sachs elaborated:

> She took men on at the level of theory, and she was formidable. She wasn't abashed at all and she never felt put down in that sense. But she always felt that she wasn't doing her best, that she wasn't accomplished. It was almost unbelievable. She was so accomplished. She produced so much. She was so formidable. I was once speaking to Nadine Gordimer about her and Nadine couldn't believe this in Ruth. Nadine, who was pretty formidable herself, was scared of Ruth, intimidated by Ruth. And yet there was a restlessness and a sense of a lack

of accomplishment about herself that she never really over-
came. If you told her, after she gave one of her speeches, "That
was well done." She would glow and beam. You'd think it was
almost patronizing to say it to her. I just feel existentially as a
person in spite of all her accomplishments and people admiring her and respecting her and so on, she had something
inside that was unfinished, incomplete, and I connected that
up with Ruth the woman in a man's world. She never fully
resolved that. For me she is a very strong, continuing, active,
emotional, mental kind of presence. Often one wonders, how
would Ruth have responded and reacted?—and you can't say
for sure. In terms of things going on—what would her critique
have been? It is a pretty fruitless enterprise except that the
continuing reminder is to be alert, to be critical, but critical
in an engaged way. Critical not just in the pleasure you get
knocking down something that deserves to be knocked, but
with the view to improve, to advance.[471]

Ruth's funeral was held on Monday, August 23, at Llanguene
Cemetery. Marcelino dos Santos, the vice-president of Mozambique,
and a personal friend of Ruth and Joe's, represented FRELIMO, and
Moses Mabhida, the General Secretary of the South African Communist Party, gave the eulogy. Over 3,000 people enveloped Joe, Shawn,
Gillian, Robyn, and Tilly. Dos Santos acknowledged Ruth as a South
African freedom fighter who "was strengthening the unity between
the Mozambican and South African peoples." He also said, "No
bomb, no threat, will make us drop our support for the ANC and for
the people of South Africa."[472] Mabhida linked Ruth's murder with
other freedom fighters assassinated by the regime, and he connected
Ruth to Nelson Mandela and Oliver Tambo. He concluded saying,
"Ruth fought for the unshakeable unity of revolutionary theory and
revolutionary practice. She left behind her a solid body of work that
cannot be destroyed by any number of bombs."[473]

When the speeches ended, Ruth's family scattered flowers and soil
on her grave as an invitation for the gatherers to follow. The ANC
choir sang "The Red Flag" and Umkhonto we Sizwe songs as the
coffin was lowered into the ground. Ruth's friend Zé Forjaz designed
Ruth's gravestone, as well as those of the soldiers who were killed in
the Matola Massacre. Albie Sachs:

Ruth's funeral – Robyn, Shawn, Gillian, Joe with Tilly seated
(courtesy of UWC Robben Island–Mayibuye Archives)

I felt so much for her mother seeing her daughter being buried. To see Joe weeping. Joe was so tough—he just seemed so tough. To see him red-eyed and weeping was very, very distressing. We threw flowers into the grave and sand and the singing was exquisite, very beautiful. I kept thinking that Ruth would have been very pleased and proud with the organization and the singing and the lack of clichés. It wasn't a cliché, death. She didn't like formalism and routine. She wanted things to be real and appropriate and in that sense fresh.[474]

Condolences were expressed to Joe and the family from throughout the world—heads of state, political parties, unions, and individuals. Memorial services were scheduled in the Angolan camps, Lusaka, and London. But they were banned in South Africa. Official yet personal messages arrived from ANC and SACP leaders Oliver Tambo, Yusuf Dadoo, and Alfred Nzo, and national leaders and diplomats including Samora Machel; Sam Nujoma of SWAPO in Namibia; Aristides Pereira, president of Cape Verde; Sékou Touré, president of Guinea; and Kenneth Kaunda, president of Zambia. Walter Sisulu sent a letter from Robben Island Prison, and there were many other letters, including one from colleagues at Durham University and another from one of her students. Ros de Lanerolle asked, "Did she know how powerful she remains?"[475] Danny Schechter eulogized, saying, "I owe you all a debt as do so many others. For the rest of my life I'll have been proud to have known her."[476] Gavin Williams honored Ruth as a "friend, colleague, and critic";[477] and Michael Wolfers said, "She would want her memorial to be a renewal of the struggle."[478]

Three letters stand out. Rica's letter touched her closeness to Ruth:

I loved her as a friend and comrade in a special and unique fashion. I always felt that despite her monumental intellect and sparkling mind, which put her far above most of us, she never made me feel inferior. On the contrary, she had a knack of giving the impression that what I had to say was more important or more useful than anything she had to offer.[479]

Jack and Ray Simons mourned:

We tell ourselves and others that we are fighting a war, but that is no comfort. We loved Ruth dearly, admired her greatly as a comrade, committed revolutionary, brilliant writer and speaker. Her death will be a great loss to us all—which of course is what the regime intended. We shall continue the struggle but are the poorer without her.[480]

Wolfie Kodesh's letter, though totally respectful of Ruth's intellect and activism, directly addressed both Ruth and Joe. He recalled Joe telling him over thirty years earlier of his love for Ruth. He said, "Life is funny. Somehow I could think of many a person whom the enemy would most likely make an attempt at assassination. But I never thought those bastards would do this to Ruth."[481] Wolfie linked Einstein and Jack Simons with Ruth as people you just do not kill. He also shared that many years earlier, at one of the famous Slovo-First parties, and after a bit too much liquor, he asked Ruth if she was still in love with Joe. According to Kodesh, her reply was that her "admiration had increased ten-fold for you over the years. 'What is love?' she asked me. I could not answer—but there is no doubt that she had stars in her eyes when she said that about you."[482]

After the funeral, Tilly First returned to London while Joe and his daughters went for a brief holiday to the beach town of Pemba in northern Mozambique. Little is known of this trip except that after about five days Robyn returned to the United Kingdom and Gillian and Shawn left shortly after their sister. Joe saw them off at the airport in Maputo, and he was clearly grieving. At home he would play the Holly Near song, "It Could Have Been Me, Instead It Was You," again and again. Then, two weeks later, he boarded a plane to visit his daughters in London and attend a large memorial that the ANC had arranged for Ruth.

Joe, Gillian, Shawn, Robyn, and Tilly attended the London memorial service at Hampstead Town Hall on September 8, 1982. Ruth Mompati, the ANC's chief representative in the United Kingdom, hosted the event. Paul Joseph remembers the poignancy of her acknowledging Tilly and saying, "She was not just the mother of Ruth. She is the mother of all of us."[483] Ruth's friend Ronald Segal gave the eulogy. He honored Ruth First as a writer, revolutionary, intellectual, feminist, and teacher. He also acknowledged the other South African revolutionaries that had been assassinated by the apartheid regime. Segal's talk began with a call to action in Ruth's name:

> Ruth First's life was essentially a political act. And her death was, of course, a political act as well, of a hideously different kind. She would have wanted our celebration of her life, and our grief and our rage at her murder, to be, above all, a political act. We will not disappoint her. Let those who killed her know that if their motive was to intimidate or dismay us, we are not to be intimidated or dismayed. Indeed, those of us who were falling asleep have been aroused; those of us who were growing tired have been reinvigorated; those of us who have been separately leading our own lives have been made aware again of where together our lives should lead. The revolutionary movement, to which she gave so much of herself, will find in us only a reinforcement of purpose, of resources and of effort.[484]

Segal ended, calling Ruth his "dearest friend":

> I cannot conclude without a few words of a more personal kind about someone who was, for so many years, my dearest friend. She was fascinatingly full of paradoxes: seemingly less concerned with the risks to her life than with having her hair done; plainly disapproving whenever Joe and I played cards for money

but unable to resist spending much of the little that she had on a pair of Italian shoes; commanding on the platform and in debate, but shy and uncertain in private encounters with those she did not know; profoundly cultured and conscious of all the books she had not read, the pictures she had not seen. She had a striking elegance of body and of mind. And without ever making a single concession to them, from her own high standards, she worried about what others might think of her. She had an enormous capacity for friendship. She was warm and sensitive and generous and always unswervingly loyal. She was such fun. I admired her for what she did. And I love her for what she was. I will feel the loss of her to the last moment of my life.[485]

Being in London was not easy for Joe. Besides the tension that often appeared between his daughters and himself, he was forced to deal with Ruth's estate. Upon his return to Maputo, he moved out of the house he had shared with Ruth and into a smaller house in the FRELIMO-protected neighborhood. He would later move again into a garage apartment at Moira and Zé's house. In the introduction to his book, *Joe Slovo: The Unfinished Autobiography*, Helena Dolny recalls that it was a very tough year. He drank heavily for a while, but he knew that he needed to grieve and recover. He entered into a romantic relationship with Dolny, who simultaneously was planning to end her marriage to Ed Wethli. On his first New Year's Day without Ruth, Joe wrote to Helena:

Maputo was a bit deadly during the remainder of the festive season. Drink, good food and other jollities, but for me also a time of sadness. Went alone to the graveside on New Year's morning with a few flowers from the hedge of my new house. Listen, H, don't get sad for me: these are times of sweet and tearful memory.[486]

Joe continued his nightly "Route 66" adventures, which included a good amount of alcohol. However, he also began a regimen of exercise and writing in addition to his continuing responsibilities with Special Operations. In January 1983, he wrote a letter of gratitude to the many people who had sent condolences after Ruth was killed. His letter reminded people that the regime killed Ruth because of her "boundless energy and intellectual productivity in opposition to racist savagery"[487] and that "in keeping with their past, they acted in the only way fascist thugs know: if you cannot deal with an idea—kill it."[488] Joe also shared his feelings for Ruth:

> During the 33 years of our married life Ruth and I enjoyed a warm companionship and stimulating mutuality. It was not without its moments of contest which sometimes perturbed those of our acquaintances who were not yet aware of the chemistry of our relationship. Ruth expressed well an aspect of our spirited comradeship in a letter during one of our unavoidable separations: "Oh for a good row in close proximity." For me there is no measure to gauge her loss.[489]

Joe began daily swimming and autobiographical writing. He'd rise in the morning and go for a swim at Club Navale before beginning his days of meetings and writing. He registered at the health club as Joe Kaplan, the name on one of his false passports and the surname of Yusuf Dadoo's wife's family. In Mozambique everyone knew his true identity so the alias was rather silly. In fact, Rashid recalls that an immigration officer at the Maputo Airport once teased Joe, saying that he thought Joe Slovo was a better name. Morning swims became Joe's norm when in Maputo, and Zé Forjaz believed that Joe forced himself through his grief because "he had things to do. He had a country to make, a mission to fulfill. So he just kept going."[490]

Part of his grieving process was telling stories of his life into a microcassette recorder for what became his posthumous book, *Slovo: The Unfinished Autobiography*. When Joe was in London for Ruth's memorial, Barney Simon had suggested that he write his own story— and at least for a short time, Joe obliged. *Slovo: The Unfinished Autobiography* is crafted with a totally different presentation than Joe's political writing, which increased in 1984 through his time in exile, and when he returned home to South Africa in 1990. Creating his memoirs was therapeutic for Joe, yet he stopped the process after only a short time. He had notes for many chapters that never came to fruition. In one of his notebooks, he explained part of his motivation for writing: "My selective memories have a predilection for the ludicrous and the comic which lightens and makes it possible to bear more easily the heaviness and often tragedies of struggle."[491]

Joe's travel intensified and Special Operations continued as Joe worked closely with Rashid. Operations such as Blackout II sustained the assault on South Africa's power grid, and there was an attack on the Koeberg nuclear power plant that stopped it from coming online. In addition, a major strike on South African Air Force Headquarters occurred in May 1983. The attack on the military headquarters on Church Street in Pretoria was labeled "Operation Ruth First." Joe objected to the name, and the operation was not viewed as successful. The intention had been for the explosion to occur after civilians had finished their workday, but detonation was premature and nineteen people awaiting their afternoon bus were killed, contradicting the mores of ANC armed propaganda. The killing of nineteen people fueled the South African government's branding of the ANC as a terrorist organization. However, the significance of the attack for cadres in the camps and people on the ground in South Africa, including the revolutionary group United Democratic Front, illustrated even more poignantly than prior incursions that the regime was not invincible.

During Operation Ruth First, Joe was attending the groundbreaking May 1983 Politburo meeting, held outside of Moscow where SACP leaders and South African labor leaders met together for the first time in decades. In September, Joe was due in Prague for a meeting of the SACP Central Committee, but detoured to London, where his comrade Yusuf Dadoo was close to death. Joe and Dadoo had worked together in London and Slovo believed that Dadoo, who came from a privileged family, had made great personal sacrifices for the struggle. "Yusuf was truly one of nature's real socialists; he not only believed in the aphorism that all property is theft, but also lived it."[492] Joe spent time with Dadoo at the hospital and they spoke about politics, the Party, and the meeting that Joe was en route to in Prague. When more family and friends came to visit, the two men made a plan to meet the following morning. Joe arrived at the hospital to find Yusuf asleep, and when he awoke he seemed close to death. But in a short time he was again talking politics and Joe delivered Dadoo's final statement to the Central Committee meeting in Prague. The final visit became personal and even joyful with family and other friends and even a final glass of scotch, with the doctor's approval. Later that evening, Yusuf Dadoo died and Joe had lost another comrade. In the 1980s, Joe mentioned to Vladimir Shubin that sometimes before he made decisions, "He would think, what would Doc [Dadoo's nickname] do?"[493]

After the Prague meeting Joe returned to Maputo. Hugh Macmillan, whose article, "The African National Congress of South

Africa in Zambia: The Culture of Exile and the Changing Relationship with Home, 1964–1990," is seminal scholarship on the ANC in Zambia, remembers seeing Joe often in Lusaka after Ruth's death. In the middle of the year, Joe moved from his house to Zé and Moira's. It was during this period that he worked daily on further Special Operations projects.

Joe made multiple trips to London, where at times he and his daughters met with a therapist to talk about Ruth's death as well as the history of their family dynamics. Mac Maharaj remembered that he would return "totally drained and he would go back to these processes in spite of the havoc that it was wreaking on him."[494] In Maputo, the tension continued between Joe's unit and the political unit, but there was also some cooperation. Ten years later in interviews with Padraig O'Malley, Mac Mahraj accused Joe of being a hypocrite, saying that though he wrote about political struggle, he only practiced military struggle. However, in 1983, Mac Maharaj had been recruiting people to join Joe's unit—the military-political schism was not a clean one.

In retrospect, it is difficult to perceive the military-political divide as the schism that participants thought it to be. Borders appear to have been crossed all of the time. For example, Ronnie Kasrils passionately recalled trying to facilitate a merger, eliciting the wrath of both Joe and Mac. Yet he continued to work under both men at different times throughout the remaining years of the struggle. In addition, all of those in both military and political units remained central targets of the South African government, and the regime continued to eliminate people, as had occurred in the Matola Massacre and the assassination of Ruth First. In some ways, it is astonishing that they did not kill Joe during his years in Maputo. The ANC security division in Mozambique informed him that he was the regime's number-one target. It was later learned in Truth and Reconciliation Commission testimony the extent to which the regime wanted to kill him. In Williamson's testimony, he said he was frustrated at not being able to assassinate Joe and admitted to being one of the people who told the South African press that Joe was a KGB colonel. Williamson added that they did not even know if the KGB had the rank of colonel. He told the Commission that special arrangements had been made for Joe Slovo, "The Slovo Suite," in the basement at the infamous South African government interrogation and torture location, Daisy Farm.

Why the South African regime was unable to assassinate Joe Slovo remains a question. Joe did carry a gun, but he never stopped his "Route 66" rounds and was not extra cautious with self-protection. He casually visited friends at night and was clearly in the open when he lived at and then visited the Forjaz home. Zé recalls that Joe practiced rituals and was sometimes "reckless and lackadaisical"[495] in his local travels. Joe visited Sue Rabkin, Dan O'Meara, Rashid, Colin Darch, Moira and Zé, as well as numerous cooperantes. Helena Dolny reflected on the setting for Joe's nightly travels:

> So I think the intensity of personal relations is something I haven't encountered anywhere else in the world. I remember leaving the crèche with my daughter and thinking there are about 18 houses I could walk to and have a cup of tea. And especially after Ruth died that's what Joe did. What we called "Route 66." He would drop in and drop in and drop in. Part of it was also recruitment. He was recruiting for special ops. He was sizing people up. Who were the people who would become the gunrunners? Who were the people who had international passports? Who were the people who had British passports who would not need visas to go to Swaziland, Lesotho, or South Africa?[496]

Dan O'Meara recalled these visits, during which they would talk politics and sometimes play music and sing, just as they had done on beach holidays. Joe talked with him about the necessity of the ANC's connection with the Soviet Union being more practical than ideological. "We cannot run the revolution without them. Without them we are not at the stage yet that we can do it. He was pretty clear-eyed about that."[497] In addition, sometimes Joe visited O'Meara with Alexei Makarov, his Russian friend who was working in the Soviet embassy in Maputo and later became Russia's ambassador to South Africa during the negotiation stage leading up to the first democratic election in 1994. Dan O'Meara:

> He and Alexei were clearly good friends. Alexei, Joe, and I spent a very drunken afternoon with two guitars in my apartment. We played music and told stories and Alexei told jokes, and I thought if this man isn't a senior KGB agent he would be shot for telling the jokes. I would always wonder, Okay, Joe's

Joe and Alexei Makarov (courtesy of Helena Dolny)

walking around with this guy? Clearly Joe is a key guy for the Soviets in the South African world and he is very close to Alexei. So who in the hell is Alexei? So I thought about this. The little I knew about Alexei I liked, and I was impressed by his mind. He had the capacity to analyze the world, and he knew about South Africa.[498]

Colin Darch, Ruth's colleague at CEA, also hosted Joe, and he noted that going from house to house to see friends was common in Maputo and was signified by the Portuguese word "passear." He remembered two jokes Joe would tell:

Some guy comes to South Africa and the security police arrest him and they're beating the crap out of him. And he says, "Why are you beating me up. I'm an anti-communist." And they say, "We don't care what kind of communist you are."

Three guys are in a camp in Siberia, and they say to the first guy, "What are you in here for?" "My watch was always ahead of time and I would arrive for work early so they arrested me for industrial espionage." The second guy says, "My watch was always behind time so I would always get to work late so I am in here for industrial sabotage." And the third guy said, "My watch was always on time so they thought I had friends in the West."[499]

Both Dan O'Meara and Rashid believed that Joe was at risk because everyone in Maputo, including South African agents, recognized the cars he drove. Rashid pointed out that all ANC members' cars were known to the regime. Cars that were stolen in Johannesburg were often brought to Maputo as well as Harare and used in the struggle. Often these cars were nondescript, but at one point Joe drove a top-of-the-line BMW. Not exactly an anonymous ride, but thankfully, as Rashid recalls, a young comrade who was supposed to be taking the car to be serviced got drunk and totaled it. Joe then drove a less ostentatious automobile. Though he went to great lengths to protect the cadres involved in Special Operations, Rashid said, Joe himself was in the public domain:

> Joe had a very different philosophical way of dealing with it. There was no holding Joe back, or getting Joe to go hide in a house. Joe would go out every evening. He would drive and go and see so-and-so. He would start early evening and invariably he'd end with us so we'd have a meal. There was a social network. Joe was not one to sit at home. Joe in that sense was not scared. He understood that he was enemy number one. He understood that the regime was out there to get them.[500]

Ruth's book *Black Gold: The Mozambican Miner, Proletarian and Peasant* was published in 1983. Ruth had tangled with the publisher because she did not want to be listed as the sole author; the book was a collective Center of African Studies effort, and the endurance and editing of Gavin Williams and Ros de Lanerolle brought the book to fruition. Before Ruth was killed, she and Joe visited Williams, who was then teaching at Oxford, and they consulted on the manuscript. The book cited Ruth as author; Moira Forjaz was listed on the title page for her photographs, images still available in galleries in Maputo and Lisbon that are in the tradition of David Goldblatt in South Africa and Dorothea Lange in the United States. Alpheus Manghezi, who worked at CEA, is also acknowledged, and his oral histories of Mozambican workers with renditions of their work songs are found in each chapter. In addition, Ruth had written an "Authorship and Acknowledgements" section in which she enumerated every person who contributed to the study and stated unmistakably that the book was a collaborative effort.

Public tributes to Ruth First continued in 1983. Ruth's friend AnnMarie Wolpe wrote a biographical article in the academic journal *Feminist Review*, and Ann Scott, Ruth's co-author of *Olive Schreiner*, eulogized Ruth in *History Workshop*. A British television program, *20/20 Vision*, produced a show on Ruth's life, and Ronald Segal in conjunction with Shawn, Gillian, and Robyn established the Ruth First Memorial Trust. Oliver Tambo wrote to Segal in July:

> In view of reports I have received, suggesting the Ruth First Memorial Trust does not enjoy the full support of the ANC, allow me to reiterate and reaffirm the ANC's full support for the trust and its objectives. We shall miss no future opportunity of expressing our strongest support for the Trust and I should like, on behalf of the NEC of the ANC, and on my own behalf, to wish the Trust a place, among our people and the friends of our struggle, worthy of Ruth First.[501]

In South Africa, despite the banning of memorials for Ruth First, Luli Callinicos launched an academic seminar on Ruth's work at the University of the Witwatersrand. She invited various people to talk about books Ruth had authored, including academics Jacky Cock, Tom Lodge, Patrick Pearson, and Eddie Webster. All who were invited to the seminar were left-wing academics, though several people chose not to participate in the seminar. "I was surprised but they were terrified. This one person said, and he had known Ruth, 'Well, those who lived by the sword have died by the sword.' It was disgusting."[502]

Fear was understandable; the South African government was revving up oppression at home, which became even harsher in the following years with numerous states of emergency declared in the country. Concurrently, the regime was placing a great deal of pressure on the border states, including Mozambique, to ban the ANC from operating in their countries. FRELIMO was experiencing both the economic and political effects of the South African regime. The number of Mozambicans working in South African mines was reduced from approximately 100,000 to 40,000 and shipping through the Indian Ocean was making port in South Africa rather than going through Mozambique. In addition, the South African regime was arming, training, and funding the counterrevolutionary group, Mozambican National Resistance (RENAMO); thus the Mozambicans were worried about their own existence. Although it was unknown then, South Africa had already entered into a secret agreement with Swaziland that led to more frequent arrests of ANC cadres in that country. In 1983, the South African government made, at the very least, three military incursions into Mozambique. In May, the regime attempted to bomb Matola residences and sent a military drone into Maputo. Then, in October, ANC headquarters in Maputo was bombed. Gavin Williams connected Ruth's assassination to South African pressure on Mozambique:

> Not only did the South Africans deprive Mozambique and the South African liberation movement of an able and independent thinker, they also demonstrated again their capacity to attack their enemies, and the friends of their enemies, wherever they are. In this way they hope to convince neighboring governments that they have no choice but to cooperate with Pretoria on South Africa's terms.[503]

Simultaneous to the attacks, the South African government had begun secret talks with FRELIMO. There was dissidence on the South African side. The foreign ministry sought to make an agreement with Samora Machel for propaganda purposes in the West while the military position was to support RENAMO or simply attack Mozambique. Formal meetings between the two governments began in late 1983, and in January 1984 President Machel met with Oliver Tambo and an ANC delegation. Joe Slovo was included in the group. Machel had conferred with Tambo in the latter part of 1983 regarding the pressure he was experiencing from South Africa. During the next two months, the Mozambican government assured the ANC that Joe and his South African comrades would be able to remain in Mozambique. Clearly, Machel and other FRELIMO leaders were struggling, anxious about a South African invasion. The Mozambican minister of information, José Luis Cabaço, insisted years later that Samora Machel believed what he said to the ANC delegation. Zé Forjaz was in the Mozambican government at the time and remembers the reality as "they controlled us and we knew they controlled us."[504]

On March 16, 1984, the Mozambican and South African governments signed the Nkomati Accord. FRELIMO agreed to limit the number of ANC diplomatic mission members in the country to ten people and vowed not to allow MK military operations to originate from Mozambique. For its part, South Africa agreed to further trade and pledged not to support RENAMO. Of course, South Africa quietly reneged on its part of the agreement. The agreement was abysmal for the ANC. Even though Joe knew that FRELIMO believed in the struggle, he viewed the Nkomati Accord as betrayal. Perhaps more than anything else, the ANC was infuriated by the fact that FRELIMO touted the Nkomati Accord as a victory for Mozambique. Shortly after the signing, Joe was involved in meetings with Mozambican leaders to facilitate the process. Just three days after the agreement, he was summoned by one of the ministers, Sergio Vieira, and was lectured about the ANC being disingenuous about property and weapons within Mozambique. As deeply as Joe was wounded by the Mozambican actions, he could not help but remind Vieira that he had carried a gun for protection within the struggle since Vieira was a child. Joe was given a set of discussion points on how FRELIMO and the ANC might work together without breaking the Accord and how the two organizations might explain to the world that the agreement was not a victory for South Africa. Vieira spoke about protecting ANC members who were at risk, meaning Joe, who was like a "red rag in front of a bull."[505] At the same time, Joe was informed that final plans needed to be implemented within a few days.

Five days after this meeting, Joe was summoned to meet with Mariano Matsinhe, the Minister of Security. Like Vieira, Matsinha first spoke of the close relationship of FRELIMO and the ANC. He told Joe that he was worried about his safety, but that it was time for the Nkomati Accord to be executed. Joe had already prepared a list of the people that the ANC wanted to maintain in Mozambique. However, the regime was on high alert and, of course, people like Joe Slovo were not going to be among those who remained in Maputo. The removals occurred quickly. Even while Mariano Matsinhe was briefing Joe on the expulsions, the Mozambican security force was searching Joe's house, and at least one member of the team absconded with various possessions. When Joe left the meeting, he sought out his comrades to convene an organizational meeting. En route, he passed his own house and saw armed police on the property. He decided not to stop, never imagining that Mozambican security would enter his house. He discovered a scene he was not expecting when he arrived home:

The burglar-proofing had been smashed and was lying on the kitchen floor, every moveable in the lounge was left in complete disarray with books churned up and lying on the floor. The bed sheets were mostly off the bed and lying on the floor, every cupboard was left open. The three weapons, which were stored openly, were taken away as well as a little recording machine and a wristwatch. Two zip bags hidden in a box and containing money had obviously been tampered with and both bags were found open with money exposed at the top.[506]

The treatment of ANC members and the expulsions were haphazard. Joe was angered by the ransacking of his house, though Sue Rabkin recalled the Mozambicans being polite and even shameful about the job they were doing. Rob Davies was at the airport when ANC members were evicted. He remembered the absurd situation as names were called and people other than those called boarded the planes—"He would shout 'Gebuza' and somebody else walked through onto the plane."[507] The urgency of the raids and evacuations corresponded to a South African delegation visiting in early April and FRELIMO wanting them to see that Mozambique had done its part in implementing the Nkomati Accord.

Joe Slovo, however, could not be anonymous. Although he was well aware that the Nkomati Accord severely hampered Special Operations, Joe took his cue from Oliver Tambo, who publicly noted Mozambique's dilemma, thanked FRELIMO for their camaraderie, and asserted that it was time to proceed with the struggle. In addition, Joe Slovo was beginning his relationship with Helena Dolny and was in the midst of even more travel for the struggle against apartheid. Zé Forjaz spoke about Helena and Joe's relationship: "Helena is such an intelligent and beautiful person. I think he felt very grateful that she as a younger person cared for him. And she really appreciated his enormously warm personality. Because he was a warm guy—the opposite of the image they tried to paint of him in South Africa."[508]

In November, Joe was again in Moscow for a meeting that became known as the Sixth Congress of the South African Communist Party. A new SACP constitution was approved and resolutions made about ideology, mobilization, and armed struggle. Quiet discussion took place about having preliminary conversations with Pretoria. The meeting was especially significant for Joe: Moses Mabhida was elected to the SACP's top post, General Secretary, and Joe Slovo became the National Chairman, second to Mabhida. For Joe, this signified a change in responsibilities, with much greater Party involvement while continuing as an MK leader from his new base in Lusaka.

10 — Lusaka, Marriage, and the Beginning of the Journey Home

TRAVELING WITH A COUNTERFEIT Mozambican passport, Joe continued his trips to Moscow and many other destinations. Though he came to admire Mikhail Gorbachev in early 1985, he certainly did not anticipate the dismantling of the Berlin Wall and the subsequent changes of governments throughout Eastern Europe. Although he had been effectively removed from Mozambique in June 1984, Joe visited Maputo often and combined seeing Helena Dolny with political work amid the South African freedom fighters who had been permitted to stay in Mozambique. In Moscow late in 1984, he appeared upbeat, past the dismay he experienced after the Nkomati Accord. Sustaining approximately a six-week traveling cycle to Maputo, in August 1984 Joe returned to deliver the FRELIMO-ANC–sponsored Ruth First Memorial Lecture at Eduardo Mondlane University.

"Some Key Concepts of the South African Struggle" was the title of Joe's lengthy oration, in which he connected Ruth to the movement. During 1985, events moved quickly in Joe Slovo's life, as well as in the struggle against apartheid. Lusaka was even more dangerous than Maputo, with a constant threat of South African invasions and the reality of local crime. Similar to life in Maputo, safe houses were established and people who were unknown to the South African regime joined the struggle, living double lives. This was also the year when Joe and Helena Dolny solidified their relationship. Helena and her husband, Ed Wethli, had begun to plan their divorce in 1984, and

Commemoration for Ruth in Maputo—Zuma on left, Mabhida third from
left, Ganhao, and Modise (courtesy of the Ruth First Papers Project,
Institute of Commonwealth Studies)

Joe was hopeful that Helena would move directly to Lusaka. However, Helena and Ed had two daughters, and they crafted a plan to live
separately for a year in Maputo while they co-parented their children.
Helena began to prepare for her life in Zambia, and Ed searched for
a position outside of Mozambique. She began a new position that
included quarterly meetings in Lusaka, and with the help of Harold
Wolpe, Pallo Jordan, and her eventual doctoral advisor, Lawrence
Harris, wrote a proposal for a Ph.D. at Open University. She saw the
necessity of having her own identity within the reality of Joe's work:
"I had no expectation of him not being assassinated, so if he was
going to get himself assassinated, which was a reasonable expectation
given that Ruth had been assassinated, this was not an unreasonable
fear. I wanted a reason for being in Lusaka that was my reason."[509]

Helena Dolny did not commit to move to Lusaka to join Joe until
late 1986. Thus Joe's "Route 66" life continued the first year he lived
in the Zambian capital. He saw Ronnie Kasrils, Pallo Jordan, and,
spent time with Rashid. More young people were now involved in
the struggle, and they became Joe Slovo's Lusaka family. Janet Love
was living in Lusaka when Joe moved there from Maputo, and he
would be instrumental in organizing her return to Johannesburg to
engineer clandestine communications networks for the forthcoming
Operation Vula. In Lusaka, Janet organized meetings between people

underground with Joe. Her reflections speak deeply on the definition of family in exile:

> The word that always sticks with me in terms of exile is "dislocation." You were constantly being dislocated from people you cared about deeply, either because they were sent off somewhere else or you were sent off somewhere else, or because they were killed or because they just had to make themselves scarce because they were going to be dispatched on some other activity or mission. I think what was more the reality in Lusaka to the extent that it was possible to be able to switch off the reality of being involved in struggle, being involved in exile and for a couple of hours to stand up and prepare with whatever was around a decent meal and have some wine or whiskey and really just talk about nothing and everything—to be able to talk about what was happening in the world at large, to be able to talk about the dynamics about something at the emotional level. Somehow there was normality in one of the most abnormal situations.[510]

Gonda Perez and Jaya Josie welcomed Joe at their house, a safe facility that was owned by the University Teaching Hospital where Gonda worked as a dentist. There were also dinners at Claire Bless's home, which was owned by the university where she taught Social Psychology. All three recalled political discussions, humor, music, and a great deal of eating and drinking on these occasions. Joe especially enjoyed the southern Indian curry that Jay and Gonda prepared when he visited. Josie recalled discussions about cruel MK commanders as well as traitors. They discussed black consciousness, the writings of Herbert Marcuse and Rosa Luxemburg, and the Soviet Union. Josie reflected on being with Joe in Lusaka:

> Joe operated from his heart. He was very emotional about people. If he liked somebody he would feel commitment. But he also had a very sharp brain and he saw Gorbachev as perhaps bringing in the changes. A lot of what happened in the Soviet Union and outside of South Africa was peripheral to Joe's thinking. For him the focus must be on South Africa, and that was his main goal.[511]

Though Albie Sachs's thoughts on Joe in exile are derived mostly from the period in which they both lived in Maputo, they can summarize Joe's life after moving to Lusaka: "Joe was often the target but meanwhile he has a life. So there is Joe the lover, Joe the person, Joe who could strum a guitar. I don't think he was all that musical, but he played music. Joe the raconteur. Joe enjoyed food, a good discussion, a good debate. But the core of it all was Joe the revolutionary."[512]

As in Maputo, Joe Slovo lived "behind open curtains."[513] Perez remembers him liking Rod Stewart, a rather odd preference when compared to the folk and rock songs that he sang. He also liked, seemingly beyond his boundaries, the Chicago mystery writer Sara Paretsky, who created the V. I. Warshawski detective stories. Perez's memories are a testament to Joe's humanity: "Joe—you couldn't call him fatherly but certainly a person I looked up to and respected and loved. I loved Joe for everything he stood for. There were no taboo subjects with Joe. You could talk to Joe about everything and anything. He loved life."[514]

Joe Slovo's Special Operations strategy and planning, political work, and extensive writing were all connected. By observing three months—April, May, and June 1985—it's possible to get a vivid snapshot of him. In April, again working directly with Rashid, and concurrent with the ANC agreeing to meet with some South African business leaders, Special Operations targeted large corporate concerns, including Anglo American, and headquarters were bombed after workers had left for the day. In May, Joe was again in Moscow, just two months after Mikhail Gorbachev had come to power proclaiming a new way, *perestroika*, that theoretically asserted the marriage of socialism and democracy. Visiting as a delegate to the fortieth-anniversary celebration of the Soviet Union's defeat of Nazi Germany, it was one of the rare times that Joe visited Moscow and did not spend all of his time in Communist Party meetings or lecturing South African cadres who were taking military training. Vladimir Shubin recalls the portion of the visit that occurred outside of official events: "On Victory Day, we strolled in Gorky Park, listened to the spontaneous singing of songs and reading of poetry, watched a fireworks display in the evening at the Lenin Hills near Moscow State University, and joined a group of singing students including some Africans."[515]

The most important 1985 political event for Joe Slovo was the Kabwe Conference, which took place in Zambia from June 16, the date that became Youth Day commemorating the Soweto Uprising, to

Joe at the Kabwe Conference (courtesy of Helena Dolny)

June 23. For months prior to the conference, regional ANC branches had discussed the armed struggle, human rights within the ANC including grievances and executions of traitors, and other organizational issues. Kabwe was attended by 250 delegates and the conference was significant for Joe for two reasons: the focus was on internal mobilization and the foundational documents used to prepare for the meeting were at least partially penned by Joe Slovo, "Strategy and Tactics" and *The Green Book*; and the conference delegates voted to make the ANC totally non-racial, opening the way for Joe Slovo to join the Executive Committee.

Reaffirming and solidifying the necessity of combining the political and military wings of the struggle, the conference called for regional politico-military committees. In addition, the ANC was now involved with struggle groups like the United Democratic Front that was fomenting protest within South Africa. Launched as a non-racial coalition in 1983, the UDF led protests and strikes that severely challenged the apartheid regime through people's power, and by the end of the decade it would progress to a mass democratic movement. The essential goal at Kabwe was to transfer the struggle from an emphasis on armed propaganda to one of an insurrectionary people's war, or as the ANC said in a published statement two months earlier, "Make apartheid unworkable. Make the country ungovernable."[516] However, a plan for operationalizing a people's war within the country was not systematically conceived at Kabwe. Mac Maharaj asserted that the two most thoughtful, theoretical, and tactical leaders, Joe Slovo and Chris Hani, were not charged with actualizing a strategy. Though Joe might have shared Maharaj's concern at the time, Sue Rabkin recalled that at the end of the meeting, the formal acknowledgments went to Oliver Tambo and Joe Slovo, whom comrades hoisted on their shoulders and carried out of the hall. Rabkin's reflections on Joe Slovo might also explain why it was he, with Oliver Tambo, who would energize Kabwe plans the following year:

> He loved Tambo and the other way around. He used to say to me, Tambo is a better communist than members of the Communist Party. Joe was very much an activist. He got his hands dirty. He didn't sit around giving orders. He worked bloody hard and nothing was too low for him. I experienced that first-hand, but he also knew he was in the leadership. So he didn't take nonsense. He expected some kind of a response, some kind of respect, which he got. I think the point was that he talked a lot and he expounded his theories a lot and that enabled every-body to engage with him and to find a way forward.[517]

Following the conference, Joe completed an interview for the British newspaper *The Guardian*. Jonathan Steele, one of Ruth First's co-authors of *The South African Connection*, interviewed him. The article, as well as Joe's writing throughout the remainder of the struggle, revealed a renewed energy and often included a breadth of ideas and politics that suggest Ruth's influence. As Albie Sachs said: "Probably her biggest contribution was as Joe's alter ego, Joe's critic."[518] Sachs's assertion is potent; and his elaboration on the idea brings depth to Joe and Ruth's relationship:

> Ruth would make sure that there were no clichés in his writing and would test and challenge and force him to think through every proposition, every statement, every sentence. In that sense they were fantastic intellectual lovers, sparring mates, combatants. But they had huge and deep respect for each other, really profound—intellectual, moral, emotional respect for each other. Neither was a touchy-feely, soft, warm, embracing

person. Both could show extraordinary compassion in particular moments, particular situations. Both could be very caring of things that were related to the struggle.[519]

In Joe's interview with Steele he connected the armed propaganda of the early 1980s with the growing vitality within South Africa and the ANC's alliance with the UDF, civic groups, and unions. He warned, "No romantic illusions must be held about the speed with which apartheid can be destroyed."[520] Joe was aware of the beginning of discussions between the ANC and representatives of the South African regime, but at this point and throughout the 1980s, he did not yet believe that armed struggle was approaching a conclusion. His emphasis in the interview focused on the weakened position of the apartheid regime through "a convergence of three essential pre-revolutionary factors: a crisis in the enemy's ranks, a clear demonstration that people are ready to struggle and sacrifice even at the risk of death, and widespread acceptance that there is an alternative source of power—the ANC."[521] Joe praised the UDF for using the Freedom Charter as a blueprint, even though it was not a socialist document, stating, "We're not Pol Pot. We're not in favor of abolishing the middle class."[522]

Joe also did an interview with the *World Marxist Review* that appeared later that year. He addressed the same topics and used similar theory and presented extended examples of the current status inside of South Africa, exemplified by the UDF and trade union participation in the struggle. He also referred to breakdowns within United States support for the South African regime.

Joe published a short article in Umkhonto we Sizwe's journal *Dawn* about the prison release of Denis Goldberg. In 1963, Goldberg left Cape Town and traveled to Johannesburg where Joe asked him to work with MK on securing weapons. Goldberg was arrested in the raid on Lilliesleaf Farm on July 11, 1963, and was one of eight people convicted of sabotage in the Rivonia Trial. He spent twenty-two years in prison until he agreed to reject armed violence in return for his release. He struggled with the decision, as he knew that other political prisoners, including Nelson Mandela, were not willing to make the same concession.

Joe's *Dawn* article was written after Goldberg took refuge in an Israeli kibbutz where his daughter lived. Joe was critical but understanding:

One cannot agree with the decision that he took, i.e. signing an agreement to give up the possibility of violent struggle. I am sure he does not agree with it in any case. We cannot agree that he chose Zionist Israel as a haven, moving from one prison to another. But at the same time we can understand and sympathize with a man who has played a very important role in the history of our struggle and we hope the wounds he has suffered will be healed and will find a place to continue struggling against this regime that blackmails him.[523]

After a brief respite in Israel, Goldberg moved to England. Before the end of the year, he met with Joe, first in Lusaka and then in London, to discuss his role in the struggle. In their first conversation, Joe suggested to Denis that before reinvolving himself in the struggle, he should get reacquainted with his family. Interestingly, in 1979 while still in prison, Goldberg had facilitated a meeting between Joe and Baruch Hirson, an avowed Trotskyist, whom Goldberg had befriended during their decade in prison together. Joe, of course, condemned Trotsky and even more so South African believers. Hirson volunteered to deliver messages from Goldberg to the ANC and MK. Goldberg's reflections were of Hirson and Slovo "swallowing their pride."[524] On the other hand, Slovo, unlike many members of the SACP, was willing to speak with Hirson, even though they'd had many theoretical and philosophical scuffles in the 1950s and early 1960s in Johannesburg. In the London meeting Goldberg was surprised by Joe's demeanor and observed that he had changed and was a nicer person. When Joe viewed this as something of a backhanded compliment, Goldberg explained that he appeared sensitive to how hard the prison release decision had been. Joe responded, in reference to the political struggle: "We had to learn that people are not made of steel, or blocks of wood. We asked too much of our activists and when they cracked we rejected them. We had to understand what human limits are and it's been a very painful lesson for the whole movement."[525]

Deaths were increasing in the struggle. Barney Molokoane, one of Joe's commanders of the Sasol attack, was killed in South Africa, and in late November David Rabkin, Sue Rabkin's husband, died in training in Angola when a faulty explosive detonated. Chris Hani and Joe spoke at the funeral in Luanda that was attended by Sue, their children Franny and Job, David's mother who was en route to Harare to meet the family for a short holiday, as well as comrades. In his eulogy, referring to recent successes in the struggle, Joe said, "If we are where we are today it is because of the likes of Dave."

As 1986 unfolded, Joe, Oliver Tambo, and other NEC members met to plan the escalation of the struggle within the borders of South Africa. Tambo and Slovo were authorized to direct a strategy, and they decided, with top secrecy, to transition senior MK leaders into the country, mobilizing military activity and underground political work—the people's war. In his extensive interviews with Padraig O'Malley, Mac Maharaj recalls that Joe Slovo and Oliver Tambo came to his house and asked him to write a short proposal dedicated to this task. Maharaj's plan, after discussions with Tambo and Slovo, was debated, edited, and approved by the two leaders. Entailing a two-year process with enormous preparation, strategizing with movement people already in the country, selfless cooperation by anti-apartheid activists in the Netherlands, and support from the Soviet Union, Operation Vula became a reality when Maharaj entered South Africa in 1988.

In late February 1986, Joe traveled to Moscow for the 27th Congress of the Communist Party of the Soviet Union. At the conference, Gorbachev stressed the necessity of settling regional conflicts throughout the world. He spoke of political negotiations but emphasized that discussions were unsuccessful when one side, assumed to be the South African government, was holding a gun aimed at the other side. According to Vladimir Shubin, Joe arrived from Lusaka in the early hours of the morning shortly before Gorbachev's main address. Joe was impressed by the Soviet president's stand and admitted to Shubin, "The proof is I did not fall asleep."[526]

Joe was aware of meetings between the ANC and University of Cape Town professor Hendrik van der Merwe in reference to possible negotiations, but he did not think the time had come for serious negotiations with the South African regime. Julius Browde, his colleague from when he was a lawyer in Johannesburg, was traveling between Johannesburg and Lusaka in 1986 as a representative for Frederik van Zyl Slabbert and Alex Boraine's organization, the Institute for a Democratic Alternative for South Africa (IDASA), a group that was trying to facilitate negotiations, or as Oliver Tambo teasingly said, "talk about talk about talks." Tambo set up a surprise reunion between Browde and Slovo, and Browde remembers Joe speaking at the subsequent meeting between Browde and exile leaders:

Joe at Moses Mahbida's funeral. Left to right: President Chissano, Joe, President Machel, President Tambo (courtesy of Helena Dolny)

I put the thing to them and it met with a mixed reception. Joe said, "Look, man, we've got to bide our time. You know people have asked me how long it will take for the ANC to take over in South Africa and I have told them about five years. But I must be truthful; I've been saying that for twenty years. While I appreciate what you're doing, forget it, it's not going to work." They knew more than I did.[527]

In March of 1986 Joe found himself in Maputo for the funeral of the General Secretary of the South African Communist Party, Moses Mabhida, a leader of the Party since 1979. Mabhida had suffered a stroke while visiting Cuba the previous year, and was flown to Mozambique with the blessing of President Machel who had admitted publicly by this time that the South Africans had not fulfilled any of their Nkomati Accord obligations and were still funding and training RENAMO. In 1985, captured documents from a RENAMO soldier, the Vass diaries, revealed without question that South Africa was supporting RENAMO and working to destabilize the FRELIMO government. Referring to South African President P. W. Botha, Machel told Frederik van Zyl Slabbert, "I cannot fight a war against him. But tell him, like Hitler's war ended in Berlin, his war will end in Pretoria."[528]

Machel, partially in reaction to continuing South African dirty tricks within Mozambique, allowed ANC members to attend the funeral of Moses Mabhida. Both Tambo and Machel offered eulogies and Joe also addressed the gathering:

> The racists hate South African communists with a special venom. To discredit what we stand for they spread the myth that communists are a strange people from faraway places who import foreign ideas from Europe, which are dangerous for Africa. The answer to all these outpourings lies before us in this coffin. Comrade Baba Mabhida, the leader of South Africa's communists, personalized the real essence of our land and its people. He was nurtured by its very soil, which he loved with a deep passion. It is no accident that all these working-class and communist leaders also became outstanding figures in a national movement.[529]

Moses Mabhida's funeral was solemn and respectful. Joe and his comrades were inspired when 20,000 people in a township just outside of Port Elizabeth defied the government's ban on political meetings and paid homage to their dead leader. Young people shouted "Viva" to the SACP, Marx, and Lenin. The *Los Angeles Times* reported: "Red Communist flags bearing the yellow hammer and sickle were raised by the dozen at a sports stadium in Zwide, a black township outside Port Elizabeth on South Africa's Indian Ocean coast. Placards praised the South African Communist Party and that of the Soviet Union."[530]

Seven months later, Samora Machel met his demise in an airplane crash over South Africa. This "accident" appears to have been orchestrated by the South African regime in retribution for Machel's continuing condemnation of South Africa's clandestine support of RENAMO's operations against the Mozambican government. Numerous FRELIMO leaders died with the Mozambican president in the crash, including Ruth's colleague, the founder and director of CEA, Aquino de Bragança. Joe was greatly shaken by the crash. He connected the deaths to the South African regime's killings of ANC freedom fighters. In his condolence letter to FRELIMO he wrote, "Your incalculable loss is also a tremendous loss for Africa and the world community."[531] Related, at least in terms of the price that blacks in southern Africa paid for their freedom, Polly Gaster recalls a statement Joe made at the time of Mabhida's funeral. He asked her whether she had noticed that white comrades wrote all of the South African prison diaries. "He thought it was because as bad as it was for whites, it was bearable. But for blacks it was hell and they didn't want to speak about it."[532]

Throughout the year Helena Dolny was readying herself for her move to Lusaka. Ed Wethli had found a job in Zimbabwe's second city, Bulawayo. This was a difficult time for her, since she and Ed had made the decision that their daughters would be safer living with him rather than with her and Joe. Tears still come to her eyes when she speaks of this decision more than twenty-five years later:

> I remember walking with Joe on the beach in Mozambique and I had in my pocket an index card and it had pros and it had cons. I still have that. The cons were all like, do I lose my identity? What do I do? What about the kids? The pros were almost like negative pros. They were the ANC is conservative, Christian, and patriarchic. And if I go to Lusaka as somebody who is twenty-seven years younger than Joe I will be treated as a young floozy. And I'm not prepared to be treated as a young floozy. So it was saying if I'm going we have to be married. So Joe agreed that we would get married. I remember him saying afterward that he hadn't expected it to make a difference to the way he felt, but in fact he did feel different.[533]

Jaya Josie also spoke with Joe about marriage:

> I remember when Joe was grappling with getting married again. It was just Joe and I sitting down and he was grappling with the issue of age. He said, "What will people think?" So I said, "Is that all that's bothering you, Joe?" And he said, "No, it's difficult." He was worried about his kids and they were older than Helena. In the end he loved Helena, and Helena loved him, and they were quite happy to get on with things.[534]

Helena did not move to Lusaka until December. In the interim, Joe was in the Soviet Union and the GDR a number of times and also visited cadres in various border states. Similar to his interactions in the Angolan camps and Mozambican cadres' houses, James Ngculu recalled him motivating young MK soldiers in Zambia. Joe shared a

Time magazine cover photograph of Palestinian youth throwing rocks at Israeli soldiers and asked the young cadres, since MK was now moving to a people's war, "What do you think would happen if the rocks were grenades?"[535]

Joe continued to write articles on the struggle for *Dawn* throughout the second half of the 1980s. The journal was the official organ of Umkhonto we Sizwe and was restarted in 1978 through the efforts of Mzwandile Piliso and Ronnie Kasrils. In addition to Joe and other leaders' contributions, there were also articles and poems by young people in the camps. Even more important, *Dawn* was read in the camps by the rank and file. "It acted as the communicator and educator not only for those in the camps but also those inside the country, when it was smuggled into South Africa and the forward areas," Ngculu said.[536] Joe's 1986 articles included a historical, present, and future trilogy. All three articles conformed to *Dawn*'s mission of teaching young soldiers the story of the armed struggle. Joe explained the beginnings of the campaign as initially symbolic and a call for change: "Nobody in their wildest imaginings dreamt that one could actually overthrow the regime or bring about a revolution through overturning a few pylons and putting some rather weak homemade explosives in relatively innocuous targets."[537] In "The Sabotage Campaign," Joe reviewed the early history of MK and wrote of going into exile to promote the struggle on the African continent. In "1976 to the Present," he traced the origins of armed propaganda and the movement toward a people's war within South Africa. "The Second Stage" reviewed historical attempts to send MK cadres back into South Africa and asserted the imperative of leaders clandestinely returning to the country through Operation Vula.

In July, Joe traveled to London to participate in a rather innocuous BBC interview on the armed struggle. Knowing that "talks about talks" were in progress, he offered one impactful statement: "I wish there were, but there is no way forward in South Africa without the armed factor in the struggle. To cancel a movement like ours, to abandon it, even if it does occasionally have blemishes, is to counsel us to submit to surrender."[538] More important for Joe while in London was the 65th Anniversary Meeting of the South African Communist Party. He delivered the keynote address, speaking about the history of the Party, the longtime connections to the ANC, and the SACP's present and future roles in, first, the struggle, and then democracy in South Africa. Joe acknowledged the failures in Party history, bureaucratic elitism, and non-democratic practices, but also addressed Party successes and the marriage, albeit with obstacles, of the working class and nationalist movements: "But perhaps one of our most signal achievements in the sixty-five years of our existence has been a truly indigenous elaboration of the theory of South African Revolution."[539]

Joe emphasized the leadership role of the ANC with the SACP and trade unions as partners. He had had conversations with Congress of South African Trade Unions (COSATU) labor leader Jay Naidoo the year before at a World Council of Churches conference in Zimbabwe, and they had met again at a 1986 meeting of the British Trade Union Congress in London. Naidoo described that meeting as "crucial, as it consolidated my relationship with the senior leadership of the ANC in exile."[540] Joe Slovo and Chris Hani, he stated, were more open than other leaders of the ANC-SACP alliance because they were willing to have conversations with struggle organizations and people who did not have ANC or SACP pedigrees.

In the speech, Joe asserted that the Freedom Charter, a democratic document, remained the blueprint for a new South Africa, acknowledging that it was a document for both socialists and non-socialists. Joe cited the support of the Soviet Union and praised the mid-1980s spark within the country as he listed four tenets of a democratic South Africa: Majority rule as stated in the Freedom Charter; Individual equality; Diversity within a united, democratic South Africa; an initially mixed economy.

Outlining the differences between a new Freedom Charter government and the apartheid regime, Joe also emphasized the moment:

In the meanwhile, mass political struggle coupled with an intensification of revolutionary violence remains the imperative. We have never relished the path to violence. But it is plain for all honest observers to see how tightly closed have been all other avenues for meaningful change. . . . And let me emphasize this: if a real possibility emerges of moving towards the total abolition of apartheid, without escalating violence, there is no sector of our liberation alliance which would reject such a path or refuse to talk to people of goodwill about how to get there. In present circumstances to expect the ANC-led liberation alliance to unilaterally abandon violence is to ask it to abandon the people's aspirations. The absence of violence is dependent on the presence of democracy. In any case, it is difficult to think of an example in history of a movement going to the negotiating table having abandoned the very tactic which has played such an important role in getting the enemy to sit around it.[541]

In August, Joe went to Berlin with Chris Hani to meet with Oliver Tambo, who was hospitalized for heart treatment. Joe and Tambo discussed negotiations, Operation Vula, and their relationships with the Soviets, Cubans, East Germans, and Chinese. Shortly thereafter, at Tambo's request, Joe visited Moscow and spoke with Vladimir Shubin about arranging a meeting between Tambo and Gorbachev. The ANC believed that Gorbachev's popularity in the West might help to ease relationships with the United States and possibly even England. However, the meeting did not materialize until November.

Back in Lusaka, Joe was in constant meetings. He again worked closely with Ronnie Kasrils, and there were consultations with others who had taken more commanding roles. Joe was meeting with Rashid formally, once or twice a week, and informally, every second day to discuss both politics and military operations. People like Janet Love, and, of course, Mac Maharaj, also worked with Joe planning underground activities. As was typical of Joe Slovo throughout his life, he continued to perform thoughtful gestures for friends and colleagues. For example, he would bring gifts to friends in Lusaka from both Moscow and London. On a larger scale, he arranged a scholarship for Claire Bless's daughter to attend medical school in Cuba and made a point of checking on her when he was in Cuba later in the decade.

Also in 1986, Joe Slovo broke new ground in September when he led an ANC-SACP group to China. The Chinese government quietly made contact with the ANC and SACP in the early 1980s, and Joe met with a delegation in Lusaka in 1985. After discussions with the Soviet Union, Joe assisted in the restoration of relations between the SACP and China. The breadth of ANC associations in the world was growing quickly. In early November, just after attending Samora Machel's funeral in Maputo, Joe traveled to the Soviet Union for the Tambo-Gorbachev confab he had helped to arrange with Vladimir Shubin earlier in the year. Joe was a member of Tambo's delegation, but he did not participate in the president's discussions. However, he did attend a meeting the following day at the Ministry of Defense. The Soviet general Valentin Varrenikov, who was ill-prepared for the meeting chaired the session. Shubin recalls passing notes and chuckling with Joe during the event. The discussions in Moscow were about arms as well as negotiations and possibilities of peace in South Africa. It also became evident to the ANC through Gorbachev that the South African government was courting Moscow.

Later in the same month, Joe accepted the post of General Secretary of the South African Communist Party. The appointment occurred at the Central Committee meeting of the SACP that took place in Bulgaria. The position of General Secretary was all-encompassing work, and Joe soon relinquished his role as the MK Chief of Staff to Chris Hani, but continued working steadfastly on the underground struggle and his leadership role in Operation Vula.

The same month that Joe began his work as General Secretary of the SACP, Helena Dolny moved to Lusaka. Helena and Joe maintained two houses in Lusaka, one that was a public place and the other a secret, secure house where they spent their nights. As a couple, they enjoyed friends like Rashid, Pallo, Gonda and Jay, and others, meeting for meals and other social occasions. But Helena explained that their lives became more domestic than Joe's "Route 66" lifestyle:

I think that Joe needed a lot. That's a strange statement to make. He was absolutely focused on his work—zoned in. Then what he liked was coming home and leaving it at the door. So he was pretty good at coming in and relaxing. I like cooking. Joe liked eating. We listened to music, cooked, talked about our day. Lusaka was less sociable. Lusaka was a twosome life. We spent a lot of nights alone.[542]

Helena's daughters visited her in Lusaka, but more often she would make the drive to Bulawayo to see them. The distance, of course, was heart-wrenching, and Helena recalled returning to Lusaka after such stays: "I'd come back and Joe would have made a beautiful meal and candles, and I would just sit there and weep."[543] Friends of Joe speak about how happy Helena made Joe. Gonda recalled Joe's normalcy after Helena arrived in Lusaka:

Joe was different and not different. He was still the same loving and affable person. He clearly now had someone in his life, so he didn't visit that often but we were invited to visit him. We saw him in the domestic situation, washing dishes and helping in the kitchen.[544]

Planning their wedding for September 1987, they decided they would marry at a registry office in London with each of them asking their best friend to attend the ceremony. Joe chose Harold Wolpe, and Helena invited Gill Walt. Although Joe had been in London in June and July, he had not informed his daughters, whom he was not inviting to the ceremony, about his forthcoming marriage. But they were aware of the wedding because Nic Wolpe, AnnMarie and Harold's son, had asked them their thoughts about their father's plans to remarry. Helena's analysis of Joe not telling his daughters provides insights into Joe's fears and insecurities:

With my 20-20 vision I could possibly say that Joe was an emotional coward. But the girls gave him a hard time. They gave their parents a hard time. When Joe would go to London there was no way he could have lunch with his three daughters. There was sibling rivalry. He needed to have lunch with each one.[545]

It is one thing to look at the relationship that Ruth and Joe had with their daughters within the family vacuum, but there are more systemic considerations to take into account—the sacrifices of families involved in the struggle. Ruth and Joe were not the only couple in the struggle whose children suffered. Mandela discussed the issue at great length when apartheid ended, and numerous families in the ANC and SACP lived through years of separation. In the late 1980s, all three of Joe's daughters spent some time in Africa and he saw them quite often in London. Gillian writes about visits with Joe in her memoirs, and friends of Joe recall seeing Robyn in Lusaka. Both Shawn and Joe have discussed spending time together on the set when Shawn's film, *A World Apart*, was shot in Bulawayo, the city where Helena's children lived with their father. Shawn's words capture the relationships within struggle families in one sentence: "He was a great man to have as a father, but he really was an atrocious father."[546] Joe often visited the set and he and Shawn had the opportunity to speak about the past and about Ruth. He read drafts of the script and even wrote one of the scenes that relates directly to race and the children of South African freedom fighters. The scene is one in which the character that represents Shawn is asked to compare her fate with her father in exile and her mother in prison to the realities of black children whose mothers and fathers are forced to leave their homes just to make enough money to support their families. Joe has written of enjoying seeing Shawn at work, and she recalls his elation when the film won an award at the Cannes Film Festival. She also recalls that he was affected deeply by her indictment of both himself and Ruth. Shawn concluded by saying, "I don't think for one moment he would have ever claimed to be a good father."[547]

A parallel script on the complexities of Joe Slovo's family and political lives would be difficult to construct. What is certain, however, is that his political realities became even more complicated at the end of the 1980s. The Soviets were beginning discussions with the South African government and urging the ANC to do the same, though in reality those talks had already occurred clandestinely. In collaboration with Oliver Tambo, Joe continued to lead Operation Vula. Struggle leaders, like Mac Maharaj and Gebuza, had reentered South Africa, as Conny Braam, Ivan Pillay, and Tim Jenkins were working on Vula from outside the country. In 1987, there were over three hundred MK military operations inside South Africa. As in Lusaka, Joe and Rashid shared evening political and military conversations over whiskey. Sometimes they were joined by Joe Modise, and at other times the discussions followed social dinners with Helena and Joe. The more formal discussions and decisions occurred in the morning after coffee rather than liquor. Rashid noted that the process was different than in Maputo, but more important, Joe's insights were critical because of his deep connections to international politics.

Joe was attending meetings in London, East Germany, and the Soviet Union to negotiate within the context of continued armed struggle. He also traveled to Cuba at least twice, and made a side trip from the Soviet Union, this time with Helena in 1989 to visit his birthplace in Lithuania. In 1987 alone, Joe journeyed to the Soviet Union on at least four occasions. In a delegation with Tambo in May, the ANC reluctantly accepted the Soviets' beginning conversations with the South African government. In September, Joe attended a meeting in Moscow of the Soviet Solidarity Committee, at which time negotiations were discussed. During the same visit, he spoke at the Africa Institute, stating: "We don't say there will be no moment for us to make a compromise, but we cannot support now the scheme which would mean perpetuation of their minority rule, like the veto for minorities."[548]

These words provide glimpses of the formal negotiations that Joe would participate in a half decade later, and his assertions at the Moscow commemoration of the 70th anniversary of the October Revolution in November 1987 are poignantly directed toward the continuation of armed struggle. Sitting on a stage with Oliver Tambo and Sam Nujoma, the first president of Namibia, Joe condemned imperialist world forces and praised the Soviet Union for their support of revolutions in Mozambique, Angola, Namibia, and Nicaragua. He concluded his talk, saying: "There are certain regional conflicts when the prospect of political settlements or real negotiation does not yet depend on diplomatic maneuver but rather on the building up of the strength of the liberation forces and escalating blows against the Apartheid regime."[549]

Articles about Joe appeared in *Time* and *The New Republic* in the United States. The one-page *Time* article was less about Joe and more about fanning Cold War flames. Steven Mufson, who later wrote a book on the struggle, *Fighting Years,* wrote *The New Republic* essay. Mufson's article, patronizingly titled "Uncle Joe," described some of Joe's history based on interviews he conducted reporting for the *Wall Street Journal* in Africa. Mufson made an interesting distinction when he contrasted the regime's demonizing of Joe Slovo with young South Africans lionizing his life in the struggle: "As the tenth anniversary of the Soweto uprising approached last year, pupils in Soweto rechristened their government-run school Joe Slovo High School. . . . 'Slovo is truly colorless,' says one black student activist. 'He's just Slovo.'"[550]

Joe's new works included articles in *Umsebenzi* and a thirty-eight-page SACP discussion pamphlet, "The South African Working Class and the National Democratic Revolution." One of the *Umsebenzi* articles was a tribute to Oliver Tambo on his seventieth birthday, "A Comrade, a Brother, and a Friend," in which Joe thanked the president for his continuing support of the ANC-SACP alliance. The pamphlet, "The South African Working Class and the National Democratic Revolution," succinctly portrays his thoughts on the future of the South African revolution. The pamphlet's introduction reviews the questions that faced the struggle throughout—class struggle versus national struggle, stages of struggle, class disparity, and the role of the working class in liberation. It is important to note that throughout the pamphlet, Joe refers to academic and political critiques of the struggle that illustrate how aware he was of the literature, publications, and statements of the time, both at home in South Africa and throughout the world.

Joe next to Arafat in the Soviet Union (courtesy of Helena Dolny)

Class struggle versus national struggle, Joe stated, was a false debate. He simultaneously emphasized the uniqueness of South Africa, where race is essential to class disparity. He addressed racism and national oppression and emphasized the greater costs to the working class. He introduced the fluidity of class struggle, and used Lenin's critique of "pure revolution" to open up discussion of class alliances and stages as part of revolutionary struggle. Joe's six-page section on "The Black Middle Strata and the Emerging Black Bourgeoisie" were particularly interesting because they appeared to build on the thesis that Rob Davies and Dan O'Meara presented, and which Joe critiqued, at the UNESCO conference in Maputo in 1982. Though clearly stating that the South African regime had co-opted black people in promoting the black middle class, in terms of the struggle he asserted: "Class purity will surely lead to class suicide and socialist-sounding slogans will actually hold back the achievement of socialism."[551] He continued with a warning:

The question, therefore, is not whether they are participants in the struggle. The real question is whether the working class, by refusing to establish a common trench, helps push them right into the enemy's lap. On the other hand, by engaging with them on common minimum platforms, the working class is able to forge a stronger opposition and also to neutralize some of the negative potential of the middle class.[552]

Three stages of development were introduced in the pamphlet: national democratic, socialist democratic, and communist. The pamphlet distinguished between bourgeois-democratic and national-democratic, and argued that national democracy actually challenges the power elite—the bourgeoisie. Joe explains the first stage as a bridge to working-class leadership and a socialist state. He explains the necessity of economic safeguards against the ruling class during the first stage, stating: "A speedy advance towards socialism will depend, primarily, on the place which the working class has won for itself as a leader of society."[553] Political education of the working class, alliance of struggle groups, and the importance of the ANC, SACP, and COSATU are emphasized as the path to power. The pamphlet ends stating the ultimate importance of a non-racist, socialist/communist state. "The winning of the objectives of the national democratic revolution will, in turn, lay the basis for a steady advance in the direction of deepening our national unity on all fronts—economic, political and cultural—and towards a socialist transformation."[554] Large selections from Joe's pamphlet were used as one of the texts for the Political Education Workshops in Lusaka the following year. Accompanied by Jack Simons, Joe taught political theory and issues to young cadres until his return to South Africa in 1990.

Besides working with Ivan Pillay and Tim Jenkins on secret technology for use by Operation Vula inside South Africa, Joe went to West Germany where he participated in a meeting of IDASA, the organization that Julius Browde had brought to his attention earlier in Lusaka. It is somewhat difficult to comprehend Joe sitting at a table talking about formal negotiations at the same time he was leading underground assaults, but he was able to invest himself fully into both endeavors. The IDASA meeting included prominent South Africans, Soviet academics, and ANC leaders. Joe was one of the facilitators of a discussion that was viewed as an introduction of the South African and Soviet academics, an attempt to ameliorate misconceptions that each group had of the other.

In January 1988, Joe was unable to attend the commemoration of a memorial for both Ruth and Aquino de Bragança at the Center of African Studies in Maputo. The director of CEA, Sergio Vieira, spoke at the ceremony, as did Mac Maharaj, Immanuel Wallerstein, and Rhodes University professor Peter Vale. A white marble stone, with a plaque that read "Killed in the cause of science, progress, and peace," was dedicated, and it still remains standing in the courtyard where the Center is housed on the campus of Eduardo Mondlane University. Though Joe could not get to Maputo, he did write about Ruth in the introduction to a new edition of *117 Days*. The five-page essay is both biographical and political and concludes:

> *117 Days* is part of the inspiration which will inevitably lead to a society of justice and harmony in our land, and peace in the region. Of all Ruth's many books, it is by far the most intimate and personal. It is also a chronicle of signal bravery, all the more moving because Ruth showed no awareness of the courage with which she faced her tormentors.[555]

Travels continued at a fast pace. There were numerous difficult discussions in the ever-changing Soviet Union in 1988. Joe appeared pleased with Gorbachev's initial position connecting socialism and democracy, and had reason to be satisfied when he was assured by the Soviets that they would not only continue their financial support of the SACP, but would raise the amount of aid. Joe led a delegation to Moscow in April and he and Chris Hani were told that the Soviets grasped that the ANC was in a much better position to understand what was happening in South Africa than were the Soviets. However, when Slovo and Hani drafted a statement that included the term "armed struggle," they were asked to delete the word *armed*. At this point, however, Joe appeared unaffected. He presented a talk at the Institute of Social Science during the same visit and firmly stated: "We may be coming into the world when the struggle between the classes, between the oppressed and oppressors, would be carried out at the negotiation table, without using the traditional forms. . . . The question is not to talk or not to talk, but with whom to talk about what."[556]

But negotiations were not Joe Slovo's focus in 1988. In Lusaka he spent time with Ivan Pillay at Mac and Zarina Maharaj's house, which served as the communications center for Operation Vula. Along with Oliver Tambo, he authorized Mac to organize a system that would allow them to communicate with Nelson Mandela who was now allowed to have visitors. This particular aspect of Joe's role within the ANC leadership would continue for the two years till

Mandela's release in February 1990. Tension emerged when UDF and COSATU members within South Africa and some ANC leaders in exile believed that Madiba was plotting his own agreement with the de Klerk regime. Mac Maharaj became an integral player in easing the tension; Joe was definitely involved. The communication with Mandela was limited to Joe and Tambo, and part of his role was assessing the convergence of Mandela's and other conversations with government representatives, and the continuation of Operation Vula and other clandestine missions.

A new operation that Joe led was the movement of weapons into South Africa. His idea was to create an overland tour company to smuggle arms into South Africa. Joe asked longtime friend Mannie Brown, who lived in London, to organize the company and "Africa Hinterlands" was born. Brown interviewed people for the mission, and Rodney Wilkinson, who had been one of the cadres who detonated the Koeberg nuclear power station, was involved in the organization both in the United Kingdom and Africa. The actual overland tour truck is housed at the Rivonia Museum in suburban Johannesburg. In addition, Australian Tom Zubrycki and Mannie Brown's son, David Brown, made a documentary film, *The Secret Safari*. Africa Hinterlands driver Stuart Round described the journey and the mission in the 2012 book *London Recruits: The Secret War against Apartheid*. A customized Bedford truck in which weapons were stored under the seats had been shipped from England to Kenya. The trip originated in Nairobi, with the tourists having no idea about the clandestine nature of their holiday. En route there were stops to visit various game parks in Kenya and Tanzania. The tour then went to Lusaka where weapons were loaded onto the vehicle. The journeys continued through Zimbabwe and Botswana, and ended in South Africa, at which point the cargo was delivered.

Operation Vula was in full motion when Africa Hinterlands began. Mac Maharaj and Gebuza had gone to South Africa in July and underground cadres that included Janet Love had begun working to fight apartheid from within the country. By the end of the year, tension arose from Mac toward Joe; a rivalry between the two men had originated earlier in Maputo. According to Mac, Joe disappointed him before he left for South Africa to operationalize Vula because Joe revealed the mission to the SACP Politburo. Mac perceived this as a breach of security, though according to Mac Joe thought that it was necessary because Operation Vula needed Party support. It is difficult to assess the validity of the argument, as Joe's perspective cannot be ascertained. The anger of Mac as well as his wife Zarina toward Joe was magnified at the end of 1988.

In October, Zarina had a serious automobile accident that subsequently required treatment in Harare and eventually the United Kingdom. From her perspective, Joe treated her poorly at the time and she was particularly upset because she believed that he had not relayed the severity of the accident to Mac, who was underground in South Africa. Like her husband, Zarina Maharaj clearly had issues with Joe Slovo. Unlike people in Maputo and Lusaka who spoke cheerfully about Joe's "Route 66," Zarina resented it. "He would always turn up unexpectedly, even at our place, for a meal or whatever. He always came at mealtimes. He never took a dirty plate to the sink, we all had to do it."[557] Believing that Joe was unsupportive, Zarina felt used by his commandeering her house as the communication center when Mac was underground with Operation Vula.

The accident had a long-lasting effect on Mac and Joe's relationship. Helena Dolny recalled, "Joe had enormous, enormous respect for Mac. That is just beyond doubt. I remember him saying the problem with Mac is he's just too complex. He makes things too complicated. Sometimes keeping it simple works better."[558] Operation Vula continued into the 1990s and during that time Mac's anger toward Joe persisted. Rashid refers to the issues between the two men during the Maputo years as a healthy rivalry. While the argument can clearly be made that the conflict accelerated in later years, Joe and Mac worked very well together after Vula in the negotiation process.

The 1989 calendar year began with Operation Vula military actions in South Africa. Concurrently, Joe flew from Lusaka to Havana via Moscow for the 7th Congress of the South African Communist Party. The meeting, held at a conference center just outside of Havana, was historic because for the first time since the ANC and SACP were banned there was representation from within South Africa as well as the border states, and England. Harold Wolpe was in Havana for the conference and with Joe and Jeremy Cronin wrote the conference's primary document, "The Path to Power." Norman Levy recalls the mood of the SACP in Havana as "upbeat and optimistic" with very little discussion of the unbanning of the Party, even though that was to occur in the coming year. "The Path to Power" chronicled a plan for the imminent democratic revolution. The revolution was explained as a staged process beginning with one person, one vote, and including economic and social rights for all people. The socialist phase would be reached through reorganizing property rights, ending oppression of the working class, evicting foreign capital, and shifting ownership of certain entities to the public sector. Theory was much easier than practice at this point.

A lively discussion ensued on the proposal as well as talks on process. Delegates debated armed struggle versus negotiations, even though by 1989 the latter might have been a fait accompli. For some 7th Congress participants the issue was not yet an either/or proposition. Joe contended that armed struggle was still essential and that "The Path to Power" was not an invitation to the government to sit at the negotiating table. At the same time, he knew that negotiations, although not yet formal, were in process. Levy recalled, "Slovo did not think that an insurrectionary situation and the negotiation process were incompatible or contradictory. The mobilization of mass action would help to create the necessary leverage for a positive breakthrough."[559] "The Path to Power" argued for the importance of working-class actions, similar to actions of the armed struggle at the time, as the avenue toward democracy in South Africa. Sue Rabkin recalled herself and others vehemently opposing the proposal. There was disagreement around the stages outlined in the document, with concern about the plan not facilitating movement directly to a socialist state. However, at the conclusion of the discourse, Party members voted to enact the document and Joe presented the Congress's concluding statement:

> The test of a good policy is that it becomes negated by its own achievement. We have fulfilled the mission which exile gave us. Less and less can we hope to lead effectively from the outside. This growing limitation is not a measure of failure. It is a measure of success. It is ever more vital that more and more of us should be where the action really is.[560]

The Congress adjourned with the singing of the ANC's anthem, "Nkosi Sikelel' iAfrika," and a verse of "The Internationale."

While in Moscow in 1989, Joe took the opportunity to again visit his Lithuanian birthplace. On the train from Moscow to Vilna, Joe and Alexei Makarov drank vodka and spoke seriously of the changes in the Soviet Union and the future of South Africa. Helena accompanied Joe on this trip and she wrote about Joe having a more extended stay with his two aunts whom he last saw in 1981. This time he also met cousins, one a committed Communist and the other part of the independence movement. One of Joe's aunts served as their family historical guide in Obelei and Joe and Helena walked through the house that he left when he was ten years old. They continued on for a weeklong holiday to Palanga, a resort town on the Baltic Sea. One of Joe's aunts, Bela, was vacationing there. Enjoying coffee each afternoon and communicating in broken Yiddish, they both learned a great deal about each other's lives. Bela generously recalled Joe as a lively child. She told him and Helena about his *bris*, saving him from a fall out of a window, and his teasing of dogs with a stick he often carried. Taking a deep breath, Bela explained that she and her sister were the family's only survivors. Politically, he discovered that it was not the Nazis, but Lithuanian Nationalist surrogates who massacred the Jews of Obelei.

Joe and Helena were deeply moved by Bela's stories. There was lightness in his spirit as he told his aunt his best Stalin jokes. One was on Stalin's selection of a commemorative statue of Pushkin—the winning design was of Stalin reading Pushkin. In another, Franklin Delano Roosevelt asks Stalin about the treatment of Jews and tells him that there is a village of two hundred Jewish people who do not have a rabbi. Stalin promises to investigate and he gets an explanation from the Party secretary of the district:

There are three possible candidates. The first has been to Party school but hasn't been to the school for rabbis. The second has been to the school for rabbis but hasn't been to Party school. There is a third who has indeed been to the Party school and the school for rabbis. But he's Jewish.[561]

Joe's train conversation with Alexei Makarov was representative of his political and intellectual life in 1989. Secret negotiations between the regime and ANC were accelerating while the clandestine Operation Vula expanded within South Africa. Joe's writing, speeches, and interviews were also more prominent. In a gesture of peace toward the West in October, prime minister de Klerk released ANC leader Walter Sisulu, who had been imprisoned since his conviction for sabotage in the Rivonia Trial. In recalling the many phone calls he received when he was released, Sisulu said that Joe, "not a chap to be easily excited, was emotional when he spoke to him."[562]

When Sisulu and Govan Mbeki, who had been released from Robben Island two years earlier, were honored shortly after their release at First National Bank Stadium in Soweto, Joe sent a message that was read to the throngs who celebrated Sisulu and Mbeki's release. "We have no doubt that it is not de Klerk but the mass of the people who have brought about your release. It is their gathering strength, which opens up the possibility of creating a further stepping-stone towards the destruction of racism."[563] Simultaneous with Sisulu's release, the regime used a photograph of Joe, the Communist, and Democratic Party leader Wynand Malan in an attempt to denounce the new opposition party.

Earlier in the year Joe did an interview with Radio Freedom and participated in a panel discussion that was published in *World Marxist Review*. Themes included questions on whether the South African regime was really interested in democracy or was using pronouncements of peace to discredit the ANC and gain further favor with Western nations. In the radio interview, Joe spoke about the possibility of alliances and even support from Afrikaner intellectuals and students. The panel discussion foreshadows his forthcoming booklet, "Has Socialism Failed?"

I have absolutely no doubts that when socialism recaptures this potential, which it is trying to do through perestroika, of creating a really new life for people with all the expectations that we have been talking about for 70 years, the whole strength of the working-class movement in the rest of the world and the freedom forces will be influenced beyond recognition.[564]

Much of Joe's thinking was an attempt to connect the changes in the Soviet Union to possibilities for a new South Africa. In spite of de Klerk's release of Sisulu and Mbeki and Joe's own knowledge about the ever-increasing unofficial discussions between South Africa and the ANC, Joe was still attempting to understand how the struggle would soon lead to a new, majority-governed South Africa. He had begun gentle criticisms of the Soviet Union when he lived in Maputo, and would soon fervently support Gorbachev's reforms in print. Yet the South African government and media continued to demonize him as a Soviet agent. Hugh Macmillan taught at the University of Zambia when Joe lived in Lusaka and his thoughts on members of the SACP underground do not concur with the regime's portrayal of "terrorist communists": "There was no doubt that many of the brightest and most articulate intellectuals in Lusaka in the 1980s, such as Chris Hani, Mac Maharaj, Thabo Mbeki, Jack Simons and Joe Slovo, were members of the Party, but no one who knew them could imagine them all taking the same line on any subject for long."[565]

During 1989, Joe met with well-respected journalist Allister Sparks, who had been the editor of South Africa's premier newspaper, the *Rand Daily Mail*. He was writing for the London *Observer* and the *Washington Post* when he met Joe at an ANC meeting in Lusaka. Joe told him that they did not have similar political views but that he respected his writing. Sparks recalled Joe saying, "Of course you want a February revolution and I want to go on to October."[566] Allister Sparks was enthralled by Joe's humanity and decided to write a profile on him connected to the theme "the hunted man." Subsequently, Sparks interviewed Joe four times in 1989, and gained insight into how people were manipulated by the apartheid regime:

> I didn't know Joe until I met him in exile. I knew of him but people didn't talk warmly about him—he sounded like an extremist. He was communism or nothing. So I didn't like the sound of this guy at all. Then you meet him and he's this warm, effervescent, witty, utterly charming individual. Then you see that he is a pragmatist and then you see that he is one of the people who truly saved the country.[567]

Macmillan's statement became even truer when the Berlin Wall fell. For the regime, Joe Slovo was still "Enemy Number One" despite the monumental changes that were forthcoming in 1990.

11—Home

WHEN JOE SLOVO ARRIVED back in South Africa on April 29, 1990, after twenty-seven years in exile, he was viewed in contrasting ways by people who had never left the country. Black South Africans saw him as a hero, and the chief rabbi, Cyril Harris, scolded South African Jews who condemned him—past and present. But there were many white South Africans who still perceived Joe Slovo as a Communist "terrorist." Joe's Mozambican friend Zé Forjaz remembered a story—possibly apocryphal as Gillian Slovo tells it very differently—that Joe, shortly after his return to South Africa, stopped at a red light and the man in the lane next to him said, "You look exactly like Joe Slovo." "I am Joe Slovo," replied Joe, to which the man said, "Fuck you, Joe Slovo." For Zé Forjaz, it was the type of story that defined Joe: "a lively and lovely person."[568]

The South African regime continued to think otherwise. Joe had told Rashid in late 1989 that a huge announcement from the apartheid regime was coming. Joe was well aware of the unofficial negotiations between the ANC and South African government. Thus it was no surprise in February when the country's president, F. W. de Klerk, unbanned the ANC and SACP and released Nelson Mandela. Everywhere in the world there were news reports with footage and photographs of Nelson and Winnie Mandela walking arm-in-arm after the future president was released from prison. Yet when formal negotiations were to begin, one of the regime's primary demands was the exclusion of the Communist Joe Slovo from the official process.

The ANC refused the government's demand to bar Joe, and he became essential in nurturing the process that led to South Africa's first democratic election in 1994.

Just prior to de Klerk's speech, Joe Slovo's essay "Has Socialism Failed?" was published as a pamphlet by the SACP. Connected to the Gorbachev revolution in the Soviet Union, and critically received by both SACP and non-Party South African socialists, the essay served to nurture a thoughtful political solution to the end of apartheid. The document is twenty-eight pages, and the underlying premise is that socialism without democracy is a contradiction in terms. Joe went to great lengths to argue that the merit of socialism over capitalism was not impugned by the failure of the Stalin and post-Stalin Soviet Union or the collapsed socialist regimes in Poland, Hungary, East Germany, and Czechoslovakia. Instead, he asserted that the bureaucratic state socialism in each of these countries distorted the canons through the practice of democratic centralism, thus alienating and demeaning the working class as well as other citizens. As Joe was writing "Has Socialism Failed?" he told Allister Sparks, "You know, I must thank Ruth for whatever extent I am a civilized being."[569] Joe's statement was potent due to his and Ruth's long-term battles about Stalin, the Soviet Union, and other Communist leadership throughout the world. Joe addressed the SACP's responsibility for accepting the Stalinist doctrine and went so far as to assert that saying he and his comrades were misled provided an inadequate explanation. He continued to hedge on this issue, however, even during negotiations. In 1992, in an interview with Padraig O'Malley, he voiced his oft-repeated explanation:

Well, it is a difficult question to answer but it is nevertheless a fact. I mean if you just look at it in relation to a visit to Moscow of a delegation for four days or even spending a couple of weeks there as part of a sort of official, formal relation, one didn't really have access to anybody or anything other than official levels. One never really had an opportunity of discovering what was going on on the ground, of speaking or making contact with the dissidents. This was diplomatically impossible.[570]

Vladimir Shubin challenged this justification:

Joe was always in a hurry and that was counterproductive, because he was—almost—not aware about real life in our country, with its achievements and problems. This made him say after August 1991 something like he had been an official guest and could not see much—I don't remember the exact phrase—but that was entirely his fault.[571]

Joe credited Gorbachev and perestroika as possible facilitators of a new, democratic South Africa. He also contended that Stalinism had not guided the SACP for many years. An interesting contention, since he was on record referencing the efforts of Brian Bunting and others in the SACP to evict Ruth from the Party in the late 1970s. In addition, in a gentle critique of "Has Socialism Failed?" Pallo Jordan noted that besides vast evidence of SACP intolerance of dissenting views, the Party exhibited "praise and support for every violation of freedom perpetrated by the Soviet leadership, both before and after the death of Stalin."[572] One of Ruth's allies in these continual political confrontations with Joe, Hilda Bernstein, reminded Joe of various Party contradictions:

> We were sitting around and Joe said to me, "Have you read my pamphlet?" And I said, "Yes, I read it." And he said, "What did you think of it?" And I said, "It made me very angry." And he said, "Why did it make you angry?" I said, "Because all those years that Ruth and I were saying these things we were marginalized, we were pushed aside, we were considered to be in a sense betrayers and so on and you supported it all. And now you're saying those very same things. How come, that you at the top were so clever, and the two of us who didn't count for anything were correct."[573]

Albie Sachs had different historical reflections on the hard-line position that Joe and some others in the SACP held for almost five decades:

> We disbelieved the attacks on Stalinism because they were saying that people like Moses Kotane and Slovo and J. B. Marks, whom we knew, were these horrible deceivers and liars and bloodthirsty and power-hungry people. And we knew just the opposite. If they're lying about people we know and things that we know, and their lies help to perpetuate apartheid in South Africa and perpetuate colonial domination, then the lies must

extend to the slave labor camps and all the rest. But the tension, the contradiction, was we were the most challenging in all sorts of ways in terms of lifestyle and critiquing the society and the conventions of society. So in some ways we were very closed and agents of history, and in other ways we were very open and very willing to accept science and the ability of ideas to liberate and emancipate. Looking back now it was a strange contradiction, which we lived through. In some ways closed through ideology and theory; in other ways that same ideology and theory subjected everything to critique and analysis and debate and argument. We tended to be on the whole a lively, spirited, challenging people rather than dour, bureaucratic-minded, faithful blind followers. There was a lot of joy, a lot of spirit. There were disagreements all the time—debates, arguments, analysis.[574]

"Has Socialism Failed?" concluded with discussions on the need for SACP collaboration with trade unions and a democratic vigilance to ensure the assent of "people's power" in the new South African state. Joe addressed the problems of one-party rule and argued that the 7th Congress's acceptance of "The Path to Power" provided a guidebook for democracy in South Africa. Throughout the document he cautioned colleagues and comrades to remember that socialism trumped capitalism:

We continue to assert that it is only in a non-exploitative, communist, classless society that human values will find their ultimate expression and be freed of all class-related morality. In the meanwhile the socialist transition has the potential of progressively asserting the values of the whole people over those of classes.[575]

There were various critiques of "Has Socialism Failed?," two of which appeared in *The African Communist* questioning Joe's thesis. These SACP critics were still unwilling to criticize Stalin or the post-Stalin Soviet Union. In addition, there was an angry attack from Archie Mafeje, the academic Ruth had condemned on the pages of the *Review of African Political Economy* years earlier. Writing in the *Southern African Political and Economic Monthly*, Mafeje argued that it was whites in the SACP who had created the schism between the

ANC and other black organizations, namely the Unity Movement, of which Mafeje was a member. By far the most thoughtful critique was Pallo Jordan's article, "The Crisis of Conscience in the SACP." Jordan both supported and critiqued "Has Socialism Failed?" but most important, he expanded Joe's thesis historically, politically, and sociologically. Jordan provided historical reasons, although not excuses, to better understand state socialism's failures. He viewed Joe's pamphlet as an initial warning to the SACP of the necessity of facing its own history while reaching out to the people and organizations that criticized the Party, something that various SACP members were unwilling to do when Ruth First tested the Party line. And he praised Joe for challenging ideology:

> Most refreshing is the candour and honesty with which many of the problems of existing socialism are examined. Indeed, a few years ago no one in the SACP would have dared to cast such a critical light on the socialist countries. "Anti-Soviet," "anti-Communist," or "anti-Party" were the dismissive epithets reserved for those who did. We can but hope that the publication of this pamphlet spells the end of such practices.[576]

The SACP and COSATU held a joint meeting in Harare, Zimbabwe at the end of March. Referred to by Ray Alexander as the event at which the SACP and COSATU discovered each other, the meeting featured a discussion of Joe's "Has Socialism Failed?" Joe was pleased when discourse led to attendees beckoning for forums of "people's power" in the new South Africa. It was a response he had sought within the context of his teaching and writing on strategy and tactics. Jaya Josie remembered talking with Joe about the essay: "It was more to alert the socialists and communists within the South African structures about the issues and dynamics of what was happening. For him, the Soviet Union helped us free South Africa. They gave us the training. They were excellent technicians. And that was enough."[577]

When de Klerk gave his February 2 speech, Joe was in the Soviet Union. In an interview at Moscow's Sheremetyevo Airport, he told *Guardian* reporter Jonathan Steele that he was not surprised by the events. Just days earlier, he had told Vladimir Shubin that Mandela's release and the unbannings were imminent.

Joe was in and out of the Soviet Union during the early part of 1990 before his return to South Africa. With Vula still in operation,

Joe and Pallo Jordan (courtesy
of Helena Dolny)

there were meetings and discussions with the Soviets who were aiding
the operation. There were also sensitive deliberations on the USSR's
relationship with the ANC and the "former" apartheid regime. After
meetings with Foreign Minister Eduard Shevardnadze, Joe was skeptical of the new Soviet minister's understanding of the struggle or
the evils of the regime: "Soviet diplomats might have their heart in
the right place, but they look at South Africa as a chess board where
some politicians were playing; they don't understand the role of the
mass struggle."[578]

Chess was being played at the time, however, in the negotiations
between the ANC and de Klerk's representatives. Just two weeks
after de Klerk's speech unbanning the ANC and SACP, the subject of
talks in Switzerland was centered on Joe Slovo. The head of the South
African National Intelligence Service, Niël Barnard, met with Thabo
Mbeki and other ANC representatives for the first time and declared
that inclusion of Joe in the ANC negotiating team was unacceptable.
Immediately, Mbeki responded, "No Slovo, no meeting."[579] After two
Barnard phone calls to de Klerk, a decision was rendered. Barnard
explained to Allister Sparks that each side would pick its own negotiators. "If the ANC wanted to include Slovo, that was their business;
if we wanted to include Eugene Terreblanche or some other crazy
right-winger, they couldn't object."[580] Formal negotiations did not
begin until 1991. After the sitting Parliament passed indemnity laws,
Joe Slovo returned to South Africa on April 29. Flying from Lusaka

with a delegation of exiled ANC and SACP leaders that included Joe
Modise, the head of MK, Ruth Mompati, the head of the Women's
Section of the ANC, the Secretary General of the ANC, Alfred Nzo,
and future president Thabo Mbeki, Joe came directly to Cape Town
to participate in the first official talks between the ANC and the government on South African soil—the Groote Schuur Summit.

Upon arrival at the Cape Town airport, Joe spoke to the large wel-
coming crowd. He was nervous but witty and he talked about hope
and possibilities for the new South Africa. At the same time he was
not entirely trustful of the government, and he knew that Operation
Vula provided necessary insurance. Groote Schuur had been the official home of the South African prime minister under the pre-1984
constitution, which had replaced the prime minister with an executive president. The mansion sits at the foot of the incomparable Table
Mountain amid the beauty of Cape Town. For security reasons, Joe
and the other negotiators were housed east of the city at the Lord
Charles Hotel in Somerset West. The meeting ran from May 2 to 4
and concluded with an initial agreement called the Groote Schuur
Minute. Provisions were enacted for releasing political detainees,
the return of exiles, and changing government security laws. Allister
Sparks recalled that at the conclusion of the talks photographs were
taken of "a smiling Slovo standing among the men who had hated and
hunted him for so long."[581]

After the meeting, Joe flew to Johannesburg where he would live
and participate in negotiations and the reconstituting of the South
African Communist Party. Blade Nzimande, the current head of the
SACP and South Africa's Minister of Higher Education, has referred
to the time as "twenty years condensed into four years." Joe's work
within the SACP was both arduous and contested. Within the context
of "Has Socialism Failed?" he clearly believed that it was necessary
for the SACP to become the party of the masses—the party of democratic socialism rather than a party of democratic centralism. Joe
had the backing of his friend and comrade Chris Hani, whom he had
definitively supported in Angola, other allies within the SACP who
had been in exile, as well as those who had never left South Africa.
However, there was also the old guard SACP bloc and others who
remained in the country who did not support democratic socialism.
Debates abounded in Central Committee meetings and on the pages
of *The African Communist*, and some in the Party remained advo-
cates for democratic centralism. One of the young Communists who

Joe with Nelson and Winnie Mandela (courtesy of Helena Dolny)

disagreed with Joe was Blade Nzimande, who recalls Joe telling him that he felt guilty about how long it took him to write "Has Socialism Failed?" and to publicly champion democratic socialism.

"Positive culture shock" is what Joe said he experienced upon his return—blacks and whites on buses together and at least a small number of middle-class blacks living in white areas. He and Helena initially stayed in the home of Audrey and Max Coleman. In the early 1980s the Colemans were politicized as a family when their son Keith was arrested in connection with his university political activities. The family became deeply involved in the Detainees' Parents Support Committee (DPSC) and Audrey became the organization's spokesperson. In addition to publicly protesting in South Africa, she traveled in Europe and the United States and addressed the United Nations on apartheid atrocities. Helena and Joe stayed with the Colemans until December when they moved to their own home near Joe's childhood house in Yeoville. Audrey and Max Coleman have wonderful memories of Joe and Helena's sojourn with them in 1990. Audrey felt privileged that they could host Joe Slovo upon his return to Johannesburg: "There was nothing about 'I am great' about him. He was himself—he was really lovely. Joe and I had a lot of fights over the sunset clauses. But he just became our friend."[582] Max Coleman recalled their evening discussions:

Joe and Helena (courtesy of Helena Dolny)

He was with us at a very important time in the history of the country, and almost on a daily basis we had a debate on how the negotiations were going and so on. We were debaters. I didn't begin to think that we would influence his thinking. Let's put it this way, we would voice our concerns about giving too much away at that point.[583]

Audrey spoke of Helena:

Joe and Helena were a lovely couple together. Meeting Helena was a gift for me. She is I think a really special lady—very, very bright and the most loving and committed friend. And she really, truly loved Joe. He was a friend. He became a family member. They both added to our lives.[584]

Joe also got reacquainted with Hillary Hamburger when he returned to Johannesburg. She and her soon-to-be husband, Tony, became friends with Helena and Joe. "He really loved Helena and Helena adored him, and I was so happy for both of them. I just felt he's got what he deserves—real love that's there and available and part of his life and he's come home."[585]

Most important, upon returning to South Africa Joe renewed his relationship with his sister Rene and her family, the Ephrons.

Occasionally at his sister's house for Shabbat, Friday night dinners, Joe did not wear a yarmulke, but was respectful of the prayers that were said over the candles, wine, and challah. He told stories and brought out his long list of Jewish jokes that required no prodding to be voiced. In a sense, being amid Rene's family was Joe's reacquaintance with cultural Judaism. "Ah," said Barney Simon, "but Joe was Yiddish, not Jewish as in the Jewishness of religion and Israel."[586]

At the beginning Joe was juggling four different types of meetings—pre-negotiations with the government, ANC meetings, SACP meetings, and clandestine encounters with Vula operatives. The Groote Schuur Minute rekindled Mac Maharaj's confrontations with Joe. After the document was released, Maharaj chastised Joe and Alfred Nzo for what he believed was a betrayal of the Operation Vula people underground. His memories are of a hard and bitter conversation with Joe:

> In all this statement you have not said one word about the safety and security of your illegal cadres living in the country. This was the time when you should have inserted that into the Groote Schuur record. You should have told de Klerk without disclosures. You know we are committing ourselves to negotiations; you know that the movement has got people that it has infiltrated over the years, living here illegally. I won't disclose how many or who they are, but I do want you to give an undertaking that their safety will be assured. Slovo says to me, "I assumed that it's there." I said, "No, let's read it." So we read. He says it's implied. I said, "Bullshit, show me where's the implication here. De Klerk is not going to protect us by implication. Show me where you've put it."[587]

Maharaj's anger toward Joe increased throughout the early 1990s. Padraig O'Malley suggests that there was tension in all of Mac's political relationships but that it was magnified in the case of Joe Slovo. His analysis portrays the breadth that existed in the two men's work with each other within the struggle. Mac viewed it as a love/hate relationship:

> The two stimulated each other intellectually. Both were powerhouses in the SACP. Mac had a keen appreciation of Slovo's strategic sense, but he believed Slovo's actions frequently gave

a hollow ring to his words. He complained that, to Slovo, whatever was the current focus of his attention was where the revolution was. Ironically, it was a complaint that many directed at Mac himself.[588]

Maharaj's assessment of Joe self-categorizing the struggle is plain wrong. Though it is not fair to dismiss criticisms of Joe Slovo, in this case Mac's contention that he has had a lifelong lover's quarrel with the ANC connects to his relationship with Joe. His fellow Operation Vula operative, Janet Love, said, "Joe embodied a whole lot of stuff for Mac that would have been part of that lover's quarrel."[589] She also believed that Joe became something of a punching bag for Vula operatives:

He bore the brunt of a degree of frustration that I afterward thought was quite extraordinary. He absorbed all of the frustration and all of the anger of all of us. And that was quite a lot to absorb for a single individual. In that sense he was really there for us.[590]

But she realized the importance of Joe's thoughtfulness and sensitivity:

I mean, Joe was able to understand. He could have stood on his position. He could have pulled rank. He could have rightly said, What do you expect me to do about it? He could have said, Get a grip. He could have been very short-tempered with what was a kind of verbal assault. But Joe didn't do that. He kind of let people vent because he knew people had to do that.[591]

In March Joe was appointed to the ANC's Internal Leadership Committee, which also included Mandela, Sisulu, Nzo, Mhlaba, Maharaj, and Govan Mbeki. The group was to provide leadership on negotiations and underground (Operation Vula) decisions. Joe also spoke with local and international journalists. In March, he took part in a detailed interview with *New Era*. The reporter questioned Joe about "Path to Power" and "Has Socialism Failed?" After criticizing himself and his comrades for their historical demonization of social democracy as "traps of imperialism" and "traitors to the working class,"[592] Joe conceded that the social democratic states in

Joe and Mandela, Sisulu, and others (courtesy of Helena Dolny)

Scandinavian countries had been more concerned with democracy than had the communists. His caveat, however, was that those nations are highly industrialized and owed much of their success to inter-national imperialism. Joe returned to Marx and Lenin to conclude this section of the interview: "I am thinking of the tradition of direct democracy, celebrated in Marx's writing on the Paris Commune and in Lenin's reflections on the soviets or popular councils that emerged spontaneously in 1905 and again in 1917."[593]

Joe warned that leadership could not live superior to the masses and then praised "people's power" in South Africa:

The working people of our country understand the basic truth that, as long as a system based on private profit rules the roost, substantial inroads into resolving their major concerns—hous-ing, education, employment, health-care, social security—will not be possible.[594]

Both the ANC and SACP were attempting to define themselves in the months after being unbanned. Joe participated in ongoing meet-ings that included planning for the first ANC National Executive Committee meeting on South African soil, the relaunch of the SACP, and an August consult with the government. He was also still serv-ing as an above-ground shepherd for Operation Vula. On July 13 the hammer fell on Vula when the Special Branch arrested Gebuza. His arrest and the incarceration of forty other members of the ANC would not be made public until July 25.

The ANC's National Executive Committee met on July 19. Joe proposed the unilateral cessation of the armed struggle. Mandela supported the proposal and the NEC approved Joe's proposition. The plan would be presented at the next meeting with the government, scheduled for early August. Joe Slovo presenting the idea was a powerful tactic because as a leader of both the Communist Party and the MK underground army, he more than anyone else had the credentials to negotiate the plan. On July 20 Joe was onstage at a press conference announcing the July 29 launch of the SACP. The public emergence of the Party was scheduled for Jabulani Stadium in Soweto. Because the stadium seated close to 40,000 people, there was concern about attracting a large enough crowd. On July 22, at an SACP Politburo meeting, there was discussion of promoting the launch. A schism existed with Joe and Hani on one side, and Mbeki and Zuma as the opposition that did not want the Party to come out publicly. According to Mark Gevisser, Mbeki and Zuma believed that their quiet conversations with the government might be compromised if the SACP were to go public. Gevisser also wrote that Joe presented Mbeki with an ultimatum—come to the launch or leave the Party. At the Politburo meeting, Joe urged Mac to participate in the event. Maharaj had already announced his intention to leave the SACP in protest of other appointments to the new Central Committee. Yet Joe was able to persuade him to introduce speakers at the stadium.

Persuading Mac to participate became a moot point on July 25, when, like Gebuza, he was arrested for his role in Operation Vula. The government went public, claiming that Mac and others were plotting a Communist overthrow. Headlines in South African newspapers were ablaze. The *Natal Witness* led with "Red Plot Allegations Denied by SACP's Slovo" and the *Sunday Times* read "ANC Secret Cell Shock." De Klerk announced that Kasrils, Zuma, and Hani would all be arrested. None of them were detained. He also demanded the removal of Joe Slovo from the planned August negotiations. De Klerk's evidence was a handwritten document written at the secret SACP Tongaat meeting championing the continuance of armed struggle. The paper was signed "Joe." However, Joe Slovo was out of the country at the time of the SACP assembly and the writing was actually that of Gebuza, whose alias was Joe.

On the day of the SACP launch, the headline of the *Sunday Times* read, "ANC Stands by Red Joe." Mandela had announced to de Klerk that Joe Slovo would be an integral part of the negotiation team. The president did not dispute the president-to-be. Fortunately, Joe and Chris Hani's concerns about attendance were unnecessary. Crowds came from afar for the SACP launch and the estimates were that 50,000 people packed the stadium. The launch was on a cold winter Sunday afternoon, but the meeting was proud and triumphant. People from all four of the apartheid-era ethnic designated groups were present, but the huge majority were black workers. Joe was on the stage with Nelson Mandela and Walter Sisulu while other Party leaders sat in the front rows. After the singing of "The Internationale," many vivas, and a worker's song, the young UDF activist Cheryl Carolus, standing in for Mac, introduced twenty-two people who composed the interim Party leadership. There were recognitions of fallen freedom fighters, speeches addressing the past, present, and future. Nelson Mandela spoke on the ANC-SACP alliance, and he warned the government about their attempts to sabotage the coming negotiations process—a clear reference to both the "Red Plot" and security forces' incitement of violence.

When Joe neared the dais, dressed in a gray suit and wearing his already famous red socks, he was met with cheers and chants—Viva! to the SACP, Viva! to socialism, and Viva! to Joe Slovo. After presenting a short history of the SACP that he had rehearsed with Helena, Joe referenced de Klerk's charges of an SACP plot, outlining three lies as he waved his passport showing that he was in Zambia during the time of his supposed writing of the insurgent document. He concluded saying, "Government allegations of a Communist conspiracy are attempts to rubbish the Party. It is they who forced us to work in the cellars and shadows. Even now they are trying to force us back into the underground cellars."[595] At the conclusion of Joe's speech, the last of the day, amid the cheers and vivas, the dark clouds burst and rain fell on Jabulani Stadium.

Ronnie Kasrils surfaced from underground for the launch before going back into hiding. Similar to Janet Love, he recalled Joe's support:

Coming back home we were together in building the Party. The periods when I was in real difficulty he was always there and exceptionally supportive. To itemize those that's when I am on the run again in 1990–91 after Mac's arrest. I met Joe many times during the period discussing the work that I was doing and the question of bringing the underground together in case something happens. He was such a wonderful moral support in that period.[596]

On the Thursday after the SACP launch, Joe was in Pretoria for the scheduled negotiation meetings between the ANC and the government. The talks lasted fifteen hours, and on August 7 a joint statement was released as a path to negotiations. The elephant in the room was that de Klerk was focused on a shared government solution, and the ANC believed in one person, one vote. In spite of the unspoken, an agreement was announced later in the month stating that the government would facilitate the release of remaining political prisoners, finalize indemnity of freedom fighters still in exile, and lift the State of Emergency in Natal. The ANC agreed, via Joe's proposal, to suspend armed actions. These agreements, called the Pretoria Minute, were to be completed by mid-September. In addition, both parties acknowledged the violence that existed in the country, albeit with vastly different public interpretations. Tension would escalate during the meeting and throughout the pre-negotiations in 1991.

Just before the SACP launch and Pretoria Minute, Keith Coleman, Audrey and Max's son, interviewed Joe for a book he was writing, *Nationalisation: Beyond the Slogans*. Joe, influenced by Gorbachev and what was transpiring in Eastern Europe, stressed worker participation and rejected posing a question on government nationalization as an either/or proposition. Joe was also interviewed, in early September, for the Party's "Africa Report." Much of that interview focused on defining the SACP within the context of its partnership with the ANC and COSATU. Joe stressed that the recruiting hopes of the ANC and the SACP differed: the ANC's goal was millions of people, while the Communist Party hoped to attract tens of thousands. He also stated that he agreed with the regime's Constitutional Affairs Minister, Gerrit Viljoen, on the need for mechanisms in the government to thwart the imposition of Communism. "But there should equally be in-built mechanisms to prevent the imposition of capitalism," added Joe.[597]

Joe was now wrestling with connections of theory and practice amid complexities that included ANC divides, SACP divides, changes in world politics, violence to which the state at the very least turned a blind eye, as well as feeling a personal responsibility for the imprisonment of Mac and others in the Vula Operation. When Mac finessed his way into a Durban hospital rather than a state prison, Joe attempted to visit him disguised as a doctor. He was recognized by the guards and turned away. Despite Mac's difficulties with Joe, he never doubted that Joe was working behind the scenes for his release, and he never doubted Slovo's total commitment to the struggle. Mac was released on bail in November, and the government finally dropped all charges in March 1992.

In December the weakened Oliver Tambo, who never fully recovered from his stroke, returned to South Africa and participated in the first ANC consultative conference on South African soil since the ANC's banning by the apartheid regime in 1960. From December 16 to 19, the delegation of over 1,600 members commanded the National Executive Committee to set a deadline of April 1991 for the government to meet the criteria of the Pretoria Minute. The delegates also declared 1991 as "The Year of Mass Action" and asserted that government noncompliance would result in the suspension of all negotiations.

Joe and Helena traveled extensively in 1990 within South Africa, to and from Lusaka and also overseas. Finally, in December, Helena packed up their Lusaka belongings, and their first Johannesburg Christmas was spent in their newly acquired Yeoville house. When Helena's daughters Kyla and Tessa arrived in March 1991, they enrolled them at Sacred Heart, a well-known Johannesburg parochial school. Helena was finishing her doctorate but also worked at the National Land Commission and subsequently for an NGO that focused on providing services in rural South Africa. She and Joe settled into the Yeoville house with the help of Audrey Coleman and Joe's sister, Rene. Helena reflected on Joe and his sister:

I think one of the interesting things about Joe was his lack of need for family. I found it very interesting when we came to live in Johannesburg meeting up with his sister Rene who he'd only seen a couple of times over those years, and she was thrilled he was home. She was thrilled he was no longer the bad relative. She was a good relative. My kids at the time would have been seven and eleven—she was fabulous with my kids. She was absolutely wonderful helping us set up home.[598]

Joe, still absorbed in his work, spoke at trade union and district SACP meetings and continued to write for *Umsebenzi*, "Umrabulo: A Personal Column." As in Lusaka, he was able to distance himself from work when he was with family and friends. But his workday was often extremely long. There were evenings at home and Helena and Joe continued to have dinners and nights out with friends. And because Joe was not underground, Gillian, Shawn, and Robyn flew to South Africa frequently.

Joe's final official trip to Moscow occurred in April 1991. He met with one of Gorbachev's deputies, Vladimir Ivashko. In addition to discussing the present situations in both countries, they spoke about relations between the future ANC government and the Soviet Union. Joe also helped facilitate a contract for continuing Party cooperation and an agreement for the continuance of young South Africans coming to the Soviet Union for higher education. While Joe was abroad, the ANC announced that the organization had taken a decision not to participate in a peace and anti-violence conference planned by the government. The public statement chronicled the regime's support of recent violence against the ANC. Examples abounded of Inkatha Freedom Party (IFP) members leaving their urban workers' hostels and attacking ANC members while police turned a blind eye. There was also evidence of South African soldiers training Inkatha fighters—echoing South African support of RENAMO a decade earlier. In April, Joe stated that he found it interesting that "each time a process is about to take place which might signify an advance towards negotiation, towards peace, the violence escalates."[599] He wrote a press release in mid-May as the General Secretary of the SACP about extreme violence in Phola Park and then Swanieville. Phola Park was a squatters' camp on the east side of Johannesburg where members of the IFP burned down 1,000 dwellings in September 1990. Residents testified that some of the attackers were white men in blackface— most probably members of the South African security forces. Police lurked in the background and made no attempts to stop the violence. Police also aided IFP ransackers in May 1991 when they attacked people in Swanieville, also a squatters' camp. Thirty-seven people were killed and 112 shacks were burned to the ground. According to later Truth and Reconciliation Commission testimony, the police escorted approximately 1,000 IFP attackers out of the area. After writing about the horror of the attacks and police and government complicity, Joe Slovo sent a warning to the regime:

President de Klerk asserted last week that the police will continue to act with impartiality and professionalism. Those in
charge of maintaining law and order are by their actions and
inactions giving the lie to such assertions. The investment
which we have all made in working for a peaceful transformation is being seriously squandered. Unless meaningful steps
are taken to meet the demands contained in the ANC's open
letter all future talks will be at risk. And we will all be losers.[600]

Ongoing closed-door negotiations about negotiations continued
and Joe spent much of his time at Shell House, the ANC's headquarters in Johannesburg. In July, the ANC held its first National
Conference since the 1950s. This meeting, unlike the earlier consultative conference, was open to all members of the organization. Set
in Durban, almost 2,500 delegates attended the conference. Also in
attendance were European diplomats and Joe's closest Soviet colleagues, Vladimir Shubin and Alexei Makarov. The conference
elected Mandela as president and Sisulu as deputy president, thus
avoiding having to choose between the great rivals, Thabo Mbeki
or Chris Hani, for the position. Surprisingly, Cyril Ramaphosa was
chosen as Secretary General, a symbol of change within the ANC and
the formal negotiations that would begin later in the year. Ramaphosa's election was concurrent with the election of a more progressive,
more radical National Executive Committee that included Joe Slovo.
Thabo Mbeki had been the key pre-negotiations' representative for
the ANC, but it appeared that his role would now be less prominent. Mandela's approval was needed for the NEC representatives
as well as Ramaphosa's election as General Secretary. Because of the
government's conservatism, the progressivism of the people elected
was seemingly incongruous in the context of imminent negotiations.
However, it was Joe Slovo who had already led the ANC compromise,
shutting down the armed struggle.

Just days after the Durban conference, NEC held a post-confer-
ence meeting in Soweto to select a twenty-member working committee
whose role would be to manage daily ANC business. Joe was again
elected, as were radical former exiles including Chris Hani and Ronnie Kasrils, as well as younger UDF progressives. At the conference,
Cyril Ramaphosa was chosen to lead the appointed negotiating committee. Again, Joe was part of that grouping with other committee
members including Mbeki, Maharaj, and Valli Moosa.

July also marked the seventieth anniversary of the South African Communist Party. Although the general conference would not transpire until December, Joe addressed a celebratory seminar at the University of the Western Cape. His speech included a history of successes and failures as well as plans for the present and future. Joe's history was a rather weak portrayal of the Party's foundational belief in "colonialism of a special type," as exemplifying their break with Stalinism long before perestroika. He explained that the Party was in the process of defining its role in the new South Africa and opined that this definition would be addressed in depth at the SACP's December conference. After discussing the historical and present ANC-SACP alliance, he concluded: "We have no double agenda. As a Party we do not hide our socialist objectives. It is our duty to spread the message of an ultimate socialist society now."[601]

Amid an intensely hectic time, Joe, Helena, Tessa, and Kyla moved from their house in Yeoville to another in Observatory. Across from the Yeoville house was a block of flats, and the ANC was concerned that Joe was slack about his own security. Dan O'Meara recalled Joe walking him to his car one evening at the Yeoville house: "If I was a hit squad that wanted to take him out I would have rented the whole block. So I said to Joe, 'For Christ's sake don't come outside.' And he stood in the street for about five minutes talking."[602]

More important at this time, Joe learned of a serious health issue. A month earlier, he was talking with a French reporter in his ANC office after business hours. When they readied to leave, they found that the door was locked. Exiting through a window panel above the door, Joe fell and bruised his chest. X-rays were negative, but the pain continued. Concerned, Joe saw his doctor, Fazel Randera, later a Truth and Reconciliation commissioner; in the early 1990s he treated almost all of the struggle leaders who lived in Johannesburg. At the request of the ANC, he had traveled with Nelson Mandela on international trips. The Randeras were social friends of Joe and Helena's. They seldom spoke politics and they shared relaxing times. During one of Joe's general checkups, Randera was being shadowed by medical students. Joe engaged them as peers. Fazel recalls Joe's humor:

I looked at their faces, and you know, body language often says a great deal. Their mouths were open because here they were for the first time meeting somebody they had read about, and he was a live person and he was having a wonderful conversation with them. When they left they were full of admiration.[603]

Randera also has tender reflections on Joe and Helena as a couple:

My recollection is of a very warm, strong relationship—an equal relationship, a very loving relationship between both of them. I can't actually recollect there ever being a time when there wasn't respect for each other. Very quickly you could see that both of them brought their own selves into that house. This was very much their home. The books, the music, the picture frames and Helena organized it all—that was a lovely house.[604]

Fazel Randera ordered blood tests. When the test results indicated something was amiss, he asked a pathologist for a second opinion. Both Randera and the pathologist suspected cancer, and Joe proceeded to have bone marrow testing. The test concluded that Joe had multiple myeloma. It was Randera's responsibility to inform him of his medical condition. Besides the confirming tests, Fazel knew the literature—in his words, "It wasn't a rosy picture that was emerging."[605]

For me it was one of the most difficult conversations to go to a person I respected, a person I had now come to see as a friend. And you can imagine then having to go and say, look here, you came back to your country having fought for this moment. I went to his house and he was all by himself, and that was even worse in a sense, because Helena wasn't there. We sat down and I then went through what had happened and why I had asked for this bone marrow test and what has come out of that. I think the shock and disbelief was there. It wasn't immediate that he started to ask me further questions—there were long moments of silence. Then he said, All right. You are telling me that I've got a cancer, so where do we go from here?[606]

When Joe was diagnosed, Helena was in Magaliesberg, an hour's drive from Johannesburg. She had gone there to work on her dissertation away from family and other distractions. She planned to be away for five days, returning home for Friday dinner with Joe:

Joe and I spoke on Wednesday and I felt there was something amiss in his voice. So I came home a day early. I worked through the night to try to finish what I'd set myself to do. And that evening Joe told me what he'd learnt earlier in the week. I was gob-smacked. He'd been told this news some three days ago, and decided not to tell me during our phone conversations, because he knew that I needed the solitude to focus and finish writing! To this day I'm amazed at his stoicism, fortitude and his way of loving me—that he didn't want to give me news that would throw me off balance when I was on my very last lap toward the finish line of submitting the Ph.D.[607]

Referred by Randera, Joe consulted with an oncologist, Daniel Vorobioff. Immediate and aggressive treatment was necessary. At the time, the prognosis for multiple myeloma was a two- to three-year life expectancy. Chemotherapy was the prescribed care. He shared his diagnosis with his daughters, Shawn, Gillian, and Robyn, and they soon came to South Africa, and met with his doctor. Randera remembered that they cautiously queried whether Joe might receive treatment in the United Kingdom. After meeting Randera, they were satisfied with Joe's care.

Joe, challenged by dealing with cancer and death, continued his intense involvement in pre-negotiations and planning the SACP's 48th Congress in December. He also had meetings with South African journalist Charlotte Bauer regarding a possible biography. Amid treatment and ANC/SACP responsibilities, he chose to not commit to the project. Helena recalled that Joe understood his mortality, meaning that his choice was to live in the present rather than review the past:

I reckon I saw Joe more than many other partners. If Joe wasn't at Kempton Park (negotiations), he wasn't socializing very much at all. He was resting. He'd have chemo and we worked it out that he needed to have chemo on a Thursday and he needed not to be working Friday, Saturday, Sunday. He needed to be flat-out resting. So we would do this whole engineering of diaries and that would be a week when the kids went to stay with Ed. And maybe we would go away. Like, there was a farm in the Free State that we went to a few times. We'd take music and Joe would probably spend a lot of that time quietly—not talking a lot at all. If he didn't do that it seemed to take him longer to recover. But if he was actually flat Friday, Saturday, and Sunday, he felt he could be up and running by Tuesday.[608]

After his initial chemotherapy regimen Joe felt much stronger. He immersed himself in Party work and negotiations. The key negotiator from the ANC, Cyril Ramaphosa and from the government, Roelf Meyer, had been meeting continually with the consent of both Mandela and de Klerk. While other people were important in the impending negotiations, it was the work behind the scenes and in subsequent meetings between Ramaphosa and Meyer that engineered the success of the two-year talks. In October, Joe was purposely seated next to Meyer at a dinner for foreign correspondents. The two men spoke throughout the evening about how Ramaphosa had nurtured the possibilities of negotiations. It was during that month that all political parties gathered at the Patriotic Front conference—another meeting for negotiating negotiations. At that meeting, Joe stressed the need for the initiation of negotiations. The talks began two months later.

December is often a quiet month in South Africa. That was not the case in 1991. The 8th Congress of the South African Communist Party and the onset of formal negotiations between the ANC and the government both occurred before the New Year. SACP membership grew substantially after the 1990 launch. By the time of the 8th Congress, Party enrollment had increased from 5,000 to 21,000 people. Held in Nasrec, just outside of Soweto, the meeting included 414 delegates from 300 branches throughout the country. There were also observers from thirty worldwide Communist Parties, including those of China, Italy, Senegal, Nicaragua, United States, Cuba, Mozambique, France, India, Israel, England, Germany, Portugal, Soviet Union, Austria, Brazil, and Spain. Amid the activities, Joe relinquished his post as General Secretary to Chris Hani. He adopted this decision partially due to his cancer and partially because of his responsibilities in negotiations. His most important reason, however, was that he believed Hani should lead the SACP.

Intense discussions and debates abounded in the 8th Congress. The Party replaced "Path to Power" with a new credo: "Manifesto of the South African Communist Party: Building Workers' Power for Democratic Change." Although the document did not fully endorse Joe's requirement of democracy for substantive socialism, it did address the difficulties for socialism globally and approved the necessity of negotiations, issues directly connected to Joe's mission.

From the Party Congress, Joe moved directly into formal negotiations. He was now hopeful because he believed that de Klerk was
aware of the necessity of compromise. Joe spoke of de Klerk as a pragmatist and an opportunist. The former because he understood that
apartheid rule was over. Yet de Klerk, as an opportunist, would fight
to limit the change and thwart the ANC. The December 20 meeting,
Convention for a Democratic South Africa (CODESA), was held at
the World Trade Centre in Kempton Park, a Johannesburg area close
to what was then Jan Smuts Airport. Over 200 delegates representing the various political parties and the government contributed, and
CODESA I, as it became known, was for the most part a planning
session for five working groups with the responsibility of researching,
debating, and bringing consensus to a subsequent meeting, CODESA
II, in May 1992. The five groups were tasked to address political
participation, the constitution, interim government, Bantustans, and
time frames. The working groups met separately beginning in January. Joe was in Working Group Two, the constitution committee.
Due to the high stakes involved, the ANC and the government had
assigned their primary negotiators to this committee. Ramaphosa and
Moosa joined Joe, and Gerrit Viljoen and Tertius Delport opposed
them. The crucial issue was majority rule versus shared government.
On the day when reports were to be presented, May 15, all of the
other groups had made good progress, but Working Group Two was
unable to reach an agreement and CODESA II collapsed. There was
little joy and even more work for Joe and the negotiation team. There
was an opportunity, however, to celebrate Walter Sisulu's eightieth
birthday. Rica Hodgson organized a party with family, friends, and
comrades, and Joe teased Sisulu about his disruptions of Communist
meetings in the 1940s.

After the breakdown of CODESA II, the ANC, SACP, and
COSATU endorsed mass action. Concurrently, there was an escalation of IFP violence in the country. The violence reached a peak in two
events: the Boipatong Massacre in June 1992 and the Bisho Massacre
in September. Boipatong was a continuation of IFP members vacat-
ing hostels and attacking local residents. With forty-six people killed,
Mandela publicly condemned de Klerk and officially ended negotiations. "Official" is the key word in this case as Ramaphosa and Meyer
continued to meet secretly. At Bisho, unlike Boipatong and prior
violence, the ANC was also culpable. As part of the reaction to Boipatong, the ANC announced that it was going to demonstrate against

Bantustans within the borders of these false states. Ronnie Kasrils led demonstrators in Bisho, the Ciskei capital, and the Bantustan army fired en masse, killing twenty-nine people. Again the ANC, this time voiced by Ramaphosa, accused the South African government of complicity. However, they were cognizant of their responsibility as they had led people to slaughter.

The cessation of talks at the time of the Bisho massacre prompted Helena to encourage Joe to take a week-long holiday on the Seychelles Islands in the Indian Ocean. Although Joe was feeling good, he continued to experience fatigue and it was not easy to get him to leave his responsibilities in South Africa. He believed that there was always the chance of the negotiations reconvening. Her compromise was that if they did resume, they would immediately come home:

> He was never at ease with being ill. At first he didn't want to tell anybody that he had cancer. But I figured out that people would use it to exclude him from the political process. In fact, he found that people would say, "You don't need to come. You need to rest." But in actual fact they didn't want him there for whatever reason. So he wanted to appear to be robust and healthy. There was one time when I wanted to go on holiday. It wasn't happening and it wasn't happening and I invited Cyril [Ramaphosa] for breakfast. There was a hiatus in the talks. I said, "This guy's pulling the wool over your eyes. He needs a break. He's not going to ask you for one so I'm saying he needs one." And we went to the Seychelles for two weeks.[609]

When Joe returned to Johannesburg after the trip, he made a point to comfort Kasrils regarding Bisho. He said, "My God, I heard about this on the radio in the Seychelles and I was so worried that you'd been shot or killed. He really was supportive and sympathetic to what we had tried to do."[610] Before Joe had gone on vacation, and with official negotiations suspended, he had written a document that helped relaunch formal negotiations that eventually led to the country's first democratic election in 1994. In August, "Negotiations: What Room for Compromise?" was published in *The African Communist*. Joe explained that compromise was inherent in successful negotiations—it was a political process. He also asserted that though it would be impossible for the ANC to achieve everything that the struggle intended, it was a stage in moving toward democratic liberation. There were some premises that Joe viewed as non-negotiable, most important: (1) no minority veto and (2) no permanent power sharing. The line in the sand had to exist because concessions on these types of issues would block possibilities of a non-racial democratic South Africa.

The next topic in "Negotiations: What Room for Compromise?" provided the drama. Joe proposed a "sunset clause" that called for compulsory power sharing in government for five years. Although the idea of a sunset clause within the context of the negotiations was first voiced publicly in Joe's article, there is some disagreement about who initiated it. Kader Asmal gave credit to Thabo Mbeki, while George Bizos claimed that it was Mandela's idea. Most believed, however, that it was the brainchild of Joe Slovo, the man Allister Sparks once referred to as "a sheep in wolf's clothing."[611] Whether originator or not, Joe was the perfect person to promote the idea, and there was great irony in the fact that the head of the South African Communist Party, the KGB agent, the "Red Devil," was the person proposing the compromise.

There was immediate debate and discussion when the article appeared in *The African Communist*, and even more so once it became part of the official negotiations. Kasrils questioned the notion, as did SACP stalwart Harry Gwala. Winnie Mandela accused the ANC of being in bed with the National Party. "The only thing red about Slovo is his socks," said one member of the SACP.[612] Pallo Jordan also voiced criticism. Even though he disagreed with both the substance and process, he understood Joe's intentions:

The debate between Slovo and myself around the sunset clause is very much misunderstood by many people. It was not whether to negotiate or not—it wasn't that. The issue was how far are you prepared to go. Joe was the one who sort of batted for it from his side, so to speak. It surprised me coming from him, considering the very left positions he had in Lusaka. When I responded to Joe's sunset clause I raised the issue of people acting as if they had been given the mandate of the membership to make deals without actual consultation, and also that we will have democracy, one person, one vote, but the state structure will remain in the hands of the old regime—and what does that mean? I think that where Joe was clever in that debate was that he insisted on a resolution first in the leadership bodies rather than going to the grass roots. Because if he had gone to the grass roots I'm sure it would have gone the other way.[613]

Joe was reading Tony Benn's *Office Without Power* at the time and his thinking on the sunset clause was twofold. He knew that politics was an important part of the negotiation process and that making state bureaucrats secure in their jobs would ease much of the white opposition to negotiations and a democracy premised on one person, one vote. Also, as a politician, Joe believed that the country needed the expertise of the people who filled government jobs. Great numbers of people who were involved in the struggle did not have the civil service education, training, or experience. He warned his colleagues, "We can win political office, but we won't have political power."[614]

Rusty Bernstein viewed Joe as "one of these people who's born to be a politician. I mean, whatever he does, you know everybody likes him and wants to shake his hand."[615] For Zé Forjaz, "Joe was easy with everybody. From every side of the political spectrum, he was the least bigoted person I have met in my life."[616] It was Dan O'Meara, however, who spoke of Joe's political acumen as it related to the sunset clause:

He had a real understanding of what he used to call the "configuration of forces." Politics was not just about the hard line; it was about the art of the possible. I mean, people try to depict him as KGB. I can talk about that because I have some insight into that in Mozambique. It just absolutely misses Joe Slovo. He had a very nuanced sense of what could be done and what couldn't be done in South Africa and in politics generally. I think because not just he but because huge sections of the ANC leadership had seen the wheels fall off in Mozambique and Angola because both FRELIMO and the MPLA went way beyond what their political base could support. He understood that if they tried to do that in South Africa there would be a bloodbath. And that a bloodbath might eventually bring complete black power in South Africa, but it would destroy the economy and ruin any possibility of South Africa becoming a decent country. So by first of all saving the negotiations with the National Party, Joe was one of the two most important architects of the new South Africa.[617]

Allister Sparks enlarged upon O'Meara's reflections:

So here was the far left—this is what leadership is all about. You are the extremist but play the pragmatist and you're able to take everybody with you. And that was the skill of what Joe did. I think he was the single most important factor in getting our negotiations concluded the way it was. Joe loved every minute of it.[618]

Sparks named the continuance of negotiations in 1993 the "Cyril and Roelf show" in recognition of Ramaphosa and Meyer as the major mediators. Mandela and de Klerk met in September 1992 and after a great deal of haggling signed a Record of Understanding agreeing to resume negotiations. The new round began April 1, 1993, and one of the foundations for the talks was Joe's article in *The African Communist*, now titled "Negotiations: Strategic Perspectives." Joe was present at the April 1 resumption of negotiations. The negotiations began quickly but were temporarily aborted ten days later when Chris Hani was gunned down in his driveway by right-wing extremists. Hani's murder was a plot crafted by Clive Derby-Lewis and executed by Janusz Walus. The murderers were quickly apprehended because Hani's neighbor, an Afrikaner woman, recorded the license plate number of the car Walus was driving as he sped away. Police later found that Walus had a list with names, addresses, descriptions, and photographs. Presumed to be a hit list, Joe was listed second, between Mandela at the top and Hani as number three—a continuance of the many assassinations and threats of the 1980s. In an interview following the murder, Joe sat at Chris Hani's desk, and as after Obadi's murder in the Matola Massacre, appeared truly despondent. As in Maputo, he was totally resolute on the need to carry on the fight for a democratic South Africa. The difference, of course, was this time it was at the negotiating table and not fueled by Special Operations incursions. Padraig O'Malley asked Joe to speak about the political impact of Hani's assassination:

The loss of Hani to the SACP was an irreplaceable one. It's something which goes without saying. I think in the end if an evil deed like that can have positive effects I think it didn't serve the purposes of those who perpetrated the act, and that is to try to demoralize people, to weaken the struggle as a whole.

They didn't succeed. I think it had the exact opposite effect. It was a real moment that helped to instill into the government a greater sense of realism about what they were going to face if the process just dragged on and on without any kind of solution.[619]

Joe suffered another blow two weeks after Hani's assassination when Oliver Tambo died after a long-term illness. Two of Joe's closest comrades were now dead as years of struggle were moving toward fruition.

Violence errupted in the country after the assassination, but the ANC was determined to continue negotiations. Speaking from a position of strength, Ramaphosa sought and received the consent of Nelson Mandela to move forward. At an ANC press conference with Ramaphosa, Joe proclaimed, "Any suggestion of calling off the negotiations would be playing into the hands of the murderers, whose purpose is to stop the process. We must defeat them."[620] The negotiations intensified throughout May and June, sometimes including 48-hour marathon sessions. Mac Maharaj remembers those meetings, with him, Joe, and government negotiators sharing continuing concerns and issues of distrust. South African photographer David Goldblatt remembered seeing Joe at a negotiations session that began at three in the afternoon and concluded well after midnight. He told Joe: "I watched you. The strain showed—you had been at it since 9 a.m. I was told—but you kept on, seemingly inexhaustible, never losing what I can only describe as a sort of—forgive the term—benign quietude."[621]

Both Billy Cobbett and Janet Love worked for the ANC negotiation team. Their memories are of Joe as the great mediator when the tensions rose. Cobbett commented:

Joe was always such a huge presence and such a voice of authority. He also didn't open his mouth just to say something. He always thought things through. Of course, he could get animated. But at this time the main person was Cyril. But the two people he trusted the most were Mac and Joe. As a team we were very disciplined. The work was unbelievably long. It was truly sixteen hours a day. Without being dramatic, it was scotch, cigarettes, and coffee I remember as my main diet. It was hugely intense.[622]

Love spoke to the same theme:

We'd finish the negotiations at nine o'clock at night. You'd have the various National Party representatives on one side and the ANC representatives on the other side of a series of issues and negotiations, all very fraught, and thereafter we'd be finished for the day and people would go and have a couple of drinks. Joe could tell jokes from that moment well into the morning without repeating a single joke. He had the most extraordinary ability to mimic. He could put on all sorts of accents. He was just phenomenal. He used to have me in stitches. Joe—I think what he portrayed so much was the humanity, and I say this not in a trite way, the humanity in the ANC for a lot of the people in the Party. Here was this person who was the "devil incarnate" in all of their psyches who not only proved to not have any horns and tail—he did have red socks. So he had all of these images he'd conjure up for all of these NAT people; he literally sat down and went with Piet, joke for joke. His ability to just relate at the human level was hugely disarming because it smashed all sorts of misconceptions and preconceptions.[623]

The May and June negotiations led to the determination of the date of the first democratic election in South African history: April 27, 1994. Despite his total involvement, his importance to the negotiations, and the successes, Joe sometimes questioned the process as well as the progress. He was well known for saying, "We will snatch defeat from the jaws of victory." Helena remembered his frustration and his reference to talks as "the setting for a Lewis Carroll–*Alice in Wonderland* fantastical story, that you had to pinch yourself sometimes to believe what you were hearing and seeing."[624]

A negotiation setback again occurred on June 25, 1993, when right-wing groups protested at the negotiations site, the World Trade Centre. Initially, the crowd was celebratory, with placards calling for an Afrikaner state. There were ominous signs as well: some of the congregants were armed and dressed in black military uniforms embossed with the swastika symbol of the Afrikaner Resistance Movement (AWB). Eventually, protesters drove a military vehicle through the front of the building and members of the crowd, turned mob, stormed the building threatening black delegates and trashing the premises while the police stood by and did nothing.

Neither right-wing violence nor later IFP and PAC attacks could hinder the negotiation process, however. In November, an agreement was made on the constitutional issues and the April election was formally approved. Between May and the end of the year, Joe Slovo lived as if his cancer did not exist.

A monthly column penned by Joe, "Red Alert," had appeared in *Business Day* beginning in late 1992. The articles were a mixture of politics, history, and humor. One of his first commentaries was about Ruth's murder, reconciliation, and de Klerk's complicity in IFP violence. He connected Ruth's assassination to negotiations. "More than once, sitting opposite government teams at the negotiating table and facing, among others, luminaries of the security establishment, I wondered which of them gave the nod for the killing of my wife and the likes of David Webster and Steve Biko."[625] Joe also "wondered" about de Klerk: "Unlike his church, he refuses to confess his own complicity in apartheid's crimes. This covers at least a share of the political responsibility for the torture, and cell and death squad killings, of so many hundreds of political activists."[626]

In May 1993 Joe's essay was titled "'Kill a Boer' Is Music to the Ears of the Generals." After writing about the roots of the song within the cruel treatment of black farmworkers, Joe explained that the song energized the hatred and violence of South African white supremacists. From a personal perspective, he recalled that he was not pleased when, during a recent speech commemorating the life of PAC's president, some in the crowd chanted, "One Slovo, one bullet." Finally, there were two articles on Eastern Europe and capitalism — or more accurately, socialism over capitalism. Joe explained that he still wanted to write a sequel to "Has Socialism Failed?" that would be titled, "Has Capitalism Succeeded?" In the same commentary, he concluded with a Boris Yeltsin joke: "Yeltsin was asked what things were like. Came the reply, 'Things are not really that good but I can confidently predict that they are certainly better than next year.'"[627]

Gillian visited South Africa in 1993 and she wrote of Joe appearing healthy and energized. In his SACP role, Joe visited China in October. Walter Sisulu led the delegation, and Joe spoke of progressive changes in the Chinese economy. An ironic analysis by Joe Slovo since he was simultaneously telling Padraig O'Malley, in correspondence to his constant mantra of "people's power"—that it was for the people, not politicians, to take the lead on South Africa's economic system. During breaks in negotiations, Joe and Helena took short holidays, sometimes to the countryside and other times to the sea at Plettenberg Bay. They occasionally stayed with the Colemans, and in one instance they visited Ruth's brother, who had a house at the ocean. In Johannesburg, they saw the Randeras as well as Barney Simon and continued to enjoy dinners with the Hamburgers and other friends like Gonda Perez and Jay Josie, who had settled in Yeoville. Jaya remembers he and Joe doing tricks for the children:

> Joe could interact with anybody. Whether it's the person doing the cleaning or the children. I was fascinated [watching] him with children, from little babies [on up]. Before he died, my daughter was a little baby and I have a picture of her with him and she used to laugh and laugh. But he interacted with children with a basis of great respect. He'd make a point. He'd walk into a place where there were children and he would go and greet them and talk to them and they loved it.[628]

Joe Slovo, throughout his life, was a wonderful, dedicated, and loyal friend. Thus, it was no surprise that in November 1993 he spoke at the launch of Ronnie Kasrils's memoir, *Armed and Dangerous*. Kasrils still gets a twinkle in his eye recalling Joe talking at the book party:

> I had asked him to speak and we had a lovely, witty, interaction joking at each other's expense at that book launch, which took place at Rockey Street Doornfontein just opposite where his family had had a fruit and vegetable stand. This was at a restaurant opposite and we joked about that, and I can remember saying that most Jews had started in Dornfontein when they arrived and after some years had moved up over the ridge into Yeoville, which was slightly better, and then they began the migration farther north to ultimately Houghton and other places. Joe, though, started off in Yeoville and went south. And he just laughed louder than anybody there. He loved that kind of joshing, you see.[629]

Teasing aside, Joe tried to live more modestly than many of his peers during negotiations and when the ANC came to power. He was clear in his vision when he spoke in the 1980s about the struggle not being for black people to drive Mercedes Benzes. His move to Yeoville when he returned to South Africa was significant. Most of his peers lived in more upscale neighborhoods. The Observatory home was certainly not posh. Julius Browde recalls Joe and Helena inviting him and his wife, Selma, to dinner. Browde joshed with Joe about the house being too modest for his new position in South African society. Joe, however, became quite serious:

> He said to me, "Look, I want to tell you something. This house is good enough for me. I'm not going to go into any big ministerial house." And I thought that was very interesting. "It's got everything I need. It's convenient for me. The school is near here. What do we want?" he said. He didn't drive big Cadillac motorcars or a Mercedes Benz.[630]

Life remained hectic in the early months of 1994 leading to the April election. Gillian visited but Joe was working constantly. He spoke to "People's Forums" campaigning for the ANC and was involved in final negotiations and in meetings with the Transition Executive Council (TEC)—something of an ANC shadow government. As a leader in TEC, Joe traveled in March to the former bantustan Bophuthatswana when the South African Army removed Chief Lucas Mangope who was trying to sabotage the coming election. In addition, he participated in meetings with Chief Buthelezi of the IFP who resisted participation in the government up until the very last moment. Dan O'Meara encountered Joe on a plane coming to Johannesburg:

> It was two days before the election. What he told me at dinner when I came back to Johannesburg a couple of weeks later was that—this is obviously Joe's version of events and I'm sure Thabo has a very different version—Thabo had been put in charge of negotiations with Inkatha and that he had totally screwed them up. Joe persuaded Mandela to let Ramaphosa and others intervene, and it was Ramaphosa who got Butelezi turned around. Joe and Ramaphosa had to intervene, literally, to save South Africa from a bloodbath.[631]

As the election approached, Joe was again feeling ill and weak, but there was no time to stop, not even time for medical tests. Cognizant of the realities that would confront him and the new government after the election, and despite knowing that his cancer was affecting him, Joe Slovo felt euphoria in knowing that the first-ever democratic election in South Africa was moments away.

12 — Election, Ministry: To Rest in Soweto

ON APRIL 27, 1994, the African National Congress, with Nelson Mandela as the first president, came to power. People throughout the country stood in line for hours, some in tumultuous rainstorms, to cast a vote in South Africa's first democratic, non-racial election. Joe Slovo was one of the masses who voted for the ANC that day. He and Helena cast their ballots in Johannesburg, and they spent the evening dancing at the ANC celebration at the Carlton Hotel. Two weeks later, on May 10, they sat in the VIP seats, alongside the past cabinet, other struggle leaders, and dignitaries that included Fidel Castro, Hillary Clinton, Julius Nyerere, Yasser Arafat, and the president of Israel, Chaim Herzog, to witness Mandela's inauguration at the Union Buildings in Pretoria. More than 50,000 people attended the event and listened to Madiba's oration on regeneration and reconciliation.

The day following the inauguration, Mandela announced his cabinet. Since the first government was one of national unity, there were to be cabinet ministers representative of the various political parties — not only those from the struggle. Joe had anticipated an appointment in the Justice Ministry, and many people were surprised when he was chosen Minister of Housing. His selection was foreshadowed in one of his 1992 interviews with Padraig O'Malley:

> I don't think within five years we'll be able to solve the housing problem of South Africa, but I think people are very patient

and very understanding in general and this is something I've been convinced about since coming back to the country. I think it's a question of honesty and honest politics, and really getting down to trying to do something using the resources that are available in the best possible way. I think people will understand that, and they will accept that we're not going to have a Utopia in 1995.[632]

Although there has been political analysis of Joe's appointment by Mandela as Minister of Housing as a devaluation of the left, what is evident is that Joe, unlike some of his fellow ministers, immediately engaged in his work. His first act was hiring a new Director General to be the housing expert in the Ministry. The man he hired, William (Billy) Cobbett, had a different perception of the debates surrounding Joe's appointment:

It was either the smartest thing Mandela ever did or some less than generous thing of sidelining. The popular read was that it was a stroke of genius to put the most popular guy after Mandela more-or-less into what was agreed was a difficult challenge. The message I took was that they were taking housing seriously after all.[633]

Joe contacted Cobbett the day after his appointment was made public:

I was at the National Housing Forum and everyone was shocked—they've appointed Joe Slovo Minister of Housing. Then within a short space of time on the same morning, maybe within an hour of it being announced, my pager went off, and it was please ring Joe Slovo. So I phoned and he said, "I suppose you've heard I am Minister of Housing—I want you to be my Director General." I said, "Okay."[634]

The two men became acquainted during the negotiations. Billy was an expert on urban issues and was the National Coordinator of Local Government, Housing, and Electrification for the ANC. In cooperation with Janet Love, he had organized facilities for CODESA. As a leader in the National Housing Forum, he officially represented the ANC on housing issues and workers' hostels when the negotiations intensified. Finally, Joe knew him well and respected his abilities when they both served on the Transitional Executive Council.

The first day of the new government was officially Monday, May 16. Joe and Billy met in Joe's garden the day before to discuss plans and to review the report Joe had received from his predecessor. Billy recalled the discussion: "Joe and I sat together and I had already thought about how to handle the whole transition and had sketched out a whole series of meetings with the private sector. This would be the minister who would hit the ground running."[635] Due to bureaucratic red tape, Billy's appointment as Director General was delayed. Instead he was named as a special advisor until the official appointment was made. Whatever the title, Joe viewed Billy Cobbett as his technical expert on housing. Actually, his opinion of Cobbett was much more than that of a technician—he respected his expertise and came to trust him fully as a colleague and friend. Billy Cobbett's appointment at thirty-six years old was representative of Joe Slovo's lifetime as a leader in the struggle against apartheid. At every stage, Joe recruited a younger deputy whom he trusted and respected, but did not micromanage. Initially it was Obadi, then Rashid, and now Billy.

On his first official day in the office, Joe called a full staff meeting for two in the afternoon. The meeting included everyone on the Ministry staff—highest bureaucrats, secretaries, and janitors. There were approximately 250 people, mostly white Afrikaners, many who still considered Joe Slovo a Communist terrorist. Billy recalled, with irony, that as a result of Joe's "sunset clauses," he was "in charge of a whole bunch of civil servants who actually owed their jobs to him."[636] They listened closely as Joe addressed the meeting:

> Joe walks into the room, you couldn't have filmed this, everyone stood up. This is about Joe Slovo, the most hated white man in the country for this audience, walking in as their boss. He spoke to them for about twenty minutes. He told them a joke about Che Guevara and they didn't know who Che Guevara was. He told them a joke about Castro and Che Guevara—Castro was the other bogeyman. Then he tells them that we are going to work together and it was all Kumbaya sort of stuff. He introduced me and says things like my door is always open which no one believes because the previous ministers' doors were not open.[637]

The bureaucrats did not believe Joe's collaborative efforts or his open-door policy because not only was it alien to their Ministry experience, it challenged their sense of hierarchy with the Minister as God, and at the very opposite extreme, their perceptions of Joe Slovo. Joe and Billy actually staged disagreements to instigate discussion among the staff, but it was very difficult to change a culture that was so ingrained. Shortly after they began their tenure, Cobbett recalled that two senior bureaucrats, men who could not help but call him "sir," approached him and said, "Sir, if we would have known you were like this, you being the ANC, we would have voted for you."[638] Billy's administrative assistant, Melinda Coetzer, recalled Joe at the Ministry:

> You go through life and meet so many people from all different walks of life, however, it seldom happens that you get the opportunity to meet someone that greatly confirms the statement: Never judge a book by its cover. When he walked into your office, his humbleness and warmth just somehow warmed up your heart.[639]

Billy noted that Joe clearly had issues with the "trappings of office."[640] He had a huge office that he thought unnecessary, and he never became used to the security that was assigned to him. In fact, he fought and subverted his own protection. On the second day, already immersing himself in his work, Joe displayed his aversion to formality. Joe and Billy had spent the morning scheduling meetings with people connected to the housing industry—banks, builders, and civic organizations, and Joe was hungry for lunch:

> So he said let's go and have a hamburger. So none of this chauffeured car shit. Joe and I walk down Walker Street. I think it was the first day but it wasn't later than the second day. So we walk a block into the local square, tiny shopping mall, sit down and you can see people just watching. And there's the Minister walking down the road, walking into a café, and we order hamburgers. The whole place was crowded, these women in their beehives and they just cannot believe that they are seeing Joe Slovo out there in public and he's eating a hamburger.[641]

Joe Slovo would also tease himself, often looking around the room if someone addressed him by his title, as he could not relate to being

Joe in Parliament with de Klerk at his left (courtesy of Helena Dolny)

called "Minister." But most important, Joe was absorbed in his work of attempting to provide good housing for the poorest sector of South African society. There had been no specific mandate from the ANC regarding housing. The mission was enormous, as were the complications of taking over systems, personnel, and industries that were firmly established under the apartheid regime. During the first few weeks in office, Joe asked Billy, who knew everyone in the industry, to summon leaders from the banks, builders, and civic organizations to meet with him at his office in Pretoria. Due to Joe's status and popularity within the ANC, no one dared reject an invitation. At meetings, Joe always introduced himself as the novice:

It was part of his strategy and tactics to be disarmingly honest about how little he knew. He would say when he met with the banks, I am here to learn from you. When he met with the civic associations, to all of them, he said, "You know me. You know what I used to do. I used to blow up power stations and now I am coming to you." As an icebreaker it was brilliant. It was also, as everyone knew, the truth.[642]

Joe and Billy set the agenda but also asserted that housing was a collaborative effort. Joe's Housing Ministry, unlike all of those before him, would be available and would listen to the voices of the stakeholders. There was a mission: unlike past governments that uti-lized housing policy to solidify, magnify, and facilitate apartheid, Joe's plan was to establish housing for an egalitarian, non-racial future.

When he began his role in the Ministry, Joe arranged a meeting with Zé Forjaz, who had been Minister of Housing in Mozambique. Zé noticed that Joe was not healthy, but he was impressed by Joe's zeal to provide housing for dispossessed people in South Africa. His advice, when he met with Joe, stemmed from the housing policy fail-ures he had experienced in Mozambique. He told him not to build people houses but rather to facilitate the building of affordable hous-ing. This was also the message that Billy brought to Joe, derived from his experience in the field as well as from his numerous consultations with experts throughout the world. Though it was the antithesis of the promises the ANC would have preferred, giving people houses was not economically possible. Joe understood the reality.

As Billy and his top deputies worked on policy, Joe quickly learned the political aspects of the process. Less than two weeks after becoming Minister, he spoke in Parliament, arguing that the gov-ernment's role was to orchestrate housing, but not to build houses. He also outlined the pressing problems and differing views of the housing stakeholders. He told the legislators, "The cornerstone of my approach will be to seek an end to the undeclared war between com-munities, the state and the private sector."[643] On June 9, Joe repeated the message, albeit with more detail, at a breakfast meeting of the Finance Week Breakfast Club. The meeting was at the Sandton Sun Hotel and Joe concluded his talk with a struggle-like challenge:

> Housing is not a privilege; it is a fundamental human right. To live in an environment of degradation is to produce a degraded people. We have striven endlessly for freedom and liberation. Now it is time to deliver. The April election—in itself a mira-cle—did not deliver liberation; it has only provided us with a launching pad to build a liberated South Africa. The complex-ity of our task is not an inseparable obstacle, it is an historic challenge, which we must face and overcome. And together we shall overcome.[644]

In addition to maintaining the mission of the struggle, Joe Slovo did not neglect his friends. He escorted Ronnie Kasrils when he was sworn in as Deputy Defense Minister in July. Kasrils recalled Joe saying how lucky we were, people like him and me. "He said we had been through a decade-long struggle and had survived that and had actually lived to see freedom and then served in the government. And he said this was such a rare thing."[645] Nevertheless, Joe was not always thoughtful. Whether because he was so involved in his mission, or because of his worsening health, or a combination of both, he was not fully aware of Helena's undertakings:

> So it was just excitement for Joe to be here but with total absorption. Joe in the end did not know what I was working on. So he becomes Minister of Housing and he asks Billy Cobbett to be his Director General and then he says to Billy, "We need a rural housing policy. We need a task team. Who can be on this task team? Who knows about rural housing issues?" And Billy said, "Well, actually, your wife."[646]

There were trips to various townships and rural locations as Joe and Billy viewed the beginnings of new housing projects. In most cases, the visits helped Joe feel hopeful about the possibilities. People were grateful that he came to their communities, but his message was always honest. Billy Cobbett:

> We went into townships and there his popularity was just legend. He would give a very simple explanation of what we were trying to do and "Comrades, it's going to take time but we're on the case." He would give encouraging but not unrealistic assessment. But people had so much faith and belief in him that he really couldn't do much wrong.[647]

Billy also recalled a visit to the Eastern Cape that affected Joe very differently. The "trappings" of government, the showy security that Joe abhorred, and corruption were all part of this particular trip:

> We flew down to the Eastern Cape with a few shocks when we arrived—there were ten limousines lined up at the airport and ten guys with submachine guns. And all of them doing these super-duper fast maneuvers to make sure nothing happened to us—not nice. And then we came to the premier's house and we're surrounded by bodyguards. This Joe didn't like at all. Then we went with the MEC, the Assistant Minister, and he

commandeered a helicopter and we went and visited some small towns. But there was this one amazing scene. A group of people were marking out plots for their own settlements, but these were not the poor. These were people who arrived in 4 by 4s and in our view were taking advantage of the change in circumstances to grab a bit of the pie. Joe directly challenged these guys. I remember him saying to this one guy and feeling his suit, "My friend, your suit is more expensive than mine." Just wanting to make the point to this guy, "You're not the poor. This is not why we did what we did. We didn't come into power to enrich you."[648]

Joe understood clearly at this point that the reality of all South Africans owning reasonable housing was a lengthy process. He was quoted as saying that "the goal was a million houses in five years." After just a few months in office, however, the newspapers were already printing articles criticizing the lack of government housing projects. Continuing tensions between the Ministry and the provinces were sometimes exacerbated by the construction industry. In addition, Joe was experiencing greater fatigue; his health was declining. Parliament was in session when Joe's relapse occurred, so he sought treatment at Groote Schuur Hospital in Cape Town. Helena accompanied him to hospital, and she said that in spite of his health, "I watched with envy and admiration as Joe judiciously applied his energy to his ministerial responsibilities."[649] In August, after completing another round of chemotherapy, the prognosis was not positive. During treatment, Joe had followed the same type of calendar he utilized during his earlier treatment. He usually had chemotherapy on Thursday and did not return to work until Monday. He had total confidence in Billy and knew that the people working with Billy were competent and committed to their mission. When the doctors informed Joe that the chemotherapy was no longer effective, they also told him that he had approximately three months to live. It was at this point that he shared the severity of his condition with Billy Cobbett. And Billy, though shaken, understood that Joe was warning him of the need to accelerate their work; there was much to accomplish and Joe's time was limited.

With Helena's prodding, she and Joe continued to enjoy short holidays to the countryside or the sea. When he was given the final prognosis, it was Joe who asked Helena what they should do in the remaining time they had together. In the past, they had planned to travel to Italy during lulls in negotiations, but were always forced to cancel their plans due to Joe's work and responsibilities. In August 1994, they agreed to make the trip. Helena, having yet to attend her formal doctoral graduation, added travel to Brussels, to participate in the Open University ceremony. Prior to leaving on their journey, they participated in an SACP fundraiser. Although this was not a particularly important event, the invitation, in the form of a postcard, featured Joe. The card portrayed a photograph of Joe dressed in a business suit. But true to form, he was also wearing his red socks. The title of the invitation was "Keep Your MPs on Their Toes" and the dress code read, "Anything that goes with red socks."

Despite feeling weak and sick, Joe was intent on making the trip. Helena's and Ruth's colleague from Maputo, Marc Wuyts, was also graduating, and Ruth's closest Maputo colleague and friend, Bridget O'Laughlin, lived in Brussels. Also, a number of the cooperantes from the Mozambican days were living in Belgium. Helena and Joe saw all their friends at a special dinner. "We had this celebratory evening and everybody knew it was going to be the last time they saw Joe. He was on morphine. He was beginning to look gaunt. By this time he was on his way out."[650] Joe was feeling horrible, but the trip was important. It was something he and Helena had looked forward to for a long time. Besides the physical pain, he was clearly struggling with his own mortality. Bridget O'Laughlin expressed to Joe in a subsequent letter how generous he had been to meet them, considering how bad he was feeling. In later correspondence with Helena, she wrote, "What scared me in Brussels was not so much the exhaustion in Joe's body, but the fear in his face—which I have never seen before."[651]

The couple stayed with friends in Tuscany and Rome. They visited the Vatican and did a small amount of touring. Joe wanted to see Michelangelo's paintings. When they returned to Johannesburg, Helena observed that Joe was feeling somewhat better. He saw his doctors and a homeopath and went back to work. It would soon be time to propose legislation for a new housing bill, and Joe's political skills were necessary to get the bill passed. Gillian, her husband, Andy, and daughter Cassie had arrived in South Africa to live just as Joe and Helena returned from Italy. Confirming Helena's assessment of Joe's improved health after traveling in Italy, Gillian found her father thin but vibrant. She would soon recognize, though, how tired he appeared after days spent working on housing policy. Just as had always been the case, there was also conflict. Gillian was working on her memoir—*Every Secret Thing*, and sought to know things about Ruth and Joe's lives, and Joe viewed her queries as an imposition. But he had formulated a plan to spend an hour each morning continuing to record his own story. Joe had begun recording his life after Ruth's assassination, but the project had not been sustainable because his daily leadership of Special Operations, as well as other struggle responsibilities, took precedence. The same thing happened in 1994. Joe was living in the present and knew that his time was short. As Helena remembered:

> He gets diagnosed with cancer and he doesn't want to speak about the past. He wants to focus on the now and the future. I think it's a psychological state. So here's Joe, for the one time doing the most creative thing. He's not blowing things up. He's doing housing policy. He's trying to do value-added to the country. He's in Joe Slovo heaven on earth.[652]

Joe was still working very hard, and when he was home, whether it was in the ministerial house in Cape Town or in his and Helena's home in Johannesburg, he opted for peace and quiet when out of his role as Minister. Helena writes about Joe loving to sit in the back garden of their Observatory home: "I would often find Joe sitting on the *stoep* after breakfast, gazing down the folds of the lawn and the jacaranda tree, deep in thought. 'Don't assume I'm loafing,' he once said. 'This is the most important time of my day, it's my thinking time.'"[653] Knowing that he needed to get legislation to Parliament before the end of the year, the pace of engineering housing policy accelerated even more in the coming months. Joe negotiated with provincial leaders, and his public pronouncements varied depending on whether his message was equality or conciliation toward the housing stakeholders—sometimes it was both. Kasrils recalled the spirit Joe brought to the work, even at this point, when he was feeling so ill: "Slovo would roll up his sleeves, consult all the role players, be prepared to knock heads together and get on with the business of rectifying things."[654]

October was especially intense as Joe publicly fast-tracked selling the housing program throughout the country. He spoke to various groups, negotiated with bankers, and put forth his policy of starter homes that were affordable for the poor through cooperation of builders, banks, national and provincial governments, community organizations, and individuals. One of the key elements of the policy was the personal involvement of homebuyers, who would, according to the policy, build incrementally as they became more prosperous in the new South Africa. Of course, there were stakeholders who did not support Joe's policies. He spoke to bankers in Krugersdorp early in the month and challenged them to help poor people, not just middle-class South Africans. In his speech, Joe provided examples of the lack of housing for the impoverished and addressed the issue of homelessness in the country.

The most important event in promoting the new housing policy was the Botshabelo Summit in late October. Joe presented the housing policy vision and again challenged each of the stakeholders. The main issue continued to be soliciting the banks to fully participate in the proposals. Bankers verbalized a liberal party line of helping poor people, but they seldom came through. There was debate from the different constituencies, and the disagreements did not just emerge from the stakeholders. There were also issues between the Ministry and provincial leaders.

One element that was essential to the policies that Billy Cobbett had written with Joe was that starter houses would be improved incrementally, through the work and growing prosperity of homeowners. Segments of the banking and construction industries did not favor the policy, and there was a motion from the floor to delete "incremental" from the policy statement. Joe intensely refused to change the wording. He knew that removing the word *totally* changed the policy he was proposing. In addition, he was quite clear that the policy was the most supportive way to assist the poor; Billy remembers:

This was not left for the technicians. It was not for me to respond. It was Joe. This was the challenge he took head on. He knew how fundamental this was. By the time of the Botshabelo Summit, Joe was very well versed on who was who in the zoo—and what their political interests were. Of course, we are talking about a political animal of extraordinary abilities. The housing side is only a small part of understanding banking interests, building interests, community interests. You don't need to be a housing expert to see what's in play. So him taking on the challenge to incrementalism was something he understood full well, anticipated, and dealt with decisively. And he convinced the floor and it was basically about honesty and pragmatism. He was basically being invited to make the kind of undeliverable promise on behalf of the ANC, which we knew we couldn't deliver. He refused.[655]

As November got under way, Joe collaborated with Billy Cobbett, John de Ridder, and other advisors on the comprehensive "white paper" on housing. In an interview with Padraig O'Malley, Joe admitted there were continuing "hiccups" being experienced in the Government of National Unity, but he remained positive about housing for the masses of South African people. He discussed homelessness, the recalcitrance of the banks, as well as rent boycotts:

> In the short term, I would say the breakthrough with the banks will bring about a complete transformation in relation to that 20 percent segment that I am talking about: for those who are earning sufficient to attract credit. And that's a substantial bit of the cherry, one in every five. From the point of view of the mass, the 60, 65 percent, we will deliver bricks and mortar, but it's a question of the scale of that brick and mortar. We will not be able to start off giving them three- or four-bedroom houses, but with the subsidy provided we will be able to put up a permanent small structure, maybe 20, 25 square meters, which, through the other structures that I've described, these housing depots that we're going to set up in every area, will start the process of enabling people themselves to begin augmenting and improving.[656]

Shortly after the O'Malley interview, Joe met with a delegation of homeless South Africans, a small representation of the estimated nine million homeless people in the country. He engaged with them as peers, discussed the pros and cons of various solutions, and urged them to organize as small groups to leverage both his Ministry and the provincial and local government. At the conclusion of the meeting, the homeless people thanked Joe. "Don't thank me," he responded. "That's my job and I'm being paid too much for it!"[657]

Joe's frailty was becoming more noticeable. He overheard Helena telling Gonda Perez about his prognosis, and though he did not join the conversation, he was cognizant of the look of shock on Gonda's face. He asked her to return the next day and Helena and Joe sat with Gonda and shared more about Joe's diagnosis. "That is the kind of thing that made Joe so special. He loved us. You felt the love in those little gestures."[658] She related one of them:

When Joe was dying he was preparing Helena for his dying. He took her to see a movie, *Three Colors: Blue*, about living and dying. And just after Joe died Helena wanted me to go with her and see this movie again that Joe so loved. The two of us sat through this movie crying and holding one another and then we went and had coffee, and I just let her talk.[659]

Joe often needed oxygen in the evenings amid medication to control his pain. Yet he still visited with friends and attended events that were personally important. Ronald Segal had a house on the sea in Cape Town in 1994 and had wonderful memories of Joe visiting and playing hide-and-seek with his one-year-old granddaughter. Joe made a point of attending Hillary and Tony Hamburger's wedding later in the month. Hillary recalled how joyful the day was as a small group of close friends witnessed their sharing of vows in the garden of their home: "I had soreness every time I caught sight of Joe. He was quiet. He was withdrawn. He really was on his way out and he died six weeks after the wedding."[660] Well-known South African poet Lionel Abrahams attended the wedding and later wrote a poem about Joe. Abrahams had invited Ruth and Joe to hide in his home to escape state security before they went into exile. Although not a great fan of Joe, his poem, "At Revolution's End," honored his place in the struggle as well as in the new government. In addition, Abrahams described Joe's condition:

He is at last a cabinet minister
in the achieved glorious government,
at last is tasked to build,
 but he has to formulate a policy
to meet approaching death . . .
He has been sitting at his table
remote at the core of silence
which even his magnificent daughters
seem reluctant to breach.
A white shadow covers him,
a slow flame slowly consumes
his material life.[661]

The same week, Ronald First's son, Trevor, died. Almost twenty years later, Ronald recalled Joe paying his condolences: "The really very warm action by Joe when Trevor died was that he came to prayers, despite the fact that the cancer was already destroying him."[662]

Shortly before he was to meet with Parliament on new housing policy, Joe went on holiday to Cintsa with Helena, Tessa, Kyla, Helena's mother, and Gillian's daughter, Cassie. They were enjoying the tranquility of the town and the sea, but three days after arriving, Joe fell and fractured his shoulder, exacerbating his illness and pain. Wearing a sling, and joking about his fall, Joe Slovo nonetheless appeared before Parliament on December 7, 1994. The white paper, titled, "A New Housing Policy and Strategy," was 81 pages with sections on every possible issue related to facilitating housing for the masses of people in South Africa. According to Billy Cobbett, just as Joe Slovo was the only person who could have successfully facilitated the Botshabelo Summit, he was the only person, both because of his political acumen and the breadth of his humanity, who was capable of shepherding the white paper through the cabinet and Parliament. The preamble of the document addresses all of the stakeholders, speaks to homelessness, and introduces what the Ministry of Housing had worked toward during Joe's seven months as Minister:

Throughout the document, a partnership between the various tiers of government, the private sector and the communities is envisaged. This is seen as a fundamental prerequisite for the sustained delivery of housing at a level unprecedented in the history of this country. It requires all parties not only to argue for their rights, but also to accept their respective responsibilities. . . . We believe that of all of our resources, nothing compares with the latent energy of the people. The housing programme must be designed to unleash that energy; not only to get the houses onto the ground, but also to give meaning to the notion of a people centred development.[663]

When Nadine Gordimer was asked by friends outside of South Africa about Joe Slovo, her response was that he was "the man who knows how, and when the time demands it, to beat AK-47s into bricks and mortar!"[664] However, presenting the white paper to Parliament was essentially Joe Slovo's final act as Minister of Housing. Yet nine days later, feeling desolate and very ill, Joe, accompanied by

Helena, attended the 49th Congress of the African National Congress in Bloemfontein. Ronnie Kasrils recalled how difficult it was for Joe:

> He was so brave. He came with Helena and he sat through the sessions in the awful heat. He had to keep going out to get fresh air and I went and joined him and he was sucking ice, which they had in a thermos, and he said to me, "Look, it's so hot, do you want to have some of this ice, it's a great relief." I didn't want to take any from him; there was a limited amount. But it just struck me the way he cared for other people.[665]

The key event at the Congress was the presentation to Joe of the ANC's highest honor, the Isithwalandwe-Seaparankoe Award. Acting on the decision of the National Executive Committee, Mandela presented the award, enumerating Joe Slovo's multiple contributions to the struggle—mediating work in the ANC-SACP alliance, Umkhonto we Sizwe, strategy and tactics, and his work as Minister. Madiba also elaborated on Joe as a model of non-racialism. "I am not sure, Comrade Joe, if you ever thought of yourself as a white South African. In a country in which there is a racially oppressed majority, non-racism is not an outlook that can be simply taken for granted."[666]

Joe's response to the presentation was brief: "As far as I'm concerned, what I did, I did without any regrets. I decided long ago in my life that there is only one target, and that target is to remove the racist regime and obtain power for the people."[667] Thenjiwe Mtintso was among the crowd that gave Joe a standing ovation. Thenjiwe was a young Black Consciousness devotee when she met Joe in Maputo. At first skeptical, as was the case with many members of BC toward white people in the struggle, she soon became a member of the SACP and came to view Joe as a teacher and mentor. At the 49th Congress she said to Joe, "We felt you were there for us, and want to thank you for your life." "What you're saying is I'm dying," was Joe's retort, to which Thenjiwe responded, "No, I'm saying thank you, I love you."[668]

Just after Christmas, Gillian, Shawn, and Robyn traveled to Johannesburg, staying close by Joe and Helena in the home of Joe's friend Mannie Brown. At Joe's request, Helena invited a small number of people to come and visit, including Harold and AnnMarie Wolpe. Rica Hodgson recalled the sadness:

When Joe was dying I went to the house very, very often. We took food every day, comrades did 'cause there were so many people dropping in all the time to see Joe, to see Helena. And the girls were there. So it was a difficult period, it was very hard for him. And he was dying, one knew he was dying; there was no hope for him then. I think Joe would have preferred it if he was just left alone with Helena but that wasn't to be.[669]

When Rashid came to see Joe, there was a final request. Just as Joe had challenged Rashid when Obadi was killed and during their Special Operations camaraderie, there was one last mission:

Just before Joe died I went to see him and he was telling me about the book that he had been working on that subsequently Helena had to finish. He said to me that the part he had never written was the whole question of Special Operations and a more detailed account of MK. And I said to Joe that I would do it, and he said to me, "We owe it to the comrades who fought so bravely and valiantly in the struggle to tell their story." The other thing that he said is that we must bring the truth out about why we had to adopt certain forms of struggle and tell the story the way it really was. That's going to be an interesting approach. I know I owe it to the comrades. I have an undertaking for Joe, the comrade who had been my mentor.[670]

After the 49th Congress, Helena was Joe's primary caretaker. Robyn, Shawn, and Gillian also alternated caring for their father. Billy Cobbett returned from a family trip to England to be at Joe's side. Billy reflected sadly on the last weeks of Joe's life:

I had a phone call from Helena and I was told he's bad, come back. I immediately flew back and I moved into the house. We had an extremely close mutual respect, which was just wonderful—the kind of relationship where you don't have to talk when you're together. He let me minister him physically. He was very weak so I used to help him walk. No, I looked after him. We would take turns—me and Helena sitting up with him during the night. We had shifts. I'm talking about the last week of his life.[671]

On New Year's Eve, family, Helen and Fazel Randera, Jaya Josie, and Gonda Perez gathered in the garden that Joe enjoyed so much to watch fireworks. Gonda recalled that Joe was unable to eat—he would take small sips of ginger ale with ice. Filled with emotion, he hugged the people who had gathered. Even that gesture was difficult as his bones were fragile. On January 4 Joe had a painful day—Helena, Gillian, Robyn, and Shawn were all with him, as was Billy. Fazel Randera nursed him through the night and he recalled Joe's anxiety and pain:

Helena had taken the first shift and then I'd taken the second shift. She was off her feet; she was totally exhausted. Joe had woken up after she had gone to sleep and was saying, "Where is Helena? Where is Helena?" And I said, "Joe, Helena is just resting for a little while. She will come to you in a little while." He looked in the mirror and my recollection is of him saying, "I think it's time."[672]

Madiba came to visit the following day. Two days later he told Helena, "When I visited Joe and he stood and embraced you, I think he was saying good-bye."[673] In her epilogue to *Slovo: The Unfinished Autobiography*, Helena Dolny paints the portrait of Joe's death:

Just before 3 a.m. Billy and I sat together, sensing the lengthening space between each beat of Joe's pulse, listening to the ever-slowing rhythm of his breathing. Then there was silence, all breathing had stopped. Billy called Fazel. Together they turned Joe on his back, arranged his head on the pillows. At last Joe's face had the serenity that we had not seen, even while resting, for some weeks. Shawn, Gillian, and Robyn joined us. We played Mahler's Fifth at a more celebratory volume. We each took a glass in our hands and, and reiterating Joe's last word to Madiba, toasted Joe's departure. "Cheers."[674]

An hour after Joe died, Billy began making calls and arrangements. Mandela arrived soon thereafter, and with the ANC taking over, just as they did when Ruth was killed, there was an unending stream of people coming into the house for two or three days. The family, in collaboration with the ANC, made unofficial and official arrangements and plans. The former included a gathering on

January 14 of approximately 120 family and friends at Johannesburg City Hall, where Joe and Ruth had led protests a half-century earlier. Gonda presented each person with a red carnation as they entered. Joe was fond of the flower because it had been used as a symbolic memorial during the Spanish Civil War. People sang and laughed and cried and expressed their love for Joe. The Johannesburg Orchestra played Joe's favorite music, Beethoven's *Eroica* and Mahler's Symphony no. 5, and musicians played folksongs that Joe had sung and strummed on his guitar. Joe's best friend, Harold Wolpe, said he could not imagine not talking with the friend who called him only "Wolpe" and whom he referred to only as "Slovo." He also spoke of Joe's specialness:

> One of the reasons why Joe's political judgments inspired great trust was the profound confidence he had in his own theoretical, analytical and political abilities. What was remarkable, however, was that he was a man that was entirely without pretensions, who retained always the common touch in his relations and, indeed, perhaps paradoxically, a wonderful modesty.[675]

Pallo Jordan shared some of Joe's favorite jokes, and at a later memorial in Cape Town, he cited Marx's eleventh thesis on Feuerbach: "Philosophers have interpreted the world in different ways; the point however is to change it."[676] For Pallo, that symbolized Joe Slovo. Cyril Ramaphosa laughed as he spoke of Joe's humor and said that being with Joe was being part of history. Barney Simon shared powerful, human memories of Joe. The two men never talked politics and Simon was most affected by Joe's humanity. He spoke of Joe's amazing hugs and connected a Hasidic tale that said that God created man because "he" loved to hear stories. Apologizing for bringing "religion" to Joe's memories, Simon thought that if the story were true, "Joe had to be one of the Lord's biggest favorites."[677] Joe's Russian friend Alexei Makarov remembered the memorial as a party where he felt Joe's presence.

The official state funeral followed the day after at Orlando Stadium in Soweto. Forty thousand people crowded into the stadium and there were eulogies from President Mandela; Barney Pityana, who would soon become chairperson of the South African Human Rights Commission; John Gomomo, representing COSATU; and Charles Nqakula from the SACP. Jeremy Cronin recited the Bertolt Brecht

Mandela at Joe's funeral
(courtesy of Helena Dolny)

poem, "In Praise of Communism." The crowd inside the stadium was subdued and the speeches were on the whole uninspiring, except, ironically, the formal eulogy by the Chief Rabbi of South Africa, Cyril Harris. The rabbi's sermon portrayed Joe's bravery and kindness, concluding with a Jewish proverb, "Yes, a resounding yes. The world is a better place, thanks to you, Joe, and your remarkable life."[678] The issue at the heart of the rabbi's sermon was Joe Slovo's commitment to social justice:

> The second motivation is humanitarian—it springs from a deep sense of identification with the oppressed, the ability to hear their cry, an acute awareness of the realities of poverty, a personal anguish at the suffering of fellow human beings. This was Joe Slovo's way. His humanity was boundless and inspirational; he became the true champion of the oppressed. Let not those religious people who acquiesced, passively or wrongly, with the inequalities of yesteryear, let not those religious people dare to condemn Joe Slovo, a humanist socialist, who fought all his life for basic decency, to reinstate the dignity to which all human beings are entitled.[679]

On the streets of Soweto, along the 12-kilometer drive to the cemetery, the South African people celebrated Joe Slovo. They danced, laughed, and sang "Hamba Kahle Umkhonto" in a tribute to Joe's life. At graveside, masses of people congregated, and there was fear as the crowd pushed aggressively toward Joe's grave. Helena gave a speech for the family reminding mourners at Avalon Cemetery that people always spoke of the Communist influences on Joe's politics, but Dadoo, Sisulu, Mandela, and Tambo also helped to form his life in the struggle. Though Joe Slovo was incredibly important to South African history, Helena recalled that South Africa "contributed to the making of Joe."[680]

Joe Slovo is one of two white South Africans that lie in rest at Avalon Cemetery in Soweto, one of Johannesburg's massive black townships. As friends and comrades laid flowers and stones on Joe's coffin he was lowered into his grave, not by the South African military, but rather Umkhonto we Sizwe cadres, Joe Slovo's comrades in the fight against the apartheid regime. Burying Joe Slovo in Soweto was more than appropriate as respect for his lifetime of commitment to the struggle against apartheid. Also apropos was the marker made for his grave, a vertical stone that was designed by his friend Zé Forjaz and was engraved with a hammer and sickle.

Epilogue

TRIBUTES TO RUTH FIRST and Joe Slovo have accelerated in recent years. There are communities, roads, schools, university buildings, lectures, fellowships, scholarships, and awards named in honor of them as heroes in the struggle for democracy in South Africa. The accolades are well deserved. Ironically, when you speak with people in South Africa today, few young adults, teens, or children know Ruth or Joe's substantive contributions to the struggle against apartheid. They do not know either person's political significance. Young professionals, young workers, college or high school students, and children may have heard the name Joe Slovo, but it is less likely that they have heard of Ruth. Those who recognize Joe's name seldom know anything about him, politically or personally. There are exceptions: an African National Congress Youth League branch is named for Joe, and there is a person on Facebook who uses the name Joe Slovo and is deeply involved in Occupy Johannesburg. When I visited Ubebele, a therapeutic early childhood center in Alexandria, a sprawling Johannesburg township, one child's young mother was named RuthFirst Ramakgopa. She was well aware that she was named after a South African freedom fighter. These examples are exceptions to the rule, however. Few young South Africans know of the contributions or the sensibilities that Ruth and Joe represented regarding social justice and the revolution against class disparity and racism in the world.

Ruth and Joe's incomparable roles in the struggle against apartheid is the reason that it is important to substantively commemorate their lives. Gillian Slovo provides insights on her parents in her book *Every Secret Thing*, and her sisters, Shawn and Robyn, keep Ruth and Joe's spirits alive in their films. Donald Pinnock, Gavin Williams, Ronald Segal, and most recently, Barbara Harlow, portray Ruth's ideas and actions in print. Of course, we also have Ruth's writings. There are various articles on Joe as well as his many articles and the posthumous *Slovo: The Unfinished Autobiography*, but the need to teach both Ruth and Joe's stories continues—their courage and deeds. Unfortunately, Pallo Jordan's eulogy of Joe, "I have no doubt that the life and work of this remarkable man will continue to inspire radicals,"[681] as well as Ronald Segal's promise after Ruth died, "The revolutionary movement, to which she gave so much of herself, will find in us only a reinforcement of purpose, of resources and of effort,"[682] remains unfulfilled.

In 2010 Zwelinzima Vavi and Helena Dolny reminded us that huge contradictions remain corresponding to Ruth and Joe's ideas and actions—their revolutionary legacies and the current reality in South Africa. Vavi told a University of the Witwatersrand audience attending the Ruth First Memorial Lecture: "The overriding lesson we continue to learn from her is that capitalism and imperialism have inflicted immense misery on humanity."[683] The heart of Vavi's speech is a list of class disparity and corruption, fifteen years after the end of apartheid, that would appall Ruth First—unemployment, sexism, outrageous CEO salaries, disparate housing, education and health care, government and corporate corruption, and censorship. Vavi argued that if Ruth First were still alive she would be fighting the current government, "Let the twenty-eighth anniversary of the death of Ruth First reignite our passion for economic justice, our hatred for inequality and our impatience with reformism."[684]

At the 2012 ceremony commemorating Joe's death, the SACP declared the organization's yearly theme as "Remember Joe Slovo in 2012: The Year of Building Working Class Power for a Solidarity Economy." In 2010, the same year as Vavi's talk commemorating Ruth, Helena Dolny spoke at Joe's graveside in recognition of the fifteenth anniversary of his death. Like Vavi, her message championed what Joe stood for in the struggle. Helena contrasted Joe's positions and actions with the disparity in South African society, as well as the societal and governmental corruption and hypocrisy:

When Joe became a Minister in Parliament he bought a Volvo as a safe car for me and the family to use, but the [government] car that he inherited as a Minister he did not change; he did not upgrade it. Joe loved the good life, cigars, good food, whisky—but he was always clear that you must use your own money to buy any luxuries you wanted to enjoy—that you must never use public funds for private luxuries. I remember one of his first trips to Cape Town and before leaving the hotel he was presented with a bill. His bodyguards had ordered room service and they ordered prawns. The bill was big. Joe spoke with the bodyguards—and it was the first and last time that this happened.[685]

Ruth First and Joe Slovo in the War against Apartheid is my effort to keep Ruth and Joe's names, values, and actions alive in South Africa and throughout the world. Although both people clearly had flaws, the spirit of each of their positions in the struggle against apartheid is sorely necessary in the current struggle for social justice. Recently, Dan O'Meara wrote to me about Ruth and Joe. He spoke to the essence of why their life stories are so important to portray now:

Neither Ruth nor Joe ever believed that it was "we" who have made the world unlivable. But rather "them": the rich and the powerful who put private interest and greed before public good. The mendacious, small-minded tyrants whose inhumanity created apartheid in South Africa and who have now given us the obscene worldwide apartheid that goes by the name of globalization. Ruth and Joe died trying to change the world; they died not in the arid despair of the mind, but in hope at the possibility of change, knowing that only "we" could wring such change from the grasping bloody hands of "them."[686]

O'Meara continues with a powerful statement that connects directly to both Vavi and Dolny's commemoration talks: "Unfortunately, that group of 'them' now includes many of Ruth and Joe's (and my) former comrades."[687] His statement also parallels my purpose in sharing Ruth and Joe's stories. Their actions always confronted the vile ruthlessness of power that initiated, fostered, sanctioned, and protected class disparity and racism. Ruth's work as a political activist, journalist, writer, academic, and Director of Research at the Center of

African Studies challenged commonplaces and injustices, class dispar-ity and racism in South Africa and throughout the continent. Joe, first as a radical lawyer and member of the reemerged Communist Party, Chief of Staff of Umkhonto we Sizwe, and leader of the South African Communist Party, combined strategy with action to fight unwaver-ingly against the apartheid regime. Then, with the same zeal that he employed as the chief strategist of the armed struggle, Joe was first a significant and central player in the negotiations with the govern-ment, and then as the Minister of Housing, all part of his breadth and depth in helping to fight for a democratic, non-racial South Africa.

Ruth and Joe did have human, ideological, and political fail-ings. Ruth could be overbearing and dismissive. Some colleagues in Mozambique thought that she practiced democratic centralism in spite of the fact that it was ideologically anathema to her New Left positions and her ongoing critiques of the Soviet Union, the German Democratic Republic, and other Communist states. Joe, of course, took much too long to admit the toxic nature of Stalinism as well as the bureaucratic, oppressive reality of the Soviet Union and other communist regimes. In addition, though he still spoke of democracy and socialism when he returned home to South Africa in the 1990s, both as a negotiator and as a minister, he did not choose to challenge the globalization that had already been embraced by the West, and would soon be embraced in the new South Africa.

Although it is important to recognize the shortcomings of Ruth and Joe, it is more important to remember, as presented in the pages of this book, that first and foremost Ruth First and Joe Slovo spent their entire lives daringly fighting for a non-racial, democratic South Africa with the goal of socialism and equality for all people. It is my hope that portraying their values and actions will help remind gen-erations across the board, old and young, of the possibilities when courageous and brave individuals join together to fight oppression, or, as the preamble to South Africa's Constitution states:

Believe that South Africa belongs to all who live in it, united in our diversity!

Abbreviations

AAM	Anti-Apartheid Movement
ANC	African National Congress
ANCWL	ANC Women's League
AWB	Afrikaner Weerstandsbeweging
BC	Black Consciousness
COD	Congress of Democrats
COMINTERN	Communist International
COSATU	Congress of South African Trade Unions
CPSA	Communist Party of South Africa
FNLA	National Front for the Liberation of Angola
FRELIMO	Front for the Liberation of Mozambique
GDR	German Democratic Republic
IDAF	International Defense and Aid Fund
IDASA	Institute for a Democratic Alternative in South Africa
IFP	Inkatha Freedom Party
MK	Umkhonto we Sizwe
MPLA	Popular Movement for the Liberation of Angola
NEC	National Executive Committee
NEUM	Non-European Unity Movement
NP	National Party
OAU	Organization of African Unity
PAC	Pan Africanist Congress
RC	Revolutionary Council
RENAMO	National Resistance Movement of Mozambique
SACP	South African Communist Party
SACPC	South African Coloured People's Congress
SAIC	South African Indian Congress
SWAPO	South West African People's Organization
TEC	Transitional Executive Council
UDF	United Democratic Front
ZANU	Zimbabwe African National Union
ZAPU	Zimbabwe African People's Union

Sources

AUTHOR'S INTERVIEWS

(2010)

Myrtle Berman	Pallo Jordan	Sue Rabkin
Joanathon Clowes	Peter Lawrence	Danny Schechter
Helena Dolny	Dan O'Meara	Zena Stein
Mike Hathorn	Jeanne Penvenne	Mervyn Susser

(2011)

Louise Asmal	Polly Gaster	
Terry Bell	Denis Goldberg	James Ngculu
Myrtle Berman	Hillary Hamburger	Blade Nzimande
George Bizos	Judy Head	Bridget O'Laughlin
Claire Bless	Claudia Hodgson	Correia Paulo
Clarice Braun	Rica Hodgson	Gonda Perez
Julius Browde	Pallo Jordan	Fazel Randera
Luli Callinicos	Jay Josie	Rashid
Arthur Chaskalson	Ronnie Kasrils	Albie Sachs
Max Coleman	Denis Kuny	Reg September
Audrey Coleman	Blanche La Guma	Vladimir Shubin
Colin Darch	Martin Legassick	Allister Sparks
Indra de Lanerolle	Norman Levy	Raymond Suttner
Helena Dolny	Janet Love	Kevin Tait
Pam dos Santos	Helder Macedo	Mohammad Timol
Hassen Ebrahim	Shula Marks	Terrence Tryon
Mike Feldman	Mariano Matsinha	Ben Turok
Ron First	Keith Mokoape	Gavin Williams
Zé Forjaz	Mosie Moola	AnnMarie Wolpe

(2012)

William (Billy) Cobbett	Ronnie Kasrils	Rashid
Jacques Depelchin	Linzi Manicom	Anne Scott
Paul Joseph	Jay Naidoo	Stephanie Urdang

RUTH FIRST'S WRITINGS

Books

South West Africa (London: Penguin Books, 1963).
Preface to Govan Mbeki, *The Peasants' Revolt* (London: Penguin, 1964).
117 Days (London: Penguin Books, 1965).
Foreword to Nelson Mandela, *No Easy Walk to Freedom* (London: Heinemann, 1965).
Editor for Oginga Odinga, *Not Yet Uhuru: the Autobiography of Oginga Odinga* (London: Heinemann, 1967).
With Ronald Segal, *South West Africa: Travesty of Trust* (London: Andre Deutsch, 1967).
The Barrel of a Gun (London: Penguin Africa, 1970).
With Jonathan Steele and Christabel Gurney, *The South African Connection: Western Investment in Apartheid* (Harmondsworth, Middlesex: Penguin Books, 1973)
Libya: The Elusive Revolution (Harmondsworth, Middlesex: Penguin Books, 1974).
With Ann Scott, *Olive Schreiner* (London: Women's Press, 1989).
"Libya: Class and State in an Oil Economy," in *Oil and Class Struggle,* ed. Petter Nore and Terisa Turner (London: Zed Press, 1980).
Black Gold: The Mozambican Miner, Proletarian and Peasant, with interviews by Alpheus Manghezi and photographs by Moira Forjaz (Brighton: Harvester Studies in African Political Economy Series, 1983).

Newspaper Articles

Ruth edited and wrote voluminously for The Guardian *(of South Africa) and other newspapers. Below is a summation of her years of newspaper writing; specific articles are not listed.*

Johannesburg editor of *The Guardian* (1946–1952), *Clarion* (1952), *People's World* (1952), *Advance* (1952–1954), *New Age* (1954–1962), *Spark* (1962–1963).
Editor of monthly *Fighting Talk* (1954–1963), Johannesburg.
Member of editorial working group, *Review of African Political Economy* (1974–1982).
Estudos Moçambicanos (1980–1982), Maputo, Mozambique.

Journal and Magazine Articles

"On Poetry," *Magazine of the Jeppe High School for Girls*, December 1941.
"The World Federation of Democratic Youth," *Passive Resister*, June 19, 1947.
Viewpoints and Perspectives, March 1953.
"The Bus Boycott," *Africa South*, July–September 1957, 55–64.
"Bethal Case Book," *Africa South*, April–June 1958, 14–25.
"The Gold of Migrant Labour," *Africa South in Exile*, April–June 1961, 7–31.
"South West Africa: Apartheid Colony or UN Trust?" *New Africa*, 1965, 13–14.

"South West Africa," *Labour Monthly*, September 1966, 419–425.
"Biafra," *Ramparts*, July 1968, 31–32.
"South Africa: Trial by Torture," *New Statesman*, November 1968, 656–58.
"Le Soudan du Sud—est-il un autre Biafra," *Afrique Asie*, November 1970, 28–30.
"Portugal's African Wars," *Africa: an International Business, Economic and Political Monthly*, February 1972, 47–51.
"Will Increased Investment Reform South Africa?," *Southern Africa*, March 1972, 3.
"The Great Namibia Strike," *Sechaba*, April 1972, 19–24.
"Namibie: Un Nouveau Congo," *Afrique–Asie*, April 1972, 26–27.
"Apartheid in the New Africa," *Ramparts*, April 1972, 28–31.
"Militaere Statskup i Afrika," *Den Ny Verden* 1972, 84–88.
"Protest and Politics in the Shadow of Apartheid," *New Middle East*, July 1972, 17–19.
"The Economics of Apartheid," *Peace News*, July 1972, 3.
"UN Diplomacy," *Africa*, August 1972, 50–53.
"Reinforcing Apartheid," *Africa*, October 1972, 26–28.
"Tanzania: How Ujamaa Works," *Africa*, May 1973, 40–43.
"Foreign Investment in Apartheid," *Objective Justice*, April–June 1973, 24–30.
"The South African Connection: from Polaroid to Oppenheimer," Summer 1973, 2–6.
"Embattled Territory," *Africa*, September 1973, 119–20.
"The Oppenheimer Empire," *Africa*, November 1973, 26–39.
"The Portuguese Coup—Reactions from the Liberation Movements," *African Development*, July 1974, 13–16.
"Southern Africa after Spinola," *Ufahamu*, 1974, 88–109.
"Afrique Australe: le Grand Dessin de Pretoria," *Le Monde Diplomatique*, February 1975.
With Gavin Williams, Introduction, *Review of African Political Economy* 1/3, 1975, 3.
With Aquino de Bragança, "Maputo et la Révolution en Afrique Austral," *Afrique-Asie*, July 1977, 321–25.
"After Soweto: A Response," *Review of African Political Economy*, January–April 1978, 93–100.

JOE SLOVO'S WRITINGS

Joe wrote under the alias Sol Dubula as well as under his own name in The African Communist, Umsebenzi, *and* Dawn *for over four decades. Articles are available online at www.sacp.org.za, www.anc.org.za, and www.sahistory.org.za.*

"The Congress of the People," *Liberation*, 1954.
"Southern Africa: Problems of Armed Struggle," *Socialist Register*, 1973, 319–40.
"The Enemy Hidden under the Same Colour" (London: Inkululeko Publications, 1976).
"No Middle Road," in *Southern Africa: The New Politics of Revolution* (Harmondsworth, Middlesex: Penguin Books, 1976).

"A Critical Appraisal of the Non-Capitalist Path and the National Democratic State in Africa," *Marxism Today*, June 1974, 175.
"Beyond the Stereotype: The SACP in the Past, Present, and Future," paper presented at the University of Western Cape Conference to mark the 70th anniversary of the SACP, July, 19, 1991.
"Red Alert," "Reconciliation Is Having to Say You're Sorry," *Business Day*, August 7, 1992.
"Eastern Europe a Victim of Theological Dogma," *Business Day*, January 8, 1993.
"Has Socialism Failed?" Umsebenzi discussion pamphlet, January 1990.
"Slovo Speaks, *New Era*, March, 1990, 38.
Slovo: The Unfinished Autobiography of Joe Slovo (Melbourne and New York: Ocean Press, 1997).

BIBLIOGRAPHY
Akhalwaya, Ameen. "The Communist Party Manifesto," available at www. sacp.org.za/people/slovo/manifesto.html.
Asmal, Kader. "Power in Africa," *Irish Times*, August 7, 1971.
Beavon, Keith. *Johannesburg: The Making and Shaping of the City* (Pretoria: University of South Africa Press, 2004).
Bell, Terry. *Unfinished Business: South Africa Apartheid and Truth* (Cape Town: Redworks, 2001).
Benson, Mary. *Nelson Mandela: The Man and the Movement* (New York and London: W. W. Norton, 1986).
———. *The Struggle for a Birthright* (London: Penguin Books, 1966).
Bernstein, Hilda. *The Rift: The Exile Experience of South Africans* (London: Jonathan Cape, 1994).
———. *The World that Was Ours* (London: Persephone, 2009).
Bernstein, Rusty. *Memory against Forgetting* (London: Viking, 1999).
Bizos, George. *Odyssey to Freedom* (Johannesburg: Random House, 2007).
Bragança, Aquino de, and Bridget O'Laughlin. "The Work of Ruth First in the Centre of African Studies: The Development Course" (1984), available at Mozambique History Net: www. mozambiquehistory.net/ people/aquino/writing/mozambique/19840000_aquino_bridge.
Bram, Conny. *Operation Vula* (Johannesburg: Jacana Publishers, 2004).
Brandenberger, David. *Political Humor under Stalin* (Bloomington: Slavica, 2009).
Bunting, Brian. *Moses Kotane* (London: Inkululeko Publications, 1975).
Butler, Anthony. *Cyril Ramaphosa* (Johannesburg: Jacana, 2007).
Butler, Jeffrey. *Journal of Interdisciplinary History* 3/4, Spring 1973, 804–7.
Callinicos, Luli. *Oliver Tambo: Beyond the Engeli Mountains* (Cape Town: David Philip Publishers, 2004).
Campbell, James. "Beyond the Pale: Jewish Immigration and the South African Left," in *Memories, Realities and Dreams: Aspects of the South African Jewish Experience,* ed. Milton Shain and Richard Mendelsohn (Johannesburg, Cape Town: Jonathan Ball, 2000).
Clingman, Stephen. *Bram Fischer: Afrikaner Revolutionary* (Amherst: University of Massachusetts Press, 1998).
Courtney, Winifred. "She Held Her Head High," *Africa Today* 13/5, May 1966.

Daymond, M. J., and Corinne Sandwith. *Africa South: Viewpoints, 1956–1961* (Durban: University of Kwazulu–Natal Press, 2011).

Dingake, Michael. *My Fight against Apartheid* (London: Kliptown Books, 1987).

Dolny, Helena. *Banking for Change* (London: Viking, 2001).

Drew, Allison. *Discordant Comrades: Identities and Loyalties on the South African Left* (Pretoria: University of South Africa Press, 2000).

Dubow, Saul. *The African National Congress* (Johannesburg: Jonathan Ball, 2000).

Dyson, Rod. "Reflections on Ruth First's *The Barrel of a Gun*," *African Communist* 49, 1972.

Frankel, Glenn. *Rivonia's Children: Three Families and the Cost of Conscience in White South Africa* (New York: Farrar, Straus and Giroux, 1999).

Gerry, Chris. "Ruth First: A Tribute," *Labour, Capital and Society*, 15/2, 1982, 3–4.

Gevisser, Mark. *Thabo Mbeki: The Dream Deferred* (Johannesburg, Cape Town: Jonathan Ball, 2010).

Goldberg, Denis. *The Mission: A Life for Freedom in South Africa* (Johannesburg: STE Publishers, 2010).

Gutteridge, William, *International Journal of African Historical Studies* 6/3, 1973, 526–27.

Harlow, Barbara. *After Lives: Legacies of Revolutionary Writing* (London, New York: Verso, 1996).

———. "Redlined Africa: Ruth First's Barrel of a Gun," *Biography* 25/1, Winter 2002.

———. "Flushed with Elation: Ruth First at the University of Dar es Salaam," www.pambazuka.org/en/category/featues/59662, 2009–10–22, Issue 454, NP.

Heilpern, John. "Bye–Bye, Blue Sky," *Nova*, January 1967, 31–33.

Hodgson, Rica. *Foot Soldier for Freedom: A Life in South Africa's Liberation Movement* (Johannesburg: Picador Africa, 2010).

Howe, Irving. *World of Our Fathers* (New York: Simon & Schuster, 1976).

Houston, Gregory. "The Post-Rivonia ANC/SACP Underground," in *The Road to Democracy in South Africa*, vol. 1: *1960–1970* (Cape Town: Zebra Press, 2004), 601.

Jordan, Pallo. "The Crisis of Conscience in the SACP," *Transformation* 11, 1990, 88.

———. "The African National Congress: From Illegality to the Corridors of Power," *Review of African Political Economy*, June, 2004, 203–12.

Kasrils, Ronnie. *Armed and Dangerous* (Oxford: Heinemann, 1993).

———. "Coming to Terms with the Legacy of Comrade Joe," *African Communist* 183, 2011, 45.

———. *The Unlikely Secret Agent* (Johannesburg: Jacana, 2010).

Keable, Ken. *London Recruits: The Secret War against Apartheid* (Wales: Merlin Press, 2012).

Krut, Riva. "The Making of a South African Jewish Community in Johannesburg, 1886–1914," in *Class, Community and Conflict: South African Perspectives,* ed. Belinda Bozzoli (Johannesburg: Raven Press, 1987).

LaGuma, Blanche. *In the Dark with My Dress on Fire: My Life in Cape Town, London, Havana and Home Again* (Johannesburg: Jacana, 2010).

Langa, A. "Ruth First: *The Barrel of a Gun*," *African Communist* 44, 1971.

Lazerson, Joshua. *Against the Tide: Whites in the Struggle against Apartheid* (Boulder, CO/Cape Town: Westview Press, Mayibuye Books, 1994).

Legassick, Martin. *Armed Struggle and Democracy: The Case of South Africa* (Uppsala: Nordiska Afrikainstitutet, 2002).

Lerumo (Michael Harmel). *Fifty Fighting Years* (London: Inkululeko Publications, 1971).

Levy, Norman. *The Final Prize: My Life in the Anti-Apartheid Struggle* (Cape Town: South African History Online, 2011).

Lissoni, Arianna. "The South African Liberation Movements in Exile, 1945–1970," PhD diss., University of London, 2008.

——. "Transformations in the ANC External Mission and Umkhonto we Sizwe," *Journal of Southern African Studies*, June 2009, 287–301.

Macmillan, Hugh. "The African National Congress of South Africa in Zambia: The Culture of Exile and the Changing Relationship with Home, 1964–1990," *Journal of Southern African Studies*, June 2009, 35, 320.

Mafeje, Archie. "Soweto and Its Aftermath," *Review of African Political Economy 11*, January– April 1978, 17–30.

Maharaj, Zarina. *Dancing to a Different Rhythm* (Cape Town: Zebra Press, 2006).

Mandela, Nelson. *Long Walk to Freedom* (Boston, New York, London: Little, Brown, 1994).

Manghezi, Nadja. *The Maputo Connection: ANC Life in the World of FRELIMO* (Johannesburg: Jacana, 2009).

Manicom, Linzi. "Joe Slovo: Ode to a Mensch," *South African Report 3*, March 1995, 16.

Mantzaris, E. A. "Radical Community: The Yiddish-Speaking Branch of the International Socialist League, 1918–1920," in *Class, Community and Conflict: South African Perspectives,* ed. Belinda Bozzoli (Johannesburg: Raven Press, 1987).

Marks, Shula. "Ruth First: A Tribute," *Journal of Southern African Studies* 10/1, Special Issue on Women in Southern Africa, October 1983.

Matthews, R. O. *International Journal* 29/3. Summer 1974, 521.

Maundeni, Zibani. "Political Culture as a Source of Political Instability: The Case of Lesotho," *African Journal of Political Science and International Relations* 4, April 2010.

Mbeki, Govan. *Learning from Robben Island* (Cape Town: David Phillip, 1991).

Meer, Ismail. *A Fortunate Man* (Cape Town: Zebra Press, 2002).

Mittleman, James. *African Studies Review* 1/1, April 1971, 165.

Mphahlele, Ezekiel. *Down Second Avenue: Growing Up in a South African Ghetto* (Gloucester, MA: Peter Smith, 1978).

Mufson, Steven. *Fighting Years: Black Resistance and the Struggle for a New South Africa* (Boston: Beacon Press, 1990).

——. "Uncle Joe," *The New Republic*, September 28, 1987, 20.

Murray, Bruce. *WITS: The "Open" Years* (Johannesburg: Witwatersrand University Press, 1997).

Naidoo, Jay. *Fighting for Justice: A Lifetime of Political and Social Activism* (Johannesburg: Picador Africa, 2010).

Ngculu, James. *An Honour to Serve: Recollections of an Umkhonto Soldier* (Johannesburg: David Philip, 2009).

O'Laughlin, Bridget. "The Politics of Production: Labour Shortage and Socialist Revolution on State-farms in Mozambique," paper given at Workshop on Revolutionary Movements, Wolfson College, July 11–12, 2011.

O'Malley, Padraig. *Shades of Difference: Mac Maharaj and the Struggle for South Africa* (New York: Penguin, 2007).

O'Meara, Dan. *Forty Lost Years: The Apartheid State and the Politics of the National Party, 1948–1994* (Johannesburg: Raven Press, 1996).

Parker, Aida. *The Citizen*, December 12, 1977, 1.

Parks, Michael. "Blacks Praise Communists at S. African Rites," *Los Angeles Times*, April 1, 1986; available at http://articles latimes. com/1986-04-01/news/mn-1451_1_south-african-communist-party.

Paton, Alan. *Journey Continued* (London: Penguin, 1990).

Pinnock, Donald. *Writing Left: The Radical Journalism of Ruth First* (Pretoria: University of South Africa Press, 2005).

———. *Voices of Liberation* (Pretoria: HSRC Press, 1997).

Resha, Maggie. *Mangoana O Tsoara Thipa Ka Bohaleng: My Life in the Struggle* (London, Johannesburg: Conference of South African Writers, 1991).

Sampson, Anthony. *Mandela: The Authorized Biography* (New York: Vintage, 1999).

———. *The Treason Cage* (London, Melbourne, Toronto: Heinemann, 1958).

Seekings, Jeremy. *The UDF: A History of the United Democratic Front in South Africa 1983–1991* (Cape Town: David Phillip, 2000).

Segal, Ronald. *Into Exile* (New York: McGraw-Hill, 1963).

———. "Ruth First: A Memorial Address," *Review of African Political Economy* 25, September–December 1982.

Sellstrom, Tor. *Sweden and National Liberation in South Africa* (Uppsala: Nordiska Afrikainstitutet, 1999).

Sellstrom, Tor, *Liberation in Southern Africa: Regional and Swedish Voices* (Uppsula: Nordiska Afrikainstitutet, 2002).

Shain, Milton, and Richard Mendelsohn. *Memories, Realities, and Dreams: Aspects of the South African Jewish Experience* (Johannesburg: Jonathan Ball, 2000).

Shivji, Issa. *Intellectuals at the Hill* (Dar es Salaam: Dar es Salaam University Press, 1993).

Showalter, Elaine. "Review of *Olive Schreiner*," *Tulsa Studies in Women's Literature*1/1, Spring 1982, 105.

Shubin, Vladimir. *The ANC: A View from Moscow* (Johannesburg: Jacana Publishers, 2008).

Simons, Jack, and Ray Simons. *Class and Colour in South Africa: 1850–1950* (International Defense and Aid Fund for Southern Africa, 1983).

Sisulu, Elinor. *Walter and Albertina Sisulu: In Our Lifetime* (London: Abacus, 2003).

Slovo, Gillian. *Every Secret Thing: My Family, My Country* (London: Little, Brown and Company, 1997).

———. *Ties of Blood* (New York: Avon Books, 1990).

Smaldone, Joseph. *Africa Today* 19/4, Autumn 1972, 91–92.
Smith, Van, *American Historical Review* 77/3, June 1972, 814–15.
Smith, Janet, and Beauregard Tromp. *Hani: A Life too Short* (Johannesburg, Cape Town: Jonathan Ball, 2009).
Sparks, Allister. *Tomorrow Is Another Country: The Inside Story of South Africa's Negotiated Revolution* (London: Mandarin Paperbacks, 1996).
Steele, Jonathan. "Interview with Joe Slovo," *The Guardian*, July 22, 1985; available at http://www.sacp.org.za/people/slovo/street.html.
Stein, Jeff. "Truth Commission Spotlights CIA Role—Our Man in South Africa," November 1, 1996, http://www.pacificnews.org/jinn/stories/2.23/961101–south–africa.
Suttner, Raymond, *Inside Apartheid's Prison* (Melbourne: Ocean Press, 2001).
Suzman, Helen. *In No Uncertain Terms* (Johannesburg, Cape Town: Jonathan Ball, 1993).
Suttner, Immanuel, ed. *Cutting Through the Mountain: Interviews with South African Jewish Activists* (London: Viking, 1997).
The Road to Democracy in South Africa, vol.1 (1960–1970) (Cape Town: Zebra Press, 2004).
The Road to Democracy in South Africa, vol. 2 (1970–1980) (Pretoria: UNISA Press, 2007).
The Road to Democracy in South Africa, vol. 4 in two vols.(1980–1990) (Pretoria: UNISA Press, 2010).
Trewhela, Paul. *Inside Quatro: Uncovering the Exile History of the ANC and SWAPO* (Johannesburg: Jacana, 2009).
Turok, Ben. *Nothing but the Truth: Behind the ANC's Struggle Politics* (Johannesburg: Jonathan Ball, 2003).
Van Zyl Slabbert, Frederik. *The Other Side of History* (Johannesburg, Cape Town: Jonathan Ball, 2006).
Wall, Patrick. *Royal African Society* 76/304, July 1977, 419.
Wallerstein, Immanuel. *American Political Science Review* 67, 1973, 657–58.
Western, John. *Outcast Cape Town* (Berkeley: University of California Press, 1996).
Williams, Gavin. "Ruth First: A Preliminary Bibliography," *Review of African Political Economy*, September–December 1982, 54–64.
——. Walter Rodney Lecture, Boston University, November 8, 1982.
——. "Ruth First: A Socialist and Scholar," *Review of African Political Economy*, 9, 25, 1982, 22.
——. "Portrait of a Modern Woman: Ruth First: Academic, Scholar and Teacher," Rhodes University, August 17, 2010.
Wolpe, AnnMarie. *The Long Way Home* (London: Virago Press, 1994).
Zug, James. *The Guardian: The History of South Africa's Extraordinary Anti-Apartheid Newspaper* (East Lansing, MI, and Pretoria: Michigan State University Press, University of South Africa Press, 2007).
Zukas, Simon. *Into Exile and Back* (Lusaka, Zambia: Bookwork Publishers, 2002).

Notes

1. Author's interview with Gavin Williams, 2011.
2. Author's interview with Albie Sachs, 2011.
3. Author's interview with Danny Schechter, 2010.
4. Umkhonto we Sizwe (MK) was the military wing of the African National Congress, launched in 1961. The literal translation is "Spear of the Nation."
5. Author's interview with Jaya Josie, 2011.
6. Author's interview with Helena Dolny, 2011.
7. Irving Howe, *World of Our Fathers* (New York: Simon & Schuster, 1976), 12.
8. Author's interview with Ronald First, 2011.
9. Donald Pinnock, *Writing Left.* (Pretoria: UNISA Press, 2005), 6.
10. Joe Slovo, *Slovo: The Unfinished Autobiography of an ANC Leader* (Melbourne: Ocean Press, 1997), 18.
11. Ibid., 24.
12. Ibid.
13. Pinnock, *Writing Left*, 8.
14. Pinnock, *Writing Left*, 8.
15. Author's interview with Myrtle Berman, 2010.
16. Pinnock, *Writing Left*, 8.
17. Ibid., 8, 9.
18. Donald Pinnock interview with Brian Bunting, 1993.
19. Dan O'Meara, correspondence with author, 2012.
20. Author's interview with Myrtle Berman, 2010.
21. Ruth First, *The Magazine of the Jeppe High School for Girls*, December 1941, 13, 14.
22. Author's interview with Ronald First, 2011.
23. Slovo, *Slovo*, 32.
24. Ibid., 37, 38.
25. Ibid., 39.
26. Ibid., 42.
27. Ibid.
28. Ibid.
29. Donald Pinnock interview with Joe Slovo, 1992.
30. Ibid.
31. Slovo, *Joe Slovo*, 43.
32. Ibid., 47.
33. Ruth First, *117 Days* (London: Penguin Books, 1965), 116.
34. Norman Levy, *The Final Prize: My Life in the Anti-Apartheid Struggle* (Cape Town: South African History Online, 2011), 27.
35. Ibid., 43.
36. Ibid., 14.
37. Ruth First to John Rheinallt-Jones, August 17, 1944.

38. Bruce Murray, *Wits: The "Open" Years* (Johannesburg: Witwatersrand University Press, 1997), 48, 49.
39. Ibid., 96.
40. Ibid., 100.
41. Pinnock, *Writing Left*, 14, 15.
42. Ibid., 15.
43. Anthony Sampson, *Mandela: The Authorized Biography* (New York: Vintage Books, 1999), 47.
44. Nelson Mandela, *Long Walk to Freedom* (Boston: Little, Brown, 1994), 91.
45. Anthony Sampson, *Mandela*, 36.
46. Ibid.
47. Slovo, *Slovo*, 50.
48. Joshua Lazerson, *Against the Tide: Whites in the Struggle Against Apartheid* (Boulder, CO: Westview Press, 1994), 55.
49. Slovo, *Joe Slovo*, 48.
50. Ibid.
51. Ibid., 49.
52. Donald Pinnock interview with Wolfie Kodesh, 1992.
53. Nelson Mandela, *Long Walk to Freedom*, 99.
54. Ruth First, *117 Days*, 117.
55. Dan O'Meara, "The 1946 African Mineworkers' Strike and the Political Economy of South Africa," *Journal of Commonwealth & Contemporary Politics* 13/2 (1975): 146.
56. A. Lerumo (Michael Harmel), *Fifty Fighting Years* (London: Inkululeko Publications, 1971), 86.
57. Gillian Slovo, *Every Secret Thing: My Family, My Country* (London: Abacus, 1997), 32.
58. Author's interview with Myrtle Berman, 2010.
59. Donald Pinnock interview with Wolfie Kodesh, 1992.
60. Stephen Mufson, *Fighting Years: Black Resistance and the Struggle for a New South Africa* (Boston: Beacon Press, 1990), 222.
61. Slovo, *Joe Slovo*, 55.
62. Ibid., 63.
63. Author's interview with Zena Stein/Mervyn Susser, 2010.
64. Gillian Slovo, *Ties of Blood* (New York: Avon Books, 1990), 253.
65. A. Lerumo, *Fifty Fighting Years*, 88.
66. Donald Pinnock interview with Joe Slovo, 1992.
67. John Heilpern, "Bye-Bye, Blue Sky," *Nova*, January, 1967, 31–33.
68. Author's interview with Myrtle Berman, 2010.
69. Immanuel Suttner, *Cutting through the Mountain* (London: Viking, 1997), 448.
70. Ibid., 449.
71. Author's interview with Myrtle Berman, 2010.
72. Gillian Slovo, *Every Secret Thing*, 38.
73. Stephen Clingman, *Bram Fischer* (Amherst: University of Massachusetts Press, 1998), 221.
74. Donald Pinnock interview with Joe Slovo.
75. Slovo, *Slovo*, 62.
76. A. Lerumo, *Fifty Fighting Years*, 88.
77. Ibid., 91.
78. Slovo, *Slovo*, 66, 67.
79. Ibid., 103.
80. Stephen Clingman, *Bram Fischer*, 194.
81. Luli Callinicos, *Oliver Tambo: Beyond the Engeli Mountains* (Claremont: David Philip Publishers, 2004), 193.
82. Elinor Sisulu, *Walter and Albertina Sisulu* (London: Abacus, 2003), 93.
83. Mary Benson, *The Struggle for a Birthright* (London: Penguin, 1966), 11.
84. Glenn Frankel, *Rivonia's Children* (New York: Farrar, Straus and Giroux, 1999), 49.
85. Ibid., 48.
86. James Zug, *The Guardian* (East Lansing: Michigan State University Press, 2007), 90, 91.
87. Gavin Williams, Walter Rodney Lecture, Boston University, November 8, 1982.
88. Ibid.

89. Ronald Segal, "Ruth First: A Memorial Address," *Review of African Political Economy* 25 (Sept.–Dec. 1982), 52.
90. James Zug, *The Guardian*, 108, 113.
91. Ibid., 147.
92. Donald Pinnock, *Voices of Liberation* (Pretoria: HSRC Publishers, 1997), 37.
93. Ibid., 38, 39.
94. Ruth First, *The Guardian*, July 5, 1951.
95. Ruth First, *The Guardian*, July 3, 1947.
96. Slovo, *Slovo*, 108.
97. Frankel, *Rivonia's Children*, 47.
98. Joe Slovo, "The Congress of the People," *Liberation* 10 (1954): 25.
99. Slovo, *Slovo*, 74.
100. Author's interview with Denis Kuny, 2011.
101. Author's interview with Julius Browde, 2011.
102. Ibid.
103. Slovo, *Slovo*, 68.
104. Ibid., 68, 69.
105. Ibid., 73.
106. Ibid., 87.
107. Ibid.
108. Ibid.
109. Ibid.
110. Ibid., 94, 95.
111. Elinor Sisulu, *Walter and Albertina Sisulu*, 146.
112. Author's interview with George Bizos.
113. Brian Bunting, *Moses Kotane* (London: Inkululeko Publications, 1975), 183.
114. Slovo, *Slovo*, 107.
115. Ibid., 108.
116. Ruth First, *Viewpoints and Perspectives* 1/1 (March 1953).
117. Gavin Williams, "Ruth First: A Socialist and a Scholar," *Review of African Political Economy* 9/25 (1982).
118. Glenn Frankel interview with Shawn Slovo, 1996.
119. In the west, a *braai* is a barbecue.
120. Author's interview with George Bizos, 2011.
121. Author's interview with Albie Sachs, 2011.
122. Ibid.
123. Gillian Slovo, *Every Secret Thing*, 36, 37.
124. Zug, *The Guardian*, 147.
125. Ibid., 309.
126. Ibid., 148.
127. Ibid., 147.
128. Pinnock, *Writing Left*, 50.
129. Glenn Frankel interview with Hilda Bernstein, 1996.
130. Glenn Frankel interview with Lionel Bernstein, 1996.
131. Bunting, *Kotane*, 194, 195.
132. Stephen Clingman interview with Joe Slovo, 1991.
133. Callinicos, *Oliver Tambo*, 222.
134. Pinnock, *Writing Left*, 47.
135. Slovo, *Slovo*, 109.
136. Lazerson, *Against the Tide*, 173.
137. Slovo, *Slovo*, 110.
138. Alan Paton, *Journey Continued* (London: Penguin, 1990), 106.
139. Author's interview with Myrtle Berman, 2010
140. Glenn Frankel interview with Rusty Bernstein, 1996.
141. Glenn Frankel interview with Hilda Bernstein, 1996.
142. Anthony Sampson, *The Treason Cage* (London: Melbourne, Toronto: Heinemann, 1958), 3.
143. Slovo, *Slovo*, 113, 114.
144. Sisulu, *Walter and Albertina Sisulu*, 157.
145. Mary Benson, *The Struggle for a Birthright*, 190.
146. Slovo, *Slovo*, 120.
147. Clingman, *Bram Fischer*, 235.
148. Sampson, *The Trial Cage*, 21.
149. Ibid., 23.
150. Slovo, *Slovo*, 121.
151. Mandela, *Long Walk to Freedom*, 212.
152. Sampson, *The Trial Cage*, 34.
153. Slovo, *Slovo*, 122.
154. Sampson, *The Trial Cage*, 168.
155. Ibid.
156. Ibid.
157. Ibid., 123.
158. Author's interview with Rica Hodgson, 2011.

159. Slovo, *Slovo*, 63.
160. Author's interview with Myrtle Berman, 2010.
161. Gillian Slovo, *Every Secret Thing*, 279.
162. Pinnock, *Writing Left*, 98, 99.
163. Ibid., 99.
164. Donald Pinnock interview with Joe Slovo, 1992.
165. Donald Pinnock interview with Mary Benson, 1992.
166. Ruth First, *New Age*, June 27, 1957.
167. Ruth First, *New Age*, September 24, 1959.
168. Slovo, *Slovo*, 127, 128.
169. Donald Pinnock interview with Wolfie Kodesh, 1992.
170. Ibid.
171. Ben Turok, *Nothing but the Truth: Behind the ANC's Struggle Politics* (Johannesburg: Jonathan Ball, 2003), 195.
172. Ibid.
173. Donald Pinnock interview with Mary Benson, 1992.
174. Ruth First letter to Nkambule, March 1959.
175. Slovo, *Slovo*, 128.
176. Helena Dolny, *Banking on Change* (London: Viking, 2001), 242.
177. Slovo, *Slovo*, 125.
178. Norman Levy, *The Final Prize*, 89.
179. Donald Pinnock, *Writing Left*, 192.
180. Slovo, *Slovo*, 135.
181. Ibid., 142.
182. Ibid., 166.
183. Ibid., 152.
184. Ibid., 165.
185. Ibid., 167.
186. Ibid., 164.
187. Author's interview with Hillary Hamburger, 2011.
188. Ibid.
189. Ibid.
190. Author's interview with Albie Sachs, 2011.
191. Ruth First, *117 Days*, 118.
192. Callinicos, *Oliver Tambo*, 280.
193. Slovo, *Slovo*, 170.
194. Gregory Houston, "The Post-Rivonia ANC/SACP Underground," in *The Road to Democracy in South Africa, 1960–1970* (Cape Town: Zebra Press, 2004), 1:601.
195. Sampson, *Mandela*, 147.
196. Slovo, *Slovo*, 179.
197. Author's interview with Ronnie Kasrils, 2011.
198. Ibid., 169.
199. Hilda Bernstein, *The World that Was Ours* (London: Persephone, 2009), 84.
200. Author's interview with Ronnie Kasrils, 2011.
201. Gillian Slovo, *Every Secret Thing*, 63.
202. Slovo, *Slovo*, 171.
203. Ibid., 70, 71.
204. Wolpe, *The Long Way Home*, 64.
205. Callinicos, *Oliver Tambo*, 292.
206. Ruth First, *South West Africa* (London: Penguin Books, 1963), 15.
207. Ibid., 14.
208. Ibid., 119.
209. Ibid., 232, 233.
210. Shula Marks, "Ruth First: A Tribute," *Journal of Southern African Studies* 10/1, Special Issue on Women in Southern Africa (October 1983): 124.
211. Ibid., 125.
212. Donald Pinnock, *Writing Left*, 220.
213. Gillian Slovo, *Every Secret Thing*, 61.
214. Donald Pinnock interview with Barney Simon, 1990.
215. Gillian Slovo, *Every Secret Thing*, 64.
216. Ibid., 71.
217. Ibid., 13.
218. Ibid., 50.
219. Ibid., 43.
220. Ibid., 37, 38.
221. Ibid., 53.
222. Ibid., 54.
223. Ibid., 65.
224. Slovo, *Slovo*, 100.
225. First, *117 Days*, 88.
226. Ibid., 103.
227. Ibid., 108.

228. Ibid., 114, 115.
229. Ibid., 122, 123.
230. Ibid., 125.
231. Ibid., 127.
232. Ibid., 129.
233. Ruth First to Joe Slovo, 1963.
234. Ruth First to Joe Slovo, 1964.
235. Ruth First to Joe Slovo, 1964.
236. Ruth First to Joe Slovo, 1964.
237. Bernstein, *The World that Was Ours*, 231.
238. Ibid., 230.
239. Frankel, *Rivonia's Children*, 293.
240. Rica Hodgson to Ruth First, June 1965.
241. Barbara Harlow, *After Lives: Legacies of Revolutionary Writing* (London, New York: Verso, 1996), 122.
242. Ronald Segal to Ruth First, June 1964.
243. Ruth First to Peter Worsley, April 1965.
244. Ruth First to Nadine Gordimer, January 1965.
245. Kasrils, *Armed and Dangerous*, 100.
246. Vladimir Shubin, *The ANC: A View from Moscow* (Johannesburg: Jacana Publishers, 2008), 65.
247. Ibid., 51.
248. Author's interview with Ronnie Kasrils, 2011.
249. Glenn Frankel interview with Robyn Slovo, 1996.
250. Glenn Frankel interview with Shawn Slovo, 1996.
251. Glenn Frankel interview with Robyn Slovo, 1990.
252. Author's interview with Rica Hodgson, 2011.
253. Author's interview with Myrtle Berman, 2011.
254. Ibid.
255. Gillian Slovo, *Every Secret Thing*, 110.
256. Donald Pinnock interview with Joe Slovo, 1992.
257. Slovo, *Slovo*, 53.
258. Colin Legum to Ruth First, April 5, 1966.
259. Ruth First to Colin Legum, April 12, 1966.

260. Gavin Williams, "Walter Rodney Lecture."
261. Author's interview with Danny Schechter, 2010.
262. Ibid.
263. Stephen Clingman interview with Joe Slovo, 1991.
264. Author's interview with Ronnie Kasrils, 2011.
265. Slovo, *Slovo*, 178.
266. Author's interview with Ronnie Kasrils, 2011.
267. Ibid.
268. Arianna Lissoni, 12.
269. Author's interview with Ronnie Kasrils, 2011.
270. Ibid.
271. Janet Smith and Beauregard Tromp, *Hani: A Life too Short* (Johannesburg, Cape Town: Jonathan Ball, 2009), 69.
272. Shubin, *ANC*, 65.
273. Author's interview with Ronnie Kasrils, 2011.
274. Danny Schechter, "The Day I Joined the Revolution," in *London Recruits: The Secret War against Apartheid*, ed. Ken Keable (London: Merlin Press, 2012), 54, 55.
275. John Heilpern, "Bye-Bye, Blue Sky," *Nova*, January 1967.
276. Barbara Harlow, "Redlined Africa: Ruth First's *Barrel of a Gun*," *Biography* 25/1 (Winter 2002): 155.
277. Ibid., 165.
278. E. S. Reddy to Ruth First, October 1967.
279. Ruth First to Colin Legum, December 1968.
280. Mary Benson to Colin Legum, December 1968.
281. Colin Legum to Mary Benson, December 1968.
282. Colin Legum to Ruth First, December 1968.
283. Ruth First to Colin Legum, February 1969.
284. Author's interview with Ronald First, 2011.
285. Author's interview with Rica Hodgson, 2011.

286. Ibid.
287. Ibid.
288. Glen Frankel interview with Hilda Bernstein, 1996.
289. Ibid.
290. Ronald Segal to Ruth First, October 1969.
291. Ruth First, *The Barrel of a Gun* (London: Penguin Africa, 1982), x.
292. Ibid., 5, 6.
293. Ibid., 8.
294. Ibid., 465.
295. Kader Asmal, "Power in Africa," *Irish Times*, August 7, 1971.
296. Immanuel Wallerstein, *The American Political Science Review* 67 (1973): 657.
297. Nhlanhla Ndebele and Noor Nieftagodien, "The Morogoro Conference: A Moment of Self-Reflection," in *The Road to Democracy in South Africa*, vol. 1, 585.
298. Harlow, "Redlined Africa: Ruth First's *Barrel of a Gun*," 167.
299. Author's interview with Ronnie Kasrils, 2011.
300. *The Road to Democracy in South Africa*, 1:592.
301. "Strategy and Tactics," ANC, 1969, 13, 14.
302. Ibid., 16.
303. Ibid., 33.
304. Callinicos, *Oliver Tambo*, 334.
305. Joe Slovo, *The African Communist* 95 (1983): 89.
306. Author's interview with Ronnie Kasrils, 2011.
307. Ibid.
308. Ibid.
309. Joe Slovo, *The African Communist* 38 (1969): 50.
310. Ibid., 52.
311. Ibid., 60.
312. Ruth First to Jack Simons, April 1970.
313. Author's interview with Polly Gaster, 2011.
314. Author's interview with Ronnie Kasrils, 2011.
315. Author's interview with Pallo Jordan, 2011.

316. Ibid., 91.
317. Shubin, *ANC*, 87.
318. Ibid.
319. Ruth First to Idris Cox, 1971.
320. Ruth First, Jonathan Steele, and Christabel Gurney, *The South African Connection: Western Investment in Apartheid* (Harmondsworth, Middlesex: Penguin Books, 1973), 281.
321. Ibid., 295, 296.
322. Gavin Williams, "Ruth First: A Socialist and Scholar," *Review of African Political Economy*, 1982. 22.
323. Mark Gevisser, *Thabo Mbeki: The Dream Deferred* (Johannesburg, Cape Town: Jonathan Ball, 2010), 121.
324. Ibid., 122.
325. Author's interview with Pallo Jordan, 2010.
326. Ibid.
327. Ibid.
328. Joe Slovo, "A Critical Appraisal of the Non-Capitalist Path and the National Democratic State in Africa," *Marxism Today*, June 1974, 175.
329. Ibid., 180.
330. Ibid., 185.
331. Ibid., 187.
332. Gavin Williams, Letter of Recommendation, June 29, 1973. Available at the Institute for Commonwealth Studies, Ruth First Papers Project, London.
333. Gavin Williams, "Portrait of a Modern Woman: Ruth First: Academic, Scholar and Teacher," Rhodes University, August 17, 2010.
334. Ruth First, *Libya: The Elusive Revolution* (Harmondsworth, Middlesex: Penguin Books, 1974), 256.
335. Author's interview with Gavin Williams, 2010.
336. Chris Gerry, "Ruth First: A Tribute," *Labour, Capital and Society* 15/2, 1982, 3–4.
337. Author's interview with Judith Head, 2011.

338. Ibid.
339. Author's interview with Albie Sachs, 2011.
340. Glenn Frankel interview with Robyn Slovo, 1996.
341. Ibid.
342. Joe Slovo, *The Enemy Hidden under the Same Colour* (London: Inkululeko Publications, 1976).
343. Ibid., 25.
344. Ruth First and Gavin Williams, "Introduction," *Review of African Political Economy*, V. 1, N. 3, 1975, 3.
345. Author's interview with Gavin Williams, 2011.
346. Author's interview with Rica Hodgson, 2011.
347. Ruth First to Joe Slovo, August 1975.
348. Available at the Institute of Commonwealth Studies, Ruth First Papers. London.
349. Ruth First to Joe Slovo, November 1975.
350. Ibid.
351. Joe Slovo, "No Middle Road," in *Southern Africa: The New Politics of Revolution* (Harmondsworth, Middlesex: Penguin Books, 1976), 113, 114.
352. Ibid., 196.
353. Nadja Manghezi, *The Maputo Connection: ANC Life in the World of Frelimo* (Johannesburg: Jacana, 2009), 137.
354. Author's interview with Ben Turok, 2011.
355. Aquino de Bragança and Bridget O'Laughlin, "The Work of Ruth First in the Centre of African Studies: The Development Course" (1984), available at Mozambique History Net: www.mozambiquehistory.net/people/aquino/writing/mozambique/19840000_aquino_bridge, 159.
356. Kasrils, *Armed and Dangerous*, 138.
357. Ibid., 137.
358. Author's interview with Pallo Jordan, January 2011.

359. Gillian Slovo, *Every Secret Thing*, 115.
360. James Ngculu, *An Honour to Serve: Recollections of an Umkhonto Soldier* (Johannesburg: David Philip Publishers, 2009), 82.
361. Author's interview with Pallo Jordan, 2011.
362. Author's interview with Albie Sachs, 2011.
363. Author's interview with Dan O'Meara, 2010.
364. Linzi Manicom, "Joe Slovo: Ode to a Mensch," *South African Report* 3 (March 1995): 16.
365. Ibid.
366. Aida Parker, *The Citizen*, December 12, 1977.
367. De Bragança, A. and O'Laughlin, B. (1984), The Work of Ruth First in the Centre of African Studies: The Development Course [online]. 160.
368. Author's interview with Colin Darch, 2011.
369. Letter from Jack Simons to Ruth First, March 1977.
370. Eleanor Sisulu, *Walter and Albertina Sisulu*, 348.
371. Ibid.
372. Author's interview with Ronnie Kasrils, 2011.
373. Author's interview with Pallo Jordan, 2011.
374. Author's interview with Ronnie Kasrils, 2011.
375. Ibid.
376. Howard Barrell's interview with Joe Slovo, 1989.
377. *The Greenbook*, Report of the Politico-Military Strategy Commission to the ANC National Executive Committee, August 1979. Available at http://www.anc.org.za/docs.php?t=The%20Green%20Book. n.p.
378. Ibid., 467.
379. Ibid., 531.
380. Author's interview with Albie Sachs, 2011.
381. Author's interview with Shula Marks, 2012.

382. Author's interview with Helena Dolny, 2010.
383. Author's interview with Dan O'Meara, 2010.
384. Author's interview with Colin Darch, 2011.
385. Author's interview with Dan O'Meara, 2010.
386. Bridget O'Laughlin, "The Politics of Production: Labour Shortage and Socialist Revolution on State-farms in Mozambique," paper presented at Workshop on Revolutionary Movements, Wolfson College, Oxford University, July 11–12, 2011.
387. Ibid.
388. Ibid.
389. Bragança and O'Laughlin, "The Work of Ruth First in the Centre of African Studies," 160.
390. Tebello Letsekha interview with Bridget O'Laughlin, 2011.
391. Bragança and O'Laughlin, "The Work of Ruth First in the Centre of African Studies," 161.
392. Ibid.
393. Tebello Letsekha interview with Bridget O'Laughlin, 2011.
394. Ibid.
395. Author's interview with Colin Darch, 2011.
396. Bragança and O'Laughlin, "The Work of Ruth First in the Centre of African Studies," 162.
397. Author's interview with Bridget O'Laughlin, 2011.
398. Ruth First to Jules Lewin, September 1979.
399. Ibid.
400. Radio Mozambique, 1982.
401. O'Laughlin, Wolfson College paper.
402. Bragança and O'Laughlin, "The Work of Ruth First in the Centre of African Studies," 165.
403. Radio Mozambique, 1982.
404. Author's interview with Dan O'Meara, 2010.
405. Ibid.
406. Ibid.
407. Ibid.
408. Author's interview with Colin Darch, 2011.
409. John S. Saul, "Laying Ghosts to Rest: Ruth First and South Africa's War," *This Magazine* 17 (December 1983): 5.
410. Author's interview with Rashid, 2011.
411. Nadja Manghezi, *The Maputo Connection: ANC Life in the World of Frelimo* (Johannesburg: Jacana, 2009), 137.
412. Author's interview with Ronnie Kasrils, 2011.
413. Author's interview with Rashid, 2011.
414. *New York Times*, June 3, 1980.
415. "Public Enemy Number One," *Newsweek*, June 30, 1980.
416. Author's interview with Rashid, 2011.
417. Author's interview with Sue Rabkin, 2010.
418. Author's interview with Paul Joseph, 2011.
419. Author's interview with Dan O'Meara, 2010.
420. Author's interview with Colin Darch, 2011.
421. Manghezi, *The Maputo Connection*, 127, 128.
422. Author's interview with Rashid, 2011.
423. Ibid.
424. Ibid.
425. Author's interview with Sue Rabkin, 2010.
426. Letter from Joe Slovo to Jack Simons, November 1981.
427. Author's interview with Pallo Jordan, 2011.
428. Ruth First and Ann Scott, *Olive Schreiner* (London: Women's Press, 1989), 4.
429. Author's interview with Ann Scott, 2012.
430. Allison Drew, *Discordant Comrades* (Pretoria: UNISA Press, 2000), 30.
431. First and Scott, *Olive Schreiner*, 18.
432. Donald Pinnock interview with Wolfie Kodesh, 1992.

433. Gillian Slovo, *Every Secret Thing*, 120.
434. Slovo, *Slovo*, 18.
435. Radio Freedom interview with Joe Slovo, 1982.
436. Author's interview with Rashid, 2011.
437. Author's interview with Dan O'Meara, 2010.
438. Ibid.
439. Author's interview with Rashid, 2011.
440. Author's interview with Sue Rabkin, 2010.
441. Ibid.
442. Ibid.
443. Author's interview with Pallo Jordan, 2010.
444. Donald Pinnock interview with Joe Slovo, 1992.
445. Donald Pinnock interview with Barney Simon, 1990.
446. Author's interview with Hillary Hamburger, 2011.
447. Donald Pinnock interview with Hilda Bernstein, 1993.
448. Ibid.
449. Zarina Maharaj, *Dancing to a Different Rhythm* (Cape Town: Zebra Press, 2006), 119.
450. Ibid., 118.
451. Spencer Hodgson to Joe Slovo, 1982.
452. Ruth First to Jack Simons, May 1982.
453. Author's interview with Dan O'Meara, 2010.
454. Author's interview with Pallo Jordan, 2010.
455. Bridget O'Laughlin's testimony to Truth and Reconciliation Committee.
456. Author's interview with Pallo Jordan, 2010.
457. Joe Slovo to Oliver Tambo, August 1980.
458. Author's interview with Albie Sachs, 2011.
459. Ibid.
460. Author's interview with Dan O'Meara, 2010.
461. Donald Pinnock interview with Barney Simon, 1990.
462. Joseph Hanlon, "Why South Africa Had to Kill Ruth First," *New Statesman*, 1982.
463. Gavin Williams, "Portrait of a Modern Woman: Ruth First: Academic, Scholar and Teacher," Rhodes University, August 17, 2010.
464. Author's interview with Bridget O'Laughlin, 2011.
465. Author's interview with Pallo Jordan, 2010.
466. Author's interview with Dan O'Meara, 2010.
467. Author's interview with Albie Sachs, 2011.
468. Fernando Ganhao, Ruth First Memorial Speech, Maputo, 1982.
469. Ibid.
470. Author's interview with Albie Sachs, 2011.
471. Ibid.
472. Marcelino dos Santos, Ruth First's Funeral, Maputo, 1982.
473. Moses Mabhida, Eulogy for Ruth First, Maputo, 1982.
474. Author's interview with Albie Sachs, 2011.
475. Ros Anslie to Joe Slovo, 1982.
476. Danny Schechter to Joe Slovo, 1982.
477. Gavin Williams to Joe Slovo, 1982.
478. Michael Wolfers to Joe Slovo, 1982.
479. Rica Hodgson to Joe Slovo, 1982.
480. Jack Simons and Ray Alexander to Joe Slovo, 1982.
481. Wolfie Kodesh to Joe Slovo, 1982.
482. Ibid.
483. Author's interview with Paul Joseph, 2012.
484. Ronald Segal's memorial address for Ruth First, London, 1982. The speech was published in *ROAPE*, 54.
485. Ibid.
486. Slovo, *Slovo*, 8.
487. Joe Slovo, an Open Letter, January 1983.

488. Ibid.
489. Ibid.
490. Author's interview with Zé Forjaz, 2011.
491. Slovo, *Slovo*, 7.
492. Ibid., 58.
493. Author's interview with Vladimir Shubin, 2011.
494. Padraig O'Malley interview with Mac Maharaj.
495. Author's interview with Zé Forjaz, 2011.
496. Author's interview with Helena Dolny, 2011.
497. Author's interview with Dan O'Meara, 2010.
498. Ibid.
499. Author's interview with Colin Darch, 2011.
500. Author's interview with Rashid, 2011.
501. Oliver Tambo to Ronald Segal, July 8, 1983.
502. Author's interview with Luli Callinicos, 2011.
503. Williams, "Ruth First: A Socialist and a Scholar," *Review of African Political Economy*, 9, 25, 1982.
504. Author's interview with Zé Forjaz, 2011.
505. Memorandum from Joe Slovo on meeting with Sergio Vieira and Fernando Honwana, March 1984. Available at the South African History Archives, University of Witswatersrand, Johannesburg.
506. Joe Slovo memorandum on the Raids, March 1984. Available at the South African History Archives, University of Witswatersrand, Johannesburg.
507. Ibid.
508. Author's interview with Zé Forjaz, 2011.
509. Author's interview with Helena Dolny, 2011.
510. Author's interview with Janet Love, 2011.
511. Author's interview with Jay Josie, 2011.
512. Author's interview with Albie Sachs, 2011.
513. Ibid.
514. Author's interview with Gonda Perez, 2011.
515. Shubin, *ANC*, 217.
516. ANC, African National Congress National Executive Committee Statement, April 1985. Available at http://www.anc.org.za/show. php?id=140.
517. Author's interview with Sue Rabkin, 2010.
518. Author's interview with Albie Sachs, 2011.
519. Ibid.
520. Jonathan Steele, interview with Joe Slovo, *The Guardian*, July 22, 1985; available at http://www.sacp.org.za/people/slovo/street.html/.
521. Ibid.
522. Ibid.
523. Joe Slovo, *Dawn* 9/2 (1985). N.P.
524. Denis Goldberg, *The Mission: A Life for Freedom in South Africa* (Johannesburg: STE Publishers, 2010), 195.
525. Ibid., 256.
526. Shubin, *ANC*, 233.
527. Author's interview with Julius Browde, 2011.
528. Frederik Van Zyl Slabbert, *The Other Side of History* (Johannesburg, Cape Town: Jonathan Ball, 2006), 47.
529. Joe Slovo, Eulogy for Moses Mabhida, Maputo, March 26, 1986.
530. Michael Parks, "Blacks Praise Communists at S. African Rites," *Los Angeles Times*, April 1, 1986; available at http://articles.latimes.com/1986-04-01/news/mn-1451_1_south-african-communist-party.
531. Joe Slovo, "Message to the FRELIMO Party and Government of the People's Republic of Mozambique on the Death of President Samora Machel." Available at the South African History Archives, University of Witswatersrand, Johannesburg.

532. Author's interview with Polly Gaster, 2011.
533. Author's interview with Helena Dolny, 2011.
534. Author's interview with Jaya Josie, 2011.
535. Author's interview with James Ngculu, 2011.
536. Ngculu, *The Honour to Serve: Recollections of an Umkhonto Soldier* (Johannesburg: David Philip, 2009) 132.
537. Joe Slovo, "The Sabotage Campaign," *Dawn* (1986): 25; available at http://www.disa.ukzn.ac.za/index.php?option=com_display dc&recordID=DaSI86.1681.57 85.000.000.1986.
538. BBC, *Focus on Africa* interview, July 4, 1986; available at http://www.sacp.org.za/people/slovo/military.html.
539. Joe Slovo, speech delivered at the 65th Anniversary Meeting of the South African Communist Party, London, June 30, 1986; available at http://www.sacp.org.za/docs/history/65yrs.html.
540. Jay Naidoo, *Fighting for Justice: A Lifetime of Political and Social Activism* (Johannesburg: Picador Africa, 2010), 109.
541. Ibid.
542. Author's interview with Helena Dolny, 2011.
543. Ibid.
544. Author's interview with Gonda Perez, 2011.
545. Author's interview with Helena Dolny, 2011.
546. Suttner, *Cutting through the Mountain*, 452.
547. Ibid., 453.
548. Shubin, *ANC*, 252.
549. Joe Slovo, Speech Extracts, *Umsebenzi* 4/1 (1988): 3.
550. Steven Mufson, "Uncle Joe," *The New Republic*, September 28, 1987, 20.
551. Ibid., 10.
552. Ibid.
553. Ibid., 20.
554. Ibid., 38.
555. Joe Slovo, "Introduction," *117 Days* (London: Bloomsbury, 1988), 8.
556. Ibid., 256.
557. Paidrag O'Malley interview with Maharaj.
558. Author's interview with Helena Dolny, 2011.
559. Author's interview with Norman Levy, 2011.
560. Joe Slovo, *Umsebenzi* 5/2 (1989): 17.
561. Helena Dolny reviews the trip in Suttner, *Cutting through the Mountain*, 242.
562. Eleanor Sisulu, Walter and Albertina Sisulu, 539.
563. Joe Slovo, letter read in Soweto, October 29, 1989.
564. Joe Slovo and Ken Gill, "We Belong to One Family, *World Marxist Review* 32 (May 1989): 12.
565. Hugh Macmillan, "The African National Congress of South Africa in Zambia: 1964–1990," *Journal of African Studies*, 35, 2, June 2009, 322.
566. Author's interview with Allister Sparks, 2011.
567. Ibid.
568. Author's interview with Zé Forjaz, 2011.
569. Author's interview with Allister Sparks, 2011.
570. Padraig O'Malley interview with Joe Slovo, April 1992; available at http://www.nelsonmandela.org/omalley/index.php/site/q/031v0.
571. Author's interview with Vladimir Shubin, 2011.
572. Pallo Jordan, "The Crisis of Conscience in the SACP," *Transformation* 11 (1990): 88.
573. Glenn Frankel interview with Hilda Bernstein, 1996.
574. Author's interview with Albie Sachs, 2011.
575. Joe Slovo, "Has Socialism Failed?," SACP, 10. Available at http://www.sacp.org.za/docs/history/failed.html.

576. Pallo Jordan, "The Crisis of Conscience in the SACP," 75.
577. Author's interview with Jay Josie, 2011.
578. Shubin, *ANC*, 293.
579. Allister Sparks, *Tomorrow Is Another Country: The Inside Story of South Africa's Negotiated Revolution* (London: Mandarin Paperbacks, 1996), 118.
580. Ibid., 119.
581. Sparks, *Tomorrow Is Another Country*, 124.
582. Author's interview with Audrey Coleman, 2011.
583. Author's interview with Max Coleman, 2011.
584. Author's interview with Audrey Coleman, 2011.
585. Author's interview with Hillary Hamburger, 2011.
586. Suttner, *Cutting through the Mountain*, 224.
587. Padraig O'Malley interview with Mac Maharaj, October 2004.
588. O'Malley, *Shades of Difference*, 345.
589. Author's interview with Janet Love, 2011.
590. Ibid.
591. Ibid.
592. "Slovo Speaks," *New Era*, March 1990, 38.
593. Ibid.
594. Ibid., 39.
595. Kasrils, *Armed and Dangerous*, 335.
596. Author's interview with Ronnie Kasrils, 2012.
597. Ameen Akhalwaya, "The Communist Party Manifesto," available at www.sacp.org.za/people/slovo/manifesto.html.
598. Author's interview with Helena Dolny, 2011.
599. Padraig O'Malley interview with Joe Slovo, April 1992.
600. Joe Slovo, Press Release on the Swanieville Massacre, May 13, 1991.
601. Joe Slovo, "Beyond the Stereotype: The SACP in the Past, Present, and Future," presented at the University of Western Cape Conference to Mark the 70th Anniversary of the SACP, July 19, 1991.
602. Author's interview with Dan O'Meara, 2010.
603. Author's interview with Fazel Randera, 2011.
604. Ibid.
605. Ibid.
606. Ibid.
607. Helena Dolny to the author, 2012.
608. Author's interview with Helena Dolny, 2011.
609. Ibid.
610. Author's interview with Ronnie Kasrils, 2012.
611. Author's interview with Allister Sparks, 2011.
612. Sampson, *Mandela*, 460.
613. Author's interview with Pallo Jordan, 2011.
614. Sparks, *Tomorrow Is Another Country*, 182.
615. Glenn Frankel interview with Rusty Bernstein, 1996.
616. Author's interview with Zé Forjaz, 2011.
617. Author's interview with Dan O'Meara, 2010.
618. Author's interview with Allister Sparks, 2011.
619. Padraig O'Malley interview with Joe Slovo, November 30, 1993.
620. Sparks, *Tomorrow Is Another Country*, 189.
621. Slovo, *Slovo*, 216.
622. Author's interview with William Cobbett, 2012.
623. Author's interview with Janet Love, 2011.
624. Author's interview with Helena Dolny, 2011.
625. Joe Slovo, "Reconciliation Is Having to Say You're Sorry," *Business Day*, August 7, 1992.
626. Ibid.
627. Joe Slovo, "Eastern Europe a Victim of Theological Dogma," *Business Day*, January 8, 1993.
628. Author's interview with Gonda Perez, 2011.

629. Author's interview with Ronnie Kasrils, 2012.
630. Author's interview with Julius Browde, 2011.
631. Author's interview with Dan O'Meara, 2010.
632. Padraig O'Malley interview with Joe Slovo, 1992.
633. Author's interview with William Cobbett, 2012.
634. Ibid.
635. Ibid.
636. Ibid.
637. Ibid.
638. Ibid.
639. Author's interview with Melinda Coetzer, 2012.
640. Author's interview with William Cobbett, 2012.
641. Ibid.
642. Ibid.
643. Joe Slovo to the South African Pariliament, May 25, 1994, available at the South African History Archives, University of Witswatersrand, Johannesburg.
644. Joe Slovo, "Address to the Finance Week Breakfast Club," June 9, 1994.
645. Author's interview with Ronnie Kasrils, 2012.
646. Author's interview with Helena Dolny, 2011.
647. Author's interview with William Cobbett, 2012.
648. Ibid.
649. Dolny, *Banking for Change*, 46.
650. Author's interview with Helena Dolny, 2011.
651. Bridget O'Laughlin to Helena Dolny, November 1, 1994.
652. Author's interview with Helena Dolny, 2011.
653. Slovo, *Slovo*, 11.
654. Ronnie Kasrils, "Coming to Terms with the Legacy of Comrade Joe," *African Communist* 183 (2011): 45.
655. Author's interview with William Cobbett, 2012.
656. Padraig O'Malley interview with Joe Slovo, 2004.
657. Slovo, *Slovo*, 279.

658. Author's interview with Gonda Perez, 2011.
659. Ibid.
660. Author's interview with Hillary Hamburger, 2011.
661. Lionel Abrahams, "At Revolution's End," in Slovo, *Slovo*, 202, 203.
662. Author's interview with Ronald First, 2011.
663. White Paper, "A New Housing Policy and Strategy," 1994, available at the South African History Archives, University of Witswatersrand, Johannesburg.
664. Slovo, *Slovo*, 215.
665. Author's interview with Ronnie Kasrils, 2012.
666. Slovo, *Slovo*, 204.
667. Ibid., 225.
668. Ibid., 285.
669. Author's interview with Rica Hodgson, 2011.
670. Author's interview with Rashid, 2012.
671. Author's interview with Billy Cobbett, 2012.
672. Author's interview with Fazel Randera, 2011.
673. Slovo, *Slovo*, 202.
674. Ibid., 293.
675. Ibid., 267.
676. Ibid.
677. Ibid., 262.
678. Ibid., 234.
679. Ibid., 232, 233.
680. Ibid., 235.
681. Ibid., 271.
682. Ronald Segal, "Ruth First, a Tribute," *Review Journal of African Economy*, 9, 25, 1982, 52.
683. Zwelinzima Vavi, Ruth First Memorial Speech, Johannesburg, University of Witswatersrand, 2010.
684. Ibid.
685. Helena Dolny, Joe Slovo Memorial Speech, January 6, 2010.
686. Dan O'Meara to author, 2012.
687. Ibid.

Index

Page numbers in italics refer to photographs and their captions.